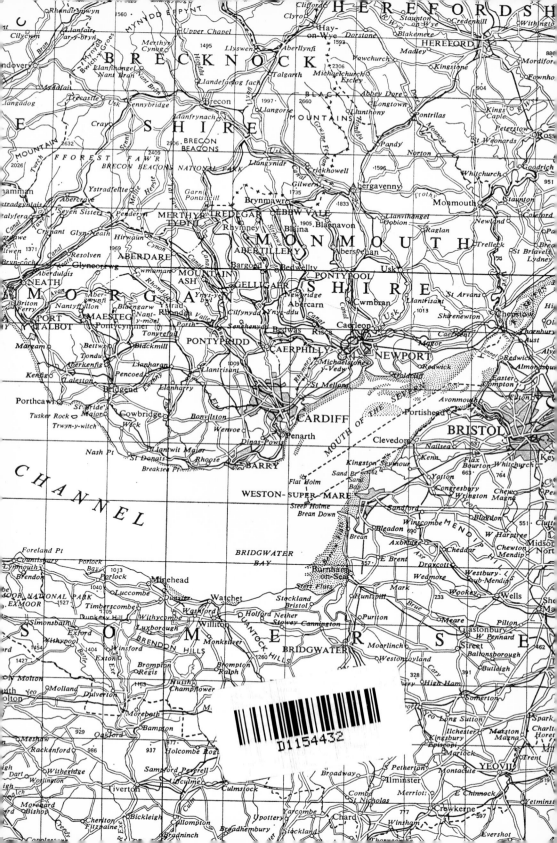

by the same author

THE MINERS
Being Volume One of
A HISTORY OF THE MINERS' FEDERATION OF GREAT BRITAIN

THE MINERS: YEARS OF STRUGGLE
Being Volume Two of
A HISTORY OF THE MINERS' FEDERATION OF GREAT BRITAIN

THE MINERS IN CRISIS AND WAR
Being Volume Three of
A HISTORY OF THE MINERS' FEDERATION OF GREAT BRITAIN

A HISTORY OF THE SCOTTISH MINERS

————

FACTS FROM THE COAL COMMISSION
THE POLITICS OF OIL
THE GENERAL STRIKE MAY 1926: ORIGIN AND HISTORY
WILLIAM MORRIS: A VINDICATION
A SHORT HISTORY OF THE RUSSIAN REVOLUTION

I   NANTGARW PITHEAD GEAR

SOUTH WALES MINERS

GLOWYR DE CYMRU

A History of the
South Wales Miners' Federation
(1898–1914)

BY

R. PAGE ARNOT

1967

GEORGE ALLEN & UNWIN LTD
RUSKIN HOUSE · MUSEUM STREET · LONDON

PRINTED IN GREAT BRITAIN
in 11 on 12 point Baskerville type
BY UNWIN BROTHERS LIMITED
WOKING AND LONDON

TO THE MINING COMMUNITY OF SOUTH WALES
TO WHOM THE BRITISH PEOPLE OWE SO MUCH
ON WHOM HAS FALLEN SUFFERING AND DISASTER
BEYOND THE NORMAL DANGER OF ANY COALFIELD
WHOSE RECORD OF STRUGGLE AND OF COURAGE
IN FACE OF ADVERSITY
RANKS HIGH AMONGST THE MINERS OF THE WORLD

FOREWORD

WE are proud and honoured to present this history of the formation and often turbulent years of the South Wales Miners' Federation.

The author, R. Page Arnot, the eminent historian of the British miners, in this volume records the struggle and sacrifice of our forebears to safeguard, improve and advance their living standards. It tells of the part they played in the fight to establish the Minimum Wage Act, of their endeavours industrially and politically to reduce the hours of work of those employed in the industry, and of their efforts to secure the passing of the Coal Mines Act designed to make the work of coalmining safer and healthier and to prevent the all-too-frequent appalling mining disasters.

Within its pages there is recounted the debate, the argument and counter-argument for and against the Sliding Scale Agreement which for so long determined the wages which were paid to the miners of South Wales as distinct from the wage systems in the other districts of the British coalfield.

In reading this history one is able to follow the forces and influences which worked to compel the miners of South Wales to unite, first among themselves and later within the Miners' Federation of Great Britain, so as to face the common enemy—the coal owners—and, more importantly, against the system which made possible their ruthless exploitation.

This history needed to be written and should be read by all who wish to learn something of the tremendous impact and influence that the miners' organisation wielded in shaping the social, industrial and political life of the whole of the people of South Wales.

This volume is another piece in the fabric not only of the history of the miners but of the workers of Britain and of the world, which is offered in tribute and respect to those who paved the way and as an inspiration to those who follow.

GLYN WILLIAMS	*President*
EMLYN WILLIAMS	*Vice-President*
DAVID FRANCIS	*Secretary*

CARDIFF
1st January, 1967

South Wales Area
National Union of Mineworkers

PREFACE

WHEN first asked, I was somewhat reluctant to undertake the task of dealing with Welsh mining history. But then, having thought it over, I agreed: for with a background of three volumes already written on the history of the British miners, it seemed that it would not be so difficult for me to handle the material available in the district records. These records however turned out to be in a deplorable state, and in no way comparable to the extensive, often verbatim records of the Miners' Federation of Great Britain. Of the printed minutes of the Executive Council of the South Wales Miners' Federation nothing before 1908 was available. Unfortunately the minutes from 1908 onward for a quarter of a century are not very informative—and are therefore in startling contrast to the very full minutes of the last thirty years. Such a statement as, under the heading Ebbw Vale, "The question was discussed and it was agreed to refer it to a committee" is followed at the next meeting by a minute that the sub-committee had not yet reported and then at a later meeting that the sub-committee planned to give its report in a further fortnight's time, whereafter nothing further appears in any minute whatever.

With nineteenth-century trade union records, however, the matter was really desperate. For example, without the reports of the Amalgamated Association of Miners to which from 1869 to 1875 the Welsh colliers adhered, there can be no full history of that troublous period. In April 1875 minute No. 101 of their nine-day conference stipulates that 7,000 copies of the report (like that of their other spring and autumn conferences) shall be printed in English and 2,000 copies in Welsh. Equipped with a single such report of the Amalgamated Association of Miners I began my search for others: and after six years' search have now gathered two more out of a possible ten or eleven. Yet thousands of these reports were in print less than a hundred years ago, while the poems of Sappho and the speeches of Demosthenes were preserved in manuscript for more than two thousand years. It may be that further search in libraries and elsewhere from South Wales up through the Midlands to Lancashire will disclose where the missing reports can be found. I hope for the future that not only in mining but in all other industries due heed may be paid to the value and importance of trade union records and the need to protect them from the salvage zealots as well as from casual pillage by irresponsible collectors.

In these circumstances the decision was taken in 1965 to prepare a first volume dealing with events leading up to the formation of the South Wales Miners' Federation and the first fifteen years of its varying fortunes.

Since much of the period covered lies within active human memory I took the opportunity in the later fifties to spend time in converse with older miners, many of whom had been chosen for this purpose by union lodges. With their aid I was able to garner many rich memories of which only a few could be used in the final presentation of the history. Sometimes as I went through the valleys I marvelled why so little of this seems

A*

to have been done before. This remarkable folk-memory tends to be left ungathered. Yet I feel it to be a task of the same order, though it may be of less importance, as the gathering of folk music by Robert Burns at the end of the eighteenth century or more recently by Cecil Sharp and, in the Hebrides, by Mrs. Kennedy Fraser. In this I had to bear in mind the fallaciousness of human memory. So wherever possible a check was made both with other memories and with available documents—though I have learned to treat with some reserve documents purporting from one side or another of a controversy to furnish a record of events.

But the supposed phenomenon of what has been given the cant name of "total recall" is also to be viewed with suspicion. Those who claim to possess this happy faculty of "total recall" have almost certainly a shaping imagination which dramatises the past, remoulds it, insensibly alters it, turns it into something much easier to recollect, into a more rounded, poignant and dramatic story. The best anecdotes are usually of this kind, but as material for history they should be offered with a grain of salt.

I did not turn historian until near to my sixth decade and quite a long while after some industrial happenings earlier in the century in which I had been deeply engaged. This participation in events had the disadvantage that I could readily be accused of harbouring a standpoint acquired through close experience of industrial conflicts. But this need not mean that the relevant facts cannot be found in my narrative clearly and fairly set forth. As to well-known personages, I have throughout given their standpoint by frequent quotation from their own speeches or writings, which I believe to be the fairest way of conjuring up these figures of over half a century ago.

Those who have a mind to it can sit in judgment weighing the evidence and decide upon the wisdom or folly, honesty or knavery of those representatives of great interests who appear in these pages. It is not my business. I have done the investigation and set out the significant facts. Readers must make up their own minds.

History and geography, blest pair of sirens, whose songs were sung to my infant ears at school in Scotland, have now everywhere been expanded and transformed into the similitude of sciences. Again, the Historical Association, celebrating its diamond jubilee this year, could recall what a lowly place was that of its study within each university when this century began. So, too, the study of Labour History has been climbing upwards amongst the university disciplines. There may come a day when only those who have studied it in college will be expected to write and when the passionless historiographer will have a professional monopoly of the subject. Then the broad sweeping treatment that enabled G. N. Trevelyan to write *Clio A Muse* will be out of fashion, utterly condemned, or handed over to the mercies of historical novelists. In the meantime chronicles like this of mine may serve a useful purpose.

The main sources for what is written here are given already in my previous books on trade union history in the coalfields: and further bibliographical details I leave to a later volume. Meantime for those who cannot wait I here should like to refer to the treatment of Welsh history in the books issued in recent years from the University of Wales Press: and in particular to the bibliographies given in *The Rhondda Valleys* by Dr. E. D. Lewis—an example of a limited area treated with a fullness which might well be imitated by other local authorities in South Wales. Indeed, just as every village or parish mentioned in Domesday Book has its history crying out to be written, so each valley in the coalfield deserves its separate history and not only each valley but each colliery. Records are available, the labourers in the field are relatively few. Those who belong to the Society for the Study of Labour History might well push forward the idea that the National Coal Board will be only fulfilling its plain duty, neglected by so many generations of coal owners, if it were to endow sufficient fellowships or scholarships to cope with the task.

I have in the main dispensed with reference footnotes, for in this I found myself in agreement (for the first time since I met him in controversy in 1919) with the view of the late Lord Norwich that footnotes had become an excrescence to be excised from the pages of books unless for special reasons. Moreover, those who are neither professionally engaged in the academic world nor aspirants thereto do not like a profusion of reference footnotes. This is true of the miners for whom this book is written in the first place, and I believe it is also true for the general public for whom it is written in the second place. In this matter the customer, as usual, is right, and I bow to his wishes or prejudices whichever they may be.

I have, however, inserted in parentheses a brief form of dating, which I hope will preserve, from page to page, the sequence of events for the reader. The quotations thus dated are nearly all from the proceedings of the South Wales Miners' Federation or of the Miners' Federation of Great Britain or from parliamentary proceedings reported in Hansard: and in this way they give the necessary references.

My predecessors in this subject have placed me under a debt of gratitude: the Rt. Hon. Ness Edwards whose books, begun forty years ago, have been to some extent my guide particularly because his fundamental approach was one which I have since made my own: Dr. Eric Evans whose assiduity in pursuit of not always easily ascertainable facts has been all the more helpful in that his general outlook is remote from my own.

This book however could not have been written at all nor could the visits to mining communities in valley after valley have been undertaken and pursued without the help, guidance and companionship in the quest of Prof. Dr. Ronald Frankenberg. He left Manchester University to undertake the meritorious but highly unusual activity of education officer for the South Wales Miners' Federation: and now in his further moves in anthropological sociology he still retains a keen interest in the coalfield and the Welsh people whom he came to know so well and about whom it is my hope he will write further studies and continue and complete the work I have begun in this volume.

The book was read before it went to the press by Arthur Horner, former President of the South Wales Miners' Federation and ex-General

Secretary of the National Union of Mineworkers, and also by his successor in the last two posts Will Paynter. After it had reached the stage of proofs it was read by some of those who had taken part in the twelve-month lockout and ten-month strike of the 12,000 miners in the Cambrian Combine. To W. H. Mainwaring, a former Member of Parliament, one of the survivors of the Unofficial Reform Committee of 1909 and a main author of *The Miners' Next Step* I also record especial thanks. The members of the South Wales Miners' Federation, their agents, Executive Council members and their retired officials, their Members of Parliament past and present, all have been of great service and help. The same applies to friends in the political sphere and in the academic world.

The same does not apply to some former coal owners who were members of the Monmouthshire and South Wales Coal Owners' Association. The trustees of this now defunct body refused to allow me to inspect their records which are housed, largely at the public expense, in the National Library of Wales. Whether they meant to feed fat an ancient grudge against me dating from the First World War, I cannot tell: but Welsh Members of Parliament who in 1961 took the question up as a matter of public interest were politely informed that in law there was nothing could be done. So all I can do is to record that this book would have appeared much earlier had these gentlemen taken a different view of their duties as trustees.

R. PAGE ARNOT

46 Byne Road, London, S.E.26.
December 9, 1966.

ACKNOWLEDGEMENTS

To Amgueddfa Genedlaethol Cymru (National Museum of Wales) for courtesy in supplying photographs facing pages 97, 128, 224, 225, 256, 320.

To the trustees and staff of the British Museum for their courtesy and help in the matter of books and periodical press.

To the National Coal Board for their courtesy and help in supplying the frontispiece.

To *Radio Times* Hulton Picture Library for their courtesy in supplying reproductions of the illustrations facing pages 97, 129, 160, 161, 192, 224, 225, 257.

To the staff of Beckenham and Penge Libraries for their courtesy and help especially in the matter of state papers.

To the family of William Brace for the photograph facing page 96.

To A. F. Adams of Treharris for the 1898 photograph facing page 48.

To Sidney Schuman for the graphs on pages 91, 93, 101, 217, 338.

To Hywel Francis for procuring the maps on pages 68, 73, 174, 203, 265.

To the Labour Research Department for their skill and care in compiling the Index.

CONTENTS

ILLUSTRATIONS

MAPS AND GRAPHS

The endpapers are reproduced from Ordnance Survey maps with the sanction of the Controller of Her Majesty's Stationery Office. Crown Copyright Reserved.

The names of many of the men, traced by Mr. Arthur Adams of 53, Fell Street, Treharris (with their picturesque nick-names in brackets) are given in the list below:

William Jones ("Check")
William Jones, Brynteg ("Groano")
Dai Walter Davies ("Brecon")
Tom Williams ("Becker")
Dai Francis, Fell Street
Ben Andrews;
Tom Jones, Webster Street ("Ogmore")
William Evans ("Sneedles")
Dai Jones ("Cardi")
Tom Theophilus
Sam Davies, Railway Terrace
John Prosser
John Williams ("Troedyrhiw")
John Harris, Gresham Place
Will Lowe
Tom Clapham
Danny Williams ("Ponty")
Ned Jones
Dai Parcel ("Crow")
Will Nicholas
Johnny Evans
Joe Phillips ("J.P.")
Ben Davies ("Cefn")
Will Tovey
Jack Davies ("Carter")
Dai Walter Griffiths
Jack Walters
Gwilym Evans' father
Rees Griffiths ("Swansea")
John Broadstock
Jack Carlick
Dan Tanner
Walter Manuel

Danny Evans ("Ginger")
Penry Morgan
George Morgan
John Thomas ("Shoni Bully")
— Trotman
— Rowlands
Dick Jones ("North")
Hugh Edwards ("Hugh the Northman"), father to Allan Edwards
Rees Jones ("Traffic")
Will Davies, 1, Railway Terrace
Mike Keenan
John Harding
Dai Edwards
Jim Rees (father to "Jimmy the Rogue")
Will Davies ("Willie Black Pipe")
Will Curtis
Banfield Morgan
Phil Sam
John Humphreys
Tom Sherry
Gabriel Evans
"Old Excel"
John Phillips ("Morriston Monkey")
Will Morgan
Tom Roberts ("Tom Merthyr Vale")
Dai Thomas Griffiths
Lewis Jones ("Lewsin Short")
Bob Thomas ("Dubber")
Dick Owen
Tom Evans ("Fe")
Enoch Davies ("Beech")
Georgie Evans ("Pug")

(Plate facing p. 48.)

CHAPTER ONE

BEFORE THE FEDERATION

I. THE BACKGROUND

OF all the continuing miners' associations that covered twenty coalfields in Great Britain the latest was the South Wales Miners' Federation which within two years came to be the largest. This rate of growth was unusual among trade unions. Still more unusual was its origin, not from a short victorious strike but from total defeat at the end of a lockout of over twenty-two weeks, complicated on either side by a series of inner conflicts. The usual effect of such prolonged and complex struggles had been demoralisation following upon defeat. But to understand South Wales and its miners we must first look at the world outside.

The last three years of the nineteenth century, when the South Wales Miners' Federation came fully into being, marked the close of the Victorian epoch. When the Princess Victoria came into the world the industrial revolution opening around 1760, though well advanced in manufacture, had as yet affected movement by land or sea only to a small extent. These were still the days of the stagecoach, the barge on the canal with its towpath for horses, the coastal barques, the packet across the Channel or the full spread of sail for the East Indiaman and the transatlantic vessels. Indeed for the Princess Victoria in her childhood travel was hardly swifter than it had been seventeen hundred years earlier when the Roman Emperor Hadrian journeyed from York to the Mediterranean.

By the end of the century there had been a transformation. Forms of energy that man had tamed or contrived for his use over thousands of years had changed. The water-mill had given place to the steam-engine, the sailing-ship to the steam-ship, the traction teams of flesh-and-blood to the iron horse. This transformation depended on coal. Heating, lighting by gas or electricity, power from the steam-engine—all came from coal. Into fire-box and furnace there was shovelled ton upon ton of coal from more and more pits that were sunk to deeper and deeper seams and worked by a growing army of men underground. Britain had been in the forefront of this change: and still in 1870 this one island had an output of coal greater than all the other countries of the world taken together.

Nowhere was the abruptness of this transformation more apparent than in Wales, the historic principality on the west of the island, and especially in its southern coalfield, with rich seams extending in an ellipse across three counties. There, between the mountains and the sea were tree-clad hills and verdant valleys: and hidden in the bowels of the earth beneath them lay the carboniferous strata—bituminous, anthracite and hard steam coals. At the northern outcrops the ironmasters from the end of the eighteenth century relied upon adjacent coal mines for their manufacture. But the coal seams that were to be the mainstay of the industry were not opened up on any scale, nor were the railways built, nor did the remoter wooded valleys of Glamorgan lose their pastoral charm until well on in the nineteenth century. Then came the deluge. From a supply of eight million tons in the late 'fifties, when very many ships still waited on the wind to fill their sails, the coal output of South Wales leapt up to seventeen million tons in 1877 and 35 million tons in 1897, while the coalfield from third or fourth place in Great Britain rose to first place. Capital poured into South Wales mining and labour followed. The coalfield became an industrial whirlpool drawing in manpower from the neighbouring English agricultural shires of Hereford, Gloucester and Somerset; and, beyond Bristol Channel, from kindred Cornwall and Devon; and from all the rural areas of the thirteen Welsh counties. Between 1837 and 1897 there had been a doubling of the population of Great Britain but a sixfold increase in the number of miners: in the South Wales coalfield the rate of increase was even greater.

The Diamond Jubilee in 1897 of the reign of Queen Victoria, widely celebrated and made into a festival of the British Empire as well as a sort of jamboree of European monarchs, was also treated as a summit of historical progress from which to survey the achievements of the past. From this vantage point the people of Britain were called to look backward for sixty years and witness how much had been accomplished in the accumulation of material wealth, in the progress of science and technology, in the flowering of art and literature. Changes in the condition of the people themselves were not forgotten. The socialist Sidney Webb wrote a monograph on "Labour in the Longest Reign." It was remembered too that when Victoria ascended the throne in 1837 children of five and six were toiling underground in the coalfields of Great Britain.[1] But no stress was laid on that stormy period of the Chartists, the first political party of the working class, whose agitation had mounted to a point where miners of Monmouthshire and South Wales were ready to take part in the Newport rising of 1839. Nor amid the celebrations in that summit year of 1897 was there any emphasis upon the existing

[1] *The Miners*, Chapter 1; and *The Scottish Miners*, Chapter 2.

conditions of mining, hours of labour or level of wages, which the Welsh miners themselves deplored as deteriorating from season to season and from year to year.

It was for this reason in the autumn of the jubilee year that the Welsh miners sought a ten per cent increase in their wages, and for this purpose decided by ballot vote (41,880 to 12,178) to end the agreement that governed wages in the coalfield. The requisite six months' notice was sent to the employers on September 30, 1897. Here then our story begins.

2. THE SLIDING SCALE

Wages in South Wales were settled not by individual or collective bargaining but by the price of coal. This system had begun in 1875 when a five months' lockout by the owners to enforce a reduction in wages had resulted in the dissolution of the Amalgamated Association of Miners. The terms for a resumption of work were a reduction of 12½ per cent and the establishment of "a sliding scale of wages to be regulated by the selling price of coal." To operate this sliding scale agreement a joint committee of workmen's and coalowners' representatives was set up and was to be "kept on foot by the employers and workmen." The expense of the workmen's side was to be supported by a levy of 2d. a month deducted from wages in the colliery office and then handed over to the miners' agent, "who thus became," wrote Professor Jevons, "very largely a servant of two masters."[1] Under these conditions effective trade unionism in South Wales virtually disappeared, nor did it re-emerge in full vigour for nearly a quarter of a century. It is true that leaders of the old union continued to be the representatives of the workmen and that behind those chosen as miners' agents there were some local associations of miners. But the peculiar form of the sliding scale joint committee, with the equivocal position of the agents, tended for the most part to suffocate trade unionism in the valleys of South Wales.

In all this period the leading figure was William Abraham, better known by his Bardic title, Mabon, who at first represented the miners of Loughor in the far west of Glamorgan although his birthplace was Cwmavon on the Afan River running down to Port Talbot. Born in 1842, his record of activity dated back to before the 'seventies. By 1877 he had moved to the Rhondda valleys where he was chosen as miners' agent. By 1885 he had been elected Member of Parliament for the Rhondda: and he was to hold his seat through seven successive General Elections and to remain a miners' M.P. for nearly a third of a century. Like other mining M.P.s, William

[1] *The British Coal Trade*, by H. Stanley Jevons (1915).

Abraham was a Liberal, and like all of them except Burt of North-umberland, a devout Christian, spending much of his time as a lay preacher. From the pulpit he taught "the identity of interests of capital and labour." He did not possess the developed political and economic standpoint of some of his colleagues. Abraham was, however, the possessor of the "hwyl," that peculiar eloquence found amongst the Welsh nonconformists, and this, together with a remarkable singing voice, he was wont to use with great effect at conferences and demonstrations. The workmen were by no means whole-hearted believers, as Mabon was, in the principle of the sliding scale, and oft-times he was hooted down by his angry constituents when he was defending the agreements reached with the owners. But Abraham had a taking way with him, and he knew how to play upon the national characteristics of his countrymen, even if it meant the splitting of the Welsh-speaking miners from the English-speaking miners. A colleague from Scotland told in his reminiscences[1] how on a speaking tour he discovered "the secret of Mabon's vast influence over the Welsh miners":

If any friction arose and pandemonium threatened—so easy to rouse, so difficult to quell—Mabon never tried to restore order in any usual way. He promptly struck up a Welsh hymn, or that magical melody, "Land of my Fathers." Hardly had he reached the second line, when, with uplifted arms, as though drawing the whole multitude into the circle of his influence, he had the vast audience dropping into their respective "parts", and accompanying him like a great trained choir. It was wonderful, almost magical and the effect was thrilling. When the hymn or song was finished he raised a hand, and instantly perfect silence fell. The storm had passed.

From the beginning the operation of the sliding scale was super-vised by a joint committee of employers and workmen, at first of five from each side but by 1890 of eleven from each. The eleven em-ployers acted on behalf of the Monmouthshire and South Wales Coal Owners' Association. This formidable body which, under another name, had come into existence in 1873 soon represented collieries with three quarters of the total output of the coalfield, and even more by the end of the century, although a number of impor-tant collieries still remained as "non-associated."

From 1880 to 1899, that is, throughout most of the years of the sliding scale, the chairmanship of the joint committee was held by Sir William Thomas Lewis (1837–1914) who in 1875 had been the initiator of this automatic regulator of wages.[2] From the beginning

[1] *My Life for Labour*, by Robert Smillie, M.P., with a foreword by J. Ramsay Mac-Donald, M.P., 1924.
[2] Lewis' rise from junior clerk to colliery proprietor is told in *The South Wales Coal Trade and its Allied Industries* by Charles Wilkins (1888).

in 1875 to the end in 1902 William Abraham occupied the post of vice-chairman.

The employers were well pleased with the sliding scale committee. Their secretary in the summer of 1895 dedicated a book of records to Sir William Lewis whose "great work" he predicted, "in maintaining the cordial relationship existing between the employers and employed will be gratefully remembered for many years to come." Elsewhere in this dedicatory letter to the Chairman it is stated:

> The Sliding Scale system has been an important feature in preserving the friendly relationship existing between employers and employed in South Wales, and it is worthy of record that during the 20 years period whilst the system has been in vogue, the workmen of the South Wales district have, with but very few exceptions, loyally abided by the arrangement, and have resisted every attempt made by the workmen of other districts to bring about a combination for securing wages in excess of those justified by the actual state of trade at the time being.[1]

A diametrically opposite opinion of the system, that "under its operation the condition of the men has gradually gone from bad to worse, whilst trade unionism has become all but extinct" was expressed in the weekly paper edited by J. Keir Hardie who in the 'nineties had been agitating in the South Wales coalfield. In fact, not a few stoppages occurred during the operation of the system: and the many revisions of the agreement were made because the workmen from time to time were dissatisfied with the Sliding Scale.[2]

In their sociological study of trade unionism[3] Sidney and Beatrice Webb stated with particular reference to the coal miners of South Wales:

> Not a third of the 120,000 men are even professedly members of any trade union, or in any way represented in the negotiations, and of the organised workmen a considerable proportion, forming three separate unions, each covering a distinct district, expressly refused to agree to the 1893 Sliding Scale, and withdrew their representatives from the joint committee.
>
> In this case the associated employers, in alliance with a minority of the workmen, enforce, upon an apathetic or dissentient majority, under pain of exclusion from the industry or exile from the district, a method of remuneration and rates of payment which are fiercely resented by many of them.

---

[1] *Records of the several coal owners associations of Monmouthshire and South Wales, 1864 to 1895*, compiled by W. Gascoyne Dalziel. (Cited hereafter as "Dalziel.")
[2] *Successive Sliding Scales and Agreements thereunder*

(1st) December 11, 1875.	(4th) January 15, 1890.
(2nd) January 17, 1880.	(5th) January 1, 1892.
(3rd) June 6, 1882.	February 17, 1893.
November 7, 1887.	March 28, 1895.
	September 1, 1898.

[3] *Industrial Democracy*, published early in 1898: and within three months translated into Russian by V. I. Lenin then in exile in Siberia.

They went on to describe the system by which a compulsory deduction from pay financed officials who represented a "small minority."

We have, in fact in this remarkable case, an instance of collective administration without democratic control.

These words, written in the year 1897, serve to explain something of the ferment found amongst the colliers in South Wales.

3. RESISTANCE TO THE SLIDING SCALE

The sliding scale arrangements of South Wales could never be completely insulated. In other coalfields a forward movement in wages[1] had such repeated success that it led to the formation at Newport on November 26, 1889, of the Miners' Federation of Great Britain. Within a week notice was due to be given in South Wales to end the third sliding scale, adopted seven years earlier in 1882. Great hopes were entertained by those who formed the new body that it would not be long before all the colliers west of the Severn would also be "free from sliding scales" and thus be able to join up. But these hopes were not to be fulfilled. Some eight weeks later, at the first conference of the new Miners' Federation of Great Britain, its chairman, Ben Pickard, in his opening address referred to "the South Wales element" as the "great lever" that had been used at Newport to prevent strike action being taken to gain the shorter working day. "We had definite pledges from the South Wales men," said Pickard, "that, if the matter could be adjourned, . . . they would never adopt such a 'rotten system' again" as this sliding scale and would obtain both an advance in wages and an eight hour working day. Pickard rather bitterly summed up, saying: "Well, they held meetings and reiterated their intentions; and what they said they would not do, now we have it on record that they will do: they have adopted another rotten sliding scale." He added, as a parting shot: "I hope the Ocean colliers, and Monmouthshire men generally, will break away from the South Wales men." (22.i.1890).

This 4th Sliding Scale, signed on January 15, 1890, laid it down that the standard of wages upon which future advances or reduction were to be made "shall be the several rates actually paid at the respective collieries for the month of December 1879." Such wages were to be "equivalent to a standard nett selling price of coal of 7s. 10½d. and under 8s. per ton." The selling price of coal (delivered

[1] The originating circular for this movement, sent out from Barnsley on September 10, 1888, by Ben Pickard, M.P., Secretary of the Yorkshire Miners' Association, began with the significant words: "All Miners now free from Sliding Scales are invited to attend a Conference . . ."

free on board at the coalfield ports) was to be ascertained by two accountants, one appointed by the employers and "the other by the workmen," in a quarterly audit. For each rise or fall of 1s. in the price per ton, wages would rise or fall by 10 per cent (or 1½d. per ton = 1¼ per cent).

Under this 4th scale, prices per ton (which had been as low as 8s. 0½d. in April 1888) were rising rapidly. They rose from 11s. 1d. in the last months of 1889 to 13s. 7½d. in the midsummer 1891; while wages, which stood at 32½ per cent above standard in January 1890 rose within eighteen months by 25 per cent until they touched 57 per cent by the summer of 1891. At that point, the associated owners, finding themselves dissatisfied with the operation of the agreement, gave six months' notice on July 1, 1891. They wanted to cut the rate (of rise or fall in wages) from 10 per cent in the shilling to 8¾ per cent (or 1¼ per cent = 1·7d.) They were willing to concede a two-monthly instead of a quarterly audit. The workmen mostly preferred shorter accountancy periods as the quarterly audit sometimes brought with it a time-lag between the date of a rise in coal prices and the corresponding automatic rise in wages. But under the new scale a reverse effect set in. Wages fell with each successive two-monthly audit throughout 1892 and within eighteen months had tumbled from 53¾ per cent in the last weeks of 1891 down to 10 per cent above standard in the midsummer period (June 1 to July 31) of 1893.

The insistence of the employers upon this new sliding scale had been accepted without much resistance from the representatives of the Welsh miners. This brought biting comment in mid-January from Sam Woods, vice-president of the Miners' Federation, who at its third annual conference held in Staffordshire made reference to the wage reduction in South Wales. He spoke of their submission "in a most humiliating manner"; "the humiliating vacillation"; "most abject position"; "a semblance of an organisation" which in consequence of "the absence of vitality" had "to succumb to the terms of the employers . . . " They had accepted and were bound hand and foot by a new sliding scale: "that scale," Woods said, "was declared in 1889 by their leaders to be rotten, and it is now still more rotten than ever." In Monmouth, however, a small union adhered to the Miners' Federation of Great Britain and represented the Federation outlook and spirit against the sliding scales. "It is a matter," said Woods, "to feel proud of, to find our Monmouth friends and others in the locality stoutly refusing to sell their liberty and become mere vassals in the hands of their employers." (*13.i.1892*).

From Monmouthshire in the east of the coalfield in the late 'eighties, and later in the western valleys of the coalfield, there sprang up this resistance, sedulously fostered by the Miners' Federation of Great Britain.

In Monmouthshire the leading figure was William Brace (1865–1947) who was born in Risca, went to the pit there at the age of twelve and afterwards worked both at Celynen and Abercarn collieries. At Celynen a story went round (and is still repeated) that young Brace[1] used regularly to go up the mountain and there test his speaking powers under a spreading tree and against the south west gales. Certainly Brace's rhetorical prowess developed early: and even in his eightieth year he still "had a voice like a bell." He was to become the most fluent and the most polished orator of his generation in the conferences of the miners. While still working at Abercarn pit Brace in 1890 was elected miners' agent (at a salary of 28s. 6d. a week) for the Monmouthshire and South Wales District Miners' Union. His little district persisted as an enclave of the Miners' Federation of Great Britain in the wasteland of the sliding scale and as a standing reproach to those whom he deemed to have abandoned the older and better traditions of the Welsh miners. These traditions were perhaps maintained in his own mind through his acquaintance with Tom Halliday,[2] president of the Amalgamated Association of Miners during its struggles in the 'seventies. Looking back from the vantage point of half-a-century later, the Rt. Hon. William Brace in his house on the hill above Newport recalled earlier times:

In those days not only people from other coalfields but from other counties were considered foreigners. County was against county. I was thrilled by the idea of a national union. The Union we formed in the eastern and western valleys of Monmouthshire had only a few hundred members. It was seven to ten years of real battling. On Monday morning I left my house, came back on Saturday, addressing two meetings every day. In Glamorgan I could get no accommodation. They would not put me up in the inn; colliers who agreed with me dared not put me up . . . Oh, it was a bitter struggle! Mabon, you know, brought a slander action against me. (*8.ix.1945.*)

Brace had been carrying on a campaign outside his own county of Monmouthshire and throughout the valleys of Glamorgan. There he had fiercely criticised the actions as well as the policy of the revered William Abraham who for his part was not behindhand in retaliating. Mabon in his speeches used to tell the miners not to heed

[1] According to Sam Fisher, sen. who was born in the same year as Brace and had known not only William but his brothers George, Tom and Mark, the family was originally called Moon: but the mother had been left a widow with six children; and Brace was the name of a stepfather. (*Interview at Wattsville, Crosskeys, on 23.ix.1958*).

[2] "I knew Halliday," said Brace. "He was not a Welshman but came from Lancashire after the breakdown of the old Amalgamated Association. He made a living selling oil and odds and ends around the collieries. His dwelling was in Cardiff and there I used to see him." (*Communicated in an interview on 6.ix.1945.*)

Brace who was bringing "an English influence" into Wales—a nationalistic periphrasis for the influence of Ben Pickard or rather of the older miners' associations. Mabon was alleged to have said that Brace was "simply a tool in the hands of the Miners' Federation of Great Britain" which had decided to spend large sums in recruitment for their Union. Mabon denied that he had used the words imputed to him by Brace. However that may be, Brace let fly at Mabon and the result was an action for slander. It was almost unprecedented that trade union secretaries should go to law against one another. It was considered by some rather a horrifying thing to do, by others that the M.P. must have had very great provocation. When the case of Abraham v. Brace came up for hearing at Swansea in the Glamorganshire summer assizes of 1893, Counsel for Abraham said that on 2nd January of that same year Brace had used the following words: "To my mind it is more honourable to be a tool in the hands of the Federation (meaning the Miners' Federation of Great Britain) than to be a tool directly or indirectly in the hands of the employers of South Wales." Further, Counsel said on 20th February that the defendant variously and maliciously had spoken these words:

> I declare deliberately that Mr. Abraham was compelled to sign the new agreement because he was not in a position to refuse it—he was not in a position to offend the employers. Week after week Mr. Abraham depends upon the good will of the employers for the keeping back of his wages at the colliery office.

The plaintiff, who had been "greatly injured in his credit" by the utterance of the defendant, wanted one thousand pounds damages. It was claimed that the construction to be placed upon the utterance was that Mabon "had betrayed the interests of the men who paid him and was secretly working in the interests of the employers and against the men, that he was acting in a corrupt and dishonourable manner as paid agent and representative and was not honestly and independently doing the best he could for the men who employed him, but had betrayed their interests and was in fact receiving money from the coalowners and working in concert with them; that he had accepted a bribe from the employers and no longer deserved the confidence of the men and was unfitted to be the agent of the Workmen's Association or to be a representative of the miners on the Sliding Scale Committee."

The verdict was given for the plaintiff and damages were awarded of £500.

This had a curious sequel. Brace took no steps to pay the money and to all legal missives turned a blind eye or rather turned these missives into ammunition for the speeches in his campaign which he continued more vigorously than ever. Both men were given to preaching. It was customary for these trade union speeches also to be delivered in the chapels. Brace took to carrying round with him the legal demands for the payment of £500 and displaying them at his meetings, as he told it:

> I used to go early to the meetings often having walked over the mountain, and in the chapel I would nail up below the pulpit where everybody could see it the demand for £500 damages. As they came in to the chapel everyone went up to read it so that they knew already what I was going to talk about. I used to say it was the greatest joke that had ever been heard that Mabon wanted to get £500 from me and that if me and my Union and all our household furniture were sold up it would not come to five hundred shillings. I said this again and again. My meetings began to be crowded. People came over the mountain and flocked to hear me, and always I ended by saying "they are hoping to get five hundred pounds out of me and if everything was sold up I would not have five hundred shillings."
>
> Then one day a friend of Mabon's, a man whom I respected, came to me and said: "Mabon will not insist on payment if you will stop making those speeches. He will let bygones be bygones but you must not tell this story in your speeches." "What!" I said to him "but you are proposing to take away my story. Why, it is the very spice of my speeches." However, I agreed and so it ended. (*8.ix.1945.*)

But though the personal roughness was to be somewhat smoothed over with the lapse of time, Brace was still the opponent of the sliding scale of which Mabon for so long had been the outspoken defender. Indeed, only ten days before the Assizes Brace had presided at a special conference where 80 delegates were present "representing nearly 40,000 workmen" and the same day had sent "To the Employers of South Wales and Monmouthshire" the conference resolution on wages[1] with its request for an early interview—to which the employers did not deign to reply. The effect, however, of this conference was soon to be seen.

4. THE HAULIERS' STRIKE

On Tuesday, August 1, 1893, on the same day that the Assizes opened at Swansea, hauliers in the Ogmore Valley struck work. The next day the strikers marched over to the Rhondda Fawr where they stopped other pits of the Ocean Coal Company and also pits at Gelli, Pentre and Bodringallt. The immediate occasion of the

---

[1] "1st. That we protest against any further reduction in our wages.

2nd. That, under the circumstances, we feel compelled to appeal to you for an advance in our wages, as we assure you that we have found the present rates to be inadequate to maintain ourselves and families, and hoping you will grant us an early interview to discuss this very important question." (*24.vii.1893.*) It is understood that the demand at an interview was to have been for a 20 per cent advance.

strike, other than the electric atmosphere created by the news of the giant lockout in the English coalfields which began on the July 26th (and was to continue for nearly five months) seems to have been the postponement of the announcement of a sliding scale advance, expected on July 29th. A hauliers' committee with head-quarters in the Griffin Hotel at Pentre, sent a letter "to the coal owners of South Wales," in these words:

Gentlemen,—We, the Hauliers of the various pits of South Wales, demand an immediate advance of 20 per cent upon the standard of our wages, and that we have decided not to resume work until our request has been complied with. (*4.viii.1893.*)

Next day the owners' side of the Sliding Scale Joint Committee encouraged those whose pits were affected by the stoppage to proceed with summonses against the workmen for breach of contract: and telegrams were despatched to the collieries affected, "with instructions to the owners to retain in hand the pay monies due to the strikers." (*5.viii.1893.*) Later the same day at the Angel Hotel in Cardiff the Sliding Scale Joint Committee declared a 1¼ per cent advance in wages as from August 1st, in accordance with the report of the audit, bringing them up to 11¼ per cent above the standard of 1879, and affecting 100,000 miners in the coalfield. This done, the representatives of masters and men considered the hauliers' request and decided jointly that "no acknowledgment or reply to the letter be sent." The letter of William Brace of July 24th was similarly treated after having been read to the Joint Committee. It was believed that work would be resumed on Tuesday, August 8th, after bank holiday Monday. But the idle day witnessed many meetings throughout the coalfield. A conference of hauliers at Pontypridd assembled to hear the reply from the owners to their missive. But, since no reply had come, they passed a resolution repeating their demand for 20 per cent advance and their determination "to remain idle pending a reply from the coalowners." (*7.viii.1893.*)

These two days had not been spent in vain by the "marching gangs," the name given to the deputations appointed to go from pit to pit. These deputations, each ten men strong, appeared in Mon-mouthshire. At one mass meeting, held in Crumlin, 10,000 were present and a resolution of support from the colliers was passed. Most of the Monmouthshire hauliers now came out on strike and were joined by a considerable number of colliers on Wednesday, August 9th. The next day the Rhondda miners at a meeting decided that "all colliers at present idle" should join the hauliers in their demand for 20 per cent advance. In the first week of August Glamor-ganshire owners had been affected: but now the Monmouthshire

B

owners had to meet at Newport to concert their plans. They, too, resolved to recommend that summonses should be issued against hauliers. But on the policy of withholding pay (which so far had not yielded the hoped-for results in Glamorgan collieries) there was considerable discussion as the action of the men in the two shires was not considered to be identical: "for," wrote the owners' secretary, Gascoyne Dalziel, "whereas in Glamorganshire the strike was entirely due to the action of the hauliers, in Monmouthshire the hauliers were distinctly supported by the colliers and in the instance of one colliery the only workmen who had presented themselves for work were the hauliers."[1] So at Newport the owners decided to pay both hauliers and colliers alike the monies which they had earned previous to the strike. That weekend Mabon had a very poor hearing at Griffin Field at Pentre: where he said that hauliers leaving work without notice had committed a breach of contract, and miners going on strike had flagrantly violated the sliding scale agreement.

Other valleys had now come out on strike so that but for the pits in the Swansea District it was considered virtually a general strike in most of the coalfield; collieries with two-thirds of the coalfield tonnage were stopped.

At the Rocking Stone, the traditional gathering place well up on the hillside above Pontypridd, contingents from the coalfield marched on Monday to a great meeting of well over ten thousand men. Some set out before sunrise. Bands were out. Morgan Thomas, a haulier from Pentre with "wonderful oratorical powers," spoke from the top of the Rocking Stone and a resolution was passed:

That we, the workmen of Monmouthshire and South Wales here assembled, denounce the demoralising effect upon us, as a body, of the sliding scale, and that we feel justified in our action in demanding an advance forthwith of 20 per cent outside the scope, and that we uphold the action of the hauliers of Glamorganshire and Monmouthshire, come what may, and that we call upon the few men now at work to join in with the common cause of struggling for freedom. (*14.viii.1893.*)

The answer came the next day from a special general meeting of the associated coalowners, which resolved not to treat with the strikers but set up an Emergency Committee of twenty-one members with full powers to act. This committee immediately stimulated prosecutions against strikers and the preparation of a "list of all workmen whose wages may have been retained in hand." (*15.viii.1893.*)

[1] Dalziel, *op. cit.*

5. TROOPS TO QUELL THE STRIKERS

But three days later when the Emergency Committee met again, the reports from the collieries convinced them that "the police authorities were practically unable to cope" with "the spreading disorder." The owners, now in a state of consternation, immediately sent off a whole series of urgent telegrams calling for more military and more police. The exchange of telegrams[1] shows clearly how closely employers, magistrates, Home Office and military authorities worked with one another.

The Emergency Committee were in session all Friday, August 18th, and on to a late hour at night. First of all, after their telegrams for the immediate calling together of all benches of magistrates in the coalfield, they got into touch with the Chief Constable for Glamorganshire, Lionel Lindsay, who makes his first notable appearance in connection with the coalowners and for the purpose of repression of strikers on this occasion. They also consulted the officer in charge of the military depot at Cardiff who sent further telegrams for reinforcements. The Emergency Committee seem then more or less to have supplanted the civil authorities: for they arranged the exact local dispositions of the cavalry and infantry despatched to the area. Late that night of Friday, August 18, 1893, the members of the committee were busied with arrangements for the transport of the troops. They were able to call upon and receive "valuable and ready assistance" from the Taff Vale Railway Company and from the Great Western Railway. Some of them arranged for the billeting of the troops.

Half of the Emergency Committee had attended a meeting of the Sliding Scale Joint Committee. There they met the workmen's representatives who then issued a manifesto, dated August 18th. The manifesto began:—"To the miners of South Wales and Monmouthshire: Fellow workmen. As your duly elected representatives upon the Sliding Scale Joint Committee we feel it our duty to explain to you our position in the present unfortunate crisis." The explanation consisted in an account of the three conferences earlier that year on the negotiations over the continuance of the 1892 Sliding Scale Agreement which they had been granted plenary powers to conduct by ballot vote at the various collieries. Their manifesto concluded:

Therefore we cannot honourably encourage any attempt to violate the agreement that we have signed at your request—and, moreover, it becomes our imperative duty to ask you, in the interests of yourselves and families, as in the interests of the trade, which has already suffered almost

[1] Given in full in Dalziel, *op. cit.*

irreparable loss, to resume your work at the collieries and honourably carry out the obligations which you entreated us to enter into on your behalf. We are, your obedient Servants, (Ten signatures follow).[1]

A further manifesto, signed by the dozen representative owners, with Sir William Lewis at the top of the list, called upon workmen forthwith to fulfill "the terms of their several engagements" and ended with saying: "We have only to emphasise upon the appeal of yesterday's date of your accredited representatives."

The Emergency Committee, still on August 19th, learned of the arrival of troops (made up of detachments from the 14th Hussars, the Enniskillen Dragoons and the Devonshire and Bedfordshire Regiments) under General Sir Richard Harrison. On Monday, August 21st, Sir William Lewis "personally thanked General Harrison" on behalf of the Association for "the prompt action taken by the military authorities" whose presence, they learned from the collieries, "had had an immediate beneficial effect."

On Monday, August 21st, several meetings were held in the Rhondda to protest against the introduction of extra police and military: but two days later, wrote *The Times* of Wednesday, August 23rd: "The strike in South Wales is dying a natural death. The threats of the strikers to invade places where work has been continued have come to nothing, the presence of the military evidently checking all movements of a hostile character."

On Thursday, August 24, 1893, it was "confidently expected" that the strike would be over the following day, but at a mass meeting of colliers and hauliers at the Rocking Stone on the Friday, it was "practically unanimously agreed to maintain the strike."

Over the weekend of August 26th and 27th there was reported to be no change in the situation in South Wales. Ballots, however, took place in several districts and the results in each case were in favour of resumption of work. Meantime the Emergency Committee met frequently and took successive measures to safeguard the interests of the owners.

On Saturday, August 26th, arrangements were made for twenty-three telegraph offices to be kept open day and night, Sundays included, during the strike to enable owners to communicate with the police or the military "in any emergency." This was a further interesting example of what seems to have been almost a state of siege imposed in Monmouthshire and Glamorgan from mid-

---

[1] The signatories were:

W. Abraham	David Beynon
David Morgan (Dai o'r Nant)	Alfred Onions
T. Daronwy Isaac	John Morgan
Thomas Richards	Philip George
Thomas Davies	Lewis Miles, *Secretary*

August onwards. Before the end of the month the miners began to go back but the danger in the eyes of the employers had not disappeared. Sir William Thomas Lewis, described as "the best-feared man, and one of the wealthiest, being an agent of Lord Bute, and a very large coal owner on his own account," gave an interview to *The Times* correspondent on Monday, August 28th, in which he is reported to have said that as long as there were two sections, some idle and some working, it would not be "safe" to dispense with the military.

On Tuesday, August 29th, the Emergency Committee, finding that colliery managers and others "had fears of a breach of the peace at some of the collieries on strike," recommended the immediate "swearing in of a number of Special constables:" and on Thursday, took two decisions. One was to recommend their members not to talk individually to the press: the other was to repeat the instructions to the employers as follows:

> No members shall entertain proposals for any deviation from the terms of the Sliding Scale Agreement nor to discuss the matter with any other parties than the accredited representatives of the workmen on the Sliding Scale Joint Committee. (*31.viii.1893.*)

We turn now to the other side of the struggle, to the mass meeting held on Saturday, September 2nd, at the Rocking Stone at Pontypridd. Three resolutions[1] were passed. One called upon the members of the Sliding Scale Committee to resign and refused in future to contribute towards the maintenance of the Sliding Scale. The second ran:

> That this mass meeting of miners of South Wales and Monmouthshire pledges itself to individually connect itself, one and all, with the South Wales and Monmouthshire branch of the Miners' Federation of Great Britain, in order to protect ourselves from further oppression. (*2.ix.1893.*)

The third resolution of Saturday, September 2nd at the Rocking Stone made it clear that work would not be resumed (on Tuesday, September 5th) "until the hauliers have first received their wages." At this point the strikers received aid and comfort from the miners' agent and secretary of the Neath, Swansea and Llanelly miners who had been a member since 1880 of the Sliding Scale Joint Committee. Isaac Evans, described by the Webbs as "a short, thick-set bulldog-looking sort of man," after long experience had become bitterly opposed to the Sliding Scale and also to its chief advocate, William Abraham.[2] Now Isaac Evans was ready, together with the chairman

---

[1] Dalziel, *op. cit.*, p. 193.
[2] "Evans is very bitter with Mabon: whom he says is a fraud. He is always dining with the employers,—even when the Sliding Scale Committee meets, Mabon deserts the men's representatives to go and dine with the employers. They give him a 'good feed' some good wine and good cigars and then they can do what they like with him. Then also his eldest son has an excellent berth in Sir. W. T. Lewis' office. That also helps to shut his mouth. Evans even asserts that he knows that Mabon takes bribes from the

of the Saturday demonstration, to attend the employers' Emergency Committee on Monday, September 4th, to lay before them the hauliers' demands. The owners' Committee refused to see their former colleague: but the effect of his intervention was that the Committee that morning resolved, "That no monies are to be retained from the hauliers on account of expenses or fines."

Already, however, nearly half the men were back at work and the *Manchester Guardian* of Thursday, September 7, 1893, bore the headline, "End of South Wales Strike."

6. THE HAULIERS' STRIKE IN RETROSPECT

The Hauliers' Strike, the course of which through August and September of 1893 has been summarily traced in these last two sections, was talked of in the valleys right up to the 'fifties of the new century, that is, as long as the vivid memories of it lasted amongst the older miners. It was not commemorated by the older officials of the union most of whom had been busy in an endeavour to quench this tumultuous outburst: and thus it appeared almost as a pattern of what was later to be termed "an unofficial strike."

Without any overt preparations in the collieries where it started, with no worked-out organisation except the spontaneous and, as it seemed, contagious activity of "the marching gangs," the strike spread like wildfire to the steam-coal area and thence throughout most of the counties of Glamorgan and Monmouth. The haulier lads were many of them enrolled in the militia, for the sake of a summer holiday; and so had learned how to march in order. But beyond the choosing of a committee there was little evidence of organisation. Of those chosen to lead amid this turmoil there was only one, Morgan Thomas, who came to public attention by the oratorical powers which so stirred his hearers at the Rocking Stone.

When Ben Tillett, a leader of the 1889 London dock strike, came to address a meeting on behalf of the Miners' Federation of Great Britain, "Every point he made went home," according to a reporter[1] who summarized his speech thus—"that the men had been fooled by the sliding scale; that without organisation they were a mere rabble; and that they should join the federation."

---

employers and gives them to the other representatives on the committee to ensure their support for himself in cases of need." (Webb Collection Vol. 26, page 196 at the *British Library of Political and Economic Science.*)

[1] "The meeting was opened with a hymn to the famous 'Aberystwyth' tune, the 25,000 men singing it in unison. The words were Welsh and gutteral, and meant that oppression had followed the people and that they were surrounded by enemies, but that Heaven would help them. This hymn was followed by a fervid prayer, uttered in Welsh by a Dissenting minister. It was treated by the meeting very much like a speech, being often interrupted by shouts of 'Hear, hear.' " (*The Times, 29.viii.1893.*)

The owners' secretary made much of this in his October report on the strike, mentioning that although Ben Tillett "denounced the employers in unmeasured terms, he predicted a failure for the workmen because of the want of organisation, a prediction that has been fully verified."[1]

The force of this outburst of protest came up against the most thoroughly organised counter-force that existed amongst the employers of the British coalfields. The men on strike faced a most formidable combination. From the very first formation of a coal-owners' association in South Wales (Aberdare Steam Collieries Association of 1864) a particular object had been clearly set forth: namely, that if any member of the association "be required by the Association to resist unjustifiable demands on the part of the Colliers or Workmen for an increase of wages" and if the member in consequence of such resistance "be put on strike" then he, so it stated, *"shall be indemnified by the Association, and recouped out of its funds all losses of profit and all necessary expenses arising out of or incurred during the period of such strike."* Clauses similar to this were found in each successive association.

In the Deed of Association of the Monmouthshire and South Wales Coal Owners' Association (1890), it was made clear that if in a dispute the employer had the express backing of the Association, then he would be paid an indemnity on "any deficiency of actual daily output." This indemnity for loss of output was also on a sliding scale, with a minimum of 1s. per ton when the price of coal was under or reached 9s. per ton. Thereafter for each rise in the price of coal by 1s. an additional 6d. would be paid. For example, when the quarterly audit showed prices at 12s. 6d. per ton, the owner involved in a dispute would receive 2s. 6d. "per ton lost." Thus the employer who was not paying out any wages (and for whom an allowance was made for overheads) would be subsidised by his fellow owners, who were otherwise in keen competition with him and with one another. To meet these indemnities it was the object of the Association "to maintain a Capital Fund of at least One Hundred Thousand Pounds." Possessed of this Capital Fund, the Association dominated industrial relations in the coalfield: and by resolution, which was binding on all its sixty-six members, could direct "the stoppage of a colliery." The discipline upon the members was strict as is shown by the rubric "Regulating action of Members as to Wages"; and here article 77 stated:

No advance in the rate of wages payable to workmen, or concession

[1] Dalziel, *op. cit.*

or variation in the terms of their contracts, occasioning any additional payment to them or an advantage in the rate of their wages, shall be made or agreed to be made, without the previous consent of the Association.

For the workmen there was the institution of a "Black List" under the rubrics "Discharge Notes" and "Restriction of Employment" which stipulated that both while a strike was threatened and during "a Strike or Stoppage" at a colliery:

no workman who has been employed at a Colliery shall be hired at any other Colliery without producing his discharge or his last pay ticket from his last employment; and it shall be a condition in engaging him that his last discharge or pay ticket shall be given up by him to his new employer, who shall thereupon file and keep it, and hand it over to the Secretary when required.

Moreover, Article 91 stated that:

No workman employed at a Colliery immediately before a Strike or Stoppage thereat takes place, shall during such Strike or Stoppage be employed by any Member.

This was the body against which the hauliers came out on strike, without organisation and without funds or means of any kind.

But they were facing even greater odds. Against them were ranged the forces of law and order. Summonses for Breach of Contract were launched immediately by many of the collieries. By the middle of the month the military were being called in ("a course which had not been necessary in previous strikes").[1] As we have seen, the Emergency Committee instituted something like "a state of siege" with the telegraph offices kept open day and night and the lavish enrolment of Special Constables—in all of which both the local and national authorities gave full backing. Lastly, with the exception of Isaac Evans, Secretary of the Neath, Swansea, and Llanelly District Miners' Association (who though a signatory of the Sliding Scale of 1892 had turned definitely against it) there was no one within the Sliding Scale associations who would lend them a helping hand. Outside the Sliding Scale was William Brace, Samuel Mills and others of the Monmouthshire and South Wales District Miners' Association (Branch of the Miners' Federation of Great Britain). But they could have but little prospect of help from the Miners' Federation of Great Britain, which itself that autumn, for sixteen weeks, was engaged in the great Lockout of 1893.[2] Thus the hauliers' strike remains a portent.

After the Hauliers' Strike had been crushed, William Brace began to draw conclusions, which were confirmed when the new Hauliers'

[1] Statement by the Association's Secretary in Dalziel, *op. cit.*, page 204.
[2] See *The Miners*, Vol. I, Ch. 8.

and Wagemen of South Wales and Monmouth Association came to an end before a couple of years were out. While the 1893 Strike had been a spectacular demonstration of the influence of M.F.G.B. policy it also became clear that only a minority of local lodges would even join the Welsh branch of the Miners' Federation, so the new tactics which Brace evolved were to induce his members to enter the Sliding Scale Associations where their influence exerted from within would effect a continuous undermining of the principle of Sliding Scales. In this those who thought with him were able to gain a measure of success, but only after the Welsh colliers had gone through yet another trial of strength with the owners' association.

In 1893 Brace had witnessed the full exercise of the power of the associated owners. He had come to realise that once the automatic operation of the sliding scale had closed "its ponderous and marble jaws" upon the earnings and the livelihood of the workmen, it would require entirely new methods before a new generation could prise them open, and free the colliers for real collective bargaining and genuine trade unionism.

A general meeting of the associated coalowners resolved to indemnify all members for loss of output (at 1s. 3d. per ton lost) during the strike in accordance with the rules of the Association. This meant a payment of £70,673 as against an average of £4,750 per annum for the previous nineteen years, an indication of the magnitude of the 1893 strike.

B*

CHAPTER TWO

FOUR-CORNERED CONFLICT

I. PLANS FOR HIGHER PRICES

A CONFLICT within the ranks of the coal owners about the structure
of their industry led in 1897 to the latest of the revolts against the
sliding scale. Trends in the coal trade had been causing much
uneasiness. Prices were falling; and "undue competition" was
blamed for this. In every coalfield they sought for a remedy, but
in vain. At last Sir George Elliot, who seemed in his career from pit
boy working underground at nine years of age to his ownership of
extensive mining property at home and abroad to be the very
pattern of the successful entrepreneur, boldly put forward a project
for a giant coal trust (described in *The Times* of September 20,
1893). This would have united 3,500 collieries in one single monopoly with a governing council of nine members (in this anticipating
by over fifty years the nine men of the National Coal Board set up
in 1946) and a capital of £110,000,000. The plans seemed to be in
tune with similar developments abroad in Germany and the United
States: but its author died in December 1893, and the scheme fell
through.

In 1896 a more moderate plan was put forward. The author was
D. A. Thomas, M.P., of the newly formed Cambrian Collieries
Limited who, in a 96-page booklet[1] argued that "the fall in prices
to the present lamentable level is due to an excess of supply and to
undue competition." That year, 1896, the average selling value per
ton of coal raised at the pit ("the pithead price") had fallen to
6s. 0½d. from a high level of 10s. 3½d. in 1890. Similarly, the average
declared value (f.o.b.) per ton of coal shipped at Cardiff had fallen
from 13s. 9d. in 1890 to 9s. 7d. in 1896. D. A. Thomas, however,
did not propose to tamper with prices. The feature of his scheme
was its simplicity. He proposed to fix output only, and he held that
prices and profits and all else including the level of wages would
issue from this restriction of output. "If it were possible," he wrote,
"to get the twenty companies or collieries constituting 80 per cent of
the output to combine, the combination would, in my judgment, be

[1] Some Notes on the Present State of the Coal Trade in the United Kingdom with
Special References to that of South Wales and Monmouthshire together with a Proposal
for the Prevention of Undue Competition and for Maintaining Prices at a Remunerative
Level.

sufficiently powerful to control and regulate the steam coal trade of South Wales and Monmouthshire." Well aware of the objections raised to such schemes, namely that "by interfering with the free play of supply and demand they are opposed to sound economic doctrine" Thomas appealed to the patristics of political economy as follows:

Adam Smith, however, the father of economic science, appears to have observed that there were circumstances peculiar to the production of coal which differentiated it from the general laws of price applicable to most other commodities, and it will be seen upon a perusal of this scheme that it fully recognises that prices must always be determined by the laws of supply and demand, but that owing to the special conditions under which coal is produced, it is requisite to regulate the supply.

The scheme was that each owner should have an "allocated output." Anyone exceeding this amount would be fined so much per ton in excess: while from the proceeds of these fines owners whose output was less than their allocation would be indemnified.

The booklet, addressed both to "colliery owners and their employees," was strongly supported by the latter as represented by Mabon and other representatives, for they hoped that by this means prices would be raised and wages would follow. The scheme got so far that a committee of associated and non-associated coalowners at their meeting on February 15, 1897, finally adopted it for submission to the Monmouthshire and South Wales Coalowners' Association. But that was as far as it got: for here it fell into the hands of Sir W. T. Lewis, who, in his re-draft of the scheme, made one significant alteration. He insisted that 95 per cent of the owners must become parties to it: and it was soon made clear that he had torpedoed Thomas's scheme by this insistence. The clash between the two coal magnates was seen in politics as well as in industry. In the 1895 election the Liberal Thomas had soundly defeated the Lewis' (Tory) son and heir: but now in the coal trade the veteran chairman had stymied the scheme of this younger rising capitalist. Meanwhile William Abraham, M.P., and those who agreed with him on the Sliding Scale Joint Committee, had fervently hoped for the success of the plan put forward by D. A. Thomas: his defeat was their defeat also. William Abraham, who as Vice-Chairman of the Sliding Scale Committee never cared for too prolonged a tussle with Sir William Lewis, was ready to acknowledge defeat in the summer of 1897. It was otherwise with the initiator of the Control Scheme who continued to struggle against his kinsman of the Coal Trade (Thomas and Lewis were second cousins), nor did he spare his criticism against those who fell away and whom he regarded as backsliders and weak-kneed.

D. A. Thomas, whose firm was not then (nor at any time in the
first ten years of its existence) one of the fifty-four members of the
employers' association had, nevertheless, for a time secured quite a
hearing amongst the associated owners. In the periodical press and
in the Welsh newspapers his scheme came up for discussion into
which he easily and frequently plunged. Sometimes his appeal was
directly addressed also to the workmen, over the heads of their
representatives on the Sliding Scale. For example, when Mabon
began to falter in his support of the Restriction Scheme Thomas
sharply criticised him. In answer to a rejoinder from Mabon's
supporters on the Sliding Scale Committee Thomas wrote a long
letter in the *Western Mail* which was headed "Control of the Coal
Output" and subtitled "Reply to Messrs. Onions and Richards,"
in it he wrote:

> Mabon was in a fighting mood in June, and it is true it was only after
> his right-about-face in July, that I began criticising his attitude but when,
> through the Cambrian Association, he advised the workmen to rest
> content with their position and be satisfied with the blessing they had
> already received, I cannot see how my criticisms justify inaction on the
> part of the miners' leaders. (*22.x.1897.*)

His pertinacity and his habit of plunging into public controversy
(usual enough in the politician, as he had been for over a decade,
but unusual in the capitalist) endeared him neither to one side nor
the other, neither to his fellow owners nor to the sliding scale representatives. In short, D. A. Thomas was unpopular with leaders on
both sides.

2. NOTICE TO END THE SLIDING SCALE

The revised Sliding Scale of 1892 had not been easily made
acceptable to the workmen; and in the five years after the hauliers'
strike it had become more and more unpopular. From May 1894,
when wages stood at 30 per cent above standard there began a long
slow decline. Successive audits of the price of coal brought successive
automatic reductions in wages until in January 1896, they stood at
$12\frac{1}{2}$ per cent and by August of that year were down to 10 per cent
above standard. Prices and wages with them seemed to be tumbling
into a bottomless pit: and it was at this juncture that D. A. Thomas
brought out his appeal to owners and workmen.

When the Thomas scheme foundered the workmen on four
successive occasions in 1897 at the Sliding Scale Joint Committee
pleaded for some kind of minimum. The owners refused. Finally, in
September 1897, a conference of the colliers under the Sliding Scale
decided on a ballot. The result was a very great majority (41,880 to

12,178) for giving notice to the owners to end the Sliding Scale
Agreement. The six months' notice began to run on October 1,
1897.

What were to be the new conditions of their employment? What
sort of agreement should they seek with the coal owners? These
questions came up at successive miners' conferences during the
winter of 1897–1898. Many were for the abolition of Sliding Scales
and wanted to have instead a conciliation board as in England. Some
colliers were for a scheme to control output of the kind put forward
by D. A. Thomas. A general conference of miners in the second
week of January instructed the representatives to:

> Open negotiations with a view to improving the Sliding Scale Agree-
> ment in as many ways as circumstances might warrant between this and
> the end of March, but especially to endeavour to secure for the dove-
> tailing of a scheme for the control of the output of coal with a minimum
> which will retain wages upon a fair and equitable basis. (*11.i.1898*.)

Eventually, however, their dozen representatives were instructed
in February to open up negotiations for a Sliding Scale with a
fixed minimum and with the rise and fall of wages regulated as in
the 1890 scale.[1]

When at length a meeting took place the negotiators found the
owners in a very unaccommodating mood. Not only were they
against the new proposals but they intimated their intention to
declare a lockout as from April 1, 1898, and for this purpose gave
the men a month's notice of termination of employment. At the same
time they refused to continue negotiations except on one condition.
That condition was that the frequent democratic practice of conference decisions (and, on big issues, of ballot votes) be abandoned
and that the dozen workmen's representatives be given plenary
powers to negotiate and sign. That such a procedure could easily
give rise to a suspicion of bribery and corruption may not have been
apparent to the coalowners; they may only have desired to force the
issue together with their ultimatum.

This demand on the part of the coal owners brought divided
counsels among the twelve, a majority of whom wanted to be given
plenary powers, while a minority headed by Dai o'r Nant were for
the miners themselves having the final say. A conference of March 14,
1898, referred the question back to local meetings of the workmen,
who then mandated the delegates to refuse plenary powers. This
question now blocked pacific negotiations. Before the lockout
notices were due to expire, the workmen's representatives once more

---

[1] Under the 1890 Scale wages rose or fell by 10 per cent for each 1s. up or down in the
price per ton. Under the scale of 1892 this equivalent was cut down to 8·75 per cent per
shilling.

met the owners, only to be told by the chairman, Sir William Lewis, that they were "not desirous to treat with people that have no plenary powers to settle the question in dispute" (*25.iii.1898*). When Mabon pleaded for time (so that the workmen could be asked to grant plenary powers) the lockout was postponed for nine days.

D. A. Thomas, supporting the miners in their demands, publicly put the blame on his cousin ("Sir William carries the Coal Owners' Association in his waistcoat-pocket"), and when asked "What do you think of the question of plenary powers?" openly advised against it.[1]

At a conference on Monday, March 28th, the plea by Mabon, Onions and Richards to be given plenary powers was opposed by Brace and Dai o'r Nant, whose proposal for a ballot was easily carried. The answer to the ultimatum from the owners was given by this ballot taken on March 30, 1898: 44,872 votes were cast against giving plenary powers to the workmen's representatives and 14,500 for such a grant; and when the question was again raised a fortnight later, the mandates to delegates revealed a still higher majority, 74,548 compared to 20,538.

So, on April 4th, Mabon and the rest on the Sliding Scale Joint Committee returned to the owners empty-handed, only to be told by Sir William Lewis that he no longer recognised them as representatives of the workmen. The Sliding Scale Agreement had come to an end on March 31st: and with it their functions. Let representatives appear with plenary powers: then only could negotiations take place.

Mabon and his colleagues sought a way out of this difficulty by calling an open conference three days later at which both the colliers who paid for the Sliding Scale and all others would be represented.

This new conference of 175 delegates (representing 100,302 men) proved to be even less amenable to Mabon's arguments for a free hand. They were extremely dissatisfied: so much so that at the outset Mabon's wonted occupancy of the chair was challenged, and another was chosen in his place by 87 to 78 votes. This was John Williams of Ynysybwl, who had been checkweigher at the Lady Windsor colliery, and who had succeeded, on the death of Isaac Evans, to the position of miners' agent. The new chairman was a

---

[1] "The representatives of the men must, of course, be given some authority to negotiate, but I think the workmen would be very foolish to give plenary powers, and the leaders would be equally unwise to accept them. The men should give the representatives, in my judgment, authority within certain limits. If I were a workman I would most decidedly refuse to give authority to bind me for several years to the present scale. I would say to the leaders 'Do the best you can to get these amendments for me, but under no circumstances agree to the masters' proposals or to the scale as it now stands.' " (*Western Mail, 28.iii.1898.*)

fluent speaker and versatile, being both a lay preacher and a bard:
and was later to become a Member of Parliament. The open conference, which would not even discuss the question of plenary
powers, elected five additional members to be negotiators together
with the old twelve.

Meanwhile over most of the coalfield the miners had stopped
work by the first weekend of April 1898: they had taken but little
account of Mabon's successful plea for postponement of the lockout.
Mabon for his part addressing a meeting had said:

The stoppage knocked everything on the head, and prices, prospects,
agreements, amicable relationships, and everything necessary to create
and maintain trade prospects had been brought to an untimely end. The
workmen had placed themselves in the wrong, and the sooner they placed
themselves in the right the better. They had driven public opinion from
their side, and the workmen were condemned all round. It might not
yet be too late to save the situation and put themselves right by resuming
work next Tuesday, *if the employers would allow them to do so.*

Utterances such as these, reported in the daily newspapers and
there favourably commented upon, brought down upon Mabon's
head the most unfavourable comment as follows:

This is the merest fudge. By throwing his influence on the side of the
masters Mabon is but encouraging them to prolong the struggle. It is a
significant fact that every newspaper which backed the employers during
the recent lockout of engineers is now patting Mabon on the back and
eulogising him for the part he is playing. (*9.iv.1898.*)

The writer was James Keir Hardie, ex-M.P. and ex-secretary of
the Ayrshire Miners' Association, afterwards to be celebrated as the
founder of the Labour Party.

3. SOCIALIST AGITATORS

The colliery workmen, locked out from April 9th, might seem in a
desperate position from the beginning. They had no strike funds and
had to seek for support outside their own ranks. They were not,
however, entirely friendless. Not only were they to get help, as we
shall see, from other coalfields, but within the South Wales coalfield
they found some of the non-associated coal owners ready to grant
the desired advance in wages: and as the stoppage continued, they
began to get support in Parliament from several Liberal members.
But by far the most ardent support came from socialist bodies. The
propaganda of socialism had been carried on for some fifteen years
since 1883, but its effect, not as yet very extensive, was found
chiefly in the big towns. The villages of the coalfields, remote from
urban industrial centres, seemed to offer less fertile soil for the seeds

of socialism—except in the particular circumstance of a strike or
lockout.

It was axiomatic for the socialists that a coalfield dispute was an
exhibit of class arrayed against class: and no matter how deeply the
lodges were imbued with Liberalism, the dispute was a summons to
socialist agitation in the area concerned. Thus the Northumberland
strike of 1887 found William Morris and others agitating in that
county: and we have his description of the pitmen hearing for the
first time this new gospel of socialism. So too, it had been in South
Wales in that year of stress, as when two agitators from the Socialist
League, "laden with literature" held their first meeting at the
Rocking Stone (on August 14, 1887) to begin a week's "socialist
campaign"—which was sufficiently effective for the *Western Mail*
to give "a virulent and scurrilous report" of the proceedings and for
the *Pontypridd Herald* to say that the district for the first time in its
history had been invaded by the advance guard of socialism and then
to devote serious consideration to the new doctrines.[1]

But never before 1898 had there been such a concentration of
socialist agitators and their journals. Foremost amongst them was
Keir Hardie, chairman of the Independent Labour Party which set
up thirty branches that year in the valleys. He was also chief
owner and editor of its weekly *Labour Leader*. The Social-Democratic
Federation, also sought to make hay while the sun shone. Like the
I.L.P. they established a score or more of branches in the valleys
and they sent John Spargo from London as correspondent for
Justice. Thus throughout the whole of the stoppage the cause of the
workmen was ardently espoused by numerous speakers, while their
weekly notes and articles served to stiffen the resistance to the
associated owners. Keir Hardie's skill as a political journalist,
strengthened by his own experience of the miner's lot, enabled very
poignant appeals to be made by him on behalf of the strikers. The
following passage from his *Labour Leader* in the last month of the
lockout is typical:

The Welsh collier is fighting for a wage of 22s. a week. Surely he is
entitled to all the help which can be given him. I make urgent appeal for
renewed efforts on behalf of a starving population. I notice that a Miss
Cory, of Cardiff, is intensely concerned about the poor starving
Armenians. Is she daughter to one of the Corys who sits with Sir W. T.
Lewis on the Mineowners' Committee, and backs that gentleman through
thick and thin in all he does? If so, or whether or no, I can find her plenty
of objects nearer home than Armenia on which to exercise the charity of
her gentle nature. A starving Welsh collier may not be so picturesque as a
starving Armenian, but he is none the less human. It is doubtless very
wicked of the Sultan of Turkey to starve Armenians, but it is not one

[1] *The Commonweal.* (*27.viii.1887.*)

2 STONEBREAKING YARD, TREHARRIS, 1898

3   RT. HON. WILLIAM ABRAHAM, LL.D., M.P. (*Mabon*)

whit more wicked than the conduct of Sultan Lewis and his Cory assistants in Wales. It is in the nature of a public scandal to beg funds in Cardiff to feed Armenians whilst in Cardiff itself thousands of victims of the lockout are starving.

The socialist agitators, selling these journals, fostered groups of young socialists or socialist sympathisers who could present a challenge not only to any particular policy of Mabon but to his whole social philosophy and outlook. At the same time their comments serve to show what in some cases lay behind the lack of trust in their leaders shown by the miners, especially towards the man who had been their most prominent spokesman for over a score of years.

4. THE APPEAL TO OTHER MINERS

The colliers were plunged into this bitter struggle without resources or funds to sustain them. A request for help went to the Miners' Federation of Great Britain, which in response held a special conference in the last week of April, attended by William Abraham, M.P., William Brace, Thomas Richards, John Williams and David Morgan (Dai o'r Nant). Dai o'r Nant, one of the signatories of the original Sliding Scale Agreement of May 1875, now considered it "impracticable." After saying that "trade unionism in South Wales has been very feeble and as yet is only very feeble," and that "some may say the men were very foolish to come out with no money at their backs," he made his plea as follows:

We must admit that we stand this day on the mercy of the world and we appeal to the Federation to support us. We ask for support from the Federation not only from the central fund but to allow us to send men to the different localities. (*26.iv.1898.*)

On the next day, April 27th, after some little debate in which the objection of the other coalfields to the Sliding Scale was very clearly voiced, the conference gave them £1,000 at once followed by a weekly grant of £500 rising to £600 and also gave facilities for Welsh officials to visit the other coalfields and raise additional sums there.

Then Pickard from the chair concluded that the presence of South Wales representatives had had a tendency "to create a better feeling towards the South Wales workers," especially the declarations that the South Wales miners believed that they should have a minimum wage. He said that the minimum wage was the groundwork of the Federation and "whether a coalowner lives or dies, whether trade sinks or swims, when the collier goes into the mine to work a day he should have a wage to keep him. We live by this and we shall try our best to keep it so long as we have any humanity left. That is the dictum of the Federation of Great Britain." At this stage the Welsh representatives left the conference: and that night Pickard, improving the occasion, wrote a letter[1] to the secretary of the English coal owners, asking for a ten per cent advance.

To the Miners' Federation of Great Britain conference both Brace and Mabon put the case that the struggle was for ten per cent advance and that there would be no renewal of the Sliding Scale. But inside South Wales Mabon kept urging that consideration be given to the owners' insistence on a renewal of the Sliding Scale, and on unlimited power for the negotiating committee. Brace and those with him were able in the first stages to defeat Mabon's propaganda.

5. NEGOTIATIONS BEGIN

Throughout Mabon sought a basis for negotiation; the gap was wide. The terms put forward by the workmen on March 25th (before the contest emerged of plenary powers versus democratic ballot) had been as follows:

1. that the Sliding Scale should provide a minimum wage equivalent to a selling price of 10s. per ton f.o.b.
2. that the advances and reductions in wages above that point should be at a rate of 10 per cent for each shilling change in the selling price.
3. that there shall be a substantial advance in wages as and from April 1st next.

These terms of March 25th, never discussed, had in any case been considerably altered by the April 14th conference (at which John Williams again had defeated Mabon in an election to the Chair). Two of the questions put by the negotiating committee to the conference (which agreed to submit them to the lodges for mandated answers) were: "Shall the negotiations be for a Sliding Scale or otherwise?" and, if without a Sliding Scale, "What amount of immediate advance do you think necessary?" At the adjourned conference on April 18th, the mandates were recorded as follows:

(a) For a Sliding Scale 29,094
    Against a Sliding Scale 63,714

                    Majority against 34,620
(b) Unanimous for 10 per cent.

[1] "Dear Mr. Ellis,
After a few words with some of the coal-owners I beg to lay the following before the owners in the Federation area—
1st.—Our Federation I believe intend asking for a 10 per cent advance.
2nd.—That it would be wise for the owners to offer us the advance.
3rd.—That this advance should be made that our men may assist the miners in South Wales and Monmouthshire to do away with the sliding scale and so prevent the keen competition of South Wales and Monmouthshire.

Week after week the deadlock continued. The owners were prepared to wait until the men would yield to the preliminary stipulation that they must elect negotiators with full power to commit all the workmen to a settlement. Sir William Lewis, the originator of the Sliding Scale, clearly believed that the men's negotiators could be persuaded to accept conditions on behalf of the men which the men themselves would reject as intolerable—if given an opportunity to voice their opinion. After forty days of idle pits and growing privation the delegates to a conference held in mid-May (and confirmed on May 26th) elected Mabon as chairman and by a small majority gave him and his colleagues credentials to open negotiations and settle the dispute.

On May 31st, across the table, Sir William Lewis was pleased to learn that the negotiators now had power to settle: but to their proposals on behalf of the workmen he returned an uncompromising negative. Instead he stated that negotiations could only proceed on the basis of the terms which the owners had published six weeks earlier when they stuck up at the pithead the terms on which the lockout could be terminated.[1]

The negotiators came back on June 4th and then were told very definitely that the owners now insisted on the Sliding Scale. The negotiators were faced again by an impasse. So on June 17th once more a conference was called, with 125 delegates representing 92,504 workmen. Mabon advised that they should consider whether or not to negotiate a Sliding Scale Agreement: let there be a ballot. William Brace led the arguments against Mabon and by a vote of 77 to 9 the conference decided not to negotiate for a Sliding Scale which, by a lesser majority, they decided not to submit to a ballot again. The earlier ballot had been in their opinion conclusive. With this decision deadlock was again reached: for the owners stood fast on their insistence on a Sliding Scale. Meantime, in this ninth week of the lockout, there were incidents in the valleys which brought public discussion throughout the country and concern in the House of Commons.

Those suggestions are made with the best intentions and to create a further better feeling between the workmen and the coal owners in the Federation area.

Trusting the above will be favourably considered, and that too without prejudice.

I am, yours truly,
(Signed) B. PICKARD.

[1] These terms posted up at the pitheads on April 12th had actually been considerably worse than those of the 1892 Sliding Scale which the men had sought to abolish. The detailed terms of the Sliding Scale were worsened in such a way as to give "a further incentive to low prices and therefore low wages": the monthly holiday ("Mabon's Day") was to be abolished: the "character note," without which no man once discharged could get another job, was to be maintained: while contracts were to be made with individual workmen.

6. THE MILITARY CALLED IN

While things were again at a deadlock military forces were called for. Troops were drafted into parts of the area. Here the elected representatives and the non-elected local authorities were at once at issue. Alfred Thomas, M.P. for East Glamorgan, asked the reason for the importation of military forces into the colliery districts of South Wales, and whether, "with a view to secure peace and good order," the Home Secretary would consider the desirability of "withdrawing the troops from the district in which no disturbance has yet occurred?" Samuel Evans, Member for Mid-Glamorgan, asked—

> Whether the Associated Colliery Owners of South Wales or any other local bodies or persons have undertaken to pay, or will have to bear any, and if so, what proportion of the expenses incurred by the drafting of the military in the County and their maintenance there; whether there has been any difficulty in the maintenance of peace and order by the police; and whether he is prepared to state to the House the facts which induced him to sanction the sending of military forces to localities where negotiations are now pending for the settlement of industrial differences between employers and workmen? (*14.vi.1898.*)

To these Liberals the reply came that the responsibility lay not with the Home Office but with the local authorities and that "the reason, no doubt, was that disorders were apprehended with which the resources of the civil power would be unable to cope." A further reply on June 17th stated that the troops, numbering 34 officers and 762 men, were sent into South Wales "at the request of the magistrates and Chief Constable of Monmouthshire." The same day another Liberal (Brynmor Jones,[1] Member for Swansea) asked the Home Secretary whether he was aware that Ignatius Williams, the stipendiary magistrate for the Pontypridd Petty Sessional Division, had received a letter from the Justices of the Peace for the Division or other local authorities, "commanding him to instruct the military detachments now quartered in Glamorganshire, if necessary, to charge the crowd, to use the bayonet, and also to fire with ball cartridges; and whether the officers in command of the troops in question are bound to obey the instructions of the civil authorities?" To this the Home Secretary said that he was not aware of any such letter but that:

> The law as to the duty of soldiers when called on to assist in quelling disturbance was clearly stated by the Committee of 1894 (after the Featherstone shootings) which pointed out that an officer, if called on by

[1] Rt. Hon. Sir David Brynmor Jones (1852–1921) born in Swansea, eldest son of a Congregational minister, had a successful career at the Bar and on the Bench. He sat as Liberal for Swansea District from 1895 to 1914.

a magistrate to take action for this purpose, has absolute discretion as to the action to be taken, the arms to be used, and the point at which firing becomes necessary. He is responsible that no more is done by the soldiers than the circumstances justify, and any directions of the kind alleged in the question would neither relieve him of that responsibility nor impose on him any obligation. (*17.vi.1898.*)

This answer though purely legal in form was apt to cause apprehension as to what might happen. Other elected representatives took the matter further with the Conservative Government. D. A. Thomas, Member for Merthyr Tydfil, had already been pressing the Government for a satisfactory reason why they were not using their powers of intervention under the Conciliation Act of 1896.[1] He now sought to bring out the danger of disturbance caused by the presence of troops through the following question:

I beg to ask the Secretary of State for the Home Department whether he is aware that during Friday and Saturday last some of the soldiers stationed at Mountain Ash became intoxicated and created a disturbance in the streets; that ladies were grossly insulted, many free fights took place, and that belts were freely used, that eventually the police interfered and endeavoured to prevail upon the soldiers to return to their quarters, but in vain; whether there has been any riotous conduct among any section of the populace of Mountain Ash, or among any of the inhabitants (50,000) of the Aberdare Valley since the coal lockout began; and whether he will suggest to the proper authorities the advisability of augmenting the police force during the stay of the military, so that the normal, peaceful condition of the district may be maintained?

The Home Secretary may have been put in some difficulty by the suggestion that the police forces, previously considered insufficient to keep the peace, would now have to be increased in order to deal with the military forces; but his reply, if evasive, was fairly skilfully drafted:

It is reported that a slight disturbance, due to the misconduct of a few soldiers, took place at Mountain Ash on Saturday evening between the troops quartered there and the civil population. Steps have been taken to prevent any similar disturbance. It is the fact, I understand, that there has been no active display of riotous conduct in the Aberdare Valley, but very grave apprehensions of disturbance were at one time entertained by the responsible authorities, and there is good reason to suppose that it was only the arrival of the military which prevented it. (*21.vi.1898.*)

The night before the Home Secretary's utterance, Keir Hardie was dating from Merthyr Tydfil his editorial article headed: "STARVING WALES: men fighting gallantly and in good spirit, but the wolf is showing his fangs." Three such articles followed one another while Hardie in Wales was carrying on a campaign,

[1] This was an Act passed on August 7, 1896 "to make better provisions for the prevention and settlement of trade disputes."

addressing two open-air meetings daily and listened to by thousands of miners. The presence and intense activity of these socialist agitators had an effect not only in winning recruits for their parties but in stiffening the resistance of the miners to the owners and the owners' chairman. "Sir William Thomas Lewis," wrote Hardie on July 2, 1898, "has done more for Socialism in three months than years of effort could have accomplished."[1]

7. DEBATE IN PARLIAMENT

The longer the lockout lasted the more deeply and widely its effects began to be felt. The feeling began to grow that some outside body, and, in particular, that the Government should intervene in some way. In the middle of May members of parliament from constituencies around the coalfield had gone on deputation to the President of the Board of Trade to ask if something could be done. Then as the days passed came new parliamentary questions, which became more insistent when it was learned that the autumn man-oeuvres of the Royal Navy would have to be cancelled for lack of the requisite Welsh coal. Finally after eight weeks' lockout Brynmor Jones rose in the Commons to move the adjournment of the House in order to discuss a definite matter of urgent public importance, "namely, the widespread privation and distress arising from the dispute between employers and employed in the South Wales coalfield, and the dislocation of, and injury to, the commerce of the district by the continuance of the dispute, and the urgent necessity for putting into force the provisions of the Conciliation Act of 1896." (Friday, June 24, 1898.)

Brynmor Jones then explained the sliding scale agreement, the notice for its termination, duly given by the workmen, the owners' intervention by imposing a lockout; the story of the negotia-

[1] W. H. Mainwaring, Member of Parliament for Rhondda East from 1933 to 1959, who entered the mines at the age of 12, could remember an old strolling musician in the Swansea Valley during the 1898 struggle, who sang the following verse to the tune *Hen Wlad fy Nhadau* (Land of my Fathers).

Mae'r glowyr Morgannwg, Sir Fynwy a'r Fro
Yn ymladd yn brysur a'm bris ar y glo
Ond gwrthod mai'r meistri wneud sylw o'm Bil
Gwell ganddynt rhyw gynllun Syr Wil
Syr Wil sy'n gwrthod wneud sylw o'm Bil
O Gymru Wen, cwyd fyny'th ben i helpu'r glowr. Amen

(translation)
The miners of Glamorgan, Monmouthshire, and elsewhere
Are seriously fighting for a price on the coal
But the masters take no notice of our Bill
They prefer some scheme of Sir Will
It is Sir Will who ignores our Bill
Oh beloved Wales raise your head to assist the miners. Amen

tions and finally of what happened at the meeting of the two bodies on May 31st. Then, said Brynmor Jones, "there was an unfortunate interruption. I refer, of course, to the despatch of military troops in Glamorganshire and Monmouthshire." This, he said, had an irritating effect upon the men. He said:

Now, Sir, these men not only look upon the action of the authorities in bringing the military into the county as a kind of slur upon their character as law-abiding citizens, but they resent it as being a move on the part of the employers. They think it shows that the Government are taking sides in this quarrel. They do not understand the fine distinctions we have to draw in this House between the authority of the Home Secretary and of the justices, and I am bound to say that the action of the justices, unless it was absolutely necessary, which I do not believe, was about the most ill-advised step that could be taken in the interests of peace. (*24.vi.1898.*)

Brynmor Jones ended by referring to the Conciliation Act which the President of the Board of Trade himself had brought in less than two years earlier and called upon him to exercise his powers under that measure. He said that he hoped the President of the Board of Trade would "indicate firmly and clearly his desire to exercise the power he possesses at the earliest possible moment." The motion was seconded by S. T. Evans, Member for Mid-Glamorgan,[1] who continued by quoting the words of the President of the Board of Trade himself uttered to the deputation that had waited upon him on May 9th:

It is to all intents and purposes a national calamity when a dispute of this kind occurs and when so many men are laid idle in an industry in which the country is so deeply interested. (*24.vi.1898.*)

The men were willing for the dispute to be determined by the Board of Trade. The masters on the other hand, he said, "have not up till now exhibited any desire for Government intervention." He described the terms posted up at the collieries by the employers (like the laws of the Medes and Persians which were "not to be altered") as declaring in effect: The answer to the men's dissatisfaction with the sliding scale was: "A sliding scale we must have; we will not deal with you on any other terms than that you must agree to a sliding scale." Then he said it was not the same scale as the old one "but a much worse scale; so much worse that the men think that, rightly or wrongly, it was devised by the masters to help them to pay the additional expense which has been placed on them by the

[1] Rt. Hon. Sir Samuel Thomas Evans (1859–1918) was born at Skewen, near Neath, and after a successful career at the Bar and on the Bench was finally elevated to the presidency of the Probate, Divorce and Admiralty Courts in 1910. Before that he had been the Liberal M.P. for Mid-Glamorgan from 1890 to 1910 and became Solicitor-General from 1908 to 1910 in the first Asquith administration.

Compensation Act passed by the Government last year." He then explained "the discharge note system":

It has been conceived in order that when a workman has come, say, from a colliery where there is a strike or a lockout and seeks employment at some other colliery in the coalfield, the employers in that colliery should know from what works the workman comes; and if a workman comes from a works where there has been a strike or a lockout, there is at once a black mark put against that man, and there is no hope or chance of his obtaining any employment at all. The discharge note is insisted upon, for paragraph 12 of the master's notice of the April 11th, to which I have referred, is as follows:

No workman will be employed at this colliery without producing his discharge, or his last pay ticket from his last employment, and it is a condition of his employment that on his engagement his last discharge or pay ticket shall be given up by him to his employers. (*24.vi.1898.*)

He expressed the view that this was one of the reasons that there was now "a complete deadlock between masters and men." After then reading from the *Western Mail* of mid-June "a newspaper which sides more with the employers than with the employed—that is why I have chosen it," he said:

In connection with all the allegations of seething lawlessness in the valleys, which, previous to the arrival of the military, only gave rise to a small hustling at which even the police laugh, and of which a half-witted lad is the only trophy, the authors seem to have been worked up to a striking degree of determination. Meantime the objects of all this lethal energy, the idle collier and his wife and children, dreamily delight in the gay pageant of military display and line the roads in good-humoured thousands when the troops march out. (*24.vi.1898*).

Next, S. T. Evans referred to the conduct of some of these workmen who were allowed by their fellow workmen to continue work, namely, "the outside fitters and enginemen and other persons employed in the Albion Colliery." He went on: "There, it appears, the military were stationed near where these men had been working, and the men said that they would not do another stroke of work until the military were removed, and the military were withdrawn, and the men went on working in peace, and without molestation, to keep the collieries safe and sound for the owners." (*24.vi.1898.*)

He added sharply: "The men in these localities believe that the military were brought down by one side of the disputants, and that the importation of the military into the locality was due to the representations of the masters in the first instance, and that the object of it was to terrorise the men into terms of submission held out by the masters."

He followed this by giving details of the suffering that had taken place following the dispute as follows:

Many of the men are away "on tramp", looking for work, and the women have sold everything possible. Doleful tales are told about the manner in which the household goods have gone to the pawnbrokers. First the pictures and ornaments, then the furniture, even to the bedstead and the bedding; the plates and dishes and cups have gone one or two at a time for a few pence with which to buy bread; then they have been obliged to take away the very clothes. Only two days ago a woman went to the committee to appeal for help. She had sold her last chemise, and her only clothing was an old petticoat and an equally old dress, with a pair of boots and stockings; and she was only one of dozens that are known to be in a similar plight. A glance inside some of the houses shows how far this sort of work has gone, for there is nothing to be seen but the bare walls. Amongst the cases relieved by the committee are the following: a woman had been living with six children, all under eight years of age, upon the barest crusts. Everything she could sell went to the pawnbroker, and at last for two days all they had to eat were two raw cabbages. But this is not all the woman's sufferings. She had not paid her rent, and the bailiffs were sent to her house to distrain or evict. (*24.vi.1898.*)

Here S. T. Evans said parenthetically that the only disturbances "which have occurred, such as they are, have arisen from the fact that the arrears of rent have been enforced by the landlords in these places, while the people are suffering from starvation."

He then gave yet another case:

A coal trimmer's wife is left at home with six children while the man is away looking for work. She has been ill and had had no food, when she applied on Thursday evening, since Sunday, and was suckling a child. In an almost similar case a woman was found with a baby only a few months old. The woman had had nothing to eat for two days, and for the same period the child had been sucking at an empty bottle, and all that it had received was some water.

Finally, he implored the Government to step in and enforce a settlement:

We ask the Rt. Hon. Gentleman to intervene in the interests of commerce, of the public peace, and in the far higher and more sacred interests of humanity, to relieve the loss and suffering caused by the deadlock, the continuance of which will work untold mischief and disaster, and be an indelible blot on our civilisation.

The motion before the House of Commons was next supported by no other than Sir William Vernon Harcourt who, until a few months earlier, had been the Leader of the Opposition in the Commons and had held office in many previous administrations including Chancellorship of the Exchequer 1892 to 1895. He was one of the most formidable debaters in the House of Commons. Sir William Harcourt addressed himself to disposing of the apparent reluctance of the President of the Board of Trade to exercise his powers under the Conciliation Act and so his speech was largely an explanation from a very experienced Member to a relatively new Minister of the powers which he possessed under the Act.

He was followed by the Minister, C. T. Ritchie,[1] who had as President of the Board of Trade actually been responsible for the Conciliation Act and for piloting it through the House of Commons some eighteen months earlier. C. T. Ritchie had not been so much moved as might have been expected by the poignant plea and the stories related by the Member for Mid-Glamorgan. He held the view: "So far as the workmen are concerned, I am glad to think that there is not the great amount of distress which some people imagined, as they have, undoubtedly, in the course of their years of continuous employment, frugally and properly, laid aside no inconsiderable amount of money. That result goes to show both that they are frugal and saving, and also that they have had wages which have enabled them to be frugal and saving." Ritchie concluded his speech by saying that he believed "the moment is unpropitious for any intervention by the Board of Trade."

He was followed by William Abraham, M.P. for Rhondda Division of Glamorgan, who said:

It is true we gave notice on the 1st October to terminate the sliding scale as a wage regulator, but that did not of necessity terminate the contract with the colliery owners. More than that when the employers informed us—informed a percentage of the workmen—that they were going to give this notice to terminate the contract, we implored, we begged them not to do it. We said it was unnecessary; that we could negotiate better when the men were working than when they were not. We almost went on our knees to ask the employers not to give this notice. More than that, we begged them to agree to put the auditors to work to make the audit. True, we had no legal right, according to the document, because the agreement would be expiring on the day that the award would be commencing, but still, the audit would be our guide; the audit would be the only thing which would tell us whether our demands were right or not. By the audit, if it were against us, we would have gone back to the men and probably induced them to reduce their demand. The employers persisted in refusing to put the audit on, and in giving us notice that we could not work unless we worked upon their terms. Though we gave notice to terminate the sliding scale, it was not we who gave notice to terminate the contract. We should not have left work but for the fact that the employers gave notice to terminate the contract, and refused to let us work unless we did so on their own terms. I am sorry to have to say here that they are responsible for the state of things in South Wales. (*Hansard, 24.vi.1898.*)

There were eight further speeches in the debate after what might

[1] Charles Thompson Ritchie (1838–1906), one of a Forfar family that had gone south and enriched themselves in the valley of the Thames, where his brother became Lord Mayor of London, had been for three years President of the Board of Trade. He was to be Home Secretary 1900–2, Chancellor of the Exchequer 1902–3 and on his retirement bore the title of Lord Ritchie of Dundee for a sixty-eighth part of his life.

have seemed conclusive statements. It is noteworthy that several of them were from the Conservative side of the House and all of the Conservatives from South Wales urged the Government to take steps. Of the other speakers the M.P. for Glamorgan East, Alfred Thomas, said: "However much we condemn the unwarrantable action of those timid panic-stricken authorities who called in the military, that is only as dust in the balance as compared with the other question, namely, the continuance of the terrible dispute now raging in the counties of Monmouth and Glamorgan."

The motion was not taken to a division, which seems to have meant that those who moved it were satisfied that the Government would be likely to yield if the matter were not pressed to a vote. Yield it did. Within a day or two the Negotiating Committee had formally appealed to the Home Secretary for a Conciliator and Sir Edward Fry[1] had been appointed to that post.

8. CONCILIATION REBUFFED

It takes two to make a quarrel: and the same number to effect a conciliation with either side. This was brought home to the Conciliator by the attitude of the associated owners, who had nothing like his own reverence for laws made by the Queen-in-parliament.

When the coalowners bluntly told Sir Edward Fry on July 13th that they would not tolerate his intervention, that eminent lawyer had to swallow this rebuff and to betake himself to London. This he did after a few more days in Cardiff where he accomplished nothing —as recounted in his report written on July 28th, although not published until three weeks later, on August 19th. A long and interesting report it was. Refusal of the associated employers to hold any intercourse with him "put an end to the possibility of conciliation in the ordinary sense of the word" and left him "only the duty of attempting to bring about a settlement by influencing the men." This, however, proved a hopeless task. The men were very imperfectly organised—if, indeed, they could be said to be organised at all. He stated: "The majority of the delegates and presumably the men whom they represent were out of sympathy with the majority of the Provisional Committee; for they had repudiated all notions of a sliding scale and insist upon principles less likely to be accepted by the masters than those adopted by the Provisional Committee."

[1] Sir Edward, born in Bristol in 1827 and not destined to die until 1918 in his 91st year, was no small fry. He was a scion of the millionaire family which manufactured cocoa in Bristol: and was to be chosen repeatedly as arbiter on international disputes between nations of Europe and North and South America. Sir Edward was almost equally distinguished in science as in law and it would have been difficult indeed for the Government to have chosen a more respected jurist as conciliator.

A contemporary chronicler (in the *Annual Register*) concluded that the men had "no chance of successfully fighting against a well-organised body of masters in the condition and temper indicated by Sir Edward Fry." The miners had no reserve funds. It is true there were contributions from colliers in other coalfields and from other trade unionists. But, went on the chronicler, "it remains a mystery how they were able to stand out as long as they did." That they should surrender in the end was inevitable and the only question was how long the end could be deferred. It came on September 1st, when an agreement for the resumption of work was signed by 11 out of 15 members of the workmen's Provisional Committee.

Only one concession[1] was made; if after a year had passed the masters reduced wages below 12½ per cent above the 1879 standard, the men would have the right to give notice to end it. Otherwise, no notice could be given for four years. The *Annual Register* for 1898 comments: "Practically, of course, this peculiar provision only recognises a right in the men to strike after six months' notice against a wage falling below a particular minimum, and it may be doubted whether the concession of this recognition by the employers served appreciably to mitigate the sense of complete defeat which the issue of the struggle produced among the miners."

The day before the deed of surrender was signed the Provisional Committee had been authorised to do it on August 31st by a Cardiff conference of delegates which decided "to accept the employers' terms and to resume work" by a majority of 61,902 votes to 37,077.

The miners had earlier begun to lose hope of a successful issue; and meanwhile the effect of the long privation was telling hard on their families. After five months' lockout they now returned to work, defeated. They accepted the owners' terms. They accepted the Sliding Scale.

But the struggle had not been in vain. In the course of these months of suffering, the spirit of trade unionism had been re-created in the valleys of Monmouth and Glamorgan. From this year 1898 the South Wales Miners' Federation dates its true foundation. It now dealt with everything but the wage question and while the old Sliding Scale Joint Committee continued it was made up entirely of members of the new South Wales Miners' Federation Executive Council.

The spirit of solidarity with the colliers of the Miners' Federation of Great Britain who had sustained the Welshmen in their struggle was tried hard by the final capitulation but was not broken, as may be seen in the sequel a few months later.

[1] See Appendix III, Clause 6.

ON MEMBERSHIP OF TRADE UNIONS IN THE SOUTH WALES VALLEYS, 1892–98.

(Excerpted from Eleventh Report by the Chief Labour Correspondent of the Board of Trade on Trade Unions in 1898 with comparative statistics 1892–1897 C. 9443 of 1899.)

	TITLE OF TRADE UNION (Arranged in order of Year of Formation.)	Year in which formed	Branches at end of 1898	Number of Members at end of						
				1892	1893	1894	1895	1896	1897	1898
	South Wales									
229	South Wales Western District Miners (a)	1869	28	4,540	1,300	1,200	2,000	2,800	2,250	5,588
230	Caerphilly Miners	1881	—	1,340	1,040	(c)	—	—	—	—
231	Aberdare, Merthyr, and Dowlais Miners	1882	15	7,000	6,500	6,400	6,000	6,500	6,000	500
232	Anthracite Miners	1882	33	3,500	4,000	3,500	4,000	4,532	5,400	6,050
233	Ebbw Vale and Sirhowy Colliery Workmen	1886	—	2,500	2,400	2,500	3,000	3,250	3,500	(d)
234	Monmouthshire and South Wales District Miners (b)	1887	—	6,059	3,059	1,368	920	682	70	(e)
235	Abercarn Colliery Workmen	1889	—	35	(f)	—	—	—	—	—
236	Risca Colliery Workmen	1889	—	84	(g)	—	—	—	—	—
237	Colliery Enginemen and Stokers of Neath and District	1892	3	55	57	56	62	69	69	186
238	Hauliers and Wagemen of S. Wales and Monmouth	1893	—	—	3,004	5,500	(h)	—	—	—
239	Rhymney Valley Miners	1893	—	—	2,500	2,500	2,691	3,500	1,917	(i)
240	South Wales Colliery Winding Enginemen	1895	1	—	—	—	57	179	83	123
241	Monmouth Western Valleys Miners	1897	—	—	—	—	—	—	500	(j)
242	South Wales Miners' Federation	1898	200	—	—	—	—	—	—	60,000

(a) No. 229:—Late Neath, Swansea, and Llanelly District Miners' Association.
(b) No. 234:—This union in the Seventh Report is described as the Monmouthshire and South Wales Miners' Association (Branch of Miners' Federation of Great Britain) and as having 77 branches at the end of 1893.
(c) No. 230:—Dissolved 1894.
(d) No. 233:—In 1898 became a district of No. 242.
(e) No. 234:—In 1898 became a district of No. 242.

(f) No. 235:—Dissolved 1893.
(g) No. 236:—Dissolved 1893.
(h) No. 238:—Dissolved about 1895.
(i) No. 239:—In 1898 became a district of No. 242.
(j) No. 241:—In 1898 became a district of No. 242.
N.B.—The Board of Trade officials did not include Mabon's Cambrian Miners' Association in the list of trade unions.

Excerpts from *Justice* and from Keir Hardie's
Labour Leader 1898

SOUTH WALES DISPUTE

Since coming into this district I have seen many wage-sheets of miners, the majority of which bore testimony to wages considerably less than £1 per week—15s., 16s. 6d., 17s., 18s., &c.

In addition to this disgraceful rate of pay, wealthy colliery companies like the Great Western Company own the houses in which the men live, and take good care to get a good percentage of the inadequate wage back from the men in rack rents for miserable hovels. The housing of the workers in these industrial Welsh valleys is carried out in a lamentable fashion. Nowhere in London can be seen worse tenements than those in which some of the miners are housed in a number of these colliery towns and villages.

(*Justice*, Saturday, April 23, 1898.)

THE LABOUR WAR IN SOUTH WALES

In spite of these terrible sufferings, the miners resolutely refuse to give to their leaders plenary powers to settle. They assert that they have repeatedly been betrayed on previous occasions, and that W. Abraham, M.P., and some of his colleagues, when negotiating with the masters, are like "clay in the hands of the potter." Abraham is perhaps the most unpopular man in this district to-day, and the miners are not loth to point out that they pay him about £700 per annum for doing nothing at all.

(*Justice*, Saturday, May 7, 1898.)

*   *   *

During the hauliers' strike in Wales, in 1893, the then Liberal Government sent soldiers; now again, in the reign of a Tory Government, the same thing is done. The Welsh colliers will probably make a note of this fact. If so they will escape the blunder into which others who should know better have fallen of pretending to believe that it is the Tories who are doing this thing. The point for the men to remember is that it is a capitalist Government which is doing it, and whether that Government be named Liberal or Tory it will be done just the same.

This latest case is really an outrage on all preconceived ideas of Government. The Welsh colliers have been on strike for two months. During that time there has been no rioting, no disorder of any kind which even called for police interference. The men at their mass meetings often sing hymns, and to open and close with prayer is not uncommon. Hunger having failed to subdue them so quickly as the masters had hoped, they decided to bring soldiers, in the hope that their presence would induce a feeling of despair, if it did not provoke bloodshed, and thus lead to the victory of the masters.

(*Labour Leader*, Saturday, June 18, 1898.)

Men Fighting Gallantly and in
Good Spirit, but the Wolf is
Showing His Fangs

Merthyr, Monday Night.

The men are in rare fettle. A very tricky move is on foot to get them to resume work on the old sliding scale. If the men I have conversed with are any index to the temper of their mates, this is the last thing they will do. Mabon hints that if the employers definitely make this offer he will advise acceptance. Alderman David Morgan, on the other hand, declares he would prefer to see the men die by inches rather than accept the old terms. His is the voice of wisdom.

Soup kitchens and the stoneyard are the principal means of relief.

I regret to hear that the soup kitchens in some districts are in danger of being closed for lack of funds. I renew my appeal of two weeks ago to readers of *The Labour Leader* to exert themselves in this holy war. *These men can win.* The shareholders in some of the big collieries are writing to the papers protesting against the action of the directors in accepting the dictation of Sir W. T. Lewis.

The Taff runs through the valley, which is enclosed by high mountains all round. In this grand amphitheatre is Troedyrhiw, and behind the village is the stoneyard. Today 1,045 men are at work. They are paid 1s. per day and 2d. for each child. The old men are kept for herding off the children, whilst the young and strong are at work earning their shilling. A picturesque sight they make, and from time to time they break out into a chorus which rolls up the mountain sides with fine effect.

In the Merthyr district there are 18,000 children being fed every day at a cost of five farthings a head per diem.

(Keir Hardie in the *Labour Leader* of Saturday, June 25, 1898.)

PEACEFUL FIGHTING WALES

I have put this question to big, lithe, active men of about thirty, "What wages do you yourself earn the year round?" and I have not yet met one who would not be pleased to be guaranteed a pound a week all the year round. Therefore for the best of the men—leaving out the favourites of Fate, which usually means the manager—a pound a week is the wage, and a ten per cent advance on that would bring it up to 22s.

It is this the masters say the coal trade will not afford!

The men are paid 1s. 4d. a ton, and are asking an advance of 1½d. which the masters will not grant. On this same coal a royalty ranging from 9d. to 1s. 6d. per ton is paid the landlord. This I believe, is paid on the total output. In the men's case it is only paid on round coal, which will run to about 75 per cent of what they get at the face. The master sells the small coal, the landlord gets his royalty on it, but the poor collier who faces danger and death and toils hard in winning it gets nothing for it!

I have been trying to point out to the colliers that were the minerals national property the 9d. a ton which now goes to the landlord as royalty might then be added to their wages. Talk of a 10 per cent advance! Here is 60 per cent to be had if only the proper steps are taken. Then there are the huge profits of the colliery owners and the agents at Cardiff and elsewhere. Altogether it is safe to say that by nationalising the mines we could in Wales make the colliers' wages three times what they are without adding one red cent to the selling price of coal.

I hear of directors of collieries who are receiving £3,000 a year. These men are the first to inform the collier that the trade won't afford him 22s. a week. As a rule these men are Christians, and some of them, like Mr. Richard Cory, of Cardiff, take an active part in evangelistic work, and then never tire of warning the workers against Socialism, because all Socialists are atheists. I think, so far as the colliers are concerned, this form of scarecrow is losing its terrors for them. They are feeling that whatever promises justice to Labour must be a part of the gospel of Christ, and since Socialism promises that, it cannot be so very far wrong. At least a good many are now taking the risk of believing in it.

The debate in the House is the subject of keen comment. Not much was expected from it. Mabon's speech had nothing to suggest. He put no blame on anyone nor made reference to royalties. He uttered no condemnation of the Government for sending soldiers. The fact is, and there can be no harm in saying it, Mabon has ceased to lead. He believes the men to be in the wrong, and in consequence wishes them back at work.

(Keir Hardie in the *Labour Leader*, of Saturday, July 2, 1898.)

LEADERLESS WALES

At Tirphil last week a body of colliers were marching in peaceful and orderly procession. They were accompanied by the chief constable and a number of his men, but no occasion was found to interfere, and when at length the boundary was reached where this particular chief constable's duties terminated he openly congratulated the men and their leaders on the splendid order which had been maintained. On the other side of the boundary line there were a number of imported constables, with Chief-constable Lindsay at their head. In order to justify their presence, those men wantonly insulted a portion of the processionists, whereupon, it is alleged, that some mischief-loving urchin threw a sod at one of them. Be this as it may, the constables charged with their drawn batons, and wounded a number of men seriously. One whose life for a time was despaired of is the stationmaster, who ran in to save a child, four years of age, who was being trampled, and was so severely battered about the head that he was unconscious for a time, and even yet, at the moment of writing, cannot be said to be out of danger and is still in hospital. Several clergymen who had witnessed the whole proceeding testified that the attack of the police was wanton and uncalled for, and even the Tory paper, the *Western Mail*, has practically admitted the same thing. In spite of this provocation, the good sense of the men prevents them from doing anything to justify the presence of either the military or the mounted constabulary. . . .

At this meeting sixty constables were held in ambush, the chief-constable, Captain Lindsay, himself being in command. A magistrate, Antony Mills, J.P., with the Riot Act in his pocket, was also on the spot in readiness to do his duty. At Pontypridd a special train, with steam up, was held in readiness to convey the soldiers to the spot, the soldiers being confined to barracks, under arms, ready to march at a moment's notice. Although nearly 10,000 people were present at the meeting, neither by word or deed did they do anything to justify all the suspicion with which they are regarded by their masters, but the lesson is not being lost upon them. . . .

Given a strong lead, the Welsh people will place themselves in the van of the Socialist movement. Kindly disposed by nature, genial in their relationships one to the other, loving justice, and hating oppression, they can easily be roused to battle for the right. Up to the present they have been kept in political servitude, in the belief that Liberalism represents the rights of Labour. They are having an eye-opener just now, which they will not easily forget.

(Keir Hardie in the *Labour Leader*, of Saturday, July 9, 1898.)

Listen to what D. A. Thomas, M.P., has, testified: "He did not always agree with Alderman Morgan, but for straightforwardness and honesty of purpose there was no man in South Wales superior to him, and that was why he respected him. (Loud applause.) *If there was one leader more than another who could not be bought it was David Morgan*, and what he had done he had done because he believed it was right."

(Willie Wright in the *Labour Leader*, of Saturday, August 27, 1898.)

UNREST IN THE SOUTH WALES COALFIELD

Meanwhile, we are glad to find that the men are organising themselves, and not, as after the defeat of 1875, contenting themselves with a mere sham. At one colliery, which employs about 2,000 men, something like 1,700 paid their contributions on Saturday last, and from other collieries the reports are equally encouraging. We trust that in selecting leaders the men will bear in mind how they have been served in past years, and choose the most honest and capable men to guide the affairs of the new organisation, and that they will not forget the lessons of the late strike, chief of which, from the point of view of organisation, is the need of consistent political action. This will be found to be a much more effective weapon than the strike and much more easily wielded.

(J.S. in *Justice*, of Saturday, October 15, 1898.)

APPENDIX III TO CHAPTER TWO

SLIDING SCALE AGREEMENT 1898

MEMORANDUM OF AGREEMENT made this 1st day of September, 1898, between the undersigned William Thomas Lewis, Archibald Hood, Edward Jones, William Thomas, Edward P. Martin, T. Forster Brown, Fred L. Davis, Charles H. Eden, William Jenkins, Joseph Shaw, Henry Davies, G. W. Wilkinson, Clifford J. Cory, T. E. Watson, Henry Lewis, M. Wolstenholme, Richard Cory, Walter S. P. McLaren, and Philip Williams, and other persons who shall execute this agreement duly authorised to act on behalf of the members of the Monmouthshire and South Wales Coal Owners' Association (hereinafter called the Employers) of the one part, and the undersigned William Abraham, T. Daronwy Isaac, Alfred Onions, Thomas Richards, D. Beynon, Evan Thomas, J. Eynon, D. Morgan (Anthracite District), J. Woodward, D. Morgan (Wattstown), and D. Thomas, and other persons who shall execute this

C

agreement, duly authorised to act on behalf of the Workmen (excepting Enginemen, Stokers, and Outside Fitters), formerly employed at the Collieries of the members of the said Association of the other part:—

1. IT IS AGREED that work shall be resumed at the Associated Collieries as on and from the 1st day of September, 1898, upon the following condition:—
2. The terms and conditions of the Sliding Scale Agreement (known as the "Old Scale"), which terminated upon the 31st March last, shall, together with Clause 3 of the agreement of the 17th February, 1893, be embodied in an agreement which shall continue in force until the 1st day of January, 1903, and may be determined by six months' notice on either side, to be given on the 1st of July, 1902, the 1st January, 1903, or any other following 1st July or 1st January.
3. The monthly holiday known as "Mabon's Day" shall be abolished, and no other holiday of a like nature will be permitted.
4. The wages payable up to November 30, 1898, shall be $17\frac{1}{2}$ per cent. above the standard of December, 1879.
5. An audit of the selling prices shall be taken for the two months ending the 31st of October, 1898 to regulate wages as from the 1st of December, 1898, in accordance with Clause 12 of the 1892 agreement.
6. If, after the 1st day of September, 1899, the employers, by virtue of this agreement, reduce the wages of the workmen below $12\frac{1}{2}$ per cent. above the standard of December, 1879, the workmen shall have the right of giving six months' notice to terminate this agreement on the 1st day of any January or July next ensuing, notwithstanding Clause 2 of this agreement.

Employers' Representatives—

W. THOMAS LEWIS
ARCHIBALD HOOD
EDWARD JONES
W. THOMAS
E. P. MARTIN
T. FORSTER BROWN
FRED L. DAVIS
CHARLES H. EDEN
WILLIAM JENKINS
JOSEPH SHAW
HENRY DAVIES
G. W. WILKINSON
CLIFFORD J. CORY
T. E. WATSON
HENRY LEWIS
M. WOLSTENHOLME
R. CORY
WALTER S. B. MCLAREN
P. WILLIAMS

Workmen's Representatives—

WM. ABRAHAM
T. D. ISAAC
THOMAS RICHARDS
ALFRED ONIONS
DAVID BEYNON
EVAN THOMAS
DAVID MORGAN (Anthracite)
DAVID THOMAS
DAVID MORGAN (Wattstown)
JOHN EYNON
JOHN WOODWARD

Witness to the signatures of the parties hereto.

W. GASCOYNE DALZIEL ⎫ Joint
LEWIS MILES   ⎬ Secretaries

September 1, 1898.

CHAPTER THREE

FIRST YEARS OF FEDERATION

I. THE FOUNDING

IN the autumn of 1898 the leaders of the miners were in the process of forming a new organisation while trying to cope with the debts and the many other difficulties arising from the long struggle they had passed through. Prime responsibility for this fell upon the dozen men who on September 1, 1898[1] had signed the agreement embodying the employers' terms and who on the previous day, together with others, had been given the task of drawing up a constitution. These men with a few others made up the first Executive Council. The chief signatories of 1898, most of them miners' agents, had sat on the Sliding Scale Joint Committee—Abraham and Dai o'r Nant since 1875, Isaac since 1890, Richards and Onions since 1892. The office-bearers were from the beginning: President, William Abraham; Vice-President, William Brace; Treasurer, Alfred Onions; General Secretary, Thomas Richards, whose house at Ty Cendl, Beaufort, Monmouth, was to be for many years the office of the Union. Brace, who now became Vice-President, and his associates Ben Davies and John Williams, had always been opposed to Sliding Scales.

The formation of the South Wales Miners' Federation signified there would be an end to the old method of wage regulation. The Executive Council of the new union, though pledged to ring the knell of the Sliding Scale, had nevertheless to bide their time until over four years were passed and gone. But no one doubted that the end would come or that it signified a triumph of the more advanced trade union policy. But though William Abraham, who had typified the old policy, had been forced to give ground to his opponent William Brace, the two men were soon willing to bury the hatchet and to work together in the new trade union for the whole of the coalfield.

The M.F.G.B. Executive Committee, meeting at the Swan Hotel, Bristol, on Friday, September 2nd, were at first in high dudgeon: "seeing that the leaders of the South Wales miners have accepted and signed the old sliding scale agreement in settlement of the strike, we instruct our treasurer to stop sending at once the weekly

[1] See Appendix III to previous chapter.

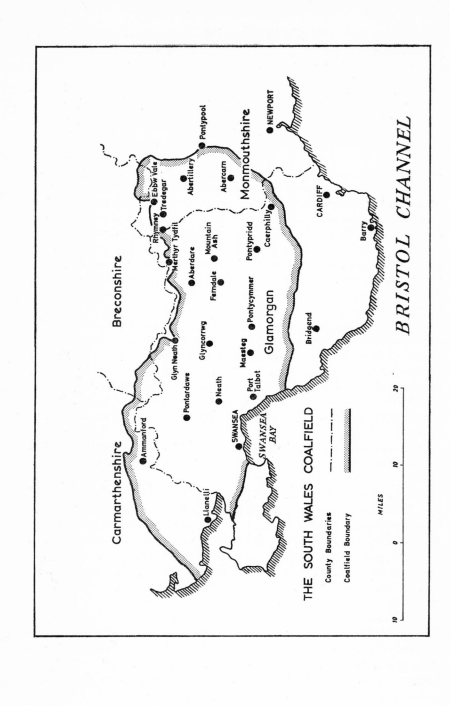

THE SOUTH WALES COALFIELD

County Boundaries
Coalfield Boundary

MILES
10   0   10   20

Carmarthenshire

Breconshire

Monmouthshire

Glamorgan

BRISTOL CHANNEL

- Llanelli
- Ammanford
- Pontardawe
- Neath
- Glyn Neath
- Glyncorrwg
- SWANSEA
- SWANSEA BAY
- Port Talbot
- Maesteg
- Pontycymmer
- Bridgend
- Ferndale
- Aberdare
- Mountain Ash
- Merthyr Tydfil
- Rhymney
- Tredegar
- Ebbw Vale
- Abertillery
- Abercarn
- Pontypridd
- Caerphilly
- Pontypool
- NEWPORT
- CARDIFF
- Barry

subscription from this Federation of £600, which was decided upon at a conference in London, on July 7, 1898," and the special M.F.G.B. Conference on September 28, 1898, confirmed this resolution. Within another month, however, their Executive Committee was considering a letter from South Wales asking that speakers be sent "to explain the principles of the Federation." This was considered "not advisable": but to all the numerous requests "from every part" of South Wales asking for information as to how they could join the M.F.G.B. the reply was steadfastly given that "they must first become organised." To the next Executive Committee meeting came a deputation headed by Mabon, Brace and Dai o'r Nant: in South Wales, said Mabon, they were now getting organised on trade union lines, and there was no mistaking the desire of the men to become members of the Miners' Federation of Great Britain: they had 30,000 members already and their numbers were growing fast: the leaders, working unitedly, had only one end in view—"to get a strong organisation, and become connected with the Federation of Great Britain, and abolish the Sliding Scale." (*18.xi.1898.*)

It was explained to the deputation that so long as the wages of the men in South Wales were governed by a sliding scale, they could not be accepted in full membership in the Federation on the wages question: but if South Wales could accept these conditions, then no doubt they would be welcomed at the annual conference.

Ben Pickard, M.P., had been the first to suggest that some opening should be found for the South Wales miners to come into the fold. It was clear to him that the aftermath of the South Wales lockout brought the opportunity to build an effective trade union and that the renewed sliding scale would be more likely to be abolished if the Welsh miners were inside the British Federation. Accordingly, when the Annual Conference assembled in Edinburgh, Ben Pickard, as first business and before his own presidential address was read, called on the South Wales delegates "to make their requisition to join." On this Mabon arose and cast his eyes around the assembled fifty leaders of the coalfields: "In making this requisition," he said, "we come as penitent Welshmen. As yet we only represent a portion of our men but I hope it will be considered ample for them to be allowed to join the Federation of Great Britain." They had 60,000 members and they had brought the cheque for £60 along with them: so he sincerely hoped they would be accepted. "Do you understand the conditions under which you will join?" asked Pickard. When this had been answered with a "Yes," the resolution was moved, and carried unanimously: "That the South Wales and Monmouthshire Trades Union, composed of 60,000 miners, be accepted as members of the Miners' Federation of Great Britain."

From its formation on October 11, 1898, the South Wales Miners' Federation grew very rapidly. Within half a year there were 92,000 members; by the end of 1899 104,212; and by the end of 1900 127,894. Then came seven lean years when the membership totals sagged downwards and touched bottom with 110,000 in 1905. Out of 132,682 employed in 1899 over a hundred thousand—a very high proportion—were in the union: but thereafter as the number employed increased the percentage of trade unionists diminished.

In the opening months, however, the builders of the union had good reason to be pleased. In his address to the Annual Conference of the Miners' Federation of Great Britain, Ben Pickard, M.P., spoke of the Welsh accession as "a very important step towards the Federation of the Miners of England, Scotland and Wales" and uttered a fervent hope that "loyalty will prove in the future strong enough" to keep them together as one united body, "not merely for one or two years, but for the next generation." (Edinburgh, *10.1.1899*.)

But would this prove equally an accession of strength in the matter of policy? The issue of this remained to be seen.

2. THE BUILDERS OF THE UNION

Who were primarily responsible for this great drive that brought about so large an association in so short a space of time? The answer is "the unknown pioneers." But particular names survive, often of those miners' agents who played a part both before 1898 and immediately afterwards in the spread of the principles of trade unionism throughout the valleys. Some of the older members of the Union in the late 'fifties had memories that went back to the days before the Union existed. Outstanding amongst these was John E. Morgan, for nearly half his adult life secretary of the Lady Windsor Lodge of which he has written the story.[1] Morgan, born in 1874 in Ferndale, said: "The trade union lodges at first were more or less secret. In the very old days I have no recollection of any meeting being held except on the mountain top. The groupings of miners had gradually evolved into an association. For example, if there was a grievance common to three or four pits, they would get together." Asked about agents, J. E. Morgan named Ben Davies and William Brace: "These were the two 'John the Baptists' who had formed a trade union lodge in this part. Ben Davies started when the miners earmarked themselves in two pits, but it was very much a patchwork. Besides Brace and Davies there was Dai o'r Nant, and

[1] *A Village Workers' Council—and what it accomplished*, being a short history of the Lady Windsor Lodge, South Wales Miners' Federation by John E. Morgan with a foreword by the Rt. Hon. Viscount Hall (Celtic Press Ltd.) with illustrations. Pontypridd (no date).

before him again there had been Tom Halliday." Morgan recollected many speakers coming down, "including Tom Mann"; and amongst women speakers he had seen Beatrice Webb in the 'nineties and had heard Enid Stacy whose husband P. E. T. Widdrington had also spoken. Asked about the hauliers' strike of 1893 Morgan replied that it had not affected them directly but "we marched in sympathy to Pontypridd." In his recollection it was the first strike that was "not confined but where the sympathy went beyond the bounds of valleys and districts."

County Alderman Jack Evans[1] who lived in a tiny two-roomed house at 30 Merthyr Road, Tongwynlais, said "I remember well the hauliers' strike, partly because it was the year of the National Eisteddfod being held at Pontypridd at the famous Rocking Stone. It was spoken of as 'the Rocking Stone strike.' The leader of the hauliers was Morgan Thomas. I myself had come from the Garw Valley and from Maesteg and crossed over the hill to the Rhondda."

W. R. Williams, J.P., of Ystradgynlais had a memory of 1898. "I remember blacklegging and demonstrations and some rough handling: but my colliery was not in this lockout. Yet we raised levies in aid of the strikers by neighbourly feeling. At that time there were S.W.M.F. tokens which the young people wore in their caps."

Edmond Stonelake of 36 Herbert Street, Aberdare, was born in 1873. "I entered the pit in 1884 but after six weeks was withdrawn as under age and so was idle until I was twelve when I began work regularly. This was in the Rhymney Valley in the old pits near New Tredegar and Rhymney. In January 1889, when I was fifteen years nine months the family came to Aberdare where there was more money (3s. 2d. a day less 2½ per cent). Why was there more money? Because of the steelworks." Stonelake had been secretary to Keir Hardie and then went to Ruskin College in August, 1901, and stayed till November. "I had then been married six years and had three children. There were 25 students. I was the only collier there. Once a week we had to scrub the place clean." He also said: "I was always a rebel. When I was a boy they stopped my money. I sought out the miners' agent. This was before there was a district organisation."

Jack Williams, formerly secretary of the Forest of Dean Miners' Association, was born in 1888 at Kenfig Hill near the Garw Valley. His father was a miner: his grandfather had been a mechanic in the mines. He himself entered the mines on his birthday in November

[1] Jack Evans, O.B.E., J.P., was a County Alderman from 1925 onwards and later sat as M.P. for the Ogmore Division from 1946 to 1950. He said: "Earlier I had been at Ruskin College from 1907 to 1908." He began work in the coalmines at twelve years of age and was a miner for 21 years. He was on the Glamorgan County Council from 1913, on the Royal Commission on National Health Insurance 1924–25 and on the Royal Commission on Justices of the Peace in 1946. He had been Chairman of the Glamorgan County Council for two years from 1939–40.

in either his 12th or 13th year and the mine at which he began was
the International. He said: "My earliest recollection as a small child
is of the hauliers' strike of 1893. I saw the riot, was in a sense actually
in the riot together with my father. The manager at Blaengarw,
whose name was Salathiel, had brought the militia to protect two
blacklegs. The Salathiel family was very widespread and were always
to be found holding post offices. I with my father had been one of
the spectators until my father joined up and I remember him pushing
away at one of the blacklegs."

Alf Palfreyman was born October 27, 1878, in Ogmore Vale,
whither his father had come from Devon to help build the railway.
When this was finished his father was engaged in the sinking of pits,
especially the Lewis Merthyr House Coal Pit. Alf went into the mine
in 1890. He remembered the flooding at the Wyndham and Ocean
Pits. At the time of the 1893 hauliers' strike he remembered seeing
the demonstration set out from Ogmore Vale to Pontypridd where
they met at the Rocking Stone. "Tom Jones was the agent then:
he had come from Clydach Vale." Palfreyman said:

> I remember very well the strike of 1898. I took part in it. I was at the
> No. 3 seam in the Aber Pit. At that pit there was no lodge committee, no
> checkweigher and no agent. Afterwards John Williams, M.P. for Swansea,
> was our agent and Tom Lucas was first secretary of the Aber Lodge where
> a publican was the treasurer. In those days we had no shovels. We left
> them there in the pit when we came out on strike. I did not get back to
> the pit. I was what nowadays they call "victimised" from September,
> 1898, until 1899. I had been active in the struggle and afterwards in the
> building of the Federation I was active. The first men who came here to
> build the Federation were William Brace and Ben Davies. They held a
> meeting on the hillside between here and Nantymoel. I presided at that
> meeting, and was again victimised for it. There is a big stone near it which
> has been christened the "Federation Stone." William Brace in those days
> was the most polished speaker we had by far.

Alf Palfreyman ran through the names of a number of other
miners' leaders who, like Brace, had all originally come from
Monmouthshire such as Tom Richards, Alfred Onions and Vernon
Hartshorn who came from Risca. Alf Palfreyman said Ogmore Vale
was the first valley in which the feeding of schoolchildren was put
into operation. "Edward Edwards the schoolmaster was the pioneer.
Edwards was a pioneer, too, of the whole labour movement here.
Otherwise things were in the hands of the Lib-Labs: and the
Anthracite in those days was backward." Alf Palfreyman said: "I
joined the Independent Labour Party in 1894. It was Edward
Edwards, however, that had pioneered the I.L.P. in Ogmore Vale."

Ted Layton, born in 1871, for 48 years on the committee of the
Naval Lodge Cambrian Collieries, remembered well the formation

of the South Wales Miners' Federation in 1898. "I joined in the first week. I attended its first demonstration held in Porth in 1899. We marched from Treherbert down to Porth where Bob Smillie was the speaker. . . . As a boy when I went to work at the age of 11 or 12 I earned about 4s. 6d. a week. The collier I worked for was getting about 18s. or 19s. The colliers used to take us lads to the pub as a tip and buy us a quart of beer each, at 4d. a quart." Before the

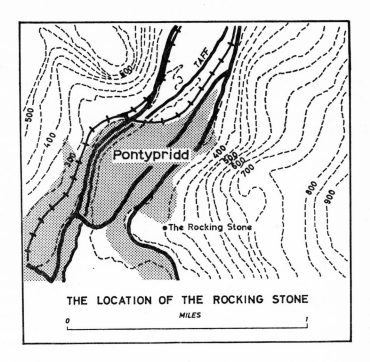

THE LOCATION OF THE ROCKING STONE

MILES

Federation there were pit committees with local funds. "In my chapel, to which I have belonged for over seventy years, both Mabon and Brace have preached." He started work at Merthyr at Abercanaid and came to the Rhondda when he was 15. "My father had eight children and an income of 15s. a week; he was a stoker in the steelworks and had his 15s. a week for a 12-hour day." In his opinion "the Union had greatly improved life; for I can remember women begging for bread around the doors." Mr. Layton worked in the Ely Pit as a labourer for 2s. 10d. a turn. Once the manager asked him to make a special effort and he emptied 14 trams of muck in a shift. "The manager would not believe me, so I left. But then I had to go back and be humiliated by begging for work." This was before 1898. "I remember particularly well the

c*

hauliers' strike in 1893 and marching down from the Rhondda to Troedyrhiw, Merthyr. We were accompanied by a man with a donkey and cart on which were casks of water for when we were thirsty. Women came out on the side of the roads with baskets of bread and cheese for us to eat. One man said his feet were sore and he was going to pawn his watch to get the fare to go by train."

Such recollections as these of the pioneers by the pioneers of trade unionism may serve to convey something of the conditions of work and of the effort it was to build a union. Little was said by them of disasters but these, too, as well as the recollection of extreme poverty, were also present in the minds of some who were interviewed. For a last example we may take Sam Fisher of Wattsville, Crosskeys, in Monmouthshire who when asked in his 94th year (having been born in January, 1865) for his recollections told us first of all:

I remember the explosion in Risca in 1880 where there had been a previous explosion in 1860.[1] I was one of a family of 9 or 10 and there was 23s. a week coming into the household. Sixty years I worked in the mines which I left in 1937. I started work at the age of 10 and for two years I was in the brickyards where I got 4s. a week. The brickyard was on the Darran. My father came from Wiltshire. I can remember that in good times my mother would get three pounds of fat bacon: and if there was a swede or a turnip it made a fine addition to the dish."

3. A FEDERAL UNION

The constitution of the new union was similar to that of other miners' associations. In what sense was it a federation? Despite its name it was not a federation of trade unions like the Scottish Miners' Federation or the Midland Miners' Federation. Its title signified only that a number of local associations, as had happened fifteen years earlier in the case of the Lancashire and Cheshire Miners' Federation, had come together to form a single trade union. But in South Wales there persisted an exceptionally high degree of autonomy in each of its twenty districts. The rules dealing with the election of officers and of the executive council, with their several duties, made it clear that a federal constitution was the aim and that the source of effective power remained very largely in the districts. These twenty districts in the main corresponded to the valleys that were such a distinctive feature of the Welsh coalfield, each separated from its neighbour by a mountain and each with its own traffic in coal through a railway running up to the valley head. In each district the miners' agent held the key position. The other three district officers (president, secretary and treasurer) came up at

[1] In the Risca explosion of July 15, 1880, 120 lives were lost: but the earlier explosion (of December 1, 1860) caused 142 deaths.

regular intervals for election or re-election. The agent, however, was to be elected by ballot vote. Once elected he did not have to submit himself for periodic election or re-election. It was this state of affairs, which already existed before 1898, that drew from Tom Richards the rueful admission a dozen years later that the Executive Council had singularly little control over the agents.[1] Noah Ablett, himself an agent, spoke scornfully of "the little chieftains" at a national conference some thirty years later.[2]

Again, while the officers of the South Wales Miners' Federation were to be elected by an annual conference of lodge representatives, the members of the Executive Council of the union were to be elected from and within each district. Thus the districts, jealous of their powers, yielded only the very minimum necessary to the new single trade union.

In the last years of Queen Victoria and still more in the reign of her successor there was frequent discussion of constitutions. Parallels were sometimes drawn between the constitutions of the United States or the German Reich or the French Republic and the articles of association that were drawn up for voluntary bodies, including trade unions, some of which had most elaborate rulebooks. But in so far as any parallels were drawn in South Wales by the union leaders who were also local preachers, they were more likely to have referred to the Book of Judges and the Twelve Tribes than to any more modern examples.

In the early years of the Executive Council a minority of the members were checkweighers who would also be lodge secretaries as a rule. But, though not every agent had a seat on the Executive Council, the agents on it had an easy majority which grew from year to year. The total number varied but was around two dozen, and the same number and to a large extent the same personnel was usually chosen to negotiate with the coal owners.

The administration, conducted for the first years from the house of the General Secretary, was on a very small scale, as was also the income from which its cost was met. A member had to contribute not less than one shilling "per lunar month," of which 6d. went to the central fund and 4d. formed the district fund, while 2d. was retained at the lodge "to defray the lodge expenses." For this shilling the members received the full aid and protection that the union could give, but no money benefits other than victimisation pay and dispute pay.

[1] "Every agent is a Czar in his own district more or less, and no one else dares interfere with him." (Tom Richards, M.P., on January 24, 1911, in M.F.G.B. debate.)
[2] "We have got the tribal system in operation, with all the little chieftains. We do not desire to continue institutions that are ossified and fossilised. We don't want the little tribes. We want one Union." (*12.vii.1932.*)

In the first ten years the total income of the central fund was rising up to an annual average of fifty thousand pounds. Out of this the cost of salaries at head office, rent, rates, stationery and printing and postage did not come to more than a thousand pounds a year. The expense of travel and meetings came always to twice and sometimes thrice as much as this, while strike pay to members cost about twenty times as much. Strikes varied in their incidence from year to year: and consequently so did the annual balance. The union as often as not ended the year with a financial loss. This, however, is not a matter to be measured in the same way as the case of an insurance company or friendly benefit society. Trade unions always could and did have recourse to levies, that is, additional contributions called by the constituted authority.

In South Wales this practice was carried further than in most of the miners' associations. Men out on strike (if sanctioned according to rule) had to be given their dispute pay from the district fund: but if more than five per cent of any district were on strike, the liability was transferred to the central fund. As districts varied in size from nearly three thousand to nearly ten thousand members (and in the case of the giant Rhondda district to nearly thirty thousand members) the liability was also very varied and certainly very difficult to estimate in advance.

Whatever the fluctuation in central, district or local funds the liability to pay out was bound up with measures to make sure that miners paid in. The early years of the Federation were marked by a series of strikes against non-unionism. By this means the new union soon had a very high proportion of the coalfield organised. But the cost of these strikes meant a very high draining away of central and district funds, so that again and again from 1899 onwards circulars went out calling for levies of up to a shilling per member in support of those out on strike.

4. A QUESTION OF TIMING

Under the Sliding Scale of 1892, accepted as part of the terms of September 1, 1898, wages varied with the rise or fall of prices. These were rising slowly till autumn 1899. Then the war in South Africa against the Boers raised prices which within eighteen months brought wages to 78¾ per cent above standard. From this zenith nominal wages declined to 48¾ per cent in the summer of 1902, soon after peace was signed. At this point, on July 1, 1902, the miners gave formal notice to end the sliding scale agreement. They sought in place of the Joint Committee another kind of negotiating body. The name of Conciliation Board was hallowed for all such bodies in Section One of the Conciliation Act 1896.[1]

A board for "the coal trade of the Federated Districts" had been reconstituted in 1899, and another "for the regulation of wages in the coal trade of Scotland" had been set up in 1900. The future of these bodies might be affected by what was done elsewhere. Therefore in the October 1900 M.F.G.B. Annual Conference, held in Saltburn on the morrow of the "Khaki" general election, the following resolution came from the Scottish district, was supported from South Wales and carried unanimously:

> That as a means to bring the districts within the Federation area into a position whereby united action can be taken when necessary, wages agreements be made to terminate simultaneously in future. (*26.x.1900.*)

Two years later at the Southport M.F.G.B. Annual Conference the Executive Committee tabled a resolution:

> That no section of this Federation enter into any wages agreement, binding such section or sections beyond the end of 1903, when the present agreement terminates, to permit of a general movement being taken to secure a minimum wage to all the districts, and to raise said minimum to a higher standard. (*7.x.1902.*)

The hope voiced by Robert Smillie from Scotland was that "ultimately they would be under one conciliation board." Objection was raised from South Wales that such a stipulation with a fixed date ("They were in thorough agreement with the principle of the resolution but . . .") might be a rock on which their negotiations in Cardiff would be wrecked. Could it not, therefore, be made into "a recommendatory resolution?" This brought chairman Ben Pickard to his feet to say that "all that talk meant there was going to be a split," and that when South Wales had been accepted in Edinburgh in 1899 it was on a definite understanding, "a solid compact that they should endeavour to work under one scheme and that they would fight the Wage Question under one scheme and not under three." Otherwise it would be "abandoning one another, everybody fighting for their own hands, and all would be attacked separately."

To this in his most soothing manner William Brace replied on behalf of the South Wales delegation and said that he quite agreed with what the Chairman had said, and that "we do not want to talk of leaving the Federation, as we have gone through great trouble and tribulation to get here. We believed from the commencement in the

[1] Any board established either before or after the passing of this Act, which is constituted for the purpose of settling disputes between employers and workmen by conciliation or arbitration, or any association or body authorised by an agreement in writing made between employers and workmen to deal with such disputes (in this Act referred to as a Conciliation Board), may apply to the Board of Trade for registration under this Act.

establishment of one Federation for the miners' unions, and now if it is the intention of the Federation to have one scheme, all we want to know is what are your intentions so far as we are concerned?" There would be some difficulty in getting the various employers to merge themselves into one central conciliation board. So Brace asked "Will the Federation make common cause with us by putting into operation Rule Twenty?[1] If the Welsh coalowners will not agree to merge themselves in one national conciliation board, will the whole of the Federation help us? Such a policy as this we are here to accept and support."

However adroitly William Brace sought to still the tempest aroused by the Neptunian outburst of Pickard, he was not as yet immediately successful. The old Chairman of the Yorkshire Miners' Association, Ned Cowey, a massive figure of a man, well over six foot tall, rose and, on behalf of Rule Twenty ("one of our fundamental principles") urged the Welshmen "not to get your hands bound behind your backs again," and added: "Do not again be shackled, fight for freedom, and I will fight with you."

But when the conference resumed the next day, Pickard was in a mood to make concessions, particularly when it became clear to all that the Miners' Federation of Great Britain were bound not to strike on a wage issue up to the end of 1903. Therefore if it came to a strike in South Wales within a few months, they could only arrange for voluntary aid from each district in support. So Pickard, from the Chair, asked if someone would move the suspension of standing orders (to enable an amendment to the resolution to be made on the spot): and when this had been carried unanimously, the first words of the resolution were altered to read: "That each section of this Federation be recommended not to enter into any wages agreement, binding such section or sections, beyond the end of 1903 . . ." (*9.x.1902*.)

At the same time it was decided to call a special conference on "the Welsh Wages Question" in the first month of 1903. Thus it was left that the miners of South Wales would endeavour to get an agreement for one year only. It was soon to be seen, however, that all this was "reckoning without mine host", for the Welsh owners had not yet spoken.

[1] Rule 20, repeatedly mentioned in the years to come, ran as follows under the heading *Defensive Action*: (*The Miners*, Vol. I, page 108, lines 6 to 10 incl.):
"That whenever any County, Federation or District is attacked on the Wage question or any action taken by a general Conference, all members connected with the Society shall tender a notice to terminate their contracts—if approved of by a Conference called to consider the advisability of such joint action being taken."

5. TALKS "BETWEEN MASTERS AND MEN"

It was not until November 4, 1902, that there was held at Cardiff
a joint meeting between the owners and workmen's representatives.
There were present the 24 members of the Executive Council (of
whom 12 had composed the Workmen's Side of the Sliding Scale
Committee in the previous four years) and nearly the same number
of owners. Four out of the six months' notice given on July 1st to
end the Sliding Scale had expired: and it was "unfortunate," said
Mabon to his District meeting, "that the employers could not have
seen their way clear to have met the workmen's representatives
months ago, to commence their negotiations." (*17.xi.1902.*) The
owners at this first meeting asked a number of preliminary questions.
First they wanted to be satisfied that the other side were duly
authorised on behalf of the workmen at the associated collieries. To
this Mabon, who in all the discussions was chief spokesman, was
able to give the required assurance as to their authority—only
to find some weeks later that the owners made difficulties about the
recognition of the South Wales Miners' Federation as a party to the
proposed agreement and would have preferred something more
nearly resembling the semi-company unionism of earlier years under
the Sliding Scale. In answer to a question about the proposed conciliation board Mabon replied: "We are desirous, if the owners
agree, to join the General Board for the United Kingdom for the
general regulation of wages. That is our desire and request."

Then came another question:

Having regard to the resolution of the Southport conference of the
Miners' Federation for what period are the workmen's representatives
prepared to make an arrangement?

Mabon's reply was:

The workmen cannot say but if the Owners would agree to join the
General Board of the United Kingdom it would be for 12 months, viz: to
the end of 1903. The workmen cannot say anything just now as to the
length of the agreement. That would depend upon the terms of the
agreement.

Finally the question was put: "How is it proposed to bind the
parties to any Award?" to which Mabon replied: "The Workmen's
representatives would sign any new agreement in joint conference
and the individual workmen would also sign it."

Thus ended the first of a series of twelve meetings that winter,
three in November, three in December, and six in January. It
seemed clear that the owners were feeling their way, were examining
the existing Conciliation Board in the federated area of England and

also considering the question of timing. Everything was very politely conducted at this first meeting. There was no expression of a hard and fast standpoint, such as used to be heard from the lips of the Sliding Scale Committee chairman, Sir William Lewis: nor did they have to endure his truculent approach to questions. For "Billy" had sometimes put on the haughty airs of the aristocrats on whom he depended, to whose favour initially he owed his rise to great fortunes and among whose ranks he sought all his life to obtain a footing. Actually, great pressure was soon to be put upon the owners' representatives, by "Billy" and other influential colliery proprietors, to adopt the stiffest attitude to the workmen.

The meeting of November 15, 1902, was taken up with stipulations that the workmen should enter into an agreement not to raise at this point the disputed issue over "Small Coal." This done, the owners, ten days later, unmasked their batteries. On their behalf William Jenkins, a member of the small but influential finance committee of the Coalowners' Association, spoke as follows:

In November last year the workmen put before the owners certain proposals confirming that they gave the owners notice in June last to terminate the existing arrangement. Since then circumstances have arisen showing that the workmen are not in a position to make an agreement except for a short period; and seeing the high wages earned by the men and as the workmen's side cannot enter into any arrangements for longer than a year, the owners submit that it would be in the interests of the workmen and of the owners that the Sliding Scale Agreement should be allowed to run for another year. (*25.xi.1902.*)

William Jenkins went on to deal with "Small Coal," saying:

The price which the owners pay for large coal covers all the value of all the labour in respect of Small Coal made and filled in transit. The owners are aware that that is not a strictly legal arrangement and that this payment is not in legal form. The owners think it is just as well in the early stage of the negotiations that they should put that question in proper form legally and otherwise. (*25.xi.1902.*)

Hence they had with the help of the lawyers prepared an agreement which everyone present was requested and expected to sign.[1] Then the owners came back to the question of the sliding scale.

At the next meeting on December 5, 1902, the owners hammered on the same nail and this dialogue then followed:

W. Abraham: Without questioning the owners' right to raise the question he might say that the workmen's representatives having carefully

[1] Weeks later Edward Jones said: "My company originally paid for 19 cwt. of large and 1 cwt. of small; but ten years ago it was arranged to pay the same price for 19 cwt. as was formerly paid for 20 cwt. About twenty years ago payment was made for 17 cwt. of large house coal and 3 cwt. of small: but ten years ago it was agreed to give the same price for 17 cwt. as was previously given for 20 cwt." (*8.i.1903.*)

considered the owners' proposal to continue the Sliding Scale are unable to agree to it.

W. Jenkins: Can the workmen's representatives give their reasons?

W. Abraham: Our side fail to agree with the owners to reinstate the Sliding Scale to regulate wages for the next twelve months.

W. Jenkins: Notwithstanding that you cannot make a longer agreement?

W. Abraham: The workmen's representatives do not admit that but it would put the workmen outside the association they are connected with. The workmen fought for a day and a half to obtain a free hand.

W. Jenkins: Then the workmen's representatives are not free people to deal with free people.

W. Abraham: That is not so. The workmen's representatives fought for their freedom and they won it. The workmen have a right to go beyond a year but it would depend upon the terms. As to the question of freedom to make an arrangement are the owners free? It is time for the owners to prove to the world that they have the freedom to treat.

W. Jenkins: The owners accept you as the workmen's representative.

W. Abraham: The workmen admit that they would rather make a short agreement than a long one but that does not prevent the workmen making a long one if they choose.

W. Jenkins: Provided the terms are good enough.

W. Abraham: Yes.

W. Jenkins: Then your reason is that there is somebody outside that says you must not renew the Sliding Scale or who tells you not to make a longer agreement than one year.

W. Abraham: No, we can do so if we choose, but we should put ourselves outside the pale of the Miners' Federation: and it is not our desire amongst ourselves to renew the Sliding Scale.

Mr. Jenkins having skilfully wrung these admissions from Abraham wound up this part of the discussion saying: "The owners take it from the workmen that the continuation of the scale for another year is not agreed to." (*5.xii.1902.*)

Yet once more at the adjourned meeting ten days later the owners came back on the same point and said:

W. Jenkins: Are the workmen quite sure having regard to all the circumstances that the continuation of the Sliding Scale will not be the best for the workmen?

W. Brace: Absolutely certain.

W. Jenkins: That is having regard to your arrangements with your colleagues in the Midlands the workmen cannot entertain it?

W. Brace: The workmen's representatives have instructions given them by their own workmen in South Wales not to entertain the proposal.

W. Jenkins: Very well then the owners must take that as being final, that the workmen will not have a Sliding Scale in any form. Is it because it is self-acting that the workmen object to it?

W. Brace: The Scale is not sensitive enough. It only recognises selling prices as the only factor and it is not a fair regulator of wages. There are several other factors.

W. Jenkins: What are the other factors?

W. Brace: Profits, Volume of Trade and selling prices.

(*15.xii.1902.*)

Then the owners said that before giving decisions on the workmen's proposals they would table some grievances. The first was an
increase in the cost of working "in recent years," from which they
concluded: "The owners' representatives feel that to meet this
difficulty it is absolutely necessary that there should be a substantial
reduction in wages as from January 1st." When Brace asked "How
do the owners account for increased cost?" Fred Davis said: "The
owners could get rid of 25 per cent of the men now working at the
collieries in this District and get the same output of coal if the men
would only work as well as they did ten or twelve years ago. Whatever the men's representatives may say, there is a systematic restriction of output." Brace replied: "I challenge that as regards
Monmouthshire." Other coalowners then spoke "from their own
knowledge" as to an "organised restriction of output being produced
by the workmen." Brace said that the workmen thought that
stoppage had "often resulted from some foolish action on the part
of the management." Boyd Harvey said: "Nearly every colliery in
South Wales has been stopped on the Union and non-Union men
question."

The coalowner Fred Davis then said:

There is another point the whole of the trade feels acutely: the loss
which results from supplying house coal to the workmen at less than cost
price. It was intended to supply workmen with coal at cost price and
when the price was fixed it was about 5s. per ton. Now the cost price is
10s. to 12s. per ton and the owners lose from 5s. to 7s. per ton. The
owners' working cost is now 50 per cent higher than when the price for
house coal was originally fixed and the workmen must help the owners in
getting rid of this grievance, and in getting the price charged to workmen
for house coal to be nearer the cost price than it is today. (*15.xii.1902.*)

A little later after this had sunk in, the following memorandum
prepared by the owners was read aloud:

That subject to the Small Coal question and the House Coal question
being satisfactorily settled, and subject to a substantial reduction in the
general wage rate throughout the district as from the 1st January next
rendered necessary by the enormous increase in the working cost, the
owners agree to the principle of a Conciliation Board, a minimum and
maximum and an Independent Chairman to deal with the general wage
question only. Detailed proposals embodying the owners' views will be
placed before the workmen's representatives at the next meeting.

When Treasurer Alfred Onions immediately protested that this
proposal was considerably worse than to renew the Sliding Scale,
there was a rapid inter-change as follows:

W. Jenkins: The owners find that the workmen have the control of the
cost of production; and it has been materially and unnecessarily
increased by the negligent working of the workmen: and the owners

ask the workmen's representatives therefore to assist them in the proposed substantial reduction in wages.

W. Brace: Do not the owners remember that if the Sliding Scale had continued they could not get a reduction before February even if the price of coal had gone down? And do the owners expect to get better terms without the Sliding Scale than they would have obtained under the Scale?

Fred Davis: We want a substantial reduction in the present percentage.

W. Brace: If the owners want a settlement of this question it would be simple madness for the owners to introduce the demand for a substantial reduction in wages . . . The proper course is to form the Board and then if the owners are entitled to a reduction they will have it.

Fred Davis: Do the workmen's representatives think that the owners are going to give way to the workmen upon all their new principles, minimum, maximum and Conciliation Board and get nothing in return especially when the cost of working is so high?

That question was left with the miners' representatives to think over during the Christmas week.

At the next full meeting from January 7 to 9, 1903, the actual proposals of the coalowners for the agreement, together with the suggested amendments put forward by the workmen, were discussed one by one. The employers proposed to add to the existing price of workmen's house coal a percentage corresponding to the percentage paid on standard wages (which at that point stood at almost 50 per cent over the standard of 1879). The workmen were also to bear the cost of haulage. On this the following remarks were made:

W. Abraham: The owners appear to be making their conditions an ultimatum.

Fred Davis: No, the workmen want to make an arrangement with the owners and they want certain things and the owners say they will agree to the workmen's things if the workmen will give the owners something in exchange, that is businesslike and there is no ultimatum about that.

W. Abraham: Is this one of the owners' main points?

Fred Davis: Certainly.

Next came the heading "Substantial Reduction in Wages." Under this William Jenkins said: "The owners feel that they want some relief from wages in some form or other and they want a reduced cost on the article which they produce and the only way by which they can achieve the desired object is to attack wages, that is the only way by which the owners think they can meet their increased cost which is entirely due to the slackness of the workmen in the first instance in producing the coal." Another employer Henry Lewis said: "These are not the only causes. The increased cost is due to legislation and due to working more expensive seams of coal and deeper seams. These help to increase the owners' cost. The owners find that their cost, irrespective of wages, has increased from 1890 by the sum of 1s. 10d. per ton. Some of that no doubt is temporary and has taken place during the last few years through the slackness of the men."

So it went on. Sharp arguments were exchanged on every item. For example, the coalowners' proposal for the minimum was 20 per cent above 1879, or half the percentage level claimed by the men. They also wanted to lower the maximum (in which they succeeded). In short the owners were willing to have a Conciliation Board only if the workmen would pay for it as for a concession. Alfred Onions said: "I would like to point out the unreasonableness of the owners' conditions. There have been Conciliation Boards established all over this country in various coalfields and I have never heard nor have the owners heard of a case where, when the Sliding Scale was abolished for a Conciliation Board, the owners have put forward demands such as for a reduction in wages, increased price for house coal and other things." To this the owners stoutly replied: "Having regard to the enormously increased cost of production the owners are entitled to some relief in some form or other." Fred Davis said that the owners thought that when they framed the clause on "house coal" they were treating the matter in a generous way. When Brace said, "There is nothing to prevent the owners from introducing the question before the Conciliation Board," the owner Edward Jones replied: "The owners refuse positively to take this before the Conciliation Board. It is a question which must be settled before the Conciliation Board is formed." Again the workmen argued that the Conciliation Board would not hurt the employers. Brace said that "if the owners make conditions thinking that the workmen will agree to a reduction in wages and an increased price for house coal to get a Conciliation Board the workmen say at once it won't be done. The men would not accept it . . . The owners have nothing to fear from the working of the Board any more than the workmen."

Again and again the point came back to the question of the duration of the agreement, whether it would need to coincide with the ending of the English agreement, that is, to "terminate within the year or as it was now within ten months, or to go on to the end of 1905." Owner Edward Jones said: "Let us decide whether the agreement is for ten months or three years, that is the crux of the owners' position. If it is for ten months it would be better not to import for a few months any of these new principles which some of the owners' side are in favour of and some are opposed to; and the only thing to do is to do the best we can for the next ten months." Moreover on the question of the minimum, while the owners were willing to consider the 30 per cent it was with the stipulation that that must be equated with a higher selling price than had been the case hitherto or than the workmen had believed to be the case.

Eventually after January 23, 1903, there was the possibility of setting out precisely what were the points of agreement and of difference.

6. THE FEBRUARY CONFERENCE

Meanwhile leaders of the Miners' Federation were becoming anxious. Their secretary had written about the question of the January conference and had been told by Tom Richards that the Welshmen were not as yet prepared to make a report and that it would be better to postpone it until the February. At the M.F.G.B. Executive Committee at the Victoria Station Hotel, Sheffield, on Friday, January 30th, Brace reported what had been done up to the present in the negotiations and he asked that a conference be called. They decided that it would be held on Friday, February 20th, if the secretary of the S.W.M.F. wrote applying for the said conference. Four days later Tom Richards wrote to apply, forwarding particulars of the negotiations "for a wage regulation to take the place of the Sliding Scale agreement that has now expired." He stated that "with the exception of the length of the term for which the agreement is to be signed, the conditions offered are considered by my Council to be fairly satisfactory." These Richards summarised as follows:

Conditions Offered

1. A Conciliation Board with an independent Chairman to be formed for the general regulation of wages.
2. The Conciliation Board without the independent Chairman to deal with disputes at the Collieries.
3. A minimum rate of wages to be fixed at 30 per cent above the standard of 1879.
4. A maximum rate of wages to be fixed at 60 per cent above the standard of 1879.
5. The Employers having insisted upon a selling price of coal being fixed at a point to be considered equivalent to the 30 per cent minimum wages, and named 12s. 3d. per ton as the price referred to, the workmen's representatives after considerable discussion offered to accept 11s. 3d. per ton as an equivalent to the 30 per cent minimum. The Committee failing to agree upon this matter it has been decided to refer the fixing of the said price to an independent person who shall be asked to state whether it shall be 11s. 3d. per ton or 12s. 3d. per ton or any other figure not below 11s. 3d. per ton or 12s. 3d. per ton or any other figure not below 11s. 3d. per ton, nor above 12s. 3d. per ton.

6. With respect to the payment for small coal it is agreed that the present practice is to continue during the existence of this agreement.
7. The Employers having asked for an increase in the price paid by the workmen for coal supplied for domestic purpose, it has been agreed to refer the matter to a sub-committee of the Joint Board for investigation and report.
8. The drafting of rules for the Conciliation Board and the arrangement of other necessary clauses have been referred to a sub-committee of the Joint Board.
9. The Employers in accepting these terms of settlement make it an absolute condition that the agreement shall continue for 3 years.

Richard's letter continued:

"but having regard to the resolution of the annual Conference at Southport, we could not accept the condition of the Employers for a three years' agreement without consulting the Federation thereon, although it is generally considered by the Council that an agreement for a longer period than the end of this year will not be detrimental to the interests of the Members of our Federation." (*2.ii.1903*.)

The negotiations for a new Agreement "between Masters and Men" had been prolonged, intricate and difficult: only in the last week of January 1903, could the heads of an agreement (including outstanding points of disagreement) be drawn up. It was not until well on in February that the special national conference could be called to consider the proposed terms for setting up a Board of Conciliation in South Wales. Before this, however, the South Wales Miners' Federation had held their annual conference. At this the terms had been approved by a fifteen-to-one majority. This approval of terms, in advance of the M.F.G.B. deliberations, might be expected to become a bone of contention and to give rise to hard feelings. So it proved to be when the special conference "to consider the proposed terms upon which to establish a Board of Conciliation in the South Wales Coalfield" assembled in Westminster on February 20th: and this was made abundantly clear by the Chairman, as he opened the discussion. Ben Pickard was in a rage, and his language was the more bitter because it was an impotent rage, as he himself partly realised. "The result," he said, "has brought a foregone conclusion" and this was because the M.F.G.B. Southport resolution had been ignored. He said: "We have been brought face to face with the position which places us under three Wages Boards within the Federation." In Cardiff there had been 281 delegates and, "only about nineteen of these delegates, according to reports in the papers, had voted against it." It would be "manifestly unfair" for them "to interfere with that result." Then his rage boiled over as he said: "I do not want to say anything that will create offence or hurt anyone's feelings, but I have gone in for united action. I do not believe in isolated action. Every tendency in that direction means mischief for somebody."

Pickard ended by saying:

We did our best to let the South Wales men easily down, and put in the word "recommendation" at their suggestion. It was agreed upon, although there were some delegates who did not want to have it in. It was made manifest, however, by more than one Welsh delegate that it would be better to make a long agreement than a short one. Therefore there are some real reasons why the recommendation of the Southport conference has been defeated. (*20.ii.1903.*)

Pickard went on to hint at expulsion, a hint which expressed his anger and suspicion rather than his settled policy: "I only know I am a Federationist: I have preached the doctrine for years . . . Ask Mr. Harvey what he did, when Durham and Northumberland would not comply." Edmund Harvey, the polished orator from Derbyshire, at once said: "I moved a resolution for them to be expelled."

To all this William Abraham made a sufficiently temperate reply, saying: "I thought that as a branch of this Federation we have a right to be heard before we are condemned; and to be so severely condemned, this is going very far beyond reasonable endurance; but, of course, we will endure it." Then he told how they had gone before the employers and definitely stated "our firm request," that they should join in one board for the regulation of wages in the South Midlands and the North; but "to that the employers turned a deaf ear." But in consequence of the resolution of Southport "we went on for days trying to arrange a scheme that would end this year. Without going into details of all that was said, the employers offered us, to renew the old sliding scale to terminate at the end of the year; we refused." Other proposals to the same end were refused by the employers who again offered the sliding scale. "We again refused," said Mabon, "and without going into details of what was proposed, after nine days spent in trying to arrange a bargain which would allow us to terminate at the end of the year, we said to the employers that we were as anxious for peace as they were." Mabon then held up a document, a copy of the proposed terms, reached after three or four days "trying to come nearer together." "We came to let you know the truth," said Mabon, "and here we are telling it: and seeing we have failed in these two attempts with the employers, being anxious for peace, we asked what they were prepared to offer for a longer period." (*20.ii.1903.*)

This statement by the President of the South Wales Miners' Federation served to cool the heated atmosphere of the conference. Delegates asked questions; and it emerged that the South Wales Executive Council had recommended the acceptance of these terms to the Cardiff Conference, "subject to the approval of this Federation." In the afternoon J. G. Hancock of the Nottinghamshire Miners' Association moved disapproval of the proposed terms. He took particularly strong exception to the employers' insistence on a selling price of coal being fixed as equivalent to a minimum wage (at 30 per cent above the 1879 basis) as well as their naming a quite unacceptable figure for this fixed price. He said:

It is a remnant of the old sliding scale. I consider the time is opportune to try to get the whole Federation under one Wage Agreement: in advising our Welsh friends not to accept the proposals, we are prepared to share with them whatever responsibility there is and we will make common cause with them. (*20.ii.1903*.)

The interventions of Robert Smillie, president of the Scottish Miners' Federation, served to reheat the atmosphere. Seconding Hancock he said:

We have had professions of loyalty from South Wales for many years. I am not prepared to accept the statement that Wales has been loyal to this Federation, in view of what has taken place. We are told no agreement has been entered into.

But the Cardiff conference had decided on the advice of their Executive Council, by a large majority, with the full facts before them, to accept. With regard to a stoppage he was prepared to advise his men to make common cause with the Welsh men.

So the debate went on: Brace made a skilful enough reply in his usual eloquent manner: but it was Abraham who signalised the failure in leadership of these federal bodies (both the M.F.G.B. and also the S.W.M.F. leadership) when he said: "When the resolution was brought before the Committee, both myself and Mr. Brace were absent: and so we did not know anything about it, until we saw it on the minutes. It was distinctly placing us to fight this battle. We believe the time has not arrived for that action."

Tom Richards moved an amendment that the employers' terms be not rejected. Finally the following resolution was proposed:

That, after fully discussing the South Wales suggested Wages Scheme, this Conference stands adjourned *sine die*, until the South Wales Federation receive the final decision of the coal-owners; and before finally agreeing to the suggested scheme, the same be laid before the Federation of Great Britain; and that delegates come to the adjourned Conference to deal with the question as to whether the same be rejected or otherwise. (*20.ii.1903*.)

It was carried against the vote of the South Wales delegates.

7. THE ADJOURNED CONFERENCE

The Welsh delegates, with the M.F.G.B. Conference resolution in their baggage, returned home and three days later, on Monday, February 23rd, met the South Wales colliery owners to whom they explained their position. Again they pressed for an agreement terminable at the end of that same year 1903 so that they could fall in line with the Miners' Federation as a whole: and they gave their reasons for it. The owners retired. On re-assembly the owners flatly rejected any such proposal and told the miners' representatives "distinctly and definitely" that everything was bound up with it being an agreement for three years: it was that or nothing.

The two sides met again three days later and, after a discussion, the following resolution was adopted by the coal owners:

That, after having heard the explanations of the workmen's representatives as to their position, that, subject to their assurance, they will come either to a definite settlement, including the three years' agreement, or negotiations shall be broken off by March 24th next. (*26.ii.1903.*)

This was the situation in the coalfield that had to be considered at the adjourned national conference on the "South Wales Wages Dispute" opening twelve days later in the Westminster Palace Hotel. (*10.iii.1903.*) Thereafter the discussion turned partly on the question of whether the miners themselves in South Wales had had a sufficient opportunity of forming a judgment on the terms. Why had there not been a ballot vote? To this the answer was given that ballot votes had only been taken two or three times up till then in the whole history of the coalfield.

Pickard then made a lengthy speech. For well over an hour he traced the history of mining unionism and its ups and downs, setbacks and successes and particularly defections and schisms. In this way, in what was perhaps his longest speech, as it was certainly his last long address at a miners' conference, Pickard unfolded the epic of the trade unionism in which he had played no small part. It was, in a way, a defence of his own life-work. In it, mingled with the racy remarks and homely proverbs, there were some shrewd criticisms. William Brace, once the "blue-eyed boy," had fallen from grace in the eyes of Pickard; who said: "South Wales, as has been told here today, have come out of great tribulation and much suffering in order to belong to the Federation of Great Britain. Mr. Brace was the chief one to quote from Scripture, in describing their way from Egypt to the land of promise." Pickard continued:

In South Wales today, I am afraid, they are putting this Federation to a severe tension. They may not know it, at the same time it is a fact. In other cases where an outside association, once having joined, failed to keep a strict and close line on this wages question, they have generally left either by one process or another. The unity of this Federation has been its safeguard; Rule Twenty has been to every man a charter that created within him that sort of feeling that first made him believe in the ideal of the Federation. (*10.iii.1903.*)

Then, tapping his breast, Pickard said:

I want to tell some of you who do not know, when we have a big stoppage, this man goes without his wages; I want you to clearly under-stand I do not preach for the men to be idle and get something myself. I always put myself in their shoes and stand exactly in the same position, and my colleagues are the same. I know I should not starve, but that does not alter the position of helping the men in their distress, that is another matter. Now gentlemen, unity of the Federation is the main string, and if we cannot act unitedly we cannot act at all. (*10.iii.1903.*)

His aim was to persuade the twenty-eight delegates from South Wales not to accept the owners' proposal but, for the sake of the wider unity, to be prepared for a lockout—in which case, his final words made clear, the other districts would join hands with South Wales. Towards the end there was a characteristic passage in this speech of Pickard, who was even more adept than Brace in quoting Scripture for his purposes:

I say if you intend to keep your wages and defy the owners, you must be prepared to act in a body and not have to wait for a man here and another there, and asking one man to do this and another man to do that. We want to be like Gideon, who was the best General to take an army in the field I ever read of; he would rather have ten men who would fight than hundreds who would not. Such men as those won the battles. They were not amongst colliers, those Gideonites certainly not, but he was fighting for humanity, for families, for husbands, wives and children. Is not that what we are fighting for? If it is not then let us say "the good Lord deliver us," and say "Amen" (*10.iii.1903.*)

So after Robert Smillie had pledged support from the Scots in the event of a stoppage in South Wales, it was agreed "that the Con-ference stand adjourned until Friday morning, at 10.30 a.m."

When the conference met again the Chairman announced that he had "spent the whole afternoon the other day in trying to draft a resolution, and thinking about it." On Thursday evening the two representatives from South Wales had approved, after slight altera-tions, of Pickard's draft, on which he now hoped for unanimity. So, after very brief discussion (for the proposed wages agreement was nearly complete, apart from the duration of it) the following resolution was put by the Chairman:

That seeing the South Wales Conference of delegates have been unable to carry out the Southport Conference Resolution on the question of

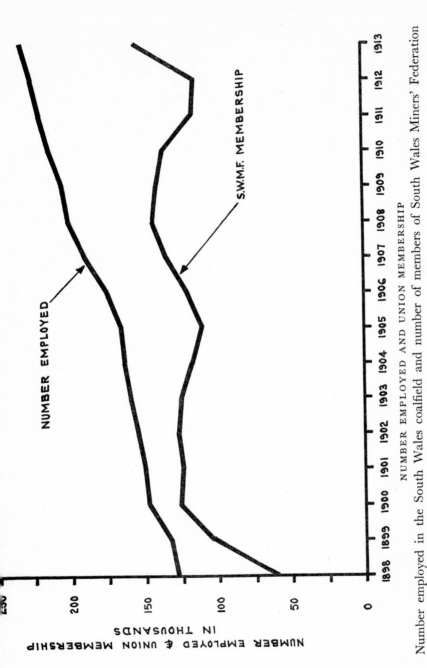

NUMBER EMPLOYED AND UNION MEMBERSHIP

Number employed in the South Wales coalfield and number of members of South Wales Miners' Federation from 1898 to 1913:

Notes

(i) The detailed figures of Federation membership are given in *The Miners* (Vol. I, Appendix *iv*).

(ii) The membership figure of associations of craftsmen and others are not shown above.

when agreements on the wage question shall commence, and when they shall terminate, this Conference cannot endorse the agreement entered into by the South Wales Miners' Conference, therefore leave the matter in the hands of the South Wales workers, and their authorised Committee, after which, at a future Conference of the Miners' Federation of Great Britain shall be called together by the President and Secretary to deal with the serious question involved therein. (*13.iii.1903.*)

It was carried unanimously by the seventy-seven delegates, who claimed to represent nearly half-a-million miners out of whom 338,304 were union members. Of these 100,000 or well over a quarter were in the South Wales Miners' Federation.

8. THE FIRST CONCILIATION BOARD

A little over two weeks later, on March 31, 1903, a memorandum of agreement between owners and men was signed, beginning as follows:

1. That a Board of Conciliation shall be established to determine the general rate of wages to be paid to the Workmen and to deal with disputes at the various Collieries of the Owners subject to the conditions hereinafter mentioned.

The remainder of the 17 clauses, plus the 9 "rules of procedure" (described by a critical Scot as "like an act of parliament") contained the following stipulations:

(*a*) A minimum wage of 30 per cent above the standard of 1879: and a maximum of 60 per cent.
(*b*) The "mineral to be gotten" and for which the cutting price was to be paid to the collier was to be "clean large coal only."
(*c*) An average nett selling price per ton to be fixed as equivalent to the 30 per cent minimum. This, named as 12s. 3d. by the owners and as 11s. 3d. by the workmen, was to be referred to an arbiter, called "an independent person."
(*d*) The price of house coal for the workmen which the employers wished to raise, was to be referred similarly.

The Agreement was to be in force until December 31, 1905, and its significance was made clear by the last clause which ran:

17. A Copy of this Agreement shall be placed in a Contract Book at each Colliery which shall be signed by or on behalf of the owners of such Colliery and also by each Workman employed thereat as one of the terms of engagement between the Owners and the said Workman.

It was clear that the demand for an equivalent to be established between the selling price of coal and the wages level was a remnant of the old sliding scale. Indeed a great deal of the wording of this prodigiously lengthy Agreement was the same as in the sliding scale

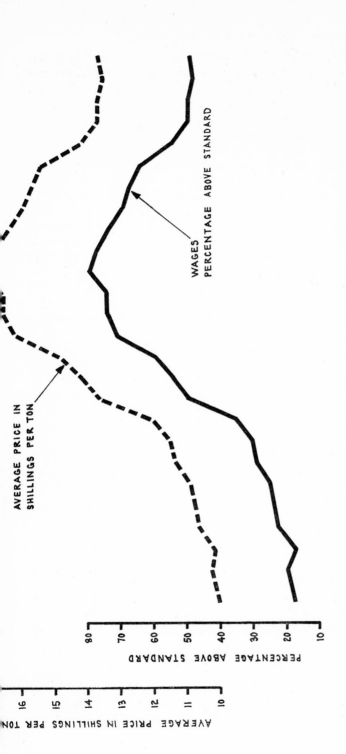

AVERAGE PRICE IN
SHILLINGS PER TON

WAGES
PERCENTAGE ABOVE STANDARD

PERCENTAGE ABOVE STANDARD

80
70
60
50
40
30
20
10

AVERAGE PRICE IN SHILLINGS PER TON

16
15
14
13
12
11
10

1898   1899   1900   1901   1902

THE SLIDING SCALE OF 1898

Notes

(i) Percentage variation in wages under the Sliding Scale automatically follows upon the two-monthly audits from October 31, 1898, to October 21, 1902.

(ii) Under the "Old Scale" of 1892, embodied in the Sliding Scale Agreement of 1898, the percentage of wages above the Standard of December 1879 is related to coal prices in such a way that wages varied (up or down) by 8¾ per cent for each shilling of rise or fall (or by 1¼ per cent for each price change of 1·71 pence) in the price per ton of coal f.o.b. at Bristol Channel ports.

(iii) The graph showing average price per ton is derived by calculation from the corresponding wage levels, using the basis of the 1892 scale.

(iv) The two-monthly audit is used throughout in the plotting of the co-ordinates.

agreements, which had suited most of the coal masters so well. Where it differed it appeared as though the owners had determined to make the workmen pay heavily for the change. For example, while under the old Sliding Scale Agreement a nett selling price per ton of 11s. 3.43d. yielded a wage equivalent of 30 per cent above the 1879 standard, the employers now wanted the figure to be set at 12s. 3d., being a price increase that upset the balance to the considerable disadvantage of the workmen. If the parties failed to reach agreement upon who should be the arbiter on the questions left over, then it ran in the agreement that the "independent person" should be nominated by the Lord Chief Justice of England or, "in case of his refusal," by the Speaker of the House of Commons. Eleven days after the signature of the agreement a gentleman from Durham was nominated. Three months later the award was given covering both the question of house coal and of the equivalent selling price. On the former the award was in favour of the *status quo*: there was to be no increase in the charge for house coal. On the latter the arbiter inclined towards the contention of the coal owners. It was fixed at 11s. 10d. a ton.

If the miners were aggrieved by the standard set for the average net selling price per ton ("taken as for large colliery-screened coal, delivered f.o.b. at Cardiff, Barry, Newport, Swansea and Llanelly"), they had no redress. They may have felt at the time (as some certainly did state it later) that this decision lessened their chance of catching up with the wage level of such coalfields as Yorkshire. But how could they cavil against the high authority who had nominated as "independent person" an associate of the millionaire firm of Pease and Partners,[1] Liberal coal owners on the North East Coast?

9. THEY CONFER AT BATH:
THE END OF PICKARD'S DREAM

At Bath where seventeen hundred years earlier the undying flame on the altar of Sul-Minerva was fed by the Romans with coal, the M.F.G.B. Special Conference met to discuss the "South Wales Wage Agreement" and, as the resolution of mid-March put it, "the serious question involved therein." In the Victoria Rooms that 11th day of June the attendance was small, so small that the contingent of twenty-six from South Wales with ten from the

---

[1] The Pease family furnished to the Liberal cabinet of December 1905 a Party Whip, J. Pease who for some years was thus "whipper-in" for Mabon, until the miners' vote ousted their president from the Liberal Party. Another member of the family became Lord Gainford who was to be vice-president of the Mining Association of Great Britain for several years.

neighbouring small coalfield of Bristol made up half the number of conferring delegates. The conference began inauspiciously: William Abraham absent, had sent "an anonymous card from South Wales" to Pickard, who had then to be placated by the Welsh delegates for what had seemed to him a deliberate affront. The chairman seemed in a wrathful mood that morning as was shown both by his opening remark: "The Annual General Meeting will be held bye and bye, and whoever lives to see it, then they will have to declare positively whether or not isolated action is to be the action of this Federation in the future," and by his frequent interjections and cross questioning of the South Wales delegates about the agreement they had signed. William Brace, in the regretted absence of Mabon, took up the task of explanation, which he performed with his usual lucidity. But unfortunately he began by saying something which invited interjection:

It is a Board of Conciliation, as you will see, on the same terms as the Miners' Federation of Great Britain.
The Chairman interjected, "No."
Replied William Brace, "We think so."
The Chairman said: "It is not like the scheme of the Miners' Federation of Great Britain."

The explanations given by Brace (and by Tom Richards in the afternoon session) covered a series of questions:

Loyalty to the M.F.G.B. Brace said: "The Agreement has been made on the distinct understanding and our men have been told as they entered into this Agreement, that they must understand, although this Agreement is for three years, if there is a conflict in any of the other counties on the wages question the Welsh workmen must be prepared to lay down their tools at one and the same time, and our men will be as loyal to that Federation as any other body of men.
We as Welshmen have as much dignity, honour, thankfulness and gratitude as anybody else in the Conference, and I hope you will make it possible for us to live in peace with you. We have come here after great struggling, and we recognise that what we have got, could not have been got were it not for the fact that we are a Branch of the Miners' Federation of Great Britain.

When Brace had resumed his seat, Pickard ended the session with a number of mordant questionings, beginning:

I should just like Mr. Brace to explain, if it is a Board of Conciliation, what is meant by Clause 7, the whole of it? If that is not a new Act of Parliament, determining the wages, what is it?

He ended somewhat ominously with these words:

If you consider all the concessions in the scheme, if the owners should not have agreed, they would be very unintelligent men. All I can say is, if we had had the owners' reasons why they have agreed to the scheme, we could have understood it better. But I am not going to try to invent any argument, it is there. I do not think I have much longer to deal with these matters, but it is the duty of the President to try to carry out the Rules and Resolutions of this Federation and which, as long as I have anything to do with it I shall do so. (*11.vii.1903.*)

So it went on during the afternoon and on the next day with explanations of all the difficulties encountered and of the exact significance of this or that clause in the agreement. Then came the point when W. E. Harvey of Derbyshire Miners' Association raised the question bluntly of the position of South Wales, and "the serious question involved in this Agreement that has now been ratified until 1905." The Federation had recommended certain things: those recommendations had not been carried out and therefore "the principle of the violation of the rules was involved." (*11.vi.1903.*)

This brought a revulsion of opinion on the next day. Pickard asked all to declare themselves, whereupon everyone spoke, in terms of the utmost amity, favouring unity with South Wales. Thereupon the Treasurer, Enoch Edwards, moved the following resolution which was carried unanimously:

> That this Conference of the Miners' Federation of Great Britain having heard the statements of South Wales in regard to their Wage Agreement, hereby agrees to adjourn any further consideration of the subject *sine die.* (*12.vi.1903.*)

In the weeks and months that followed there were repercussions. Up till that time the members of the M.F.G.B. Executive Committee as elected at the Annual Conference had formed the workmen's side of the Conciliation Board in the Federated Area of England. The Scots had thus been included, even after there was a separate Conciliation Board for the Scottish coal trade, terminable at three months' notice. As soon as the sliding scale agreement had been denounced in summer 1902, the two South Wales members of the Executive Committee had also sat upon this English Conciliation Board. But now Pickard and the others felt they must accept the new situation that had developed and draw the necessary conclusions. This was evidenced in the remarks on the South Wales agreement in the presidential address,[1] and also in the resolutions formulated by the Executive Committee and put to the 15th Annual Conference. There in the Windsor Hotel, Glasgow, on October 6 to 9, 1903, the decision was taken that Scotland and South Wales were henceforward excluded from the workmen's side of the board for the federated area. The details of this arrangement lie outside the scope of a history of the South Wales Miners' Federation: but the significance of these discussions were long to remain in the memory of all those concerned.

[1] See Appendix II.

4 RT. HON. WILLIAM BRACE, M.P.

RT. HON. TOM RICHARDS, M.P.

5 CYMMER COLLIERY, SOUTH VIEW, 1880

FERNDALE COLLIERY, RHONDDA, NOVEMBER 1871

Pickard, who clearly felt that the plans of a lifetime had been thwarted, did not live to see the effects. Before the first conference of 1904 he had passed away: and years were to elapse before there were successors able to match his calibre—or his personality.

10. THE BOARD IN OPERATION

The first conciliation board agreement was operative as from April 1, 1903. Under the rules of procedure the board had to meet once at least in each month for the purpose of dealing with difficulties or disputes arising at the several collieries. If either party desired to vary the general rate of wages, this could be considered only on four occasions in each year, namely on the 14th day of the months of February, May, August and November. But if at any such meeting the parties failed to agree then it was adjourned for a week to enable the "Chairman from Outside" to attend, and give his casting vote. Such a Chairman had still to be found. The Chairman chosen to decide for or against in case of deadlock was appointed in April 1903. The choice fell upon the Right Honourable Viscount Peel who had been Speaker of the House of Commons for ten years up to 1895, and who had retired from that office with a peerage and an annual pension of £12,000 (twelve thousand pounds sterling). This youngest son of the famous Sir Robert Peel was now in his seventy-eighth year. At the moment of his appointment the wage, as settled on December 1, 1902, after the last audit under the sliding scale, stood at $48\frac{3}{4}$ per cent above the 1879 standard in both steam and bituminous collieries and at $43\frac{3}{4}$ per cent in anthracite collieries.

By the end of that month the coal owners' auditor reported a fall in the selling price and on May 14th the owners applied for a reduction in wages. The workmen's side could not accept. On May 21, 1903, the owners' application for a reduction of 5 per cent was again considered with the chairman present at the Board. Viscount Peel refused.

Three weeks later William Brace explained why in his opinion the decision had gone against the owners:

Had we now been governed by the Sliding Scale, taking the average of the three months preceding our Agreement, the employers would have had a $6\frac{1}{4}$ per cent reduction, and taking the last month before this meeting, the selling price of coal has been reduced 9d. a ton, which would have given them a reduction of $7\frac{1}{2}$ per cent under the scale. The employers produced this as a reason for seeking a reduction in wages. On technical grounds, we objected to the audit, and we took the matter before the independent Chairman under this Agreement, we placed before him the volume of trade, and the increased value of small coal. The state of trade taking the previous months of this against last year shows we had an

D

increase of 140,000 tons in round figures. We therefore said to the employers, if they have increased the volume of trade 140,000 tons, and
reduced the selling price of coal because of unfair competition amongst
themselves, they have no right to come to this Board to ask the independent
Chairman to recoup them for their lost profit (due to reduction of prices
by competition amongst themselves) out of the workmen's wages, and we
contend the owners should not cut down the selling prices, and if they
do that they ought to be satisfied with increased volume of trade, and
not ask for a reduction. I am glad to say the independent Chairman
accepts our basis of argument and found that the owners had not made
out their case for a reduction in wages although the selling price has gone
down. (*11.vi.1903.*)

By end July prices per ton had fallen further, by a fraction of a
halfpenny. On August 21, 1903, the owners again applied, this time
for a reduction of 8¾ per cent. Viscount Peel refused. Three months
later an application was made by the owners for a reduction of 5
per cent. It was on November 5th that notices went out for a meeting
of the Conciliation Board on Saturday, November 14th. Mabon
had publicly advised the associated owners not to proceed with their
demand: and he found an ally in D. A. Thomas, M.P.; whose views
on the matter received fullest publicity.[1]

On November 21, 1903, Viscount Peel granted the application.
Wages, therefore, went down to 43¼ per cent above standard as
from December 1, 1903, with 5 per cent less in the case of anthracite
collieries.

In January 1904, Viscount Peel resigned the office of Chairman.
Both owners and workmen put pressure as far as they could upon
him: but Viscount Peel who had just another nine years to live could
not be induced to withdraw his resignation. He had had enough of
that occupation. The office of chairman remained vacant a good
many weeks. Meanwhile on February 15, 1904, there was a double
application. The owners applied for a reduction of 5 per cent, and
at the same time the workmen applied for an increase of 2½ per cent.
There was deadlock. In the absence of a Chairman the applications
of February both fell to the ground. The owners renewed their
application for a reduction of 5 per cent on May 14, 1904, at the
same time the workmen's representatives applied for an advance
of 3¾ per cent. The Conciliation Board meeting on May 14th, without
an independent chairman, decided to leave the wages as they were
for the summer months. This apparently amicable arrangement
completed the first twelvemonth of the Conciliation Board. Each
side had learned something, though most of the ground covered was
very familiar to those who had served for so many years on the
Sliding Scale Joint Committee.

[1] See Appendix III to this chapter.

EXCERPTS FROM THE RULES (1902)

The Union sought registration (under the Trade Union Acts of 1871 and 1876) from the Registry of Friendly Societies. This was given on April 20, 1899. Partial alteration of rules was certified on January 17, 1901; and again on September 5, 1902. The rules as printed in 1902 are divided into three sections and number 59 in all. The first section comprises 20 rules: the second section, headed *Districts and Lodges*, 13 rules; the third section, headed *General Management of Local Lodges*, 26 rules.

Name.

1.—The trade Union shall be called the "SOUTH WALES MINERS' FEDERATION." Its Registered Office shall be The Rise, Beaufort, in the County of Monmouth.

Constitution.

2.—This Federation shall be composed of persons employed in and about the collieries comprising the South Wales Coalfield.

3.—Its objects shall be:—

(i) To provide funds by entrance fees, contributions, levies, donations and fines to carry on the business of the Federation in the objects hereinafter specified, the same to be disbursed as provided in the following Rules.

(ii) To take into consideration the question of trade and wages, and to protect workmen generally, and regulate the relation between them and employers.

(iii) To seek to secure mining legislation affecting all workmen connected with this Federation.

(iv) To call conferences to deal with questions affecting the workmen of a trade wage and legislative character.

(v) To endeavour to secure by legislation the reduction of the hours of labour in mines to Eight Hours from Bank to Bank, and to oppose the system of Double Shift except where absolutely necessary for the purpose of ventilation.

(vi) To watch all inquests upon persons killed at the mines, when more than three persons are killed by one accident; and to seek to obtain compensation for all injuries caused by accident in and about mines.

(vii) To provide a weekly allowance for the support of members who may be victimised, locked out or on strike, and to resist any unjust regulation connected with their employment.

(viii) To prevent illegal stoppage of wages at the Pay Office.

(ix) To assist and to affiliate with kindred Associations that have the same objects as are hereinafter stated.

(x) To endeavour by all legitimate means to secure the abolition of sub-contracting in or about mines.

(xi) To provide funds for securing the carrying out of Rule 38, Coal Mines' Regulations Act, 1887, i.e. Inspection of Collieries by Workmen.

(xii) To provide funds wherewith to pay the expenses of returning and maintaining Representatives to Parliament and other Public Councils and Boards, and to request them to press forward by every legitimate means all proposals conducive to the general welfare of the members of the Federation.

District Liability

7.—Each District shall support 5 per cent of their members in cases of dispute or disputes, but exceeding that percentage in the aggregate the whole number affected shall be supported by the Central Fund, subject to the provisions of Rule 8 having been complied with.

8.—The Society will not undertake the responsibility of a strike of any dimensions whatever, nor will they provide or make any arrangements for the financial support of those who may be on strike, unless the matter in dispute has first been legitimately placed before the Executive Council or Conference, and thoroughly discussed upon just principles, exceptions to be made in cases of emergencies, such as the employers tendering notices, or violating any agreement.

Government and Election of Officers.

9.—The Society shall have a President, Vice-President, Treasurer, and Secretary, nominated by the Lodges and elected by the Conference, and an Executive Council, who shall be paid such salary as the Conference shall from time to time determine, and shall be elected as follows: Every District numbering 3,000 members will be entitled to one representative on the Council, and an additional representative for every additional 6,000 members. Small districts may amalgamate for the purpose of securing representation. Nominations for President, Vice-President, and Treasurer must be in the hands of the General Secretary 21 days before the date of the Annual Conference, and shall be printed upon the agenda sent to the Lodges.

Agents

30.—The Agent of each District shall be elected by a majority of the financial members of the District, ascertained by ballot. His duties shall be to attend all inquests in cases of fatal accidents, on being requested to do so by the District Secretary or the Lodge Secretary to which the deceased member belonged. He shall visit the Lodges and give advice, or addresses, on suitable occasions, gather all necessary information in cases of disputes, and try to settle the same in an amicable manner, and labour to promote the interest of the Federation generally. He shall also have power, in conjunction with the President and District Secretary, to call Special or District Committee Meetings. His wages shall be fixed by a majority of the delegates at the District Monthly Meeting, and be under their control during the time he is in their service. He shall give three months' notice and shall receive the same before leaving the service of the Federation. If any important matter arises in regard to the Agent, the same shall be referred to the Lodges, and the majority of the members of the Lodges shall decide the same by a numerative vote at the District Meeting.

33.—2d. to be retained at the Lodge to defray the Lodge expenses, such as rent of room, books, Officers' salaries, Committee's expenses, and

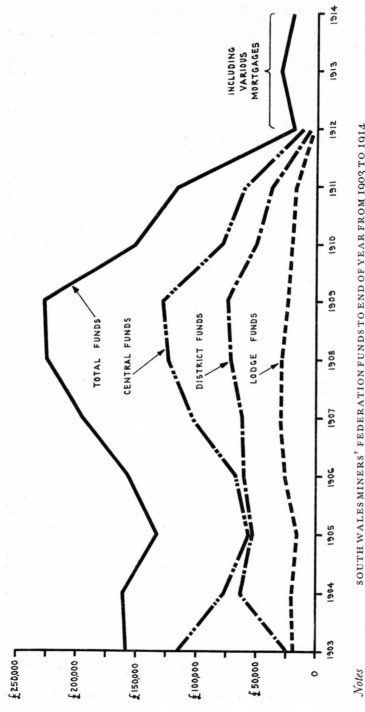

SOUTH WALES MINERS' FEDERATION FUNDS TO END OF YEAR FROM 1903 TO 1914

Notes

(i) The rise in the curve after 1912 is partly accounted for by inclusion of various mortgages.

(ii) The triple division of the funds, shown graphically above, reveals the federal structure of the trade union.

delegates' fees to District Monthly Meetings and General Federation Conferences.

39.—The Treasurer of each Lodge on his election shall sign a stamped agreement for the faithful fulfilment of his duties, the form of which will be supplied by the General Secretary, the amount of the bond to be decided by the District Secretary, in conjunction with the member of the Lodge; the President and Secretary binding themselves to prosecute the said Treasurer in case of the violation, infringing or misapplying any of the Funds to which he is entrusted belonging to this Federation. The stamping fee of 2s. 6d. must be paid by the Lodge.

Strike Pay.

46.—When the members of the Lodge have ceased work, the control and guidance of such Lodge shall be vested in the Federation. Any member or members locked out, or being on strike or victimised, and having complied with these Rules, shall receive a sum not exceeding ten shillings per week and one shilling per week for every child under twelve years of age.

The total set of rules ended with the following signatures:—

WILLIAM ABRAHAM	DAVID WATTS MORGAN
W. BRACE	ENOCH MORRELL
ALFRED ONIONS	W. E. MORGAN
BEN DAVIES	THOMAS RICHARDS.
Printed in 1902.	General Secretary.

APPENDIX II TO CHAPTER THREE

EXCERPT FROM PICKARD'S LAST ADDRESS

In his presidential address Pickard said:

For many years South Wales has been under a sliding scale. Their wages under that scale have been, as some think, regulated well; while others believe they were not regulated well. Everybody knows that advances and reductions under the Sliding Scale were as sure to follow on certain conditions as night follows day. A sliding scale was one of the buttresses of the Coalowners' great ideal of keeping men in subjection. It proved a great failure in many ways. Sliding scales do not prevent strikes or lockouts—in fact one of the biggest stoppages that ever took place in South Wales occurred under the sliding scale. So far as the effects of such stoppages are concerned, it is not my business just now to deal with them, although it may be said that that stoppage showed the daring, pluck, and courage of the South Wales Miners individually and collectively. In that regard no doubt South Wales showed great pertinacity and some skill in trying to find out what was and is good for themselves.

The sliding scale having now gone, the next question is—what has been put in its place? A new scheme was adopted, and a Board of Conciliation formed, with a wage arrangement and a maximum and a minimum. No-one 25 years ago, or indeed at a later date, would have anticipated that such a scheme could be arranged in South Wales. Everyone said there would never be a Board of Conciliation there—however, it is now an accomplished fact, and there is no doubt that the South Wales people are highly delighted with the achievement, because when all is said and done, to abolish the sliding scale and establish a new scheme in its place with a maximum and minimum wage, is one of the greatest events in the history of any Trades Union; and it is a fact that few Trades Unions have secured what is called a maximum and minimum wage rate. A great deal can be said on this matter, because the Federation itself, before securing a maximum and minimum rate under its scheme had a great battle to fight. The battle was won and eventually what is known as a living wage was secured. The existence of a minimum and a maximum principle holds up the fact that the living wage has been obtained. So far as the Federation is concerned, from the year 1893 the principles I have referred to were not merely secured then, but have been upheld and maintained ever since. Some other trades have followed in the wake of the Federation, and have obtained what they considered to be the maximum and minimum rate. Trades unionism is the only means by which such conditions have been secured. (Glasgow, *6.x.1903.*)

APPENDIX III TO CHAPTER THREE
COMMENTS by D. A. THOMAS, M.P.

The comments below were made in a speech at a political meeting, called by the Liberal Party and held in the Bedwas Bridge Schools on Wednesday, November 11, 1903. Colonel Ivor Herbert, C.B., C.M.G., the Liberal Candidate for South Monmouthshire attended together with D. A. Thomas, M.P., President of the South Monmouthshire Liberal Association. Lewis Miles, for many years Secretary to the Workmen's Side on the Sliding Scale Agreements, proposed a resolution "condemning the present Government for its attack upon Free Trade and for its criminal blundering in the conduct of the war, regretting its failure to amend the judge-made law relating to trade disputes, and urging the necessity of a national system of education based on popular control and freed from religious tests." (*Western Mail, 13.ix.1903.*)

D. A. Thomas referred to the wages question and said that the representatives of the employers and workmen would meet at Cardiff on Saturday, November 14th, to consider the application of the former for a general reduction of 5 per cent on the standard rate of wages: "I feel very strongly that, even if the employers can make out a case for such a reduction, it is a tactical error on their part to put in an application at this particular juncture, when autumn contracts are being arranged, and I sincerely trust that on Saturday they will see their way to follow Mabon's advice and withdraw it."

"Unfortunately, the commercial element is not very strongly represented on the Conciliation Board. That has always been the weakness of the Board, and the influence of the employers' representatives is too entirely directed towards reducing wages and the cost of production and not enough towards obtaining remunerative prices. It is of little use securing a reduction of 5 per cent in wages if it is promptly to be followed by a drop of 9d. or a 1s. in the selling price. A reduction in wages just now will be regarded by buyers as an indication of weakness in the market, and I have little doubt but that any such reduction will be at once given away by the sales agents."

Later he said: "One good result of the new agreement has been the excellent effect it has had on the speculative tendencies of the middleman. It has, as was anticipated, undoubtedly thus far had a most steadying influence on the market. I believe the agreement is a good one for the District, a good one for the men, and, in the long run, will prove beneficial to the employers and the trade generally."

"My strong advice to the workmen is to do everything in their power, by regular work and the avoidance of trivial disputes and unreasonable stoppages, to show how advantageous the agreement is to the employers as well as to themselves and how vastly superior for the coal trade as a whole to the old sliding scale."

CHAPTER FOUR

COAL TAX AND CONCILIATION
BOARD

1. PARLIAMENTARY REPRESENTATION

Of all "the labouring classes" within the population of Great
Britain in the nineteenth century, colliers were the first to be
represented in parliament. It was in 1874 that Alexander McDonald
and Tom Burt were elected. By 1886 there were five mining
members of parliament, two from Northumberland, one from
Durham, one from Yorkshire, and one, William Abraham, from the
Rhondda in Glamorgan. So it remained after successive general
elections, until the end of the century.[1]

The formation in February 1900 of the Labour Representation
Committee made up of a small number of trade unions together with
the three existing socialist organisations, had aroused great expectations in some quarters. But hopes of immediate sweeping successes
were quenched some months later when out of fifteen candidates put
forward at the general election of October, 1900, only two gained
parliamentary seats. One of these was in South Wales, where the
former secretary of the Ayrshire Miners' Union, James Keir Hardie,
secured election at the double-barrelled constituency of Merthyr
Tydfil.

The miners' leaders in England and Wales had taken no part in
these candidatures, nor had they shared in these expectations. A
resolution at the Saltburn M.F.G.B. annual conference in October
1900, resulted in the setting up of an electoral fund, for miners only,
by a levy of one shilling a year: and the rules for this fund, confirmed in 1902, laid it down that no alteration was to be made until
after the next general election. The allegiance of Mabon was to the
Liberal Party; which held most of the Welsh parliamentary seats.
In West Monmouth, however, the Member of Parliament was Sir
William George Granville Venables Vernon Harcourt (1827–1904).
He had been a staunch lieutenant of the Liberal leader W. E.
Gladstone, on whose retiral in 1894 he was due to become Prime
Minister. But the inclinations of Queen Victoria were in another
direction: and she chose of her own proper motion the Earl of
Rosebery. Harcourt, after the Tories came to power in 1895,

[1] For details, see *The Miners*, Chapters IX and X.

D*

continued to lead the Opposition in the House of Commons until December 1898. As Chancellor of the Exchequer in the Liberal administration of 1892 to 1895, it fell to his lot to introduce the Death Duties which, it is claimed, brought low so many landed families and compelled them to sell out their estates to the newer rich of the early twentieth century. Harcourt was a type of late nineteenth-century Whig, who carried Whiggism as far as it could go to the left: and even supported the non-conformists in their demand for disestablishment of the Church of England in Wales.

This old Squire of Malwood was on good terms with his trade union supporters. Early in 1904 Harcourt let his mining constituents know of his impending retiral with the result that a leaflet was issued, "To the Trade Unionists and Co-operators Resident in 'The West Monmouth Parliamentary Division'." It was signed by William Brace of Abertillery, Alfred Onions of Tredegar, Evan Thomas of Rhymney, William Vyce of Ebbw Vale, and James Manning of Blaina. Headed "Retirement of Sir W. V. Harcourt" it stated that the Annual Conference of the South Wales Miners' Federation had instructed their Executive Council to take the necessary steps for selection of a candidate "under the M.F.G.B. Parliamentary Labour Representation Scheme," and a conference at Tredegar in the Temperance Hall selected Tom Richards. In the subsequent by-election in November 1904, he was duly elected.

Meantime additional candidates were sought and seats were earmarked, for William Brace in East Glamorgan and John Williams at Gower. Like Burt and Pickard, like Abraham and Richards, they would be designated as Liberals in the House of Commons, where they would accept the Liberal Whip: while they spoke of themselves as Labour representatives of the miners' unions. In the socialist weeklies the habit grew up of referring to them curtly as "Lib-Labs"; but they themselves never adopted this and indeed objected strongly to this abbreviation which suggested some sort of political poultice. When Pickard (in his written address to the Birmingham 1901 M.F.G.B. annual conference) declared that he had not altered in his scepticism about the new Labour Representation Committee, he added simply: "I am yet a Liberal Labour member."

2. THE COAL TAX

The Boer War of 1899 to 1902 was costly beyond expectation and soon began to make a heavy impact on the national finances. This the Marquess of Salisbury's administration met not only by the usual recourse to loans, but also by raising tax levels (income tax went up year by year from a standard rate of eightpence in the pound sterling in 1900 to one shilling in 1901 and to 1s. 2d. in 1902) and by a number of new imposts. Amongst these was the device, almost without precedent, of an export tax on coal. This proposal, put forward as part of the annual budget in the House of Commons on April 18, 1901, caused the immediate summons of a Miners' National Conference from all districts in England, Scotland and Wales. The eighty-nine delegates who assembled at the Westminster Palace Hotel listened to the tale of the chief exporting districts: in one year South Wales had exported eighteen million tons of coal, Northumberland eight million, Durham six, while two-thirds of the coal raised in Fife went for export. They resolved:

That this meeting, representing the whole of the mining districts of the nation, hereby enters its protest against the imposition of an export tax upon coal, as, in our opinion, it is economically unsound and highly dangerous to our position as wage-earners. That the Government ought to reconsider their position, and withdraw the tax; and that we seek an interview with the Chancellor of the Exchequer, in order that we may place our views before him. (*25.iv.1901.*)

Tom Burt, M.P., who had been Parliamentary Secretary to the Board of Trade in the last Liberal administration, enlisted the help of his old House-of-Commons chief, Sir William Harcourt, to get the Chancellor to agree to meet a miners' deputation. The delegates charged the Members of Parliament present (Messrs. Burt, Pickard, Abraham, Wilson and Fenwick) to make the necessary arrangements for a meeting on the morrow with the Chancellor. This was Sir Michael Hicks-Beach (1837–1916), "Black Michael" as he was called and reputed to be of a tough character. A deputation to him at the Treasury from the liquor trade (always a prop of the Tory Party) were not only refused their object but so berated by "Black Michael" that one of the brewers dissolved into tears.

It was to this formidable personage that Pickard introduced a deputation on April 29, 1901. It was an exceptionally numerous deputation, consisting of 89 delegates, and very vocal with six speakers. On this occasion, however, there was no disturbance, and the Chancellor of the Exchequer blandly explained to them that the tax would be paid by the foreigner and no portion of it would be paid by those inside the island.

This explanation did not entirely reassure the delegates who met again the next week and agreed on a motion from Northumberland, seconded by Alfred Onions of South Wales, that "those districts that have not considered the question of laying the pits idle immediately do so by calling Council meetings during this week, and that a Conference be held next Tuesday to finally decide what shall be done." (Wednesday, May 1, 1901.) In this unanimous resolution it was also recommended "that all miners leave off work unless the tax upon exported coal is withdrawn." Within a week, however, a cooling-off process had set in. The House of Commons in the meantime had decided by 333 votes to 227 "that there shall be charged on and after the 10th day of April, 1901, the following customs export duty on coal, 1s. 0d. per ton." (*6.v.1901.*) So, when the delegates came together again, it was found that in the majority of districts the miners were against a stoppage. Only Bristol supported the four chief exporting districts. Nevertheless, Northumberland seconded by Durham moved, in the belief "that the passing of the Coal Tax will be ruinous to our industry," that the Conference should "advise all our fellow-workmen to cease work at once until this iniquitous tax is withdrawn." (*7.v.1901.*) Discussion went on for a couple of days. The Yorkshire men reported that "the newspapers had been pointing out that the men were fighting the employers' battle," and the effect this had caused in their coalfield. Eventually an amendment by Robert Smillie, seconded by W. E. Harvey of Derbyshire, was carried by 451 to 219. Put as a substantive motion and carried unanimously, this ran as follows:

The miners, having been told by the Chancellor of the Exchequer that the export tax on coal will be paid by the foreign consumer, and that there are no reasons why it should affect the workmen's wages, and believing this to have been largely the reason why the House of Commons went so strongly in favour of the tax, this conference does not see its way clear to recommend a general stoppage at this juncture. But we recommend that if any mining districts are asked to submit to a reduction of wages consequent upon the tax, a general conference be called to consider and determine whether the whole of the mines of the country shall be laid idle until such intimated reduction is withdrawn.

Notwithstanding we still strongly condemn this tax, and believe it will be used by the owners to bring about a reduction in the wages of the miners.

We also emphatically repudiate the statement made that the miners and owners are acting in collusion to bring about a general stoppage of the collieries as being malicious and untrue. (*8.v.1901.*)

It was also decided that if any district were to be asked for a reduction in wages, consequent on the coal tax, then "such district must communicate with the president and secretary, Messrs. Pickard and Ashton, to call a national conference to consider the matter."

What had induced the Salisbury administration to bring in a tax of this kind? All the traditional fiscal arguments seemed to be against it. The main reason for the tax seems to have been that more revenue was needed: and this impost brought in quite a handsome sum and was easy to assess and collect. Another reason was alarm felt by those in high places regarding the approaching exhaustion of

Britain's coal supply, which would become perceptible within another hundred years. A Royal Commission on Coal Supplies was set up, in December 1901. Pickard was asked to collaborate but declined. He was sceptical of the jeremiads and indicated his belief that it was all a "mere blind," to find arguments for continuing the tax. In this he was not followed by Ralph Young or William Brace, who both found it possible to sit on this new Royal Commission, which in the end reached estimates of supplies not very different from the figures given by their predecessors thirty years earlier.

3. CAMPAIGN CONTINUES AGAINST COAL TAX

Meantime the miners continued to press for the removal of the tax. William Abraham, M.P., presided at a three-day Miners' National Conference with a total of 117 delegates, more than half of them from the four main exporting districts. Amongst the speakers John Williams, agent for Neath, said that the whole of South Wales was "suffering from this iniquitous impost" and that the Conference should appoint "a strong deputation to wait upon the Chancellor to point out to him the advisability of abolishing the tax." (*18.ii.1903.*) Robert Smillie reminded the delegates that the tax was "popular with the general public, owing to the coalowners making such large profits. The public believes it is coming out of the pockets of the owners, but this is not so, as the tax has been paid to a great extent from the wages of the miners." The five mining Members of Parliament made arrangements for a meeting on the third day of delegates with the Chancellor of the Exchequer who was now C. T. Ritchie.

As we have seen, it was part of the regular functioning of governments in those days and particularly of the Treasury that a considerable amount of time, both of ministers and of the higher civil servants, should be devoted to meetings with the representatives of various important interests at the appropriate season of the year. For over a generation the miners' associations had been acknowledged as one of the bodies that might reasonably claim to be heard on behalf of their members. Meetings of this kind, being in the main public and indeed frequently reported in full, were not open to the sort of objection that could in a later generation be raised in parliaments that were jealous of any outside body that might infringe their privileges or suspicious of unreported backstairs influence. After half-a-dozen speeches, including one from Alfred Onions, who pointed to the reduction in wages in South Wales of 30 per cent, the Chancellor of the Exchequer, having first said that the customs export duty had not been put on simply as a war tax, replied in immense detail and at great length produced counter-figures to these adduced by the miners. On exports and weekly wages, on number of days worked and the percentage changes he got very different results, mostly through choosing a different base year or other standard for the purpose of drawing comparison. He was able to prove to himself, if not to his hearers, that coal exports were up, that wages had increased and percentages also. For example, he said that wages of all classes employed in coal mines in South Wales and Monmouthshire in 1899 were 24s. 8d., and in 1902, 28s. 2d.: that in the same district the wages of hewers in 1897 were $11\frac{1}{4}$ per cent above the standard and in 1902 were $48\frac{3}{4}$ per cent above. He ended with the words:

I think if you take the trade as a whole it is difficult for you to establish any good ground for complaint. (*20.ii.1903.*)

With thanks from John Wilson, M.P., for the "kind and courteous statement" the deputation departed. They had got nothing.

Told of this by the returning deputation, the national conference decided to adjourn and in the meantime to have the miners "balloted throughout the whole of the country in protest against the tax." (*20.ii.1903.*) Reassembled two months later, the conference heard reports from districts of meetings held and resolutions passed. What further steps could the conference, now depleted to seventy-six delegates, take to further its aims? The decision was "That the delegates present lobby members today and tomorrow on the question of the Coal Tax" and that amendments to the tax clauses of the budget be left in the hands of "the miners' representatives in the House of Commons." (*22.iv.1903.*) When the conference, with twenty fewer delegates than before, resumed on Tuesday, June 23rd, W. Abraham, M.P., still in the chair, began rather dispiritedly by giving his opinion that "the feeling against the Coal Tax appears to be waning, if this conference is any index," and though John Wilson, M.P. for Durham stoutly maintained this was not the case, an attendance of only seven of the usual sixteen districts was ominous. The next day, when the 56 delegates (42 of them from the exporting districts) came together again after the hours spent in the House of Commons lobby, they learned that their efforts had not secured victory over the tax and that their motion had been defeated by a large majority: whereupon after "an exhaustive discussion," doggedly they decided to do all in their power to secure withdrawal of the tax, as follows:

That this conference is still convinced that the coal industry generally, and the exporting districts in particular, is injured by the impost of the Coal Tax, and pledges itself to do all in its power to secure its withdrawal.

That in the meantime, in districts represented by members favourable to the tax, all possible means be used to induce them to alter their attitude. That a conference be called at a date immediately before the introduction of the Budget next year, the date of such conference to be left with the Labour Members. (*24.vi.1903.*)

Nine months later a national conference of miners' representatives met to consider the Coal Tax, and also other questions: "Employment of Chinese Labour in the Transvaal," and "Trade Disputes Bill." Political storm clouds were gathering. Charles Fenwick, M.P., reported that the new Chancellor of the Exchequer, Austen Chamberlain, had declined to receive a miners' deputation, saying that until the Royal Commission on Coal Supplies had reported he could not add anything to what had been said by his predecessors. The Conference protested both against the Coal Tax and against the Chancellor's refusal to discuss it and then plunged on the second day into a full discussion of the new system in the gold mines in the annexed territory of the Transvaal, by which "indentured labour" was imported from China and kept in "compounds" on the Witwatersrand. The indignation that this aroused (it was just 41 years after President Abraham Lincoln's proclamation to emancipate the slaves—to which speakers referred) is indicated in the terms of the resolution which was passed unanimously:

That this National Conference of miners strongly protests against the introduction of Chinese labour into South Africa, as we consider that it is a system of slavery, and purely for the benefit of the mine-owners, and against the interests of the working men; and we strongly protest against the action of the Government in allowing and approving of this abominable system of slavery coming into existence. (*11.iii.1904.*)

Within a fortnight of this conference Austen Chamberlain had second thoughts. A further national conference, assembled on April 11th, received an invitation to accompany a deputation of coal-owners, coal exporters, and shipowners whom Austen Chamberlain was now about to receive. The conference agreed and appointed fifteen delegates to meet the various owners in joint conference that evening and to go with them next day to meet the Chancellor when the miners' case would be put by William Straker (Northumberland), John Weir (Fife), and Alfred Onions (South Wales) with commendable brevity. To them and to the more voluble Clifford Cory and other owners' representatives the Chancellor replied at great length. The upshot may be seen from the resolution passed the next evening by the miners' conference:

That we desire to express our thorough dissatisfaction at the reply and especially at the unsympathetic tone of the Chancellor of the Exchequer to the deputation today, and that we continue our protest against the Coal Tax until it is repealed. (*12.iv.1904.*)

A year later the Chancellor of the Exchequer made no bones about it, when approached by William Abraham, M.P. and Charles Fenwick, M.P.; but was willing to meet delegates from the Miners' National Conference in February 1905. It was, as it turned out, an exceptionally large conference, attended by 107 delegates, all of whom formed the deputation and nearly filled the great room at the Treasury building on Whitehall. There they found Austen Chamberlain flanked by his parliamentary subordinates and by the officials of the Treasury. This time his reply was much more brief yet perhaps more sympathetic in tone; "but," he said, "the fact of your coming before the Budget statement makes it impossible that I should give you or a similar deputation the kind of answer that I might give at or after the Budget statement in the House of Commons." (*17.ii.1905.*) The miners then took the hint, if hint it was, and submitted amendment after amendment in the House of Commons debates on the Finance Bill throughout that summer of 1905. They got assistance from the Liberal leaders. One hot night in July, when Prime Minister Balfour—his administration was by this time on its last legs—had insisted on an all-night sitting, Winston Spencer Churchill, by this time a Liberal and ready to burn what he had once adored, launched a personal attack. "The Prime Minister," he said, "had shown himself unreasonable and even harsh in his leadership of the House and in the conduct of public business by refusing to pay the slightest attention to the weighty appeals which had been addressed to him by representatives of the great industry affected by the Coal Tax . . ." This led to a counter-attack from a Conservative Member who suggested that Winston Churchill was suffering from beri-beri, a disease whose "most marked and characteristic symptom" was "a terrific swelling of the head." And so it went on all that night. After the House had been in continuous session for nineteen hours Sir Edward Grey moved once more to report progress. But A. J. Balfour remained unmoved; and finally after several hours more of further debate the Coal Tax passed unaltered through the Committee stage.

For the Conservatives it was a Pyrrhic victory. The series of debates and especially the all-night sitting had brought home to the public how great was the objection to this particular tax, "which," said Keir Hardie in the House, "was wrong in principle and vicious in incidence. The export trade had only been maintained by the wages of the miners being reduced to the extent of the burden of the tax."

A few months later A. J. Balfour resigned; and on December 5,

1905, the Liberal leader, Sir Henry Campbell Bannerman, undertook to form a new administration. The new Chancellor of the Exchequer, H. H. Asquith, approached by a mass deputation consisting of the whole of the conference delegates (105, including the officials) could only reply as to his intentions in the same stereotyped terms as had been uttered by Austen Chamberlain the previous year. But unlike his predecessors he went on to say that he was anxious "to remove what I believe to be a grievous and unnecessary burden upon one of the greatest industries of the country." The miners had won their point, this time after five years of agitation. The Coal Tax was removed as from November 1, 1906.[1]

4. A NEW CHAIRMAN: AND A NEW BOARD

After the resignation of Lord Peel from the chairmanship of the Conciliation Board there was no agreement reached on a successor, so that the Lord Chief Justice of England had to nominate. His choice on April 30, 1904, had fallen on Sir Michael Hicks-Beach, inventor of the coal tax, who had resigned from the Tory Cabinet on the issue of Free Trade. When the Balfour administration was about to give up the ghost it put forward for a peerage Sir Michael Hicks-Beach who in December 1905, was created Lord St. Aldwyn.

The Conciliation Board at the beginning of June, 1904, received a letter from the new Chairman, who suggested that for the future joint audits should be made of the owners' books by accountants acting on behalf of both owners and workmen. These joint audits would include the following matters: (a) Price realised for Large Coal. (b) Price realised for Small Coal. (c) Increased cost of production (apart from wages to workmen), in rates and taxes, stores, horsekeep, pitwood, boiler coal, and general charges. (d) Increased volume of trade. (e) Percentage of Large and Small Coal in the total product. These proposals suggest that the new Chairman was keenly aware of various developments on other Boards of Conciliation.

[1] Net amount of Coal Tax paid (together with annual United Kingdom revenue) and tonnage represented.

Year	Bristol Channel Ports (£,000)	United Kingdom (£,000)	Total National Revenue (£,000,000)	Bristol Channel Ports (million tons)	United Kingdom coal exports (million tons)
1900	—	—	140	—	—
1901	478	977	153	9	19
1902	822	1,856	161	16	37
1903	893	2,055	151	18	41
1904	876	2,043	153	17	41
1905	863	2,104	154	17	42
*1906	869	2,052	155	17	41

* The figure for 1906 covers ten months only.

When the Board held a meeting in July with Lord St. Aldwyn to consider his proposals, no decision was come to.

Months passed by. Then in mid-November, 1904, the owners applied for a reduction of 5 per cent. There was no agreement. On November 21st, after hearing both sides, Lord St. Aldwyn gave his decision in favour of the employers. The wages were brought down by 5 per cent to 38¾ above standard for steam and bituminous collieries and 33¾ per cent for anthracite collieries. This was to date from December 1, 1904.

The price of Large Coal fell within twelve months from 13s. per ton to 11s. 6d., from summer 1904 to summer 1905. The employers again asked for a reduction in February 1905 of 3¾ per cent: the workmen would not agree; and on appeal Lord St. Aldwyn supported the workmen.

The employers applied for a reduction of 7½ per cent on May 4, 1905: ten days later on May 15th the workmen offered to accept a reduction of 5 per cent: and on this agreement was reached.

The owners at the end of July applied for the reduction of 3¾ per cent: the Board failed to agree: Lord St. Aldwyn on August 18th decided in favour of the owners. His decision brought the wage rate down to the minimum of 30 per cent above the standard as from September 1, 1905. It remained at that rate for another nine months, until May 31, 1906.

In the meantime, during the winter of 1905, the two sides of the Conciliation Board began negotiating a new Wage Agreement. In meetings on November 4th and throughout that month until the second week of December they at length reduced their respective demands to reach a new wage agreement to come into force on January 1, 1906, and to last thereafter for four years until December 31, 1909. This new agreement signed on December 11, 1905, contained little that was new, and indeed apart from registering that the miners should have twelve days' holiday each year, it may be regarded as a simple extension of the 1903 agreement.

The interest in it lies almost entirely in the matter of its duration and the effect this might have on other coalfields. On this already in the Victoria Station Hotel of Nottingham at the end of November, the M.F.G.B. Committee (with four out of fifteen representing South Wales) had set out its standpoint in the following resolution:

That in the opinion of this Committee, the South Wales new agreement should not extend beyond the end of next year, and we strongly recommend the South Wales miners' representatives to enter into a wages agreement for twelve months only. (*24.xi.1905.*)

At the same time they decided that a new Special Conference

should meet "to consider the South Wales new agreement." When this met in the Midland Hotel in Birmingham on Thursday, December 14, 1905, the chairman reminded the 58 delegates that three years earlier they had unanimously expressed the desirability that all agreements should end "at one and the same time": and secondly they were not only for a minimum wage ("the living wage") but that all "should do their best to raise that minimum wage." The delegates then heard from Alfred Onions that, in pursuance of "the ideals we have in this Federation," namely a higher minimum wage and simultaneous termination of all agreements, the S.W.M.F. Executive Council had been seeking the following alterations:

1. To raise the minimum from 30 per cent to 35 per cent on the 1879 standard.
2. To make this 35 per cent correspond to the equivalent selling price, and so in this way raise the general wage rate.
3. To abolish the maximum of 60 per cent.
4. To have weekly pays, now received by one tenth only of the miners, extended to be uniform throughout the coalfield.
5. To get payment for Small Coal.[1]
6. To have power to call in an Umpire when the Board representatives fail to settle local disputes.
7. To have the night-shift bonus turn (a weekly six turns for five) attached to each night.

This last was explained as follows:

Then again, we have in South Wales at most of the collieries, the night men. There are six turns for working five nights, and so if they lose one of the five nights they are only paid four turns, so that you will see it is very important, especially during slack times, if the night men lose a turn or lose a night, it means the loss of two turns. We seek to get that extra or bonus turn attached to each night by increasing the standard wages of the night men by one-fifth, so that every night will stand by itself. (*14.xii.1905.*)

Finally, the South Wales Miners' Federation sought an agreement for just twelve months, to end in December 1906, simultaneously with the ending of the agreement in the English Federated Area.

The coalowners, too, had many demands to make. In their proposals they sought (1) to reduce the minimum from 30 per cent to 20 per cent on the 1879 standard; (2) to raise the selling price per ton equivalent to 30 per cent from 11s. 10d. to 12s. 6d. and in this way to reduce wages; (3) to make the equivalent selling price per ton the only factor in determining the wage rate below a certain level; (4) to increase the price of workmen's house coal by 5 per cent. (5) a five-year agreement with six months' notice of termination.

[1] "We are asking for 6d. a ton in all small taken by what is known as *Billy Fairplay*." (Thursday, December 14, 1905.)

Alfred Onions explaining why they did not bring the provisional agreement to a conference, such as this before signing it, said:

There were men on the coalowners' side in South Wales seeking to bring about a rupture, and resorting to various methods in order to accomplish their end, and some of us know that had we not signed the agreement late on the Saturday night, a week last Saturday night, had we left it over, the probability was that the employers' representatives would have had tremendous pressure brought to bear upon us to go from the agreement we were then prepared to enter into. (*14.xii.1905.*)

The Chairman at the Birmingham conference, Enoch Edwards, then said that he thought there was one question that they must emphasise and that was, why the agreement was signed for four years? He referred to the "strong recommendation" of the national committee at its last meeting three weeks earlier and asked the Welsh treasurer "Tell us why it was made for four years." To this Alfred Onions replied: "It was really a question of bargaining and making the best agreement we could, accepting, as we believed, the lesser of two evils: that, I think, is the chief reason why we ultimately agreed to four years." (*14.xii.1905.*)

Thereafter questions and discussion began, with much forthright comment from the other coalfield associations. After the several questions had been asked and replies given thereto by William Brace and by Tom Richards, M.P., the full debate was opened by W. E. Harvey of Derbyshire who said:

Why this conference has been called I am at a loss to know. The agreement is settled, and whatever we say today will not alter it. The agreement was agreed to and signed and in the agreement there are vital principles at stake, very vital indeed. The other two sections here this day, are working with a 35 per cent and $37\frac{1}{2}$ per cent minimum, and to accept 30 per cent without the consent of this conference, in my opinion, is a violation. I say this courteously and with all respect. It is a violation of what I understand should exist in this Federation. (*14.xii.1905.*)

Robert Smillie, president of the Scottish Miners' Federation, followed with a most searching criticism on point after point in the new agreement, while on the vexed question of its duration he took the opportunity to set forth what he believed should be the aim and the strategy of a united miners' organisation. Compared with the suave language and moderate tone of Enoch Edwards it may have appeared to many delegates that the mantle of Pickard had fallen upon Scottish shoulders: but in their minds there must have remained the question how far the Welsh leaders represented fully and fairly the views of their members, and how far this was also the case with Smillie and the Scots colliers.

The debate in the afternoon opened with William Abraham,

M.P., president of the South Wales Miners' Federation in his best placatory manner saying "Notwithstanding the severe criticisms that were passed upon the South Wales delegates this morning, we still feel that you are our brethren." He then told the delegates:

You do not seem to appreciate the real enmity and antagonism of a portion of the Welsh owners to the Federation at all. You will remember the strong man amongst the owners (Sir W. T. Lewis), who will have nothing to do with our agreement and is not represented on our Board. There are a number of men inside who represent this man's views, and it is those inside who have been referred to as desirous of creating a rupture. Although we have been placed in a humiliating position, you might as well have the truth.

During the Friday morning (December 8th) we signed a provisional arrangement, and we passed a resolution that we would report to the Federation. But after a certain time, certain facts came to our knowledge— not from the employers only—that there were those enemies outside watching an opportunity of pressing their friends inside to create that opportunity.

Do you know of a case like this anywhere where a body of employers who personally are favourable to regulating wages by agreement, go and meet on a Sunday morning to try and devise means to prevent that agreement being carried out?

Had we not known about that happening on the Saturday, the probabilities are we would have come away without signing a provisional agreement. Let me tell you from the bottom of my heart, if we had come from there on Saturday without placing the initials of the Chairman of each side to that provisional agreement (because the clauses were to be re-worded and arranged) and with that body of men meeting on a Sunday, without that agreement signed at once, we would have been here today without an agreement.

It has been said this is impossible. It is not impossible, and I hope you will give us the credit of knowing our owners a little better than anybody else. We would then have had to fight against a minimum of 20 per cent if we had not signed the agreement. Now you know all.

Now I wish to say that we admit to the world that had we not been in this Federation, we would never have got this 30 per cent minimum.

Mabon ended with the fervent wish for a decision that would not reflect adversely on either standpoint saying: "All I can say before God and man, we have done all we could to save us from a great strike."

After this, though a number of other speeches were made, and the questions at issue continued to be hotly debated, the interest now lay in what reply would be given in the closing speech of Chairman Enoch Edwards.

"Whether we like it or not," said Enoch "whether we were inclined to blame Wales or not, the fact that an agreement had been made with a 30 per cent minimum is not a good omen for the Federation. I say that without reflecting at all upon South Wales. I believe they have done their best."

Finally, Enoch Edwards came to the question, what kind of resolution should be passed. Ultimately the following resolution was carried unanimously but was not given to the press:

That having heard the report of the South Wales delegates as to the signing of their new agreement that we express our regret that the South Wales representatives failed to secure an agreement for twelve months only as per resolution of the Executive Committee, but this resolution carried with it no censure on the workmen's representatives. (*14.xii.1905.*)

Then they parted, wishing one another a Merry Christmas and uttering sentiments of mutual esteem. The hatchet was buried: and with it was buried the grand design for which Pickard and the other founding fathers had toiled for so many years, the plan for one single conciliation board, where the miners of the whole island could act in unity on the wages question. A new generation had to grow up before anything resembling this could once more become feasible.

APPENDIX TO CHAPTER FOUR

CONCILIATION AGREEMENT, 1905

MEMORANDUM OF AGREEMENT made this eleventh day of December 1905, BETWEEN the undersigned—William Jenkins, W. H. Routledge, Frederick Lewis Davis, M. Wolstenholme, Joseph Shaw, Henry E. Gray, Thos. H. Deakin, William Evans, William Smith, Hugh Watts, Thomas Griffiths, Frederick Cleeves, William Walker Hood, Henry Lewis, Thomas Wilson, and Henry T. Wales, duly authorised to act on behalf of the Owners of Collieries in Monmouthshire and South Wales whose names or titles are set forth in the Schedule hereto (hereinafter called the Owners) of the one part and the undersigned—William Abraham, William Brace, Alfred Onions, Evan Thomas, David Watts Morgan, John Williams, John Thomas, John Davies, Thomas Evans, Benjamin Davies, William Vyce, James Manning, James Winstone, Enoch Morrell, John Daniel Morgan, Vernon Hartshorn, Charles Butt Stanton, John Williams, Thomas George, Thomas Harries, William Harris, William Herbert Morgan, Thomas Davies, and John Watts, duly authorised to act on behalf of the Workmen (excepting Enginemen, Stokers, and outside Fitters) now employed at the Collieries of the said Owners of the other part whereby it is mutually agreed as follows:

1.—That a Board of Conciliation shall be established to determine the general rate of wages to be paid to the Workmen and to deal with disputes at the various Collieries of the Owners subject to the conditions herein-after mentioned.

2.—The title of the Board shall be "The Board of Conciliation for the Coal Trade of Monmouthshire and South Wales" hereinafter called "The Board."

3.—The Board shall consist of 24 duly authorised Owners' Representatives and 24 duly authorised Representatives of the Workmen employed at the Collieries of the Owners, and when dealing with questions relating to general advances or general reductions in the rate of wages also of a Chairman from outside who shall not be financially interested in any Coal Mine in the United Kingdom and who shall have a casting vote only.

4.—The first Members of the Board shall be SIR MICHAEL HICKS—BEACH, BART., the Chairman from outside as aforesaid, and who is hereinafter called the Chairman, and

Owners' Representatives

WILLIAM JENKINS	WILLIAM SMITH
W. H. ROUTLEDGE	H. W. MARTIN
F. L. DAVIS	HUGH WATTS
CHARLES H. EDEN	THOMAS GRIFFITHS
M. WOLSTENHOLME	FRED. CLEEVES
JOSEPH SHAW	W. W. HOOD
HENRY DAVIES	HENRY LEWIS
J. BOYD HARVEY	THOMAS WILSON
H. E. GRAY	CLIFFORD J. CORY
T. H. DEAKIN	HENRY T. WALES
W. S. B. MCLAREN	E. M. HANN
WILLIAM EVANS	W. J. HEPPELL

and

Workmen's Representatives

WM. ABRAHAM, M.P.	JAMES WINSTONE
W. BRACE	E. MORRELL
ALRED ONIONS	JOHN D. MORGAN
EVAN THOMAS	VERNON HARTSHORN
D. WATTS MORGAN	C. B. STANTON
JOHN WILLIAMS	JOHN WILLIAMS
JOHN THOMAS	TOM GEORGE
JOHN DAVIES	THOMAS HARRIES
THOMAS EVANS	WILLIAM HARRIS
BEN DAVIES	W. H. MORGAN
WM. VYCE	TOM DAVIES
JAMES MANNING	JOHN WATTS

of whom there shall be two Presidents one elected by the Owners' Representatives and the other by the Representatives of the Workmen.

Whenever a vacancy on the Board occurs from any cause (except in the office of Chairman) such vacancy shall be filled by the body which appointed the Member whose seat has become vacant, but during such vacancy the Board may transact the business of the Board. Intimation of such appointment shall be at once sent to the Secretaries. When and so often as the office of Chairman becomes vacant the Board shall endeavour to elect a Chairman and should they fail to agree will ask the Lord Chief Justice of England for the time being or in case of his refusal the Speaker of the House of Commons to nominate one.

5.—The parties to this Agreement pledge their respective constituents to make every effort possible to avoid difficulties or disputes at the Collieries and in case of any unavoidable difference the Owners or their Officials together with their Workmen or their Agent or Agents shall endeavour to settle all matters at the Collieries and only in case of failing to effect a settlement shall a written appeal setting forth clearly the facts of the dispute and the contention of the parties making the claim be made to the Board by either or both of the parties concerned in the dispute to consider the same and no notice to terminate contracts shall be given by either Owners or their Workmen before the particular question in dispute shall have been considered by the Board and it shall have failed to arrive at an Agreement. The Board shall have power to refer such questions to a Committee consisting of one or more Owners' Representatives and an equal number of Workmens' Representatives all of whom shall be Members of the Board to consider and if so directed with power to settle and in all cases to report to the Board either a settlement or a failure to agree within three calendar months from the date of the reference to such Committee, and should the Board then fail to arrive at an Agreement within one month, or any extended period that may be agreed upon by the Board, either party may give notice to terminate Contracts. Any notices wrongfully given to terminate contracts on any question shall be withdrawn before the Board or any Committee thereof shall consider such question.

Both parties hereby respectively undertake to make every effort possible to secure the loyal observance by the Owners and Workmen respectively of any Award made by representatives of the Board on any questions which may have been referred to them by the Board.

6.—Rules of procedure for the conduct of the business of the Board are set forth at the end hereof and the same shall be deemed to be incorporated with and to form part of this Agreement.

7.—The Mineral to be gotten is clean large coal only as hereinafter described.

The cutting prices to be paid to the Collier shall be the several standard prices prevailing and paid at the Collieries of the Owners respectively.

Such standard cutting price shall be paid upon the weight of the large coal to be ascertained in manner hereinafter appearing and includes all services in respect of the small coal necessarily produced in filling the large coal in conveying it from the working places to the screen at the surface and in the process of screening that price being equal to the value of all the services involved in getting such large coal and small coal and being more than the value of the services rendered in respect of the large coal only.

The respective weights of such large coal and small coal for the purpose of paying the Collier shall be ascertained as follows:

After each tram of coal is brought to the weighing machine it shall be weighed and the tare of the tram shall be deducted from the gross weight. The coal shall then be tipped over the screen in use at the Colliery to separate the small coal passing through the screen from the large coal passing over it.

The small coal which shall pass through the screen shall be weighed and that weight shall be deducted from the gross weight of the coal in the tram in order to ascertain the weights of such large screened coal and small coal respectively, and the cutting price paid to the collier upon the weight of the large screened coal as aforesaid shall during the continuance of this Agreement be deemed to be the value of the services rendered in respect of both the large screened coal and small coal the weights of which respectively shall be ascertained as aforesaid.

8.—It is distinctly understood that Clause 7 in this Agreement is not intended to change the system of weighing and screening the coal as it at present exists, but the Owners shall be at liberty to adopt such improved methods of screening and cleaning as they may consider necessary provided that any methods so adopted shall not in any way prejudicially affect the wages of the Workmen.

9.—Clause 7 shall not apply to or alter or in any way interfere with any agreements now existing or hereafter to be made for payment for through and through coal or where small coal is now separately paid for.

10.—The Board shall at the meetings held under Rule 6 of the said rules of procedure determine the general rate of wages to be paid for the three months commencing on the first day of the month following the dates of such meetings, but should neither party desire to vary the rate of wages, the then prevailing rate of wages shall continue until the same shall be varied in accordance with the said Rules of Procedure.

(a) All Standard rates and prices shall be the Standards known as the Standards of December 1879 and 1877 respectively.

(b) The wages payable to the Workmen shall until the same shall be advanced by the Board, be 30 per cent above the several rates actually paid at the respective Collieries under the Standard of December 1879.

(c) During the continuance of this Agreement the rate of wages shall, subject to sub-section (d) hereof, not be less than 30 per cent above nor more than 60 per cent above the December 1879 Standard of wages paid at the respective Collieries and in considering any proposal for an alteration in the general rate of wages the said minimum of 30 per cent shall for that purpose be considered as equivalent to an average nett selling price of large coal of 11/10 per ton. Such average nett selling price shall be taken as for large colliery screened coal, delivered f.o.b. at Cardiff, Barry, Newport, Swansea, Port Talbot, and Llanelly.

(d) At Collieries where the Standard or basis upon which wages are now regulated is the rate of wages paid in the year 1877 the percentage payable thereat shall be 15 per cent less than at the Collieries where the 1879 Standard prevails provided that in cases where Workmen have hitherto been paid nett rates of wages or fixed or other percentages whether upon the 1877, 1879 standards or any other existing standards they shall continue to be paid such nett rates, fixed or other percentages only.

11.—At the Collieries under this Agreement all wages due to the Workmen shall be paid once in each fortnight, provided that at those Collieries where wages are now paid weekly such practice shall continue in force.

12.—The workmen shall be entitled to 12 General Holidays in each year, which shall include all Bank Holidays and Federation Demonstration Holidays the dates to be agreed upon by the Board, and the Workmen's Representatives agree that in arranging such holidays they will issue instructions to the workmen requesting them to resume work immediately after such holidays have terminated, and will use every effort to see that such instructions are complied with.

At any Collieries where "Mabon's Day," now exists, the custom of keeping such a holiday shall be forthwith abolished.

13.—The prices to be charged to workmen entitled to house coal for their own domestic purposes shall be the same prices as are fixed to be paid by the award of Sir David Dale, Bart., of the 11th day of July, 1903.

14.—During the continuance of this Agreement all notices to terminate individual contracts on the part of the Owners as well as on the part of the Workmen shall be given on the first day of any calendar month and shall terminate upon the last day of the same month, provided that if the first day of any calendar month fall on a Sunday, the notice shall be given on the previous Saturday.

15.—Subject as aforesaid the Owners and Workmen at the respective Collieries shall be bound to observe and fulfil and shall be subject to all customs, provisions and conditions existing in December, 1879, at the Collieries respectively and no variation shall be made therein by the Owners or Workmen except by mutual arrangement at the Collieries respectively or by a decision of the Board after a reference thereto in accordance with the provisions of Clause 5 of any proposal for a variation.

16.—Nothing in the Clauses of this Agreement or in the Rules of Procedure is to preclude either party bringing any matters before the Board or Independent Chairman, which they consider as factors bearing upon the General Wage Question, but any evidence brought forward as to the selling price of large coal shall be confined to the price of large coal delivered f.o.b. at the shipping ports named in Clause 10 (c) hereof in the three calendar months immediately preceding the first day of the month prior to the month in which the meeting is held to consider any proposal to vary the General Wage Rate.

17.—This Agreement shall continue in force from the 1st January, 1906, until the 31st December, 1909, and thenceforth until either party gives to the other 3 calendar months notice terminating the same, such notice to be given to the Secretary of such other party in writing or left at his usual or last known address. Upon the termination of this Agreement all contracts of service between the Owners respectively and their Workmen respectively shall cease.

18.—A Copy of this Agreement shall be placed in a Contract Book at each Colliery which shall be signed by or on behalf of the Owners of such Colliery and also by each Workman employed thereat as one of the terms of the engagement between the Owners and the said Workman.

RULES OF PROCEDURE

1.—The Constituents of the Board, *i.e.* Owners' Representatives and Workmen's Representatives are for brevity herein referred to as "the Parties."

2.—The Meetings of the Board shall be held at Cardiff or such other place as the Board may from time to time determine.

3.—Each of the parties shall appoint a Secretary and shall give notice of such appointment when made to the other party and such Secretaries shall remain in office until they shall resign or be withdrawn by the parties appointing them. The Secretaries or their respective deputies for the time being shall attend all Meetings of the Board and be entitled to take part in the discussion but they shall have no power to move or second any resolution or vote on any question before the Board.

4.—The Secretaries shall conjointly convene all Meetings of the Board and record the names of the persons present thereat and at all meetings held under Rule 6 of the Rules of Procedure full minutes of the proceedings thereof shall be taken under the conjoint supervision of the Secretaries by an official shorthand writer to be mutually agreed on by the parties which minutes shall be transcribed into duplicate books and each such book shall be signed by the Presidents or other persons presiding at the meeting at which such minutes are confirmed. One of such minute books shall be kept by each of the Secretaries, such minutes to be for the private use of the Board and not for publication. The Secretaries shall also conduct correspondence for their respective parties and conjointly for the Board.

5.—The Board shall meet once at least in each month for the purpose of dealing with difficulties or disputes arising at the several Collieries and referred to in Clauses 5 and 15 of the foregoing Agreement and the same shall be dealt with by the Board without reference to the Chairman. The Secretaries shall give to each Member of the Board seven days' notice of the intention to hold any such meeting and of the business to be transacted thereat, and, except by mutual agreement, no subject shall be considered which has not been placed on the Agenda to the Notice convening the Meeting.

6.—Should there be a desire by either party to vary the rate of wages the Board shall meet to consider the same on the 10th day of the months of February, May, August and November in every year (except where the 10th day of any of the said months falls on a Sunday when the meeting shall be held on the following day) to determine the general rate of wages to be paid for the three months commencing on the first day of the month next following the date of such meetings. Either party intending to propose at such meetings any alteration in the general rate of wages shall 10 days before the said 10th day of the months of February, May, August and November for holding such meetings give to the Secretary of the other party notice in writing of the proposition intended to be made and of the grounds thereof and the Secretaries shall enter such intended proposition and the grounds thereof on the Agenda to the notice convening the meeting. The Secretaries shall send to each member of the Board 7 days' notice of each such meeting and of the business to be transacted thereat.

At all such last mentioned meetings the questions to be dealt with thereat shall in the first instance be considered by the Board, it being the desire and intention of the parties to settle any differences which may arise by friendly conference if possible. If the parties on the Board cannot agree then the meeting shall be adjourned for a period not exceeding twelve days to which adjourned meeting the Chairman shall be summoned and shall attend and preside thereat, when the questions in difference shall be again discussed by the parties, and in the event of their failing to arrive at an agreement with regard thereto, the Chairman either at such meeting or within five days thereafter shall give his casting vote on such questions, and the parties shall be bound thereby.

7.—Both Presidents shall preside at all meetings (other than at meetings at which it shall be the duty of the Chairman to preside in accordance with Clause 6 of these Rules) but if either or both of them shall be absent then a member or members of the Board shall be elected by the respective parties to preside at such meetings according as such President who shall be absent shall represent the Owners or Workmen. The Presidents or other persons presiding shall vote as representatives but shall have no other votes.

8.—All questions submitted to the Board shall be stated in writing and may be supported by such verbal documentary or other evidence and explanation as either party may submit subject to the approval of the Board.

9.—Each party shall pay and defray the expenses of its own Representatives, Secretary and Accountant but the costs and expenses of the Chairman, Official Shorthand Writer, Joint Auditors (if any), and of the stationery, books, printing, and hire of rooms for meeting shall be borne by the respective parties in equal shares.

[Signatures of members of the Board then followed together with those of the two secretaries, W. Gascoyne Dalziel and Thomas Richards.]

THE SCHEDULE REFERRED TO IN THE FOREGOING AGREEMENT

Abercrave Collieries Co.
Albion Steam Coal Co., Ltd.
Ammanford Colliery Co., Ltd.
Bargoed Coal Co., Ltd.
Blaenavon Co., Ltd.
Blaenclydach Colliery Co., Ltd.
Blaina Colliery Co., Ltd.
Bwllfa & Merthyr Dare Steam Collieries (1891), Ltd.
Cardiff Navigation Colliery Co.
Cartwright, T. G.
Corrwg Rhondda Colliery Co., Ltd.
Cory Bros. & Co., Ltd.
Crawshay Bros. Cyfarthfa, Ltd.
Cwmaman Coal Co., Ltd.
Cynon Colliery Co.

Davis, D. & Sons, Ltd.
Deep Navigation Collieries, Ltd.
Depeaux, F. F.
Dinas Main Coal Co.
Duffryn Rhondda Colliery Co.
Ebbw Vale Steel, Iron & Coal Co., Ltd.
Evans & Bevan.
Ffaldau Collieries Co., Ltd.
Gas Coal Collieries, Ltd.
Gelliceidrim Collieries Co. Ltd.,
Glamorgan Coal Co., Ltd.
Glyncorrwg Colliery Co., Ltd.
Glynea Coal & Brick Co., Ltd.
Glenavon Rhondda Collieries Co., Ltd.
Graigola Merthyr Co., Ltd.

Great Mountain Collieries Co., Ltd.
Great Western Colliery Co., Ltd.
Guest, Keen & Nettlefolds, Ltd.
Gwauncaegurwen Colliery Co., Ltd.
Gwendraeth Anthracite Collieries Co., Ltd.
Harry, David, & Bros.
Hedley's Collieries Co.
Hill's Plymouth Co., Ltd.
Hoskins & Llewelyn.
Insoles, Ltd.
International Coal Co., Ltd.
Jones, Southwood & Co., Ltd.
Lancaster, John & Co., Ltd.
Lewis Merthyr Consolidated Collieries, Ltd.
Locket's Merthyr Collieries (1894), Ltd.
Main Colliery Co., Ltd.
Marquess of Bute
New Cross Hands Collieries, Ltd.
Newport Abercarn Black Vein Steam Coal Co., Ltd.
Nixon's Navigation Co., Ltd.
North's Navigation Collieries (1889), Ltd.
Ocean Coal Co., Ltd.
Partridge Jones & Co., Ltd.

Penrhiwceiber Navigation Colliery Co., Ltd.
Pentremawr Colliery Co., Ltd.
Pont Henry Colliery Co., Ltd.
Pontyberem Collieries Co., Ltd.
Powell Duffryn Steam Coal Co., Ltd.
Powells Tillery Steam Coal Co., Ltd.
Pwllbach Colliery Co.
Rhymney Iron Co., Ltd.
Rhos Colliery Co., Ltd.
South Wales Anthracite Colliery Co., Ltd.
South Wales Primrose Coal Co., Ltd.
Thomas, Sir Griffith
Thomas, Samuel
Tirpentwys Black Vein Steam Coal & Coke Co., Ltd.
Tredegar Iron & Coal Co., Ltd.
United National Collieries, Ltd.
Vipond, John, & Co., Ltd.
Vivian & Sons.
Varteg Deep Black Vein Collieries, Ltd.
Williams, Representatives of the late E. D.
Williams, Thomas, & Sons.
Ynyshir Steam Coal Co.

CHAPTER FIVE

SHORTER HOURS—AND THE SEQUEL

I. UNTROUBLED SEAS

As the second five years of the century began to unroll it might well have seemed to the leaders of the Welsh miners that their troubles were a thing of the past. The coal trade was prospering. Output of coal in South Wales which had gone up from nearly forty million tons in 1899 to forty-three million in 1905, leaped up to fifty million in 1908. This was an even greater rate of increase than in the United Kingdom as a whole. The coalfield was approaching its zenith. The number employed had grown. The price of coal had been rising and as the price per ton was still the main factor in decisions of the Conciliation Board, money wages had been rising also.

All the miners' aims, legislative and political and other, seemed to be coming nearer to achievement. Their trade union, the vessel that held the fortunes of the Welsh miners, was voyaging happily over untroubled seas. The horizon, as far as the eye could see from Cardiff, was clear enough: in Cardiff there was quiet and calm in the Executive Council of the South Wales Miners' Federation: halcyon days indeed for the officials. In these untroubled waters there had been little change of personnel since the formation of the South Wales Miners' Federation. The same miners' agents who had come together as the Executive Council in 1898 still gathered fortnightly in Cardiff and each two or three months sat as the workmen's side of the Board of Conciliation. On the other side, too, there was little change except that Fred L. Davis now headed the array of two dozen colliery owners at the Conciliation Board.

The horizon at Westminster, too, as viewed by the three S.W.M.F. officials, had but little cloud on it. With John Williams of Gower they numbered four out of the sixteen mining members: they were enrolled in the ranks of the Liberal Party: and they were part of the Trade Union Group which worked amicably enough with the two-and-a-half dozen members elected under the banner of the Labour Representation Committee. They may not have been privy to the 1903 secret arrangement between the Liberal Whip and the L.R.C. Secretary Ramsay MacDonald (by which some 35 Liberal seats were traded for "friendliness") or to the stipulated exclusion from this deal of candidates from the Social Democratic Federation or the Miners' Federation of Great Britain; but they were secure in their seats and could bask in the approval and friendliness of many other M.P.s from South Wales, brothers in non-conformity, national feeling and political faith.

They participated actively within Parliament in the efforts which brought about the reversal of the crippling Taff Vale judgement through the passing by December 1906 of the Trades Disputes Act which was to give some legal protection to active trade unionists for another twenty years.

In the autumn 1906 ballot vote of the Miners' Federation of Great Britain "on the question of joining the Labour Representation Committee," Mabon and his leading colleagues, as convinced Liberals, threw their influence against it: and the ballot also had an adverse result. But the cloud on the horizon grew greater when it was seen that the miners of South Wales, amongst whom Socialist influence had been gaining ground, were strong for joining the Labour Party.[1] Apart from this jolt to their pride of leadership the three officials (and a good half of the Executive Council with them) felt they had good reason to be satisfied with the progress of the South Wales Miners' Federation.

Yet, in comparison with the colliers in the main English coalfields, the Welsh miners from the beginning of the century were in a worse position. Their wages were lower. their hours longer, their housing poorer and their safety less. There was much leeway to make up. It was on the question of the hours of labour underground that a big effort was made in these years from 1905 onwards and that the first success was attained in the aim of reaching uniformity throughout the island. This was through the campaign for the eight hour day to which we must now turn.

2. THE CAMPAIGN FOR EIGHT HOURS

When the agitation for a shorter working day was growing in the last quarter of the nineteenth century, the Welsh miners had more reason than any for their strong desire that the hours of labour underground be limited to "eight hours from bank to bank": but their desire was not matched by strength of organisation. Consequently, as is narrated in full elsewhere[2] the attempt to get shorter hours through trade union negotiation or strike action, as had been

[1] See Appendix I to this Chapter.
[2] See *The Miners* (A History of the Miners' Federation of Great Britain, 1889–1910) Chapters IV, V, VI. See also Reports of Miners' National Conferences from 1885 onwards which incidentally give some particulars of the numbers claimed as "union men."

almost unanimously agreed at a miners' general conference in
November, 1889, had to be abandoned.

So the newly founded Miners' Federation of Great Britain began
the campaign for eight hours by Act of Parliament; though many of
them shared the foreboding uttered by Harvey of Derbyshire that
once they sought to secure eight hours by legislation "the grass will
grow over the graves of some of us before it is obtained." (*27.xi.1889.*)
In Parliament, accordingly, while Burt and Wilson and Fenwick
stood aloof (they represented the North-East coalfields with their
special position and attitude on the question of hours) or were hostile,
the solitary representative of South Wales joined in the campaign.
The name of William Abraham, member for the Rhondda from
1885, stood along with that of the Yorkshireman Ben Pickard as
backers of the Eight Hours Bill of 1889 brought in by R. B.
Cunninghame Graham who was the first member of parliament to
proclaim himself a Socialist, a claim to which a certain piquancy
was lent by his descent: for this Scottish laird came of a family
which many held to have a better right to the throne than the
Stuarts or their Hanoverian successors. About this and subsequent
Bills of the same kind, especially about that of session 1893, there
was kindled a great deal of enthusiasm in the Welsh valleys.[1] Miners
took the then unwonted journey to London to wait in deputation
upon Ministers of the Queen, to lobby Tory or Liberal members in
the hope of winning their support, and finally to listen in the
gallery of the House of Commons to debates that bore so closely upon
their working lives. There it was in March 1893, that the 84-year-
old Prime Minister Gladstone and Home Secretary Asquith heard
Alfred Onions in No. 10 Downing Street put the Welsh case for
shorter hours. There, too, on May 3, 1893, miners could hear one
of the Welsh coalowners take the lead in moving the total rejection
of the Eight Hours Bill: it was D. A. Thomas, Member of Parliament
for Merthyr and Aberdare who argued on the grounds (1) South
Wales could not have eight hours without the hated double shift;
(2) that it would reduce wages; (3) that the general election was no
proof of strong feeling in the constituencies for eight hours—on
the contrary; (4) that the statistics of support amongst the miners
were very doubtful; (5) that there would be a reduction of output;
(6) that there would be an increase of prices. But the Bill, though it
got a "second reading," and had the powerful support of the Tory

---

[1] W. H. Mainwaring had a memory of Mabon at Swansea in the 'nineties making
a speech on the eight-hour day and uttering the famous jingle in Welsh as follows:

Wyth awr i weithio	Eight hours to work
Wyth awr o rhyddid	Eight hours of freedom
Wyth awr i gysgu	Eight hours to sleep
A wyth swllt y dydd	And eight shillings a day

6   GROUP OF OFFICIALS, BRYNEYLLYS COLLIERY

POCHIN COLLIERS ENTERING THE TRAIN, TREDEGAR

7   TONYPANDY. SHOPPING THROUGH THE BARRICADES, NOVEMBER 1910

TONYPANDY. RECEIVING STRIKE PAY IN CHAPEL, 1910

Lord Randolph Churchill, did not become an Act: and so it turned out session after session and parliament after parliament for fifteen more years.

At length there came the new parliament elected in January 1906, and prospects seemed brighter. The Bill received a second reading in the Commons on May 11th, having been supported in speeches not only by mining M.P.s such as Enoch Edwards, W. Abraham, and W. Brace, but also by the Home Secretary, Herbert Gladstone. Gladstone, however, said he proposed to accept the suggestion for an inquiry as put forward by John Wilson, M.P. for Mid-Durham, and Thomas Burt, M.P. for Morpeth. This angered the M.F.G.B. Executive Committee which would have nothing to do with the Departmental Committee appointed by the Government to conduct the inquiry. But before the end of the year a deputation to Prime Minister Sir Henry Campbell-Bannerman received such good and firm assurance that they departed well-content: while the last word came from Mabon to Sir Henry: "You have removed us from that wintry atmosphere into a spring of hope." (*6.xii.1906.*)

Thus it was that the Eight Hours Bill, introduced in the 1907 session of Parliament on April 12th, easily passed through its second reading and was then remitted to the Grand Committee where the Home Secretary moved that they do not proceed with the Bill. So, against the opposition of the M.F.G.B. members, the Grand Committee after ten days reported the Bill to the House without amendments, "because the information at their disposal is at present inadequate to enable amendments to be satisfactorily considered." The report of the departmental committee was not yet ready.

Four weeks later the final report was issued. The miners kept up their pressure and at last, on August 1, 1907, a Government Bill for a Miners' Eight-hour Day was introduced. It was not, however, a Bill for "eight hours from bank to bank" which William Abraham, M.P. had moved as far back as 1887 at the Edinburgh National Miners' Conference.[1] The Government Bill added at least half an hour a day.

The long awaited report[2] revealed a wide disparity from one coalfield to another throughout the island. The colliers of Monmouthshire and South Wales were shown to have much longer hours

[1] "That this Conference is of opinion that eight hours should be made the maximum working day of miners underground; that where a single shift is worked workmen work not more than eight hours, and where the double shift system is in force that they work not more than seven hours—in both cases the time to be reckoned from bank to bank" (*12.x.1887*)

[2] Departmental Committee appointed to inquire into the probable economic effect of a limit of eight hours to the working day of coal miners. Reports Cd. 3426–8 and Cd. 3505–6 of 1907.

E

underground than was the case in any other coalfield: and also a higher accident rate. It confirmed the contention, twenty years earlier, of Isaac Evans of Neath that in South Wales more accidents occurred towards the end of a long day than at other times.

3. A DEPUTATION FROM THE OWNERS

In the meantime the coalowners had begun to muster their resources both within Parliament and without. To urge their case against the Bill they too went to Whitehall: and soon the Liberal minister received the Liberal member of parliament, Sir Clifford Cory, with a deputation from the Mining Association of Great Britain. The main grounds of their opposition were set forth at length by T. Ratcliffe Ellis, the Law Clerk and Secretary of the Association: it was undesirable that Parliament should "interfere with the hours of adult labour in mines"; such a measure would be "distinctly prejudicial to safety"; it would work "most unfairly" as between districts and as between collieries, and be a great hardship upon "the older and weaker men"; it would bring such a reduction in the output of coal and permanent increase in the cost "as would be disastrous" to industries dependent on cheap fuel. The coalowners acknowledged that they were "deeply indebted" to the Home Secretary not only for setting up the Departmental inquiry but also for resisting, under considerable difficulties, "the attempt of the Miners' Federation of Great Britain to force through the House of Commons their Eight Hours Bank-to-Bank Bill." Ratcliffe Ellis nevertheless sought to correct the conclusions of the Departmental Committee,[1] saying, "If, however, the true index to the effect upon production would be the time lost, not by all underground workers, but by the underground workers other than hewers, then the reduction should be calculated at 13·72 per cent instead of 10·27 per cent, and upon the output of 1906 the loss of production would be 34,444,170 tons per annum." (*8.i.1908*). Other coalowners drew a picture of a coal-famine with an alarming rise in prices that might result. On behalf of Yorkshire and the Midlands, F. Parker Rhodes spoke of "a greater coal famine than in 1872" which would happen "after the passing of this Bill."

---

[1] The Departmental Committee's estimate of the effect of eight hours was:

Reduction in Aggregate Hours Underground

	Per cent
All classes underground	10·27
Hewers only	6·20
Underground other than hewers	13·72

In their Summary of Conclusions it was stated: "That if this loss of time be accepted as a basis of a proportionate reduction of output, as it was contended by most witnesses engaged in colliery management would be the case, the loss of production would be: 25,783,000 tons calculated on the output of 1906."

Andrew McCosh of Bairds, the Scottish coal and iron masters, said that "if this Bill is passed," it would be "a disastrous matter to the general trade of the country." Even from the Durham and Northumberland coalfields Sir Lindsay Wood, Bart, the learned mining engineer and member of Royal Commissions, foretold a reduction of twenty per cent of their total output. So it went on until the assembled colliery owners must have sounded to the Home Secretary like a chorus of Cassandras: he, however, remained undaunted and after congratulating Sir Clifford Cory on his new honour, a baronetcy: and complimenting the others who had spoken on their acumen and the clarity of their views, expressed the hope that there would be "friendliness and forbearance" between masters and men: he had given nothing away.

The coalowners' forebodings were not fulfilled: and their vaticinations proved untrue. British output of coal, so far from being reduced, grew greater in the five years working of the Act up to the war of 1914–1918.[1] Pithead price of coal, instead of rising to fantastic heights, actually fell below the 1907 and 1908 average in the four years after the passing of the Act: and the same was true of the price at the ports. Average declared value (f.o.b.) per ton of coal exported in 1907 and 1908 stood at 12s. 8d. only to fall by as much as a shilling and more in the four years that followed.

4. A PROGRAMMATIC SPEECH

Amongst the colliery owners in the deputation at the Home Office there was one who made a quite distinctive statement. This was Fred L. Davis, who showed the attitude of the associated coalowners, covering four-fifths of the output in South Wales, to be at once more unyielding and also more fully calculated than that of their colleagues and rivals in other coalfields. In a series of com-

[1] The price of exported coal, in the nineteenth century, was usually well below half-a-guinea per ton apart from the upward leaps around 1873 and 1890. In the early years of the twentieth century half-a-guinea was the lowest figure.

Year	Total Output (million tons)	Average Selling Value per ton of coal raised at pit		Average Declared Value (f.o.b.) per ton of coal exported.	
		s.	d.	s.	d.
1905	236	6	11	10	6
1906	251	7	3	10	10
1907	267	9	0	12	8
1908	261	8	11	12	8
1909	263	8	1	11	2
1910	264	8	2	11	8
1911	271	8	2	11	4
1912*	260	9	1	12	7
1913	287	10	2	13	10
1914†	265	10	0	13	6

*National Strike in March and April.
† War emergency in five months of 1914.

putations, labour time lost through limitation of hours was equated with loss of tonnage and thereby with loss of pounds sterling in profits: and from this in turn Davis worked out an entire strategy of industrial relations by which it was hoped the Welsh owners would be able to recoup themselves for their as yet prospective losses. As the standpoint was set out as the deliberate policy of the owners, it is important to show the steps of this argument.

It affected the 615 collieries in the coalfield, employing in the year 1906 148,000 men underground and 26,000 on the surface (174,000 in all) to produce forty-seven million tons of coal. The argument was that shorter hours would reduce output by at least 15 per cent and increase working cost by an average of 1s. 6d. per ton: as a result the owner would have to charge the consumer 2s. per ton extra price to keep at the same level: but if the foreign consumer would not pay the higher price then the South Wales owner would be "obliged to reduce the wages of the workmen." Moreover, it was argued, the collieries of South Wales where the average working day was longer than in other districts, and where average costs were higher than elsewhere, could not be run at a profit on a single shift of eight hours. The introduction of a double shift would be necessary, although "this change of system would undoubtedly involve a serious friction between the employers and workmen, as one of the objects of the South Wales Miners' Federation, as defined in their rules, is: 'To endeavour to secure by legislation the reduction of the hours of labour in mines to eight hours from bank to bank, and to oppose the system of double shift, except where absolutely necessary for the purpose of ventilation.' " (*8.i.1908.*)

On the question of the double shift, the conclusion of the Home Office Departmental Committee was cited that this system, whether desirable or not "from a domestic and social point of view," would be an economic advantage for both producer and consumer and that after the institution of an eight hour day the coalowners generally, especially in South Wales, "would make a determined effort" to extend it.

There had been much discussion at this time about the Royal Commission on Safety in Mines from which much was expected, in conjunction with the effect of shorter hours. The South Wales owners, however, saw a different prospect. They were "strongly of the opinion that the efforts of the Royal Commission in that direction would be largely, if not wholly, nullified by a shortening of the hours of work, for a reduction of hours will certainly induce a tendency on the part of the men to devote their time to wage-earning rather than to see to the safety of their working places."

Then Davis made a statement about the Conciliation Board

agreement (due to expire at the end of 1909), which boded ill for the future of industrial relations but which does not seem to have been treated with serious attention at the time. He said:

This agreement is based upon existing conditions as to hours of work (amongst other conditions) and the introduction by legislation of reduced hours of working would be an interference with that contract which affects 7/8ths of the 174,000 workmen engaged in the South Wales collieries. This alteration of one of the main conditions of employment would necessitate the employers seeking a reduction in the basis of the general wage rate of the workmen with the probable result that a disturbance of the friendly relations between the employers and the workmen would follow. (*8.i.1908.*)

Then reverting to the cost of production, with an estimated increase of 1s. 6d. per ton corresponding to some 13 per cent in the wage scale, he went on to say that therefore the minimum wage rate of 30 per cent above the standard (which then corresponded to a selling price of 11s. 10d. for large coal f.o.b. at the shipping ports) "would require to be made co-relative to 13s. 4d. selling price; and it is quite certain that the workmen would look upon this as a very decided reduction in wages; and there is no escape from this result except by arguing that there would be no increase of cost."

With these forebodings the permanent chairman of the coalowners' representatives on the Conciliation Board made it clear that the South Wales owners were on the war-path.

5. STRIKE? OR A PARLIAMENTARY BILL?

Ten weeks later the Home Secretary received another deputation. This time it was the Executive Committee of the Miners' Federation of Great Britain headed by Enoch Edwards, M.P., who said that miners, having waited twenty years for the measure, were now disposed to achieve shorter hours by strike action rather than wait any longer, but "we have always felt it is to the best interest of the trade and the workmen and everybody concerned that we should conserve if possible that trade without strike and strife and stoppage." Smillie from Scotland spoke next: the new Government Bill was "a compromise, reluctantly accepted by the miners," since a person could be underground for half-an-hour longer than the original proposal contained in the Mines Bill. (*24.iii.1908.*) Arguments about increased cost, Smillie said, come "with very bad grace" from the colliery owners of the country who, during the past thirty years, had "made enormous fortunes out of the coal trade, even during periods when the wages of the workers in the coal industry had often reached the starvation point." Smillie ended by saying that "unless the hours were limited by legislation" it would lead to "a general stoppage of the mineworkers of the country," and he called on the cabinet to fulfil their promises.

One week earlier the 302 delegates (representing 132,105 members) at the Ninth Annual Conference of the South Wales Federation meeting in Cardiff had unanimously passed the following resolution:

That this Conference, representing the whole of the Colliery Workmen of South Wales, strongly repudiate the attempt of Colliery Owners and others financially interested in the production and Sale of Coal to represent that the operation of a Mines Eight Hours Bill will seriously reduce the production of Coal and enhance the price to consumers. We would remind the country that on every occasion when legislation has been proposed on behalf of the mining community similar statements were made which further experience proved to be entirely groundless. The Conference again repeats that they expect the Government to fulfil their pledges by giving immediate facilities for passing the Bill into law this Session, feeling assured that to reduce the hours of workmen employed underground will not detrimentally affect the interests of either the consumers of coal or the general public, while it will bring some relief and mitigation to the arduous, dangerous employment of the miners, who for 20 years have been pressing forward this reform.

Then William Abraham, M.P., said that the extreme statements as to the result were "simply suppositious and problematic." He had tried to find out "upon what basis have these gentlemen formed their calculations?" But, said he, "I waited in vain for an answer. Neither the owners nor the engineers nor anybody else have given us a word of explanation." "Well," continued Abraham, "we have to admit that the opposition to this Bill is very, very largely a South Wales opposition." After saying that the system of long hours was actually "conducive to loss of time," Abraham concluded:

We believe that the introduction of this Bill will equalise the hours, and men will be working more regularly. Yea, Sir, they will be working more regularly and there will be less days in which to drink, and less days for running about and so forth. I want to ask you with all the fervour in my nature, do not go back upon this measure for anything, and we will stand by you to the death if you stand by this Bill. (*24.iii.1908.*)

The Home Secretary, Herbert Gladstone, began his reply by recalling that the Eight Hours' Agitation had become a practical question in 1892 when Joseph Chamberlain in the House of Commons had admitted that "it would be disastrous if, after a fair and constitutional agitation, coal miners throughout the country were thrown back upon the disastrous remedy of a strike." Then after a filial reference to W. E. Gladstone who in 1893 had been "converted to the principle of limitation of hours" he said:

Gentlemen, allusion has been made to the dangers which would ensue, might ensue, if Parliament in its wisdom or unwisdom, declined to recognise the strength of your claims. Now I think every sane man in this country will agree that nothing can be more disastrous than anything in the shape of a great coal strike. (*24.iii.1908.*)

Thus, promising to press forward with his Bill before Easter, Gladstone sought to assuage the fears of the miners' leaders. But three months later Easter had come and gone and then Whitsuntide and still there was a hold up. This was due to "an agitation of a most mendacious and unscrupulous character" as explained by William Brace in Paris to the continental mineworkers:

All the power of vested interests apparently have been united for the purpose of defeating the miners . . . During the last months combinations, leagues and associations have been formed, backed by enormous wealth, taking part in every by-election in Britain, simply to oppose the miners' Eight Hours Bill. (19th International Miners' Conference,[1] *9.vi.1908.*)

To a special conference a fortnight later chairman Enoch Edwards complained "Mr. Gladstone sometime ago made a promise to give us a week's notice, but, like all politicians' promises, it was broken" and went on to say "the Home Secretary has got very weak kneed about this Bill; somebody has frightened him." (*22.vi.1908.*) On that evening the second reading began. By July 6, 1908 the Bill passed second reading with a majority in its favour of 390 for and 120 against.

There was however another Liberal Minister who had espoused the cause of shorter hours and who was less likely to be frightened, and in whom therefore the miners' leaders reposed great confidence at that time. This was Winston Churchill, who had entered the Cabinet as President of the Board of Trade on April 12th and within two weeks had been thrown out of Parliament at the ensuing by-election in North-West Manchester. As soon as Churchill had found another seat, he was cordially invited to the Miners' gala held at Porth in the Rhondda. There were a dozen speakers including the Liberal Sir Alfred Thomas and, as a fraternal delegate, Arthur Henderson, M.P., that year elected to be Chairman of the Labour Party who found it "the most magnificent workmen's demonstration that I have ever attended." But the star speaker was the young man whom Brace described as "one of the most brilliant statesmen of the day." It is very doubtful whether any liberal or conservative Cabinet Minister had ever again the honour paid to him of an

[1] Jean Jaurès, a guest at the banquet given to the delegates, all of whom (except the British) expressed socialist sentiments, in his speech said that "Europe was never so much menaced as at the present moment. When Chiefs of State were meeting one another to see how to maintain peace", he asked himself "Where is the next war going to break out?" and that it was the interest of the miners and other workers "to bind themselves together to prepare for a great future of universal peace."

invitation to speak at a miners' gala in South Wales. Churchill's oration was recorded at considerable length in the Rhondda District Minutes. Amongst other things he said that of the measures before Parliament, first of all was the Mines' Eight Hours Bill:

The Tory Party have changed their opinion about this Bill. They used to think that it was a measure which it would be unpopnlar for them to resist. Now, however, they are beginning to think that they can make some capital out of opposition to the measure. I know that because I had to fight a by-election in Manchester a little while ago. A powerful attack was then made upon the Government and upon myself as a consequence of that Bill, which the poorest voters weretold was going to be a great injury to them in their daily life.

Having referred to the excellent service rendered to the Manchester by-election by William Brace, Churchill went on to say:

By-elections are not of great consequence so far as the House of Commons is concerned but they are of great consequence so far as the House of Lords is concerned. That body would like nothing better than to throw out the Mines' Eight Hours Bill if it dared. We have to keep on showing them that it is not worth their while to dare.

I urge upon you to impress upon your fellow workers in the great cities who are not themselves connected with coal-mining that your cause is a just one, and that out of justice there never came harm to anyone in the world.

Proper and regular hours of healthy labour are the only foundation on which a highly complicated modern system of industry can stand. If you can show the people in the next few years that they did not suffer by the institution of an eight hour day for the miners, but on the other hand that they gained, you will strike a great blow, not only for yourselves but for humanity in general.

Dealing with the Licensing Bill (afterwards destroyed by the House of Lords) he said:

We ought surely to be glad that among the causes to which democracy has set its shoulder, is the noble cause of temperance. What a catastrophe it would have been to the world if the tendency of democratic voters of this country had been towards free and unrestricted indulgence of the consumption of liquor. What an injury it would have inflicted upon the development of the people. What a delay it would have caused to the extension of the franchise widely among the people and what a hindrance it would have been to their effective control of public affairs. You may be confident that when you advance the cause of temperance you will at the same time advance the cause of democracy. (*20.vii.1908.*)

The vigorous young lieutenant of Lloyd George in the campaign for social reform measures (or for "The Welfare State," as it was dubbed at a later date) might feel as he listened to the thrice-prolonged applause that his rhetoric had done something to sustain Liberalism among the colliers: and Tom Richards had said as much in speaking on the vote of thanks. But a few weeks earlier the miners, despite their leaders, had balloted to depart from the Liberal fold. All William Brace could do for the Liberal Party at the M.F.G.B. Annual Conference that autumn was to propose a delay "until after the next General Election." It was a vain effort: and so by this vote Mabon, Brace and Richards were conscripted, willy-nilly, into the Labour fold.

6. THE EIGHT HOURS' BILL IN PARLIAMENT

The Bill stayed long in the House of Commons. Its first reading was in August 1907. After eleven months the second reading had been carried in July: but thereafter the Bill went into Grand Committee for detailed discussion and amendment: and remained there into the autumn months. Then, on November 18th, it was agreed that the Bill as amended be reported to the House. Back there in the Commons it was considered on December 9th, 10th and 11th and ordered to a third reading. The motion, after a full day's debate, that the Bill be now read a third time, was challenged. A vote was taken: 264 voted for the Bill: 89 against.

The Bill now went to the Upper House. There in the House of Lords it went to second reading on December 15th: and in the Division 121 voted for the Bill, 44 against. The Bill was read accordingly and committed to a Committee of the whole House. The Lords made several amendments in Committee. The third reading was taken and the Bill was returned to the Commons on December 18th. One of the Lords' amendments was accepted by the Commons, but another, postponing the coming into operation of the Bill, met with objections. The House of Lords on December 20th, on hearing the reasons assigned for disagreeing with their amendment, yielded and withdrew that amendment. The Royal Assent was given on December 21, 1908, on which day the Bill with the old formula,[1] became law.

7. "MANY DEFECTS IN THE ACT"

The Bill, finally carried as we have seen, after long and bitter resistance from the employers, became law as the Coal Mines Regulation Act, 1908. Ashton, in his quarterly report to the

[1] "BE it enacted by the King's Most Excellent Majesty, by and with the advice and consent of the Lords Spiritual and Temporal, and Commons, in this present Parliament assembled, and by the authority of the same as follows:

i. Subject to the provisions of this Act a workman shall not be below ground in a mine for the purpose of his work, and of going to and from his work, for more than eight hours during any consecutive twenty four hours."

E*

International Miners, stated: "The Act is a long way short of what was asked for, but it may be considered a foundation upon which we can now begin to build. It is the first instalment of an eight hours' working day by legal enactment. The agitation will still continue until that which the Federation set out for is obtained, a Mines Act limiting the working hours at not more than eight per day from bank to bank." (*March 1909*).

The operation of the Act both as anticipated beforehand and as it was actually carried out after the statutory date gave rise to not a few problems and difficulties. Most of these had to be dealt with in the districts, but some raised wider questions of principle, necessitating special national conferences, district negotiations and a deputation to the Home Secretary. In the case of South Wales there were actions by the owners which not merely affected their employees, but brought into play the officials and conferences of the Miners' Federation of Great Britain and raised the question of a general strike of miners. To these various events we must now turn.

The main defect of the Act, in the opinion of the Miners' Federation, was the Sixty Hours Clause to which they were inflexibly opposed. It came in Section 3 of the Act and ran as follows:

3.—(1) The time fixed by this Act as the time during which the workmen in a mine may be below ground for the purpose of their work and of going to and from their work may be extended as respects any mine by the owner, agent, or manager of the mine, on not more than sixty days in any calendar year, but not more than one hour a day, and on any on which an extension of time is made in accordance with this section as respects any mine the time as so extended shall be substituted for the purposes of this Act as respects that mine for the time as fixed by this Act.

Would there be any disturbance where the Act came into operation, either as to wages, or as to hours in any district? On this matter the Miners' Federation of Great Britain held a special three-day conference, at which reports were given by representatives of meetings held with the owners and arrangements made for the Act's coming into operation in every district—except South Wales.

After long debate the delegates resolved "that it be an instruction to each District affiliated to the Miners' Federation of Great Britain to decline to accept any reduction in wages demanded by the coalowners consequent upon the coming into operation of the Act; and should any district be attacked upon the wage question or upon the question of extending the working hours from eight to nine under the Sixty Hours Clause, that a national conference be convened to decide what defensive action is to be taken." (*6.v.1909.*)

Six weeks later the question was further discussed at a two-day special conference which decided:

That in any District where difficulties arise due to the Mines' Eight
Hours' Act coming into operation, and failing a settlement of such
difficulties, a District so affected, before any stoppage of the men take
place, shall call upon the officials and the Executive Committee of this
Federation to assist them in their negotiations with the employers, and
any case that may arise the committee shall consider on its merits, and
act accordingly. (*18.vi.1909.*)

8. WELSH OWNERS THREATEN LOCKOUT

In South Wales no arrangements whatever had been entered into
between the two sides of the Board of Conciliation for the Coal
Trade. The owners contended that this Act as it came into operation
automatically terminated their Conciliation Board Agreement. They
consulted learned Counsel on the matter and Mr. Lush, K.C., gave
his opinion very definitely and very clearly that the coming into
operation of the Act did terminate the Conciliation Board Agreement. The miners' representatives then approached a very eminent
Counsel, Mr. Upjohn, and his opinion was contrary to that of Mr.
Lush. The owners then took the opinion of two other high legal
gentlemen, who agreed with Mr. Lush, and so the owners wanted
the miners' representatives to do likewise. They also made a further
offer, or rather a suggestion, that the solicitors of the owners and
the workmen should state a case to some high judicial authority, a
man to be selected by the Lord Chancellor. The workmen's representatives would not agree; they could not see how the Act's
coming into operation could terminate their Conciliation Board
Agreement and not have the same effect in England and in Scotland.
All this and much to-ing and fro-ing had taken up some half a
dozen meetings from the time when on February 22nd the matter
had first been raised by the owners' side. But all this while nothing
as yet had been said about conditions such as had been put forward
by owners in other districts. This was to come, after a joint committee and further meetings had failed to reach agreement on half
a dozen major points of difference. On May 21st the owners who
had already concerted their views came to a meeting of the Conciliation Board and there intimated their intention of giving notice
on June 1, 1909 to terminate the workmen's contracts on June
30th—unless before then there was a settlement of the employers'
demands. Their main demands were:

1. The acceptance of double shifts throughout South Wales.
2. Reduction in wages of daywagemen.
3. Working sixty hours as provided in the Act.
4. An extra man in every working place.

At the Special Conference of the Miners' Federation of Great

Britain in Westminster a month later Tom Richards, M.P., spoke for South Wales and gave an exhaustive summary of the stage so far reached in negotiations with the South Wales owners.

Enoch Edwards then put forward a resolution which was the unanimous recommendation of the Miners' Federation of Great Britain Executive Committee, for the M.F.G.B. national officials to assist the South Wales officials in their endeavour to reach a settlement. It was natural that the Committee should have put the resolution in this form since the National Conference had been summoned very largely on the desire of the South Wales Miners' Federation that it should be held in view of their serious situation. The Conference passed the following resolution as had been recommended:

That the President and Secretary and Mr. Smillie be appointed to assist the miners' representatives of South Wales in their endeavour to arrive at an amicable settlement of their dispute in the present crisis. Failing to arrive at a final settlement, another special conference of this Federation be called without delay. (*18.vi.1909*.)

To clear up any doubts the conference then confirmed the decision of the March conference on the questions of wages and the Sixty Hours.

At Cardiff one week later the South Wales coalowners, who had in the meantime agreed to meet with the representatives of the Miners' Federation of Great Britain, were adamant. With a view to arriving at a settlement many proposals and counterproposals were made, both by the owners and by the workmen's representatives. The meetings began at ten in the morning and went on into a late hour at night, till at the close there appeared to be no hope of reaching a settlement. It was nevertheless agreed that another meeting should be held five days later.

9. THE LAST DAYS OF JUNE 1909

All that passed in the discussion with the associated owners on Friday, June 25th, was duly recounted by Tom Richards, M.P., to a conference of representatives of the lodges in Cory Hall, Cardiff, held on Monday, June 28, 1909. Brace, too, told how the owners were seeking to put an end to the Conciliation Board agreement, "although all the other colliery owners in Great Britain, having similar agreements, have not thought it necessary to terminate their wage agreement." Unanimously the Conference "while desiring industrial peace in the South Wales coalfield," backed up their representatives and further resolved that, should the South Wales coalowners lock their workmen out at the end of the month, their delegates, due at the Miners' Federation of Great Britain Conference in London on the morrow, "be instructed to apply for the putting into operation of Rule 20 at the earliest possible date." (*28.vi.1909*.)

The next day the national conference, summoned by telegraph, met at the Westminster Palace Hotel in London, when the chair was taken by Robert Smillie (the President being still seriously indisposed) and W. E. Harvey gave an account of what had taken place on June 25th. Harvey ended his report by saying "We could not get them to shift." Then the proposal was made to adjourn for a month, to give time for further negotiations, to suspend notices for a month. "We pleaded," said Harvey, "that there was nothing to lose, but, on the other hand, there would be 150,000 men who would be out on July 1st. But the answer was 'No.' They said they would not allow the pits to work one hour longer."

"I have met employers in the Midland Counties during the last quarter of a century, and I have met employers in other counties, but I am bound to say there was not the least indication in the Welsh owners for a settlement of any kind. They are the hardest employers I have ever met in my life."

Brace moved a resolution which after demur from Charles Fenwick M.P., and Thomas Burt, M.P., was finally carried as follows:

That this conference having heard the report of the deputation to South Wales upon the matters in dispute consequent upon the coming into operation of the Eight Hours' Act, confirms the action of the deputation in supporting the South Wales representatives in their opposition to the demands of the employers, namely, for an absolute free hand in deciding the methods and the number of shifts to be worked, the application of the sixty hours and the number of workmen in a place, and the conference recommends to the workmen that if the South Wales men are locked out the Twentieth Rule should be put into operation and a national stoppage declared. (*29.vi.1909*).

Before they adjourned until Thursday, July 1st, it was agreed not only that a ballot of the whole of the men employed in every District in the Federation be taken "on the question as to whether Rule 20 of the Federation be put into operation," but also that "the men be recommended to vote in favour."

The scene now shifted from London to Cardiff on the next day. It was the last day of June, 1909, the last day before the ultimatum of the coalowners expired, indeed the last hours. For a settlement was not reached until just upon the stroke of midnight. The report of these proceedings was given by W. E. Harvey, M.P., who had travelled down together with Thomas Ashton, Enoch Edwards being ill and Robert Smillie the Vice-President of the Miners' Federation of Great Britain detained in Scotland by the acuteness of the wages question there. Harvey explained how the workmen's side had finally made their peace with the owners by withdrawing their opposition on any ground, to the introduction of double shift, except one, namely if there was a feeling that safety was concerned, if there was likely to be danger. Harvey said that with regard to the danger,

if there is a disagreement at the Board the matter has to be submitted to the Home Secretary.

I say, I said it in Wales, I say it at this conference, each side can produce evidence and bring witnesses before the Home Secretary whether Liberal or Tory. If they prove that the working of a double shift is more dangerous than a single shift he will decide against a double shift if he is a reasonable man. We have safeguarded that.

With regard to the sixty hours the owners say that they are going to have it. The Welsh representatives there—Mr. Brace, Mr. Abraham, Mr. Richards, Mr. Onions and others—laid stress upon the fact that under the Act if you try to enforce it then will come the question of law upon the matter. That will have to decide the issue itself because the men will not work it. The owners say they shall; the men say they will not; then the law must decide.

Harvey then gave what he considered to be the main clause[1] in the agreement.

When this report was given and the agreement main clause read to the assembled delegates at the adjourned national conference a Lancashire delegate moved a resolution which ran as follows:

That after having heard the report of the terms agreed upon for a settlement of the South Wales difficulties with regard to the operation of the Eight Hours' Act, this conference hereby adopts the same as satisfactory, and thanks our representatives for their services in the matter. (*1.vii. 1909.*)

Thereupon James Winstone,[2] Eastern Valleys agent at Pontnewynydd, rose to move that the agreement be not ratified by the national conference until "it has been submitted to a conference of Welsh miners and agreed to by them." He spoke in a somewhat emotional manner. George Barker, the Western Valleys agent at Abertillery, a fellow member of the Executive Council, seconded the amendment saying that the workmen were

emphatic that there shall be no double shift system in South Wales. They have decided that most emphatically by vote in our own conference last

[1] See appendix III to this chapter.
[2] James Winstone, born in Risca in 1863, lost his father, a stonemason, at an early age and so had to leave school at the age of eight and go to work first at the local brickworks and then he became colliery boy at the Risca United National Colliery. Elected checkweigher, James Winstone took an active part along with William Brace in the struggle against the sliding scale and so in his middle thirties became one of the founders of the South Wales Miners' Federation. He was the first Executive member of the Tredegar District (Eastern Valleys) and had an overwhelming majority when there was a vacancy for the agency.

Monday. I say that this agreement provides the complete machinery for the introduction of the double shift.

We have different customs in South Wales than in other districts in the United Kingdom. That brings me to this point. This Federation does not exist for introducing into a District the most objectionable systems in other Districts; it exists for the purpose of removing these objections and raising the workmen up to the highest level and not bring them down to the lowest level . . .

We have exceeded our powers as delegates and as true as I am present here today at the conference, we have provided the very machinery that the employers wanted for introducing a system into South Wales that is hateful to every miner, and believing this as I do as a free-born man, I claim the right to express my opinion.

Three voted for the amendment. The rest of the delegates were in favour of accepting the settlement. The Chairman then asked for unanimity. Smillie on putting the matter to the vote again received a unanimous vote for the resolution. This was the end of the discussion nationally of the question of South Wales, and of the possible national stoppage arising from it. But as we shall see it was a matter only of weeks before the South Wales miners were balloting on a national stoppage in relation to the Scottish miners.

10. UPS AND DOWNS OF WAGES

Meanwhile, how had it fared with the Board of Conciliation for the Coal Trade of Monmouthshire and South Wales, set up in December 1905, after twelve months of falling wages? With comparative smoothness, at any rate at the beginning, the Board had been running its four-year course ("From January 1, 1906, until December 31, 1909."). The Board began with wages on the minimum at 30 per cent above the level of 1879. From June 1, 1906, there came within eighteen months a series of increases, with the price of coal rising, until wages by December 1, 1907, reached 60 per cent above standard. Having reached maximum, they could go no higher.

Wages remained at the maximum for some fifteen months until March 1, 1909, when they were brought down, first by 5 per cent, and then within another three months by another $7\frac{1}{2}$ per cent. In South Wales, in 1907, so it was stated in the report to the International Miners' Federation, "the coal trade was very brisk, the collieries working practically full time."

A year later the report of March 1909, says of South Wales that "a severe depression set in during the last quarter and has continued since. At the present time a number of collieries producing the inferior classes of coal are stopped, and in consequence between three and four thousand men are out of employment."

This depression in the coal trade was part and parcel of the cyclical crisis in British economy of 1908–1909. To cope with large-scale unemployment there remained only the provisions of the Poor Law of 1834 against which, at that same time, Beatrice Webb was drawing up a formidable indictment in the shape of the Minority Report of the Royal Commission on the Poor Law. In South Wales, too, there was serious unemployment and widespread destitution. It was in this difficult period that the two successive reductions were made in miners' wages through the Conciliation Board. Immediately thereafter came the reduction in earnings consequent upon the shorter hours worked from July 1, 1909, onwards: while a pregnant decision in 1908 of Justice Bryn Roberts about payment for abnormal places was having an effect and was spreading a feeling of dismay amongst the colliers at a time when the questions of abnormal places and the growing proportion of small coal were assuming greater and greater importance. In all these circumstances the leaders were by no means certain that a struggle in summer 1909 would have been successful. They were therefore bound to be fairly well satisfied that they had averted a coalfield lockout even at a price of grave concessions. But the price paid was bound to weigh heavily on the consciousness of the more advanced workers in the industry and was to be the source of much future strife.

Meanwhile the leaders had paid little heed to the possible legal consequences of the refusal to work the Sixty Hours Section of the Act. But these were not slow in coming. Before the month had ended the matter of the Sixty Hours Clause in the Act came up before a meeting of the Executive Council to whom it was reported that "a number of men in the Rhondda Districts were being proceeded against in the Police Court for not working the extra hour demanded by the owners." (*31.vii.1909.*) The Council decided to assume responsibility for legal expenses. By August 21st the report of the solicitor made it clear to the Council that it was very serious litigation and so they decided that the matter should be laid before the Miners' Federation of Great Britain Executive Committee. They also decided in Cardiff "that the owners' be requested to postpone the operation of their decision of claiming the sixty hours, until the Miners' Federation of Great Britain had been consulted." (*21.viii.1909.*)

At the meeting four days later of the M.F.G.B. Executive Committee it was duly reported that at certain collieries in South Wales notice had been put up that an extra hour—one of sixty hours as provided in the Act—would be worked on a certain day. The men had refused to work the extra hour, and legal proceedings for breach of contract had been taken against them. The terms of the contract were in the agreement between the South Wales Miners'

Federation and the coalowners' side of the Conciliation Board dated June 30, 1909, whereby the hours of labour "of workmen employed below ground shall be such as are authorised by the Coal Mines Regulation Act, 1908." The judgement was given against the defendant, the damages were agreed at 2s. 6d. and the further decision was taken to deduct the damages from the wages of the workmen: another case (Lewis Merthyr v. John Keats) was similar, except that the claim had been for 5s. 11d. damages in the case of John Keats and the Magistrate fixed the amount at 5s. 9d. damages. It need hardly be remarked that the legal costs exceeded a thousand-fold the total of the damages in the series of cases of which these two were the first.

In the Miners' Federation of Great Britain Executive Committee there was a very long discussion on the issue. The Executive could not agree to take a case to the Court of Appeal except on the point of what they considered to be an illegal deduction from the men's wages. On the point of the breach of contract it was decided ultimately that a deputation be appointed to meet the South Wales Coalowners on the case and on the Sixty Hours question. Finally it was decided that the President and the Secretary and Messrs. Robert Smillie and W. E. Harvey be that deputation. The statement was made much earlier by a Northern Welshman that he could call spirits "from the vasty deep" to which Hotspur had replied "But will they come when you do call for them?" It had been easy to call for a meeting with the South Wales owners: but a fortnight later the South Wales Executive Council meeting in Cardiff learned through a letter from Gascoyne Dalziel that the owners had declined to meet the deputation from the Miners' Federation of Great Britain. The Executive Council telegraphed from Cardiff to London the words of the coalowners' letter and asked that the deputation should come down on Friday, September 17th, or if that was not feasible a special meeting should be called in London to consider the very serious situation. The Lewis Merthyr v. John Keats case went to appeal in the High Court of Justice (King's Bench Division)— Divisional Court and was heard on Tuesday, December 14, 1909, before the Lord Chief Justice, Mr. Justice Ridley and Mr. Justice Darling. The appeal was dismissed.

11. CENTRALISATION (UP TO 1908)

It was not long after the Federation had come into being at the end of 1898 that it began to be realised how the extremely federal nature of the organisation had negative aspects. Whether anything more cohesive than the structure achieved in the first set of rules could have been built at the beginning may be doubted: but very soon, both at the Council and at S.W.M.F. Conferences, proposals for improvement were brought forward. For example, at a Council meeting on June 15, 1900, the first item on the agenda was for improvement of wages by "payment for small coal," put forward by George Barker. Three days later one item on the Conference agenda was to "consider proposals from several lodges to increase the contribution to the Federation to 2s. per month," and another was "proposed amendment of rules" under which several dozen proposals from lodges showed a lively interest in the affairs of the Federation. The proposal to double the monthly contribution was, however, defeated. Again at the Annual Conference on February 9, 1903, the same proposal for 2s. monthly contribution was put forward, this time by the Executive Council: it was unsuccessful. Though defeated in each concrete proposal, those who wished to have a change made were unwearied in bringing forward proposals. Although the fifth Annual Conference in February 1904 contained no reference to this, a Special Conference was called for Monday, July 11, 1904, which concerned itself almost entirely with amendments to rules and improvements of both the structure and the finances of the Federation. The most comprehensive proposals were put forward from the Pontypridd and Rhondda District: they dealt both with structure (the nineteen districts were to become eight equal-sized divisions) and also with the meagre regular contribution, the insufficiency of which resulted in all too frequent levies upon the members. On the Conference agenda there was added the following note:

The Council having had under consideration for some time the question of Centralisation, do not approve of the foregoing propositions but desire a discussion at the conference upon the general principle of Centralisation with a view, if thought desirable, of preparing a complete scheme of re-organisation for the consideration of the members of the Federation. (*26.v.1904.*)

By the middle of 1906 some Districts, notably Ogmore and Gilfach, put forward proposals (July 27, 1906) for a "system of Centralisation": and the Pontypridd and Rhondda District (September 15, 1906). Each of those Districts sent around printed copies of their letters. They had begun a real agitation. At the Annual Conference on March 18, 1907, a vote was taken. For Centralisation there were 1,318 votes and 1,310 against. This showed that many of the Districts did not favour the new proposals: and by July of that year in a Council meeting the proposal for Centralisation was abandoned. Next year, at the March Annual Conference, Alfred Onions told how the Executive Council had received letters of protest against Centralisation from several Districts representing a majority of the members of the Federation: and Mabon from the chair further explained how the Districts had refused to co-operate. So the delegates decided:

That the question be referred back to the Executive Council with instructions to formulate a scheme, the Scheme to be submitted to a future Conference, after such Conference has discussed it, to be submitted to the whole of the Members for Ballot. (*18.iii.1908.*)

Three schemes came before the Council: and the third re-arranged the Districts and reduced them to eight in number, "leaving the constitution of the Federation in other respects as at present." It was resolved: "That the three schemes dealing with the question be sent to the Districts and a report brought to the Council." (*28.viii.1908.*)

The report of the "Centralisation Sub-Committee" opened with the words: "We desire to point out that, having due regard to geographical areas, it has been very difficult and complicated to form the Districts into equal areas, or even numbers." Thereafter it suggested the following Districts:

1. Llanelly, to West	.. ..	10,870
2. Swansea	.. ..	9,300
3. Aberavon	.. ..	6,800
4. Bridgend	.. ..	13,000
5. Rhondda Fawr	.. ..	29,500
6. Taff Fawr and Tribties	.. ..	26,900
7. Rhymney and Tredegar	.. ..	17,400
8. Crumlin and Pontypool	.. .. ..	22,100
	Total ..	135,870

The proposal to make a reduction so drastic in the number of Districts met with the approval of not one single District while Pontypridd and Rhondda wished that their own scheme should go before the Conference. So the Executive Council on October 12, 1908, having received these negative reports, called a Special Conference for five weeks later. The minute on this matter runs:

The Conference decided to vote upon the principle of Centralisation, before considering the Schemes submitted by the Council, and it was Resolved by an enormous majority to reject the principle of Centralisation. (*17.xi.1908.*)

There could hardly have been anything more conclusive in wording or in weight of numbers than this decision, which apparently wrote "finis" to nearly ten years of proposals for one or another kind of reorganisation. But, as we shall see, the need for some such change was increasingly urgent and when it arose again some four years later it had the backing of a new grouping of advanced socialists within the Federation as a whole and of a minority inside the Executive Council.

BALLOT VOTES

(on the question of joining the Labour Representation Committee)

M.F.G.B. District	Ballot of October 6, 1906		Ballot of June 5, 1908	
	For joining	Against	For joining	Against
South Wales	41,843	31,527	74,675	44,616
Yorkshire	17,389	12,730	32,991	20,793
Cumberland	492	372	2,816	1,522
Scotland	17,801	12,376	32,112	25,823
Lancashire	8,265	3,345	30,227	13,702
Nottinghamshire	1,806	11,292	2,959	5,822
North Wales	295	2,428	2,467	6,017
Midland Federation	666	13,553	10,772	19,951
Derbyshire	1,798	11,257	5,811	16,519
Somerset	1,101	1,527	2,052	1,291
South Derbyshire	136	208	656	1,072
Leicestershire	60	747	194	675
Bristol	570	352	1,074	474
Northumberland	—	—	14,331	10,169
	92,222	101,714	213,137	168,446
		92,222	168,446	
Majority against		9,492	44,691	Majority for

Durham: no ballot of 98,500 members.

TABLES FROM DEPARTMENTAL COMMITTEE 1909

TABLE A

SUMMARY SHOWING THE *mean* HOURS WORKED PER FULL DAY AND THE *average* HOURS WORKED PER WEEK FROM BANK TO BANK OF HEWERS (MEN) AND OF THE TOTAL PERSONS EMPLOYED UNDERGROUND AT COAL MINES IN THE VARIOUS DISTRICTS AND FOR THE UNITED KINGDOM ACCORDING TO THE RETURNS RECEIVED

Inspection Districts or Counties	Per Full Day				Per Week	
	Persons Working at the Face (Men) only		Total Persons Underground		Working at the Face (Men),*	Total Underground
	Number Employed	Mean Hours from Bank to Bank per man	Number Employed	Mean Hours from Bank to Bank per Person	Average Hours Bank to Bank per Man.	Average Hours Bank to Bank per Person.
		Hrs. Mins.		Hrs. Mins.	Hrs. Mins.	Hrs. Mins.
East Scotland	22,284	8 41	39,491	8 51	45 6	46 55
West Scotland	17,892	8 54	31,411	8 57	46 32	47 53
Northumberland and Cumberland	20,140	7 28	41,329	8 20	39 56	44 39
Durham County	43,825	6 49	93,193	8 17	37 12	44 10
Yorkshire	36,987	8 29	76,408	8 42	48 19	48 55
Manchester and Ireland	16,160	9 10	30,782	9 32	42 26	46 39
West Lancashire and Cheshire	13,959	9 39	34,548	9 43	52 37	54 16
North Wales	3,463	9 6	6,953	9 22	53 22	53 6
Midland	28,969	9 18	62,269	9 26	53 56	52 57
Stafford	13,939	9 8	34,308	9 17	53 33	53 59
Cardiff	27,665	9 44	61,246	9 54	55 7	54 59
Swansea	12,487	9 19	23,530	9 43	53 34	53 49
Monmouthshire	18,470	9 54	35,639	9 57	54 52	54 42
Southern (excluding Monmouth)	4,260	8 32	9,976	8 44	50 51	51 39
	280,500	8 36	581,083	9 3	47 46	49 53

* i.e. men returned under the heading 2 (a) in the classification of underground labour adopted in the form of return.

TABLE B

SUMMARY SHOWING PERSONS EMPLOYED, OUTPUT PER PERSON, HOURS OF EMPLOYMENT, PERCENTAGE OF ABSENTEEISM AND ACCIDENT DEATH-RATE PER 1,000 PERSONS EMPLOYED *underground* AT COLLIERIES IN THE VARIOUS DISTRICTS OF THE UNITED KINGDOM, ACCORDING TO THE RETURNS RECEIVED

Inspection Districts or Counties	Number of Persons employed *underground* (As per Returns)	Output per Person employed *underground* under the Coal Mines Regulation Acts in 1905.	Hours of Persons employed *underground* from Bank to Bank. Per day.		Per Week		Mean absenteeism percentage (*underground*).		Accident Death-rate per 1,000 persons employed *underground*, under the Coal Mines Regulation Acts in 1905
		Tons	Hrs.	Mins.	Hrs.	Mins.	1899	1905	
East Scotland	39,491	446	8	51	46	55	5·0	5·8	1·22
West Scotland	31,411	417	8	57	47	53	4·7	6·2	1·44
Northumberland and Cumberland	41,329	347	8	20	44	39	5·2	4·6	1·15
Durham County	93,193	390	8	17	44	10	4·3	3·9	0·93
Yorkshire	76,408	341	8	42	48	55	8·3	9·5	1·14
Manchester and Ireland	30,782	324	9	32	46	39	6·6	11·7	0·73
West Lancashire and Cheshire	34,548	327	9	43	54	16	11·1	14·1	1·51
North Wales	6,953	287	9	22	53	6	5·3	11·3	1·44
Midland	62,269	379	9	26	52	57	6·7	7·5	0·95
Stafford	34,308	375	9	17	53	59	9·3	9·1	1·50
Cardiff	61,246	302	9	54	54	59	4·3	5·1	3·71
Swansea	23,530	321	9	43	53	49	4·4	4·5	2·10
Monmouthshire	35,639	310	9	57	54	42	8·3	7·2	1·86
Southern (excluding Monmouth)	9,976	215	8	44	51	39	3·9	7·1	0·82
UNITED KINGDOM	581,083	361	9	3	49	53	6·1	7·1	1·49

Departmental Committee appointed to inquire into probable economic effect of a limit of eight hours to the working day of coal miners. First Report, Part II. Cd. 3427 (Appendix C), pp. 38 and 39.

DEPARTMENTAL COMMITTEE APPOINTED TO INQUIRE INTO THE PROBABLE EFFECT OF A LIMIT
OF EIGHT HOURS TO THE WORKING DAY OF COAL MINERS. Final Report. Cd. 3506.
(Appendix No. 27) p. 294 (652).

STATEMENT NO. 4
(See Q. 12211)

Statement showing the amount of Mortality among Coal Miners, due respectively to
Accident and to all other causes for the years 1900–02.

	Total Mortality	Accident	All other causes
All males	1,000	59	941
All occupied males	925	58	867
All coal miners	846	123	723
Coal miners, in Durham and Northumberland	763	105	658
Coal miners, in Lancashire	1,006	131	875
Coal miners, in West Riding	783	99	684
Coal miners, in Derbyshire and Nottinghamshire	675	80	595
Coal miners, in Staffordshire	846	118	728
Coal miners, in Monmouthshire and South Wales	951	169	782

APPENDIX III TO CHAPTER FIVE

Excerpt from
MEMORANDUM OF AGREEMENT JUNE 30, 1909,
SUPPLEMENTAL TO THE CONCILIATION BOARD
Agreement of December 11, 1905

2.—The workmen's representatives having declared that it is not their
intention to prevent the mutual introduction of any new method which
may lead to the better working of the pits, due regard being had for
safety and economical working, it is agreed that the Owners shall have
freedom to propose any method of working their Collieries without
being met with the objection that their so doing is a breach of custom or
a breach of the Conciliation Board Agreement. Should the workmen
allege that the proposed method of working is a source of extra danger to
the workmen employed at that Colliery this question, in the event of a
failure to agree at the Colliery, shall be referred to the decision of an
experienced and disinterested person to be agreed upon between the
Owners and the workmen's representatives on the Conciliation Board,
or, failing such agreement, to an experienced and disinterested person
to be appointed by the Home Secretary. The Owners and workmen to
be at liberty to call evidence before the person agreed upon or to be
appointed. Any other objection to the proposed method to be brought
before the Conciliation Board in the usual way and the Board shall either
decide the matter or report failure to decide within two months from the
date of reference.

CHAPTER SIX

THE 1910 WAGES AGREEMENT

I. THE NEW CONCILIATION BOARD

THE claim of the associated owners that the Eight Hours Act would abrogate the Conciliation Board Agreement and their insistence that they must be reimbursed for their hypothetical if not prospective losses by a series of immediate concessions, had aroused a spirit of resistance in the coalfield. From around 1908, when hopes raised by increased Parliamentary representation had begun to fade, a mood of militancy was becoming evident in the valleys, while the tense discussions of 1909 sharpened all the issues. Indeed, in March of that year, delegates at the annual conference in Cardiff looked to strike action on a national scale, rather than accept the employers' contention.[1]

Two weeks after a Westminster conference (June 29, 1909) had reached the point of authorising a ballot for a national strike in support of South Wales miners a not dissimilar trouble occurred at the other end of the island. A mid-July conference of the Miners' Federation of Great Britain decided that all its members "be balloted at once on the question of putting into force the 20th Rule in order to maintain the Scottish minimum of 6s. 0d. a day." The result was a large majority: total votes were 518,361 for, and 62,980 against. The miners of South Wales voted for this national strike by 125,311 to 18,356, figures that sufficiently indicate the difficulty the union leaders had in restraining their members from going on strike over local issues.

Even before the result of this ballot was known Winston Churchill, then for fifteen months in the Cabinet as President of the Board of Trade, had made up his mind that intervention was needed to avert a stoppage. Although, by means of this intervention, a strike was averted at the end of July 1909, yet it was clear that in all the British coalfields the miners were finding conditions intolerable if such an overwhelming majority was ready for all the risks of a

[1] "While realising the necessity for a mutual arrangement of the hours of working at the collieries to comply with the requirements of the Mines' Eight Hours' Act, and authorising its representatives to negotiate with the Owners for that purpose, the Conference refuse to accept the suggestion that the Conciliation Board Agreement is terminated by the passing of this Measure."
"That, failing a satisfactory agreement being entered into, we ask the Miners' Federation of Great Britain to put into force Rule 20." (*22.iii.1909.*)

national strike. The comparative quietude of the decade from 1899 onwards had departed, not to return for a generation and more.

In South Wales that autumn of 1909 the Conciliation Board, having run its four year course, was soon to end. The Executive Council, having called a conference for mid-December to consider what changes should be made in the new agreement, decided: "That we recommend the conference to tender notices upon January 1, 1910, to terminate the present Conciliation Board Agreement." (November 22, 1909). In the Cory Memorial Hall, Cardiff, this recommendation was accepted; and draft "workmen's proposals" were adopted and strengthened. Finally it was resolved by a majority of the 300 delegates, representing 141,429 members, "That it be an instruction to the Executive Council that before any new agreement is signed it must be reported to a General Conference, and afterwards submitted to a ballot vote of the workmen for approval or otherwise." (*13.xii.1909.*)

This last decision had provoked considerable discussion. William Brace, in the Chair in the absence through illness of Mabon, was naturally anxious that the condition of affairs of the previous nine years should not be disturbed. The Board of Conciliation for the Coal Trade of Monmouthshire and South Wales had worked pretty well, in the opinion of the leaders, without any question of coalfield ballots to ratify decisions. It was a new departure since 1898 for Conference delegates to insist on tying down the Executive and on supervising their stewardship by means of a ballot vote of the South Wales Miners' Federation. It was, however, part and parcel of the new spirit already mentioned that there should be this more exacting democratic control exercised over the members of the Executive Council, who of course largely made up the workmen's side of the Conciliation Board.

Before the end of the year negotiations on the new demands began. The owners turned out to have many counter-demands. To the M.F.G.B. Executive Committee, meeting in Stoke-upon-Trent, it was reported that "matters were serious in South Wales" and that within a week negotiations might be broken off. The employers had said that they "would forego the damages accruing to them by the decision of the Divisional Court, in the Sixty Hours cases only if the men agreed to work the sixty extra hours per year. The representatives of the men had said that they would not pay the damages, and the men would not work the sixty hours. The Committee resolved that if after the first meeting of the Conciliation Board on January 11th the situation should be "considered by the South Wales representatives to be at so acute a stage that a special conference of this Federation should be called, we authorise our

president and secretary to call one at as early a day as possible."
(*4.i.1910.*)

When this was reported to the Council meeting in Cardiff on
Friday, January 7th, they felt they could go ahead with a fair chance
of steady backing from the other coalfields. They then worked out
workmen's proposals for a new Board. These included an increase in
the minimum from 30 up to 40 per cent; abolition of the 60 per cent
maximum; payment for small coal; for abnormal places; and for
night work; and weekly pays. There followed a series of meetings
of the Board in Cardiff. To meet the public interest in these discussions, it was agreed at the second meeting on Wednesday,
January 19th, to publish both the owners' proposals (for they, too,
had been hatching out schemes for the future) and the workmen's
counter-proposals.

The owners' proposals, described by Thomas Ashton, the old
secretary of the Miners' Federation of Great Britain, as being "of
a reactionary nature" and such as "could not be accepted by the
workmen's side of the Board," were set out, at considerable length,
in fourteen clauses. The chief demands were for a minimum of 20
per cent; multiple shifts; abolition of six turns for five; insistence on
the sixty hours extra; the minimum to be equated with a higher level
of selling price; higher charge for house coal; and fortnightly pays.
The opposition of interests was now very open.

Here in those two sets of proposals was material enough for a
head-on collision and not much apparent ground for reaching any
common standpoint. Sure enough, in half a dozen meetings, neither
side had made headway; nor had agreement been reached on any
proposal. Moreover, the owners by mid-February were reluctant to
meet the workmen's representatives again unless the latter had got
plenary powers to make a settlement, powers that had been denied
them by the South Wales Miners' Federation in its December
Conference. All this was duly reported by William Brace on
Wednesday, February 16th, to the M.F.G.B. Executive Committee,
which decided that the stage had not yet been reached when the
national body should be called upon: before taking any action they
would await the result of the next joint meeting.

In the meantime delegates from the valleys, assembled in Cardiff
to hear a report on the negotiations from William Brace, M.P.,
instructed their representatives "to continue negotiations and meet
the owners' representatives on Thursday next, as already arranged,
with a view to terms of settlement being arrived at: and that power
be given to our representatives to either call a South Wales Conference, or a National Conference as they think desirable." (*19.ii.*
1910.) So after a fortnight the negotiations resumed on Saturday,

February 26th. At the end of that day's proceedings the spokesman for the owners read aloud the employers' conclusions:

That in view of the fact that the workmen have refused to agree to give any increase in the selling price equivalent to the minimum percentage of wages to meet the increased cost shown by the owners or to agree to arbitration as to what the equivalent to the minimum shall be: and still maintain their demand for a further payment for small coal: and for a guaranteed daily wage in abnormal places: neither of which demands the owners can agree to, the owners fail to see any advantage in discussing the other points while these remain unsettled. (*26.ii.1910*.)

Clearly it was a deadlock. The "acute stage" in negotiations envisaged at Stoke-upon-Trent early in January had now been reached. It was necessary to have recourse to the national body: and accordingly an M.F.G.B. special conference was called.

2. WESTMINSTER CONFERENCE OF MARCH 9, 1910

The M.F.G.B. Special Conference on the "South Wales Dispute" met in the Westminster Palace Hotel with a relatively small attendance, over a quarter of the 125 delegates coming from the Welsh valleys. The situation was very fully explained by William Brace, M.P., who then tabled as main items the three points of difference stressed by the owners at the last of the nine meetings held, namely, the minimum and its equivalent selling price, payment for small coal, and abnormal places. Brace explained how the equivalent of 11s. 10d. for a 30 per cent minimum had been decided through an arbiter seven years before, but that

the coalowners, however, propose now that the minimum be reduced to 20 per cent with an equivalent selling price of 12s. 4d. per ton: and that the maximum remain at 60 per cent. Then they have amended that proposal; they agree to continue to pay the 30 per cent minimum, but that the equivalent selling price to the 30 per cent be increased from 11s. 10d. to 13s. 6d. per ton. The conference will, therefore, see that under that proposal the workmen are called upon to suffer a very substantial reduction in wages. (*9.iii.1910*.)

Tom Richards, M.P. gave some further explanations. One was on small coal.[1] On the question of abnormal places, when he remarked that "we have a larger portion of the men affected by the abnormal

---

[1] Tom Richards said: "To get an ordinary wage in a place it requires anything from 75 per cent to 80 per cent of large coal to be sent out, whereas the condition of things are such that the percentage is reversed and they send out 75 per cent of small for which they get no payment at all. This abnormal place question is a very important matter in this dispute, of course, we are asking for payment for small coal, and if this were granted it would mitigate to some extent the question of abnormal places, because if men were paid for the coal whether large or small, the percentage of softs would not affect his wages."

places question than any other coalfield," there were shouts by several delegates of "Question." For this issue of abnormal places, little canvassed in the nineteenth century, was rapidly coming to the fore in every coalfield.

A great deal of time at the conference was occupied, as always at miners' conferences, with the delegates from other coalfields making quite sure that they fully and clearly understood the specific conditions of the particular coalfield under review. For, throughout the island, coalfield differed from coalfield. The conference unanimously adopted the following resolution:

> That this conference stands adjourned until our officials have consulted with the Executive Committee of South Wales, and co-operated with that body to assist them to arrive at a satisfactory settlement; failing a settlement the conference to reassemble for the purpose of deciding what next steps should be taken. (*9.iii.1910.*)

The upshot was that on Thursday, March 17th, Edwards, Ashton, and Smillie attended the Council meeting in the Engineers' Institute in Cardiff: and on the next day went along with the two dozen workmen's representatives to the offices of the Coalowners' Association. There, and also on the Saturday, March 19th, as was remarked by Enoch Edwards ten days later, "We were in with the employers and the men time after time, and at any rate we carried out the functions we were appointed to carry out: and when the meeting broke up on Saturday last we had made some sort of an approach towards a settlement. They had come a little nearer, but no settlement was effected when we left the owners." (*29.iii.1910.*) This was an understatement by Enoch Edwards: for the joint meeting on Saturday, March 19th, had ended in full deadlock. So clear was this to the Executive Council that two days later, with Robert Smillie present, their sole thought was of industrial action. They resolved to apply for "a National Conference at the earliest possible moment, and that it be authorised to take action." (*21.iii.1910.*) They also called a Conference of South Wales Delegates: which decided with unanimity

> That in the opinion of this Conference, seeing that our leaders have exhausted every means of effecting a settlement with the South Wales Coalowners, that this Conference ask the M.F.G.B. to put into operation the 20th Rule. (*23.iii.1910.*)

It is not clear from the records whether an appeal "within 24 hours" was made to the Board of Trade "to intervene"; or whether some less formal approach was made from the Welsh miners' leaders; or whether Sydney Buxton as President of the Board of Trade took the initiative, as he was empowered to do under the Conciliation Act of 1896; but intervene he did. First he had a meeting with the coalowners whom he urged should meet the workmen's representatives once more: and then he had a meeting in London in similar terms with the four officers of the South Wales Miners' Federation. This did bring the parties to the dispute together again.

On Saturday, March 26th, the owners made to the workmen their final offer for a settlement. To this they wanted a definite reply by noon on Wednesday, March 30th, the day before the expiry of the notices. They stated that if the workmen's representatives would recommend these terms for acceptance, the owners would agree that the men should continue work on day to day contracts up to and including April 9th, so as to give time for a ballot to be taken. The workmen's representatives agreed to put the terms before the men for further consideration. But before this could be done the terms had to be submitted to the M.F.G.B. Executive Committee and Conference. So the adjourned national conference did reassemble in London on Wednesday, March 29th.

3. SPECIAL CONFERENCE OF MARCH 29, 1910

Once again the other coalfields came together with the 36 delegates from the South Wales Miners' Federation to debate and decide upon the "South Wales Dispute." There were in all 150 present. As before, William Brace, M.P. was called upon by the chairman to make the opening statement. After recounting the course of events in the week that had passed Brace then read "the net result" of the negotiations and so outlined the owners' proposals, on some of which as he pointed out, there was a very strong feeling amongst the men, "so strong that in many cases they think that the terms ought to be rejected."

Earlier that morning in the Westminster Palace Hotel there had been a special meeting of the Executive Council of the South Wales Miners' Federation, recorded as follows:

The Council meeting was held at 9.30 a.m. to consider the matter of laying before the Miners' Federation of Great Britain the proposals of the owners for a settlement of the Conciliation Board dispute. Arrangements were made for making application to the Conference for putting in force the 20th rule and calling a national stoppage in the defence of the South Wales miners. (*29.iii.1910.*)

Consequently it fell to Tom Richards, M.P. as General Secretary to put this proposition for a national stoppage. This Richards did: but first of all he gave a number of lucid explanations on the questions at issue. Of these the first was on the minimum.[1] Then Richards went on to tell how the employers had proposed that if the workmen would abandon some of their claims they in turn would also abandon some claims. Thus the owners were ready to abandon their claim to sixty hours "and also relieve us of the damages they claim."

Enoch Edwards, M.P., from the chair gently chided Tom Richards for his reference to Rule 20 as "a bit unfair to the conference" and then said the matter was now open for discussion. In the course of the discussion, it became fairly clear that within a coalfield there could be differences of policy and that in South Wales there were two groups amongst the leaders. As against the older leaders, there was now a younger group (not necessarily younger in years) headed by George Barker of Abertillery, C. B. Stanton of Aberdare and James Winstone of Pontnewynydd. George Barker, who had been on the Executive Council, had later gone to China for a time, and then in November 1908, had replaced Michael Roach as agent for the Western Valleys district of Monmouthshire. As soon as he was once more on the Executive Council George Barker took up an independent standpoint and was often enough in opposition to the three parliamentarians who with Treasurer Alfred Onions were the official heads of the Federation. At the conference three weeks earlier Barker spoke mainly in explanation of the effect of the owners' demand on the minimum wage, but in his closing remarks there had been an implied criticism when he said:

Let me say that it is only through the imperfections in the machinery of this Federation that we are here. Until we improve that we shall be compelled to come here district by district when agreements are made. . . . We want all agreements to be made simultaneously throughout the United Kingdom: we should be ten times stronger and this division of opinion would not exist. (*9.iii.1910.*)

On this occasion C. B. Stanton took up the argument about abnormal places, followed by Barker and then by Winstone. These three speeches were countered by a speech from Ben Davies, once the fiery opponent of Mabon in the Rhondda. With this division in the South Wales ranks thus made clear the representatives from other coalfields now had an opportunity to speak. In most cases their standpoints brought cold comfort to the Welsh delegates.

That afternoon the Executive Committee met. Eight out of the eighteen present were Members of Parliament. At great length they went into the question. Their resolution (on which the four South Wales representatives refrained from voting) ran in its final form as follows:

[1] See Appendix to this chapter.

After having carefully considered the whole position in South Wales, we strongly urge the Conference to advise the workmen to accept the terms of settlement put before the Conference as the outcome of negotiations between the coalowners' and the miners' representatives, as we do not think the points of difference are sufficient to justify either a sectional strike in South Wales or a national struggle, with all the tremendous issues involved, this not to be taken as committing other districts of the Federation to support an Amendment of the Eight Hours Act. (*29.iii.1910.*)

This recommendation was immediately communicated to a meeting of the thirty-six South Wales representatives, attending the National Conference: after a lengthy discussion the Executive Council passed the following resolution:

That if the Conference tomorrow accepts the decision of the Committee and refuse to support the South Wales Miners in rejecting the terms of the Owners by putting into operation the 20th Rule and calling a national stoppage, we, the South Wales representatives, believing a stoppage in South Wales alone would be disastrous to the workmen, accept the decision of the National Conference and recommend the South Wales miners to accept the terms with the deletion of the Owners' Abnormal Places' Clause. (*29.iii.1910.*)

Eighteen voted in favour and three against. There were four votes unrecorded, either abstentionists or absentees.

In the next day's discussion, which began with an eloquent and closely argued utterance by Steve Walsh, M.P., who moved the adoption of the Committee's resolution, representatives of the miners' associations first made it clear that they were opposed to a national strike and then spent their time seeking to convince the Welsh delegates that they had come well out of the negotiations. Robert Brown, of the Midlothian Miners' Association (and secretary of the Scottish Miners' Federation) said:

In my opinion they have done very well. They have got rid of the sixty hours and also the question of damages. They have got rid of the double shift, met by the introduction of an overlapping shift. They have got an increase in the minimum of 5 per cent. Taking all these things into consideration it forces every reasonable man to come to the conclusion, as compared with the position put before us three weeks ago, that the miners in South Wales have something to congratulate themselves upon, and I think this resolution ought to be carried. (*30.iii.1910.*)

Thereupon George Barker, "profoundly dissatisfied," expressed his dissent and followed this with a passionate appeal that since small coal was sold "at nearly 8s. per ton," therefore it was time that they got paid for this coal, and his plaint was that

if this agreement is signed for five years it will deprive our men of this payment: I say you are putting us in a humiliating position.

Ten years ago South Wales was on strike, and within six months they

8   TONYPANDY. POLICE EATING IN THE POWER HOUSE

METROPOLITAN POLICE CARRYING THEIR BEDDING

9   TONYPANDY. GLAMORGAN COLLIERY, NOVEMBER 1910

TONYPANDY. BARRICADED SHOPS IN MAIN STREET

were defeated, and then the men turned over to this Federation, and I may say that some of the present leaders opposed us in joining this Federation years ago.

We contended then that there ought to be no more sectional strikes. We have been faithful to this Federation, and we say now that this Federation is shattering the hopes of the Welshmen. They have turned their minds towards you and founded their hopes upon you. I hope you will not throw out these grievances formulated by the men and submitted to you, upon which they ask the assistance of this Federation to help them to get, and upon which they have put their whole soul. I ask you, gentlemen, in conclusion, not to pass this resolution. (*30.iii.1910.*)

One phrase in this stung Tom Richards into an interjection which became a passage-at-arms as follows:—

Richards: When Mr. Barker has the effrontery to get up here and refer to men sitting at the head of affairs who opposed the South Wales men joining the Federation, that cannot be allowed to pass. There are men sitting at the head of affairs who would oppose any organisation, whether it be in South Wales or anywhere else, joining the Miners' Federation, who would have had at that time to bring into this Federation a disorganised body of men. I do not want to use any passion, but I retort to Mr. Barker very deliberately, that the men at the head of affairs built up this organisation, and made it possible to join this Federation, whilst Mr. Barker was doing something in China. He has done nothing absolutely from beginning to end to build up our Federation or securing any better conditions.

Barker: Mr. Richards has stated what is untrue. I was present at the birth. I was on the Executive.

Richards: Then you ran away from us.

Barker: I went to China. I had a right to go where I like.

Richards: You ran away after leading the men over the precipice.

The personal acrimony of this cut-and-thrust in public had behind it a deeper antagonism within the coalfield and the body politic: and soon this was to come to the surface in the months that followed.

4. APRIL DAYS IN CARDIFF

Back in Cardiff, the Executive Council, on Friday, April 1st, decided to issue a Circular "Recommending the Workmen to accept the proposals for a continuance of the Conciliation Board Agreement." It was a stormy conference the next day in the Cory Memorial Hall. William Brace, M.P., who was in the chair, gave a report of the proceedings that had taken place since the last conference (the interview with the President of the Board of Trade; the further meeting of the Board; and the national miners' conference) and Tom Richards, M.P. supplemented it. There was no lack of questions and speakers amongst the 315 delegates. One delegate proposed that the Executive Council "be asked to resign." Then,

F

after the Treasurer, Alfred Onions, had answered questions, came the hour for propositions. These tumbled up from the floor, all hostile. One was for rejecting the employers' terms, because nothing in them bore upon "Abnormal Places, Daymen's Wages, Payment for Small Coal"; another condemned the Council for giving the owners "the power of enforcing the Overlapping Shift" in defiance of the March 23rd Conference, and for this reason asked them to resign; a third called upon "all Members of Parliament" to resign from the Council; while a fourth was to "advise all Workmen to use their Ballot against the terms of settlement."

Brace's eloquence saved the Executive Council from rejection of their policy: and eventually it was carried:

That the Resolution of the Conference held on December 13, 1909, be adhered to, and the proposals for a settlement be submitted to the Ballot of the Workmen as arranged by the Council. (*2.iv.1910.*)

Brace boldly put to the vote the second proposition of those listed above and "very few hands were put up in its favour." But that it should have been moved at all was a portent. Nevertheless when the ballot was taken on April 6th the result was: For the acceptance of the terms[1] of settlement, 97,272 votes, Against 34,963.

There was dissension in the Council: and the trouble could not be kept within doors. So a week later there is again a Council meeting in which there is minuted a resolution upon "Members' Differences" as follows:

That this council, having discussed the practice of indulging in personal attacks on each other by Members of the Council, regards this practice as "being injurious to the best interests of the Federation as a whole, and tending to create suspicion and dissension in our ranks, express the opinion that this course should be discontinued, and each Member undertakes not to make any statement in future which in any way reflects personal discredit on any of his colleagues." (*15.iv.1910.*)

This however, in no way affected the agreement which was signed by both sides of the Conciliation Board which ended its thirteenth meeting on this matter in a spirit of amity, in which a shower of votes of thanks were passed including one to Sydney Buxton who as President of the Board of Trade had brought the contending parties together.

5. AMENDMENT TO THE ACT?

"The two sides of the Board shall unite in procuring an amendment of the Eight Hours Act, making this early starting on Saturday legal." These words proclaiming a common interest of owners and

[1] See Appendix I to this chapter.

workmen, or seeming so to proclaim, with little regard to the interests of colliers in other coalfields, may well have caused qualms of conscience amongst the socialist-minded members of the Board. But there the words were and beneath them the signatures of the twenty-seven "workmen's representatives." So at the next meeting of the M.F.G.B. Executive Committee on Wednesday, April 20th, an application was made by the South Wales Miners' Federation to consider the question of a proposed amendment to the Act. The Secretary said that on his arrival at the hotel the previous night he had received a letter from the President of the Board of Trade, asking the Committee that day to come and hear his views on the proposed Amending Bill. With the exception of the four South Wales representatives they were against any alteration of the Eight Hours Act, but as an act of courtesy it was agreed that the whole of the Committee accept the invitation. (*20.iv.1910.*)

The Committee met Sidney Buxton as arranged: and next they pondered what had taken place at the Board of Trade. The Committee felt bound by the resolutions of Conferences that they could not recommend any alteration to the Eight Hours Act, neither could they withdraw the opposition of the Federation to any amending Bill that might be introduced by the Government. It was resolved "That our Secretary issue a circular to get the opinion of districts on the question: and that a special Conference be called." (*21.iv.1910.*) The circular was duly sent out on June 14th and the special Conference was called for June 28th. But on that day when the delegates came to their customary hotel in Westminster they found there was no room in the inn because "the proprietor had a big dinner on, the Archbishop of Canterbury and friends." So, after preliminary business and chairman's remarks and after passing a resolution[1] of compliments they adjourned till the morrow. In his remarks the chairman had said:

When we were before the President he told us that he had received deputations on the question of the South Wales settlement from both sides, both parties in Wales, both parties to the agreement, both the employers and workmen. All we were asked for as a Committee was, could we give a sort of undertaking that as a Federation we would not oppose the Government if they brought in a Bill to amend the Act, the recent Act dealing with the hours, that portion of it which deals with the time that a man leaves off between the Friday shift and the Saturday shift. He said that he had the consent of the Cabinet to bring in such a Measure.

He would bring in a Bill in harmony with the views of the coalowners and the workmen, I suppose, on this overlapping shift, to make it possible

[1] "That this Conference extends to Dr. Wilson, M.P., its great pleasure and gratification at the degree of D.C.L. having been conferred upon him by Durham University, and trust he will live long to enjoy that honour." (June 28, 1910, p. 318 (M.F.G.B.).)

so that they could work six days without entrenching on the ordinary eight hours shift, and finishing on a Saturday towards twelve or one o'clock.

The M.F.G.B. Conference three months earlier, in its resolution advising the South Wales workmen to accept the terms of settlement, had expressly stipulated that this was not to commit other districts to an amendment of the Eight Hours Act. Enoch Edwards therefore made this clear to the President of the Board of Trade:

We had to tell him that as a Federation we were not disposed to sit still while the Act is re-opened. We were asked as to whether we would observe a benevolent neutrality. We felt as a Committee that while we were in this position in seeking to interpret this resolution and your general views as expressed at the Conference, we felt as a Committee we could not take upon ourselves to move any further without giving all districts an opportunity of dealing with it and bringing them together to consult them on this matter. We felt it was so vital that everybody should have an opportunity of having their say from their point of view. It is not a new point—it was raised in the early days, twelve months ago in this hotel on the hours question. (*28.vi.1910.*)

The discussion accordingly began with John Wadsworth, M.P., expressing on behalf of the Yorkshire Miners' Association their inflexible hostility to any change of the Act. A series of other districts reported in the same sense. With the exception of three small districts (Cleveland, Leicestershire and Bristol, totalling less than 17,000 members) all were against any tinkering with the legislative enactment for which they had campaigned for over a score of years. There was a strong sense of grievance in the speeches from the South Wales delegation[1] but despite this the following resolution was passed:—

That this Conference having fully considered the position in South Wales hereby re-affirms the Resolution passed on March 30, 1910, and resolves to oppose any Amendment to the Mines Regulation Act, 1908, which is not introduced or sanctioned by the Miners' Federation of Great Britain. (*29.vi.1910.*)

It was not surprising if a sense of grievance was also harboured

[1] For example, in the speech of E. Gill which ran as follows:
"We have for many years been agitating for the raising of the lower paid workmen and we wanted payment for small coal and various other matters, and we want as a district to try and make an agreement: and we failed to get what we fought for and came to this Federation: we came to an open Conference, and the official element in an open Conference recommended that South Wales, or rather said, that we must accept the terms laid down by the employers; and because the Executive of the Federation had recommended these terms the South Wales colliers had to take into consideration their wives and families. Consequently they had to vote in favour of selling themselves to the employers for five years because the Federation recommended those terms, and now you are trying to evade the responsibility of your action and tell us to break faith with the employers. If the Committee had asked the miners of Scotland to go into the bowels of the earth for another five years under those conditions they would have said, 'No.' In my opinion you are evading your responsibilities." (*29.vi.1910.*)

by some of the Welsh owners, to whom it seemed clear that on this one issue of an amending Act they had been thoroughly out-manœuvred, not by their own workmen but by the experienced and skilled parliamentarians of the M.F.G.B. Executive Committee. It was their own workmen, however, who would have to face the consequences.

6. IDEOLOGICAL CONFLICT

By the end of 1908 the South Wales Miners' Federation had been in existence for ten years. Its membership after the rapid rise of the first two years had been fluctuating. It was not commensurate with the huge increase in the manpower of the South Wales coalfield and was becoming a yet smaller fraction as the months and years went by. But the Federation was now part of the Miners' Federation of Great Britain, which by the end of that year 1908 embraced every coalfield in the islands, and had after a twenty years' campaign obtained the shorter hours legislation. By the end of 1908 also the decision to join the Labour Representation Committee (as the Union documents still called it) was accepted though the formal membership of the Labour Party was not complete for another twelve-month. These movements, whether of progress or of regress, whether institutional or legislative, had taken place without any visible alteration of policy or of general outlook amongst the agents or in the leading committee of the South Wales Miners' Federation. But there were great changes maturing amongst the members, due both to certain worsened conditions and to a growing enlightenment over the source of these conditions.

When the Federation began in 1898 it was fifteen years after the revival of socialism in Britain in the form of and through the medium of organised societies. These were the Social-Democratic Federation in 1883, the Fabian Society and the Socialist League in 1884. Here and there two of the socialist journals, *Justice* edited by H. M. Hyndman and *The Commonweal* edited by William Morris, were to be found in the valleys. These were to be reinforced in the early 'nineties by two additional weeklies both published from Manchester; they were *Clarion* edited by Robert Blatchford, and *Labour Leader* owned and edited by Keir Hardie. In the same period of years meetings were being held in one valley after another by socialist agitators and propagandists. But in 1898 the old influences still prevailed. The mass of the miners were as yet disinclined to alter their old allegiances.

The dominant influence in the Welsh coalfield was "the Chapel." This, the expression of religious dissent or nonconformity, was closely linked in many cases with a fervent support of the Liberal Party. Now both in the Free Churches, whose communicants outnumbered those of the Church of England by more than three to one in the coalfield, and also in the Liberal Party there were to be found in leading positions many of the mine owners. This tended to a certain community of outlook between the leaders of the working miners and the coal owners. The miners' leaders indeed had in nearly every case come to prominence first in the Chapel, in which as a rule they continued to act as leading laymen and often in the case of Methodists as fervent lay preachers.

Suddenly, launched in Loughor, from 1904 onwards, a fervour of religious revivalism swept through the valleys. Congregations were carried away by it. Outstanding in this activity were such men as Evan Roberts. Revivalism brooked no rival outlook, no absorption in the affairs of this world, let alone the hostility of sceptics and free-thinkers. It lasted for several years and only gradually died away. It was linked with the previous strong teetotaller and nonconformist sentiment of the majority of religious people of Wales. It was not directly concerned with the propaganda of disestablishment of the Church of England in Wales, but it stemmed from the same family of religious belief and ecclesiastical policy. Its effect amongst the miners was dramatic. Underground, hymns were being sung in seams that at one time had heard only the imprecations of frustrated colliers. It was often told later that "the ponies stopped working when the men stopped swearing at them in Welsh."

But the socialists were not only conducting education and carrying on propaganda. They were also taking part in electoral contests, local and national. Of these the election of Keir Hardie for the double-barrelled constituency of Merthyr Tydfil took place amid the jingo atmosphere of the "Khaki Election". The Marquis of Salisbury, then Prime Minister, advised the dissolution of Parliament in the autumn of 1900, a few months after the popular rejoicing over the relief of Mafeking had given a new word to the language. Hitherto all demonstrations of mass excitement had for the most part tended, from Chartist times onward, to be the result of feeling against some Government action or policy. The night of Mafeking was an example of the same sort of imperialistic fervour and jingoism as had characterised the crowds in Paris thirty years before when they cheered on the outbreak of the Franco-Prussian War and shouted the illstarred words "À Berlin, à Berlin."

The victory at Merthyr Tydfil was partly the product of a vigorous branch of the Independent Labour Party. At Briton Ferry and elsewhere throughout the South Wales coalfield there were other branches of the I.L.P., while in many parts the Social-Democratic

Federation had a local branch. Apart from this electoral victory at Merthyr Tydfil the building of socialist groupings seemed uphill work for several years.

Outside the island new developments were heralded by the Russian Revolution of 1905 to 1907. Though defeated, it had significant echoes all over the world not least in India. In the hour of its defeat it was hailed by Lenin as the "dress rehearsal" for a future victorious revolution.

On the other side of the Atlantic the foundation in 1905 of the I.W.W. (Industrial Workers of the World) was to affect (though only after a time-lapse and only to a lesser extent) the working class movement in other English speaking countries. The next year the Charter of Amiens of the French trade unions was also to have an effect beyond the boundaries of the French Republic. Thus by the end of 1905 and in the course of 1906 there was already a quickening within the body politic.

The overwhelming defeat of the Tories and the return of over fifty Trade Union and Labour representatives to the House of Commons had a marked effect. Twenty-nine of them, sponsored by the Labour Representation Committee declared themselves in 1906 to be the Labour Party. All this had aroused great expectations. Apart, however, from a few such measures as the Trade Disputes Act of 1906 these expectations were not to be gratified. Hence arose a new distinction, not only between the Lib-Labs (including most M.P.s subsidised by the M.F.G.B.) and those who belonged to the Labour Party, but within the Labour Party and within the socialist bodies. It was between new and old, between Left and Right, between the rank and file and the established leaders, between Socialism and Liberalism.

Disappointment with results in Parliament made many workers consider what they could do for themselves. Perhaps the most remarkable example of this occurred some two years later when an economic crisis in 1908 brought widespread unemployment and there occurred for the first time hunger marches pioneered by Stewart Gray, a notable leader of the unemployed.

Another example was the development if not the beginning of a new move for working-class education, heralded by a great many classes and study circles in the towns of Britain and also in some of the coalfields. In this matter of education a complete division arose which had a bearing on South Wales trade unionism and partly originated from it. In 1899 Walter Vrooman and Charles Beard, two citizens of the United States, had helped to found what was afterwards called Ruskin College. Situated in Oxford, it was a sort of philanthropic venture to begin with and had the social outlook indicated by the title of the College. In 1907 the Trades Union Congress Parliamentary Committee advised unions to send students thither: and students were sent by sundry miners' associations. Notable among these was Ebby Edwards from Northumberland. The first Welsh students sent to Ruskin were from the district organisations. Thus, from the Eastern and Western valleys of Monmouthshire there went to Ruskin College Arthur Jenkins, Frank Hodges, Ted Gill and W. J. Saddler. From the Rhondda valleys there were sent in one year four students: Jack Evans and Tom Evans, two brothers from Cwm Park, Treorchy; Noah Rees and Noah Ablett. The eldest of these and the most experienced was Noah Rees, who had been secretary of a lodge in Ogmore Vale as a boy of sixteen. Sometime before 1903 he was chosen as check-weighman at the Cambrian Colliery. The type of student that Rees exemplified emerges very clearly from his correspondence with those who sponsored his studies.[1]

Trouble was brewing in Oxford. It was in the year 1908 that there came a great disruption. Students from South Wales that year, and from some other coalfields as well as railwaymen and students sponsored by other unions, found themselves in a College where there was political strife between the governing body on the one hand and the Principal, Dennis Hird, on the other. Hird wished to include the doctrines of Charles Darwin and advanced teachings in sociology in the curriculum of the College. The orthodox university teaching was desired by the governors who finally dismissed Dennis Hird.

In the spring of 1909 the students, and conspicuously those from South Wales, went on strike, withdrew from the College and with the assistance and backing of their valley organisation continued their studious activities outside Ruskin. This led to the formation

[1] At the delegate meeting of the Rhondda District on January 28th the following letter was read:

"Ruskin College, Oxford, January 26, 1907

Dear Mr. Morgan,

I take the opportunity of writing in view of the District Meeting on 28th instant. I desire to thank the delegates and yourself and through you the workers of the Rhondda for the opportunity which I now enjoy, viz., of attempting to acquire some knowledge which be it little or much it will be my pleasure and duty to use on behalf of my class. I may say that I find it very hard to think and study and to try to commit things to a rather fickle memory, after spending some 22 years in doing something very different. The subjects taught so far are Sociology (Spencer), Economics (Marshall), Logic and Public Administration. I may tell you that Ablett of Porth and myself study together and share the same room. I might also add that we miss the Welsh steam coal, and in consequence I am personally sporting a fine mellow sample of a cold. However, I hope to be able to conduct myself in such manner that my fellow workers will not regret having sent me here.

Yours very sincerely,

Noah Rees.

P.S. Tom Evans will probably write to you as well."

Several delegates approved of the sentiments in the letter.

of the Central Labour College in Oxford late that year. At the moment it caused a great division which was maintained by the propagandists on either side. On the side of the rebellious students there was the *Plebs* magazine, founded in 1909 and having a very considerable effect in spreading the appeal of the new kind of teaching and of the forms of organisation bound up with it. When *Plebs* came to be edited by J. F. Horrabin, celebrated equally for his strip cartoons and his cartography, it attained a wide circulation maintained at a considerably later date under the temporary editorship of Maurice Dobb. On the other side the propaganda for state-aided adult education had been carried through, more by example than by precept by R. H. Tawney, whose kind of socialism with its religious accompaniment accorded ill with the doctrines taught in the new Central Labour College.

Of those who came back from Oxford to the South Wales coal-field, the students from Monmouthshire were soon to be chosen as leading representatives of the workmen. Those from the Rhondda were to play an outstanding part either in militant trade union activity or in the propaganda of ideas generated in the student body at Ruskin and spread through the Plebs League, founded in October 1908. Of all of these Noah Rees, experienced in trade union administration, exerted greatest influence as secretary of the four-thousand-strong Cambrian Lodge.

The most outstanding in grasp of theory and the most tireless propagandist of the new ideas was Noah Ablett. His nimble wits, previously exercised upon religious disputations, such as those aroused in the chapels by "The New Theology" of R. J. Campbell, had a quick appreciation of the philosophic and economic doctrines of Karl Marx.

He was ceaseless in organising socialist educational classes. Born in Ynyshir he was elected checkweigher in Mardy at the head of the Rhondda Fach: and from there exercised an influence that was to bring him into the leadership of the South Wales Miners' Federation.

F*

SUMMARY OF 1910 WAGE AGREEMENT
(Third Conciliation Board)

The content of the five-year Wage Agreement of April 1910, was in many clauses not very different from the four-year agreement of December 1905, while in some clauses the wording was exactly the same. But whereas the 1905 agreement had 18 clauses, the 1905 agreement had half as many more. Clauses 1 to 6 were much the same as before and covered the following points:—Board of Conciliation, Title, Composition, Chairman, Obligation of Both Sides to Enforce Decisions, Procedure. Clause 7 (set out in full below) with exactly the same wording registered thereby that the owners from 1900 onwards had successfully resisted the workmen's endeavour to be paid for small coal: the consequential clauses 8 and 9 remained the same as before, as did clause 11. Clause 10, however, had its figures altered: and clause 12 was the first of nine new clauses, mostly arising from the Eight Hour Act.

Clauses 21–27 were practically the same as Clauses 12–18 in the 1905 Agreement—the main change being that "Customs and Conditions" were dated back to December 1899, instead of to December 1879.

Conciliation Board Agreement, 1910. Clause 7.

"The Mineral to be gotten is clean large coal only as hereinafter described. The cutting prices to be paid to the collier shall be the several standard prices prevailing and paid at the collieries of the owners respectively. Such standard cutting price shall be paid upon the weight of the large coal to be ascertained in manner hereinafter appearing and includes all services in respect of the small coal necessarily produced in filling the large coal in conveying it from the working places to the screen at the surface and in the process of screening that price being equal to the value of all the services involved in getting such large coal and small coal and being more than the value of the services rendered in respect of the large coal only. The respective weights of such large coal and small coal for the purpose of paying the collier shall be ascertained as follows:

"After each tram of coal is brought to the weighing machine it shall be weighed and the tare of the tram shall be deducted from the gross weight. The coal shall then be tipped over the screen in use at the colliery to separate the small coal passing through the screen from the large coal passing over it. The small coal which shall pass through the screen shall be weighed and that weight shall be deducted from the gross weight of the coal in the tram in order to ascertain the weights of such large screened coal and small coal respectively and the cutting price paid to the collier upon the weight of the large screened coal as aforesaid shall during the continuance of this Agreement be deemed to be the value of the services rendered in respect of both the large screened coal and small coal the weights of which respectively shall be ascertained as aforesaid."

This was a change and for the worse. But when it came to Clause 10, it was the lack of alteration that proved significant. Wages, which at the time of signature stood at 50 per cent above the standard of December 1879, were to vary within the following limits for the five years from April 8, 1910, to March 31, 1915. They were not to be less than 35 per cent nor more than 60 per cent above the December 1879, standard: the minimum of 35 per cent was made equivalent to an average nett selling price of large coal at 12s. 5d. per ton f.o.b. The remainder of clause 10 (c) stipulated in phrasing of remarkable ingenuity (or of remarkable clumsiness if regarded from another standpoint) that 50 per cent should be equivalent to two separate selling prices.

Conciliation Board Agreement, 1910. Clause 10 (c)

"During the continuance of this Agreement the rate of wages shall, subject to sub-section (d) hereof, not be less than 35 per cent above nor more than 60 per cent above the December 1879 Standard of wages paid at the respective collieries. The minimum of 35 per cent above the December 1879 Standard of wages shall subject to sub-section (d) hereof be paid when the average nett selling price of large coal is at or below 12s. 5d. per ton f.o.b. When the nett selling price of large coal reaches 14s. and does not exceed 14s. 9d. per ton f.o.b. the rate of wages shall subject to sub-section (d) hereof be 50 per cent above the rates paid under the Standard of December 1879 and when the nett selling price exceeds 14s. 9d. per ton f.o.b. the workmen shall be entitled to claim advances in the general rate of wages in excess of the 50 per cent and up to the said maximum of 60 per cent but in cases of claims to advances above 50 per cent 50 per cent shall be taken to be the equivalent of 14s. 9d. per ton f.o.b. and in the case of claims to reductions 50 per cent shall be taken to be the equivalent of 14s. per ton f.o.b. The average nett selling prices shall be taken as for large colliery screened coal delivered f.o.b. at Cardiff, Barry, Newport, Swansea, Port Talbot and Llanelly." (1910.)

In addition to this peculiar stipulation the other provisions of Clause 10 (c) represent a considerable advantage to the employers. In the first place coal prices were rising. Consequently wages were never near the minimum of 35 per cent whose increase above the former 30 per cent proved to be of small significance. Secondly, after slight fluctuation upwards the wage level again stood at 50 per cent in December 1911. From March 1, 1912, the wage level moved rapidly upwards for fifteen months till it hit the ceiling in 1913. For 23 months thereafter it stuck at the maximum of 60 per cent. Moreover the changed equivalent of what had been taken over from the sliding scale was to the disadvantage of the workmen. Consequently on this clause there was bound to be growing dissatisfaction. In addition there were the questions of payment for small coal, and for abnormal places on which nothing had been yielded by the employers. These were grounds for growing dissatisfaction at a time when the cost of living was mounting rapidly. The wage machinery took no account of the high cost of living which affected every home in Monmouthshire and South Wales.

On the nine new clauses there was further dissatisfaction, even on one or two items which were favoured by the workmen's side as well as the owners. Thus, while clause 12 withdrew the obligation on workmen to work the permissive extended hours in Section 3(i) of the Coal Mines Regulation Act 1908, on the other hand there was to be no advance in standard rate for prices—nor, of course, any reduction. In clause 13 the custom of payment, 6 turns for 5 worked by night, was to continue: but payment for overtime (forbidden under the Act) was to cease.

In clause 14 the owners withdrew their claim for double shifts (a practice extremely repugnant to the Welsh miners) but were allowed certain afternoon shifts for which they were to pay 6 turns for 5 as though for night work. In certain circumstances they were also allowed double shifts. Clause 15 ran as follows:

"An overlapping shift shall be worked where required by the owners, such shift shall not start earlier than 6 a.m. and not later than 9 a.m. On Saturdays this shift shall start and finish at the same time as the first shift. The two sides of the Board shall unite in procuring an Amendment to the Eight Hours Act making this early starting on Saturday legal."

Clause 16 altered the Sunday shifts day work from the customary six to the legal maximum of eight hours. Mealtimes were fixed at 20 minutes by clause 17. Clause 18 fixed surface hours at $8\frac{1}{2}$ per day (excluding banksmen). By clause 19 the number and names of men accompanying an injured workman out of the pit were to be selected by the manager: while clause 20 stipulated no stoppage for funerals except by agreement with the management.

APPENDIX II TO CHAPTER SIX

ORGANISATION

Some Observations from Memory of Early Mining Conditions
(by Lewis Williams, 67 Cilhaul, Treharris, Glam.)[1]

Mention is made of the low state of organisation in the early years of the Federation. To anyone who lived through those years this is no great surprise when we remember that most of the miners were men who had come into the industry from rural areas where the nonconformist religion was very strong, and where trade unionism was regarded as ungodly and weakening the faith in Providence. Allied to that the rural areas of Wales, and indeed South Wales too, had passed through a very heavy religious revival which can almost be said to be mass hysteria. Some of the scenes that took place during 1904–5 were fantastic, when pubs were empty, horses underground refused to work because their haulier had stopped cursing, everything had become topsy-turvy, and organisation suffered, and it was as much as the leaders could do to keep the lodge in funds. Showcards became necessary every few months to whip in the non-unionists, and strikes were quite common, until some owners allowed some men to draw from the colliery office sufficient monies to clear up. Unfortunately, the same men were in arrears again very soon. Drastic methods were used to persuade some of the recalcitrants, such as marching them in front of a procession dressed in a white shirt, another was to refuse to ride in the pit cage with them, and at the same time allowing the winder to know that there was a non-unionist in the cage, with some-times very unpleasant results to the lone rider. Some lodges resorted to collecting the Federation dues from door to door, and I did this for years.

[1] Lewis Williams, well-known for his many broadcasts on the B.B.C. Welsh Region, was one of the veteran trade unionists at the Miners' Gala in Cardiff in 1964 a few days after the above was communicated to the author.

It had one very important advantage, it provided that personal touch, not only with the workman himself but with his good wife as well, something that has been lost since the dues are deducted at the colliery office. Today, I fear that a great number of the workmen are not conscious trade unionists, but should be called cardboard trade unionists. They are very much alive to their rights but fail badly in the recognition of their responsibilities. At one time a good muster of men could be gathered for a mass meeting of the workmen of one pit, today a very small attendance can be got together even from three or four adjacent pits. It proves the old adage that what you don't see you don't miss: the dues are paid through the office and are not paid at the lodge or to the collector.

CAMBRIAN COMBINE DISPUTE (1910)

I. A LOCK-OUT AND STRIKE BALLOT

IN the Welsh coalfield the year 1909 had been stormy. The year 1910 was to be stormier still. In the autumn there began in the Rhondda valley an historic struggle of long duration which had wide repercussions, from the neighbouring valleys, to every coalfield in Great Britain, and involved the civil and military authorities

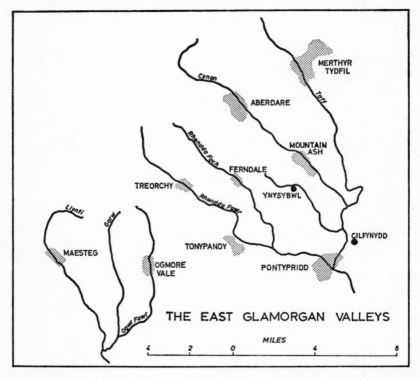

THE EAST GLAMORGAN VALLEYS

MILES

not only locally but on a national scale. The legal "Eight Hours" underground had brought many new problems, or had made existing problems more difficult to solve. To many colliers the negotiations over the new wage agreement had been anything but satisfactory. It was hardly with their goodwill that the new Board was launched in April 1910 upon its five year course. On the crucial problem of abnormal places (made more acute by the legal decisions of Justice Bryn Roberts) there had been engendered a widespread and deep suspicion which was apt to apply to any move on the side of the coal owners or the colliers. Meantime the cost of living was rising. All these and many more industrial and economic factors lay behind the "troubles" that were to mark the twelvemonth from autumn 1910, onwards. But contemporary observers were quick to note other features. In a chronicle of events[1] published in autumn 1911, and written from the standpoint of the coal owners, it was remarked:

> The causes were no less personal and political than they were industrial and economic. For over eighteen months prior to the outbreak at the mid-Rhondda collieries of the Cambrian Colliery Combine, a severe contest for supremacy had been waged between the younger and the older leaders of the South Wales Miners' Federation. The younger leaders were socialists imbued with communistic theories concerning the relations of capital and labour, and the older leaders were orthodox trades unionists.

The origin of the "Cambrian Combine Dispute" was in the Ely Pit at Penygraig in the Rhondda No. 1 District. This pit was owned by the Naval Colliery Company which in turn was controlled by Cambrian Collieries Limited whose Chairman was D. A. Thomas, M.P. Thwarted in his ambition to be one of the new Campbell-Bannerman administration following upon the triumph of the Liberal Party which he had done so much to secure, D. A. Thomas, M.P., had in the spring of 1906 returned to Clydach Vale and plunged once more into the productive side of the coal trade. He resumed his old plans for integration of the steam coal section of the industry, but now by the method of building a horizontal trust. Within a little over four years he had absorbed into his domain many collieries adjacent to Clydach Vale[2]—as well as many other concerns, including local newspapers. By 1910 these mineral properties covered nearly 8,000 acres, produced nearly three million tons of coal per annum, and employed nearly twelve thousand mineworkers. Through his acquisition in 1907 of Glamorgan Collieries, D. A. Thomas had become a member of the Monmouth-shire and South Wales Coal Owners' Association, which was no longer dominated by his old antagonist Sir William Lewis—with whom indeed he buried the hatchet at a public meeting in 1908. Thus a corpus of centralised capital, the Cambrian Combine, had now behind it the other owners associated within the coalfield.

[1] Compiled partly from Home Office papers (not always quoted with complete accuracy), it is entitled: *Labour Strife in the South Wales Coalfield, 1910–1911: A Historical and Critical Record of the Mid-Rhondda, Aberdare Valley and other Strikes.* David Evans, Educational Publishing Co. Ltd., Cardiff (1911).
[2] See Appendix I to this chapter.

The coming into existence of this large aggregation of capital had caused a growth of solidarity first among its employees and then more widely in the Rhondda and throughout the coalfield. The Cambrian Lodge was well organised. Noah Rees who was soon to become an Executive Councilman had done his work well. The twenty-six districts of the colliery with its numerous seams sent well-nigh fifty representatives to the full Lodge committee. Beyond this was a joint committee of the whole combine.

Originally as an off-shoot from this Cambrian Lodge there had come together in 1909 an "unofficial miners' reform committee" beginning in the Rhondda and rapidly spreading to whatever parts of the coalfield had been affected by the propaganda of the Plebs League whose first secretary[1] was George Sims of Bermondsey, a Ruskin College "striker."

The Ely management had decided to open a new seam, the Upper Five Foot, or Bute Seam. A new price had to be fixed for it. After test working had been carried on to make a basis for negotiations the haggling began and went on for many months. The owners alleged that the men had so worked it during the test period in 1909 as to make the average output lower than it would normally be when the seam was brought fully into operation. The matter finally came before the Conciliation Board in December 1909 and referees were appointed. On June 8, 1910, the final offer was made of a piece rate of 1s. 9d. per ton. The workmen had demanded a rate of 2s. 6d. per ton on the ground that it was a particularly troublesome seam which would result in many abnormal places.[2] There was deadlock. Two days later on June 10, 1910, it was announced that the referees from the Conciliation Board had failed to agree.

Three weeks later, on August 1, 1910, the owners posted lockout notices. The seam in question affected eighty colliers. The owners locked out the whole of the miners working in the Ely Pit including 800 men who were not affected by the matter in dispute. A suggestion for arbitration was rejected by the coalowners association and the lockout took effect on September 1st.

The Committee of the Naval Lodge thereupon issued a manifesto asking for support from the whole of the coalfield. In this they said that the Bute seam upon which there had been failure to agree over a piece price list, was

ready for operation at each of the collieries of the Combine, viz.: Cambrian, Clydach Vale; Glamorgan, Llwynypia; Britannic, Gilfach Goch; Naval, Penygraig. These four form between them a mighty

---

[1] At a later date Winifred Horrabin became secretary.

[2] "To this day," the author was informed in 1963 by Jack Jones, then agent for the Rhondda, "the Bute Seam is of a nature that presents problems in price list negotiations."

quadrangle, and from this seam alone millions of tons of coal will ultimately be worked. But the exceedingly pertinent and important fact is that nowhere at these collieries on this seam has a price list been settled; hence it is a fact of infinite moment that the Ely Pit should at this moment be made the cock-pit—the centre of this despotic attempt to force upon us a starvation price list. A price list once settled will undoubtedly be a price list for the whole of the Cambrian Combine.

On Monday, September 5th, two of the Naval pits, Nantgwyn and Pandy, stopped work in sympathy with the locked-out workmen of the Ely pit. In the Cambrian and Glamorgan collieries, meetings on Wednesday, September 7th, decided to strike a week later. On Friday, September 9th, there was a meeting of No. 1 Rhondda District of the South Wales Miners' Federation, with delegates from some forty lodges present. The senior miners' agent, William Abraham, M.P., attended this delegate meeting. There he pleaded with the three lodges not to come out on strike. "My friend D. A. Thomas," he said, "has been suffering from poor health: and I feel sure that on his holiday in France he will not benefit in health if he were to hear of such a strike as this. I beg you, I beg you to hold your hand." At this point W. H. Mainwaring, prominent in the Cambrian Lodge, stood up and said "Mr. D. A. Thomas may be your friend, Mr. Abraham; he is not our friend. But we have heard your plea. We will call off the strike, but on one condition, Mabon. The condition is that, to consider the whole matter, you grant us a coalfield conference in seven days from now." Mabon gave the required assurance. This was just what the local men were keen to have, a forum to put their case and to broaden the conflict so as to confront effectively the capitalist power that was now massed against them. There was therefore no strike: the decision to come out on strike was rescinded. The promise of the President of the union was fulfilled by the calling of a conference. On Friday, September 16th, the Executive Council in Cardiff decided:

That the Council recommend the conference tomorrow to agree that the whole of the workmen employed at the collieries of the Cambrian Combine be given permission to tender notices upon the 1st of October next, to terminate their contracts, and that a weekly levy be made upon all the members of the Federation to provide the necessary financial support.

Next day, at the conference in Cory Hall, there were 248 delegates present representing 147,430 members. The report, given by D. Watts Morgan (then an agent in the Rhondda, junior to W. Abraham) was supplemented by statements from Noah Morgan, chairman of the Naval Committee, and Tom Smith, delegate of the Ely Pit. On a card vote the Council's recommendation was rejected by 1,486 votes to 1,171. The decision was for a ballot to decide on whether the Cambrian workmen should strike alone, with the support of a regular coalfield levy, or whether the whole South Wales Miners' Federation should come out on strike.[1]

At a meeting of the Conciliation Board held on September 23rd, F. L. Davis, president of the owners' side, protested against the holding of this strike ballot which the owners looked upon as a distinct breach of the wages agreement. To this the representatives of the workmen replied that the locking out of the whole of the workmen of the Ely Pit who were not concerned in the dispute that affected some dozens of workmen only on the matter of the Five Foot Seam was equally a breach of the agreement.

Two days later it was reported that the ballot had had the following result: For granting financial support: 76,978. For giving notice to stop work, 44,868. Majority for financial support, 32,110.

While the strike notices were running throughout the month of October, the atmosphere in the coalfield, especially in the districts of Rhondda, Aberdare and Ogmore, was becoming more and more tense and critical. There was a widespread feeling that the owners were in an unreasonable mood: while similar suspicions were entertained in the ranks of the owners.[2]

Nevertheless, negotiations had begun and W. Abraham, together with D. Watts Morgan, on October 22nd met D. A. Thomas, managing director; Leonard Llewellyn, manager; and others representing the Naval Colliery Company. Present also at the negotiations was a committee representing the Naval Colliery workmen. This meeting reached the point where Mabon negotiated a price with the representative of the coalowners of 2s. 1·3d., as against the 1s. 9d. offered by the owners, and the 2s. 6d. asked for by the men. These terms "were drawn up for submission to the workmen" who did not accept them. This proposal, treated later by the owners as

---

[1] The ballot was taken nine days later on September 27th, as soon as the ballot paper could be printed and sent to the lodges, as follows:

CAMBRIAN COMBINE
DISPUTE

BALLOT PAPER

1. I AM IN FAVOUR OF FINANCIALLY SUPPORTING THE CAMBRIAN COMBINE WORKMEN FROM THE FUNDS AND BY LEVY ACCORDING TO RULE.

2. I AM IN FAVOUR OF ALL WORKMEN IN THE COALFIELD GIVING NOTICE TO STOP WORK IN SUPPORT OF THE CAMBRIAN COMBINE WORKMEN.

[2] The contemporary chronicler David Evans was quick to adopt in his opening pages the contention of the owners:

"It is here desirable to point out further that the complaints of boycott and lockout urged against the employers ignored altogether the fact that it was the refusal of the workmen to accept what the coalowners' referee considered a fair offer, and the impossibility of working the pit at a profit without a reasonable price list, that were responsible for the closing down of the Ely Pit."

having been a settlement dishonoured by the workmen, was recorded in the Council minutes as follows:

Several meetings had been held between the representatives of the owners and the workmen. The last meeting was attended by Mr. Fred L. Davis and Mr. William Abraham, M.P., the chairman of the Conciliation Board at which certain terms of settlement were drawn up for submission to the workmen. The workmen met and considered these terms which they unanimously rejected as not being satisfactory. (*28.x.1910.*)

A long discussion enfsued at the Council meeting upon "the situation created by this ailure to settle." Three days later the notices of the whole of the Cambrian Combine would run out. All sorts of suggestions were put forward to get a settlement. Eventually the Council chose a deputation consisting of John Williams, M.P., Vernon Hartshorn, John Davies and Tom Richards, M.P. The business of this deputation was to meet the joint committee of the Combine workmen "to put before them the whole situation with a view of ascertaining whether a ballot of their workmen should be taken on the question whether they should stop work or financially support the other workmen." (*28.x.1910.*)

This high-powered deputation duly met the joint committee at the Thistle Hotel in Llwynypia on the evening of Saturday, October 29th. It urged that the Combine Committee reconsider the decision to reject the proposed terms of October 22nd which the owners called "the settlement": that they give an experimental trial to these terms which might be allowed to go to a ballot vote. The committee replied that the terms, reported to them by Mabon and Watts Morgan on Monday of that week, had only three days before (Wednesday, October 26th) been rejected almost unanimously at a mass meeting of the workmen most concerned. Furthermore, they said they would not go against the decision of the coalfield ballot by which all were committed to a stoppage of all Cambrian Combine pits and to general levies in support thereof. Finally, they passed the following resolution:

That the tyrannical action of the Cambrian Combine in locking out our fellow-workmen, and endeavouring through their sufferings to force upon them the acceptance of an unfair price-list, must be resisted at all costs, and that we further pledge ourselves to be faithful to the decision of the Federation ballot, and to refuse to work for the Cambrian Combine until a fair price-list has been settled for the Ely Pit workmen, or the 800 of our fellow-workmen who are not affected are reinstated in their employment. (*29.x.1910.*)

The rejection of "the October 22nd settlement" on October 26th was followed on the 28th by a meeting of the Coal Owners' Association in Cardiff. It was "very largely attended": and those present were filled with a fierce determination to deal with this "intolerable situation." Consequently they passed a resolution to give an indemnity to owners whose pits had become or would become idle. They resolved also not to employ "the strikers" at any of the associated collieries: while this application of Rule 91[1] had already been used in September to boycott the men locked out from the Ely Pit.

Thus both sides were committed to the fray. The strike levies could only yield a meagre livelihood, if that, to the men locked out or on strike: while neither D. A. Thomas nor any other owner suffered privation. They were guaranteed, moreover, against financial loss by the "indemnity on any deficiency of actual daily output," calculated upon the average of the preceding quarter. The rate of this indemnity would vary according as the selling price per ton varied. When the price of coal stood at 12s. od. the indemnity was at the rate of 2s. 6d. a ton. The figures have not been made aailable: but it may be safely assumed (especially with the sporadic rise in selling prices that followed on the stoppages) that the four colliery companies received indemnities of several shillings "per ton lost." At no time were they likely to be in such straits financially as to compel them to yield to their workmen.

2. THE ABERDARE VALLEY

Suddenly amid this atmosphere of tension big strikes broke out in the Aberdare valley. They began in the pits of the Powell Duffryn Steam Coal Company. A notice had been posted up by the management in the Lower Duffryn colliery at Mountain Ash that one of the old customs (whereby men had been in the habit of taking home waste wood) was to be abrogated, and that in future they must have the permission of the management and indeed must pay for it. When men brought out timber the police at the top of the pit told them they must not take it any further. This, the workmen held, was a violation of a forty-year-old custom: and so they asked that it be continued until the Conciliation Board had dealt with it. The management refused and the workmen came out on strike on October 20th. On the same issue the miners at the Lletty-Shenkin colliery at Aberaman also stopped work. A formidable list of grievances against the owners was then drawn up and widely circulated, with the effect that the strikes spread to all the main pits in the Aberdare valley. This list of grievances, as read aloud to the S.W.M.F. Executive Council was followed by the statement:

---

[1] Rule 91 of the Coal Owners' Association ran: "No workman employed at a Colliery immediately before a Strike or Stoppage thereat takes place, shall during such Strike or Stoppage be employed by any Member."

This petty tyranny has culminated by the workmen refusing to continue working. We appealed to the manager; but he would not discuss the matter with us because of the poor state of our organisation, and jeered at us, stating that "we could not get the men out." (*7.xi.1910.*)

If the manager actually used those words or behaved in this way, he was soon to be undeceived. Not only the Powell Duffryn pits, but nearly all other pits and adits in the Aberdare valley had been very soon brought to a stop. Thus up to the end of October and for many weeks thereafter the Aberdare valley, as well as the mid-Rhondda, was on strike. There was, however, one considerable difference. The men of the Cambrian Combine were due to come out on strike on November 1st as the result of a balloted decision of the coalfield and after having given the due month's notice. The work-men of the Powell Duffryn Combine were out without any such decision, without having given notice and without the sanction of their Executive Council. The position of the Aberdare men, while a complicating factor, was distinct from that of the men of the Ely pit, and all the other pits of the Cambrian Combine. But the "unofficial" Aberdare strikes were in a neighbouring valley and took place in the same November and December of 1910. Consequently, it was not long before it was suggested that the two joint committees make common cause.

Meanwhile the Conciliation Board machinery had been set to work to deal with the Powell Duffryn manager's decision, and the dispute that followed. But before any settlement had been reached, there had been a great sharpening of personal difference between the general manager of the Powell Duffryn, E. M. Hann, and the Aberdare miners' agent, C. B. Stanton, the latter on October 27th having uttered words which might seem to imply a threat of murder. Negotiations were broken off and apologies were demanded. The agent and the men behind him refused. Later the matter came up before the South Wales Executive Council, which in the meantime had made it clear that they neither would nor could sanction the sudden Aberdare strike as they might incur heavy penalties for breach of the wages agreement if they were to do so. So November began with the men of Aberdare out on strike without the right to receive strike pay.

3. THE CAMBRIAN STRIKE BEGINS

It was on August 1, 1910, that the men of the Ely pit belonging to the Naval Colliery were given lockout notices: it was on November 1st, three months later, that the answer of the South Wales Miners' Federation became effective with the beginning of the official strike

of all miners employed by "The Cambrian Combine." There were
thus over a dozen pits affected in the mid-Rhondda employing in
all about 11,500 men. But elsewhere, and especially in three other
districts, many men were out and many pits stopped. In the Aberdare
valley over 11,000 men were out: the others were Maesteg and the
Western Valley of Monmouthshire. Some pits were stopped through
lockout but most through strike action, often against non-unionism.
The total, over twice as many as the Cambrian 12,000, may have
varied between 27,000 and 33,000. Thus nearly one-sixth out of the
total of 213,000 miners employed in the Monmouthshire and South
Wales coalfield had stopped work for a longer or shorter period in
that autumn of 1910.

The industry had been growing with such rapidity that there were
many in it each year fresh from adjacent counties of England or
Wales; or beyond the River Severn from the shires—Worcester,
Gloucester, Somerset—rural areas where trade unionism was still
a feeble growth. Some of the South Wales coalowners hoped that
imported labour would take the place of the strikers, especially since
the South Wales Miners' Federation, which ten years before had
numbered in its ranks three-quarters of the total number employed,
had that year only two-thirds of the miners enrolled as organised
trade unionists. The colliers were prepared for this action on the
part of the employers: and were now fully aware that the Trade
Disputes Act of 1906 had completely restored the right of peaceful
picketing on which they would rely in order to dissuade any imported labour from operating in the Cambrian pits. Under these
circumstances a clash seemed not unlikely.

For their part the owners had for a considerable time relied upon
the Chief Constables of the counties. At this time the Chief Constable of Glamorgan was Captain Lionel Arthur Lindsay. His
training had been in the Egyptian gendarmerie, a force raised to
deal with any disturbance amongst the townspeople or amongst the
toiling fellaheen of the Nile Valley; and in this service he had risen
to be Captain, Adjutant and finally Major. He had retired from this
arduous if rewarding occupation and, now in his fiftieth year, had
settled down in Glamorgan. Captain Lindsay had begun his career
as part of the British Army of Occupation in Egypt: and it may
seem that he never quite disabused himself of the notion that he
was part of a Coalmasters' Army of Occupation in South Wales. At
this juncture in November 1910, he had already made some
dispositions; and provisional arrangements had been made for
military assistance. But now at the end of the fourth day of the
strike at the pits in the Cambrian Combine, Captain Lindsay
received a stimulus to action. The stimulus was of a kind which he

had learned to look upon almost as a command: his not to reason why. He was informed that the Monmouthshire and South Wales Coal Owners' Association had been meeting on Friday, November 4th, in Cardiff, and that they requested increased police protection for their property.

Captain Lindsay took stock of the situation. Apart from local constables, he was like a Roman centurion: for he had under his command and available a little over a hundred men on foot or on horseback. He discussed the matter with the stipendiary and other local magistrates, some of whom were coalowners, on Saturday, November 5th. The decision was taken to send for extra police from the nearest large towns or cities. They got 30 from Swansea, 50 from Cardiff, and 63 from Bristol. With these, or with an equivalent number, he would garrison the "disturbed areas" and especially the mid-Rhondda in which lay the pits of the Cambrian Combine.

4. CLYDACH VALE AND LLWYNYPIA
(Monday, November 7th)

On the second day of the Cambrian strike and the sixty-third day of the Ely pit lock-out, the men who were out in the mid-Rhondda assembled in Tonypandy at what was in those days called a "miners' mass meeting." There from the lips of the chairman William John (who was soon to be chosen financial secretary for the Rhondda) they heard this significant statement:

The Combine Workmen's Committee will strain every nerve to bring the fight to a successful issue, and it is our intention to stop any man from doing any work at the collieries. We intend to prevent any of the officials from Mr. Llewellyn downwards from entering the colliery yards. (*2.xi.1910.*)

This enunciation of a policy for total abstention from work in the pits meant, if successful the withdrawal of labour of those in charge of the pumping and ventilating machinery: and this in turn would put a strain (which otherwise would hardly have existed) upon the owners' side of the conflict. This issue which had come up in the past (and was to emerge again in the future) was an acid test of the seriousness of any particular conflict in an industry where the clash of interests caused hundreds of stoppages every year: it was also an indication of the general outlook of the workmen and their leaders. Would this all-out policy be accepted on this occasion? Of this there was to be no question. The next day, a second mass meeting at Tonypandy of the Cambrian men on strike unanimously passed resolutions recommended by the Workmen's committee as follows:

(1) That steps should at once be taken to confer with the leaders of the

organisations of the Enginemen, Stokers, and Surface Craftsmen's Union, and the Winding Enginemen's Union, with a view to getting their members to cease work at the end of this week.

(2) That in the meantime no man at present working at the Combine collieries do anything other than his own particular work.

(3) That in the event of these men joining hands with the miners, the latter pledge themselves to see that when a settlement of the dispute was arrived at, all these men would be reinstated in their former positions. (*3.xi.1910.*)

Similar resolutions were passed elsewhere, and were also given publicity. On the approaching first critical days of the strike a high degree of public interest was aroused, mainly by the unusual attention paid to these troubles by the periodical press. Most weekly periodicals and practically all the daily newspapers were hostile to the strikers, whose standpoint was upheld by the handful of socialist weeklies. The narratives and notes in *Justice* and *Labour Leader* were in contrast to the general tone of the press. One narrative from Tom Mann[1] who had hastened to the fray was written during the day of Monday, November 7th and from the scene of the strike. His very informative article[2] begins with an explanation of the nature of the dispute and of the parties to it. Then the special difficulties confronting the strike committee were explained: the fact that there were at that time other colliery unions with which apparently the agents (Mabon and Watts Morgan) had made no arrangements for common action and who in the first days of the strike had continued to go to work.[3]

[1] Tom Mann, in his fifty-fifth year in 1910, had for long been internationally famous as a leading socialist agitator and trade union organiser. He had been one of the trio who led London's Dock Strike of 1889 (in which they had the help of Eleanor Marx) and at that time and for some years afterwards was well acquainted with Frederick Engels and with William Morris. He was appointed a member of the Royal Commission on Labour (1891–5), and had been secretary for a couple of years of the Independent Labour Party in the mid-nineties. Thereafter he had voyaged to the antipodes where he became the effective founder of the Australian Socialist Movement. From this he had come back in 1910 with ideas, largely shared by himself and by James Connolly, of industrial unionism, class solidarity and "direct action". Throughout the summer and autumn of 1910 Tom Mann had been conducting a vigorous campaign for these ideas.

[2] Reprinted in Appendix II.

[3] The biggest of these was the Monmouthshire and South Wales Colliery Enginemen, Stokers, and Surface Craftsmens' General Association, the number of whose branches had increased from 57 in 1907 to 64 in 1910 and which had grown in membership since it seceded from the South Wales Miners' Federation in 1903 to 7,422 in 1907 and to 9,367 by 1910.

Another, much smaller, was the South Wales and Monmouth Winding Enginemen's Association and Provident Trade Union, formed in 1895. Its membership had increased in the previous seven years, and very steadily, as follows:—

Year	Membership	Year	Membership
1903	478	1907	608
1904	532	1908	621
1905	550	1909	669
1906	575	1910	572

A third body referred to as the "Firemen or Stokers" was probably the organisation of the Firemen by which name the deputies were usually known in South Wales.

Tom Mann's article, after these explanations, continues like a dispatch from the field of action—as indeed it was. He tells how "to intercept the sections referred to," that is, members of those other unions or those who were not trade unionists at all, "it was decided that all miners should demonstrate near their respective mines at 5 a.m. in the morning": and he then goes on to tell how it fared with one such procession, and what success it had.

Actually the decision to draw the fires had been taken earlier by the trade union committee: and the members of the South Wales Miners' Federation had been alerted. Shortly after 5 a.m. on the morning of November 7th, Noah Rees, secretary of the Cambrian Lodge, together with W. H. Mainwaring and "a trumpeter" went through the streets, and roused the miners and their families. The repeated sound of the cornet or bugle was immediately effective: and in a matter of minutes hundreds were out-of-doors and forming up in processions towards the colliery nearest to their homes. Half-a-mile from Pandy, at 5.30 in the morning, men, women and children were coming to Clydach Vale to put out the fires at Cambrian Colliery. Fifty-five years later one of that lodge committee concluded "We drew the fire before breakfast in the Cambrian Colliery. There were pickets in every lane. Never had there been such picketing before. Mark Harcombe was the secretary of the Combine."

Meantime that first weekend of November 1910 the colliers had heard a rumour (which turned out to be true) that the owners were determined to import labour, mainly outside surface labour, for the Glamorgan Colliery at Llwynypia. Leonard Llewellyn had made his colliery there a fortress against trade union action. On Monday evening, November 7th, the pickets were out early: and all the Combine Collieries in which work had been going on were soon stopped—with one exception. The exception was the Llwynypia pit of the Glamorgan Colliery Company. Thither that evening of Monday, November 7th the pickets and many other strikers along with them moved from Clydach Vale eastward and from Penygraig, Trealaw and Tonypandy up the valley to Llwynypia where they surrounded the colliery about 10.30 p.m. Inside was Leonard Llewellyn and some three score officials and draughtsmen whose services had been used in keeping the workings open and free of water. Llewellyn, apparently by design, had left 300 pit ponies underground, a week after the strike had begun.[1]

---

[1] Publicity given to these 300 ponies, deep down in the mine, had its usual effect. Public sympathy for domestic animals was readily aroused: and the colliers locked out or on strike lost sympathy in a corresponding degree. His Majesty George V, who had been on the throne for five months had his sympathies keenly excited by the possible fate of the ponies: and he kept on making enquiries.

Ensconced in the colliery premises but on the surface were also 99 policemen, headed by "the Roman Centurion," Chief Constable Lindsay himself the hundredth man.

The attempt of the strikers to get into touch with those at work was refused. There was a sharp brush with the police, who were in the power station, which was nearer to Pandy Square. From the high ground of the hillside stones were thrown at the power house. The trucks below were struck. One of the boys throwing these stones remembers shouts of "Bulls-eye" each time there came a ringing sound as a stone struck a buffer. Wooden palings fencing the colliery were pulled down. Police reinforcements, however, were soon on the way from Clydach Vale and from Pandy Square. At 11.15 p.m. they reached the Eastern or rear side of Llwynypia colliery: and a quarter of an hour later they began a series of baton charges. The strikers were driven back.

Half an hour after midnight all seemed quiet. The road was clear. The fifty constables from Cardiff were sent off from Llwynypia down the valley to the Thistle Hotel at Tonypandy. There, however, the strikers were gathered in Pandy Square. At 1 a.m. the Cardiff City Police were called upon to disperse them. They immediately used their truncheons: but it took them an hour before the Square was clear.

5. HOME SECRETARY TAKES CONTROL
(Tuesday, November 8, 1910)

At 1 a.m., as we have seen, the strikers were assembled in Pandy Square, where they were soon to be "moved on" by baton charges: at the same hour Chief Constable Lindsay was telegraphing for troops, as previously arranged. His telegrams went to Shrewsbury in Shropshire, Chester and Salisbury Plain. From Tidworth on Salisbury Plain he received a reply at 3.30 a.m. that infantry and cavalry were on their way and would arrive about 9 a.m. at Pontypridd. It was not, however, until after 9 a.m. and when there began to be some surprise at the non-arrival of the soldiers that the Chief Constable bethought himself to inform the Secretary of State of Home Affairs about the situation and about what he himself had done. At 10 a.m., November 8th, the Home Secretary received the following telegram:

All the Cambrian collieries menaced last night. The Llwynypia Colliery savagely attacked by large crowd of strikers. Many casualties on both sides. Am expecting two companies of infantry and 200 cavalry today. Very little accommodation for police or soldiers. Position grave. Will wire again.—Lindsay Chief Constable of Glamorgan.[1]

[1] *Colliery Strike Disturbances in South Wales: November 1910.* Cd. 5568.

But long before the above telegram was received, Winston
Churchill (who was to make his mark as Home Secretary for the
twenty months after mid-February 1910) had learned of the troop
movements, unauthorised by him. He promptly arranged that the
order be countermanded. This stopped the movement of troops
at the railway junction of Swindon in Wiltshire, the breadth of
three shires away from Cardiff and still further miles away from
Pontypridd. This action of the Home Secretary was an abrupt check
to all the plans that had been laid by the Chief Constable and the
Magistrates (in response to the request from the owners) for the
use of soldiers.

If there was trouble in the South Wales Coalfield and an awkward
situation in the Rhondda and other valleys, there was also an
awkward situation in Parliament and misgivings in the Liberal
Party cabinet which was facing the prospect of a second General
Election in that one year 1910. The last occasion of the employment
of troops in South Wales a dozen years earlier had met opposition
in Parliament from Liberal members although at that time the
South Wales Miners Federation had not yet come into existence. Now
in 1910 there was a powerful trade union of the Welsh miners and
behind them the Miners' Federation of Great Britain. There were
nearly a score of mining members of Parliament who, together with
the other Labour members made up a contingent of 40 members on
which (together with the four score Irish Nationalists) the Cabinet
had to rely for a sufficient majority against the Conservatives.
Moreover, it had been the policy of the Home Office bureaucracy,
ever since "Bloody Sunday" of 1887 in Trafalgar Square, to draw
the velvet glove over the iron hand of authority: and they had no
wish to have their policy upset by the local initiative of magistrates
and chief constables carried out without prior consultation with
Whitehall. For all these reasons, Churchill met in a very accom-
modating spirit the representations put to him at the Home Office on
Tuesday morning, November 8th by William Abraham, M.P.,
President of the South Wales Miners' Federation. He promised that
he would avoid if he could the sending of troops into the area.

Mabon that morning (of November 8th) had read in the newspapers as he travelled up from Cardiff to London (to a meeting of the
M.F.G.B. Executive Committee) the story of the disturbances at
Llwynypia the night before. At Paddington he and his colleague
Alfred Onions had been met by an official of the Board of Trade
who told them that the Home Office authorities had decided to
send in the military: and that the Board of Trade (Labour Department and Conciliation Department) were anxious that the agent
from the Rhondda (D. Watts Morgan) and half-a-dozen local

representatives should come up to London on the Wednesday afternoon to see what could be done about the dispute. It was this information, or rather the former part of it which had caused Mabon with his colleague to go to the Home Office to interview Churchill. Mabon naturally enough claimed considerable credit for having been instrumental for delaying if not preventing the movement of the military.

Still in the morning of Tuesday, November 8th a telegram was sent at 11.15 a.m. ("Please telegraph fully as to state of affairs this morning and what necessity exists for further assistance to the police—Home Secretary") which must have come as a cold douche to the Chief Constable of Glamorganshire. Thereafter around noon a conference was held between the Home Secretary with his officials Sir Edward Troup and Sir Edward Henry and R. B. Haldane,[1] the Secretary of State for War, with the Adjutant-General.

Haldane knew all about the Featherstone shooting of 1893 having been one of the Committee of Enquiry into it. There was, therefore, the maximum of authority both as regards past happenings and present needs in this little conference, at which General Macready was also present. The result of it was that the following telegram was despatched at 1.30 p.m. to the Chief Constable.

Your request for military. Infantry should not be used till all other means have failed. Following arrangements have therefore been made. Seventy[2] mounted constables and two hundred foot constables of Metro-politan Police will come to Pontypridd by special train, leaving Padding-ton 4.55 p.m. arriving about 8 p.m. They will carry out your directions under their own officers. The County will bear the cost. Expect these forces will be sufficient, but as further precautionary measure 200 Cavalry will be moved into the district tonight and remain there pending cessation of trouble. Infantry meanwhile will be at Swindon. General Macready will command the military and will act in conjunction with the civil authorities as circumstances may require. The military however will not be available unless it is clear that the police reinforcements are unable to cope with the situation. Telegraph news Home Office and say whether these arrangements are sufficient.—Churchill.

On receiving this telegram the Chief Constable must have realised that his request for military assistance had brought results which perhaps neither he nor the magistrates had expected. Normally the Home Office had very limited powers over a county Police force, whose superior was a Watch Committee, jointly made up of County Councillors and Justices of the Peace. Now the appeal had been made to Caesar: and Caesar had taken prompt measures—for

---

[1] Richard Burdon Haldane (1856–1928), F.R.S., O.M.; Secretary of State for War 1905–12; Lord High Chancellor 1912–15 and 1924; created Viscount Haldane of Cloan in 1911.
[2] One hundred mounted police, instead of seventy, were sent eventually.

which the County would have to pay the cost. So about 2 p.m. on Tuesday, November 8, 1910, Captain Lindsay called the Home Secretary on the telephone and stated that the force of Metropolitan Police would suffice; that there was no need for the cavalry to come to the valleys that night (whereupon the order was given to halt the cavalry at Cardiff[1]) and finally asked "for a message to use if desirable."

Down in the mid-Rhondda that Tuesday afternoon workmen on strike were being paid off by the companies of the Cambrian Combine. They assembled thereafter in a great mass meeting at the Athletic Ground in Tonypandy. At this meeting the Stipendiary Magistrate Lleufer Thomas spoke to the strikers and asked them to give all the assistance they could in the maintenance of the peace. Furthermore the Chief Constable read out the following message which he had received from the Home Secretary:

You may give the Miners the following message from me:—
Their best friends here are greatly distressed at the trouble which had broken out, and will do their best to help them to get fair treatment. Askwith, Board of Trade, wishes to see Mr. Watts Morgan with six or eight local representatives at Board of Trade two o'clock, tomorrow, Wednesday. But rioting must cease at once, so that the enquiry shall not be prejudiced, and to prevent the credit of the Rhondda Valley being injured. Confiding in the good sense of the Cambrian Combine workmen, we are holding back the soldiers for the present and sending only police. —Churchill.

With its slightly veiled innuendo against the employers this was resented by the general body of the coal owners, but was well received by the mass meeting.

The strikers formed a huge procession and marched through Tonypandy, Trealaw and Llwynypia to the Glamorgan Colliery near which they drew up about 4 o'clock. The police estimated there were 9,000 in the procession which was orderly.

Yet in just over an hour there had occurred what was described as "serious rioting" in the mid-Rhondda, as is recounted in the next section. This led to a series of further telegrams; the first of these was sent at 8 p.m. to General Macready, as follows:

As the situation appears to have become more serious you should if the Chief Constable or Local Authority desires it move all the Cavalry into the disturbed district without delay.—Churchill.

[1] By 2.30 p.m. a memorandum was sent to the Adjutant-General: "We have arranged that Metropolitan Police shall leave by 4.30 and arrive at Pontypridd about 8.30 to-night. The Chief Constable Glamorgan now thinks this will be sufficient, and, after consultation with him, I have decided that the cavalry shall be stopped at Cardiff for the present. Please give orders accordingly, and inform me that this has been done. The cavalry may have to stay for a few days at Cardiff. I presume it will be easy to keep them there, and that arrangements can be made to supply the police column with forage and rations as proposed.—Churchill." (Cd. 5568, p. 5, item No. 11.)

The second telegram was sent at 8.15 p.m. to the Chief Constable of Glamorgan.

As it appears from telephone messages just received that the situation has become more serious Home Secretary has authorised General Macready, if you desire it, to move all the cavalry into the disturbed district without delay. You may communicate this to General Macready in case Home Secretary's telegram has not reached him. About 9.30 tonight, ring up Mr. Churchill, at 6823 Gerrard and inform him of situation. Signed Under Secretary Home Office.

Between 9.30 and 10.30 p.m. that evening the Home Secretary was in telephonic communication with General Macready and the Chief Constable; and it was arranged that though serious rioting appeared to be over a second contingent of 200 Metropolitan Police should be sent by special train, leaving London at 3 a.m. the next morning (Wednesday, November 9th). These arrangements were at once carried out.

Earlier that evening, at 7.45 p.m. the Pontypridd Stipendiary Magistrate Lleufer Thomas sent a telegram to the Home Office, where it was received at 9 p.m., as follows:—

Police cannot cope with rioters at Llwynypia Rhondda Valley. Troops at Cardiff absolutely necessary for further protection. Will you order them to proceed forthwith. Am ready to accompany them.

This signified that the stipendiary (and three brother magistrates) were ready "to read the Riot Act," that is, the proclamation[1] under the Act of 1716, before which it would not be usual for the military to resort to extremities.

These telegrams give a record of what was passing between Whitehall and the Rhondda. Now we must turn to what had actually been occurring at Llwynypia earlier that evening.

6. THE EVENING OF TUESDAY, NOVEMBER 8TH AT LLWYNYPIA

What had happened in the late afternoon and evening in the Valley? Leaving the Athletic Ground the miners in orderly procession marched through Trealaw and Tonypandy up to Llwynypia, where they gathered about 4 p.m. outside the Glamorgan Colliery. There a small body of mounted police made an effort to disperse them just as dusk was setting in, with a result that might have been expected. From a little after 5 o'clock a hand-to-hand conflict developed between the strikers and the police and lasted for a little

---

[1] "Our Sovereign Lord the King chargeth and commandeth all persons being assembled immediately to disperse themselves, and peaceably to depart to their habitations or to their lawful business, upon the pains contained in the act made in the first year of King George for preventing tumultuous and riotous assemblies. God save the King."

over two hours. A Home Office press statement at midnight described the evening's events as "serious rioting," but in this as well as in subsequent despatches from the military authorities there was no tendency to over-stress the seriousness of what occurred: for example the first report signed "C. F. N. Macready, Major-General" gives little more than the disposition of the troops he commanded, in Cardiff or in Pontypridd. It was far otherwise with the two sides of the struggle. Even half a century later members of miners' families, both men and women, retained most vivid memories of what they recalled as "a civil war."

On the owners' side there were similar heightened feelings at the time: and these were set out before a twelve-month passed in a book written with all the skill of a war correspondent. The author David Evans from the standpoint of the side whose cause he espouses not only against their employees whom he calls "the mob" but also against the Home Office and the military authorities. With this preliminary word of caution we may now quote some passages from this "class war correspondent."

On the conflict outside Glamorgan Colliery (lasting for over two hours from five o'clock) David Evans wrote "it is believed to have been unparalleled in recent years in the grim fierceness with which it was fought and in the bloodshed which it entailed."

Inside the colliery were some 60 men (and 400 horses) headed by Leonard Llewellyn, the general manager "whose determination," wrote the enraptured chronicler, "and courage against such heavy odds had excited the admiration of the whole country, and had drawn messages of congratulation from almost every quarter of the globe." The surface premises were held by a force of 120 police headed by the Chief Constable Captain Lindsay in person. We are told that the strikers brought to the ground "what of the frail wooden fencing had been left standing in the previous night's riot," and that there then followed "the hustling of the body of police guarding the entrance, the throwing of stones at the constables under cover in the yard, and an attack on the power house."

Two of the strikers asked for an interview with the Chief Constable inside the colliery yard, but, said the chronicler,

"The granting of that request would have been the discovery by the strikers of the strength of the defending force. For that reason it was refused, and the Chief Constable met the two men outside the gate. The interview was merely a parley to gain time and was quickly broken off." Captain Lindsay, "under these conditions," ordered the mounted men, who were stationed just outside the offices, "to clear the main road with their truncheons in the direction of Tonypandy." At the same time a body of foot constables were to operate simultaneously in the direction of Llwynypia. But "the mob offered a stubborn resistance; the police had to fight almost every inch of their way"; but after "a prolonged effort succeeded in driving the rioters some distance away" from the entrance to the colliery.

With a dervish yell and batons drawn they dashed out between 80 and 90 strong from the colliery yard and cut a way clean through the densely packed mob. Their first purpose was to split up the crowd. This they achieved with very little difficulty, the intrepidity of the movement and the determination with which it was carried out having both surprised and for the moment staggered the rioters.

Forty of the Cardiff police drove towards Llwynypia; while forty Bristol, Swansea, and Glamorgan constables drove towards Tonypandy. A passage of excited rhetoric describes what followed:

Using their formidable weapons with great effect, the rioters on several occasions temporarily checked the forward movement of the police, and among others injured Chief Constable Lindsay; but they had to give way to the determined resistance of a small body of determined men each of whom felt that he carried his life in his hand, and scores of the rioters were struck down like logs with broken skulls and left on the ground. The agony cries of the injured, the sharp hissing clash of baton against pick handle and other weapons, the sickening thud of skull blows, and the howling of a mob maddened with rage is better imagined than described.

The end of it was the complete rout of the mob; and the secured safety for the night of the power station at the Glamorgan Colliery.

After this drive in each direction for a quarter of a mile, the police in each section scurried back to the colliery. The Chronicler says that "In the course of their return, particularly along the portion of the main road between the colliery and Tonypandy, they found scores if not hundreds of rioters prone on the ground or staggering along the road "groaning from the pains of injured shoulders, arms, and heads; while at the colliery itself they discovered that the handful of men left in charge of the property had all barricaded themselves inside the power stations." These two dozen were under the impression that the 80 constables who had been on the main road had been defeated and therefore "made discretion the better part of valour by retreating inside the buildings."

With scores of batons broken, we are told that the local supplies of staves had been "completely exhausted" and the following morning "300 were brought up to Llwynypia." Whether the facts of that evening were exactly as portrayed by the coal-owners' chronicler may be questioned. Major-General Macready, writing to the Home Office three days later, discounted much of the reports. He says of "the recent attacks on mines" that "they were not as serious as the

IO   RT. HON. WINSTON LEONARD SPENCER CHURCHILL, M.P.

II   JAMES KEIR HARDIE, M.P.

reports would lead one to believe—for instance, at Llwynypia, where it was reported that desperate attempts were made to sack the power house, the attack appears to have been confined to the gateway and to the throwing of stones from the road through the windows of the power house. The wooden palings had been pulled down and there was nothing to prevent the mob, if as strong as reported, from swarming over the whole of the mine property and attacking the power house from all sides in overwhelming numbers. That they did not do this is not due to the action of the police but to either the want of leading or disinclination to proceed to extremities on the part of the mob on Tuesday night." (Cd. 5568, p. 17.)

All this happened at the Glamorgan colliery between 5 o'clock and up to a late hour that night. But there was more to come: the disturbance an hour or so later at Tonypandy in Dunraven Street in Pandy Square (from which the power house was only a few hundred yards distant) was much more celebrated in the newspapers at the time. Consequently, it is Tonypandy rather than Llwynypia that has given its name to the main disturbances on November 7 and 8, 1910.

7. THE EVENING OF NOVEMBER 8, 1910 (TONYPANDY)

The scale of events that night in Tonypandy was certainly much less formidable than what had been taking place up the valley. Windows both of shops and of private dwellings had been smashed: and stones were being flung at certain houses so that the local *five* constables had their work cut out to keep order, any semblance of order, in the central part of the town. Less than a dozen additional police were sent down by the Chief Constable from his fortress in Llwynypia Colliery and these made various charges and cleared the streets. By the time the 150 Metropolitan police arrived that night in Tonypandy (about 11 o'clock), the disturbances were entirely over. With the same heightened and telling use of words as for the rather more grim affair that had occurred up the valley, the chronicler tells the tale "about the party of three leading policemen and seven constables" who had been sent down from Llwynypia colliery to Tonypandy:

When the party reached the entrance to Gilfach Road they were warned not to proceed further as the road was in possession of the rioters, who were heavily stoning certain houses. Undeterred by this warning Inspector Hole ordered the men to draw their staffs and to charge up the hill. Relating the incident to the writer Inspector Hole said: "It was like going up the roof of a house, so steep is the hill. We were at once met

G

with a terrific volley of stones, and several of the men were struck—
Sergeant Harris receiving so violent a blow that the plate of his belt
was doubled up." It was recognised that the strikers could only be dis-
lodged by a flank movement and by a larger force, and the party retreated.
Later on however, Inspector Hole and his men succeeded in reaching
Kenry Road where they took up a position commanding that held by
the rioters. Discovering they had been outflanked, the rioters ran away.

The summing up of that disturbance, which took place by the
bridge end in Tonypandy may be given in an account of casualties.
There were nearly 80 casualties of police[1] and the authority of the
Glamorgan County Police is behind the statement that "over five
hundred persons are known to have suffered injury" but that "of
the toll in blood, broken skulls and damaged limbs among the
rioters there is no authentic record."

"One injury was fatal in the case of Samuel Rays of Partridge
Road, Tonypandy who died three days after the Llwynypia affair."
At the inquest, held on Thursday, December 15th at Porth, medical
evidence showed three scalp wounds (two penetrating to the bone)
and that the skull had been fractured over the temple and the right
ear. The jury returned the following verdict: "That we agree that
Samuel Rays died from injuries received on November 8th caused
by some blunt instrument. The evidence is not sufficiently clear to
us how he received these injuries." Evidence was given by a considerable number of witnesses for the police, including the Superintendent, the Deputy Chief Constable, an Inspector and a Sergeant.
But the main evidence was that of Captain Lindsay, who said that at
the colliery it had been for a long time a case of 'touch and go.' The
crowd, he said, had retaliated blow for blow, and it was a question
whether the police would succeed or not. The batons were smashed
by the weapons in the hands of the mob, and his officers complained
to him "What's the good of a thing like this against a mandrel?"

8. CHURCHILL BETWEEN TWO FIRES
(Wednesday, November 9th)

On the Wednesday morning all was quiet in the valleys after the
disturbances of the previous two days. All was quiet too at Westminster. There in the Westminster Palace Hotel just opposite the
Wren-restored end of Westminster Abbey there was a conference

---

[1] Official List of Police Casualties at Llwynypia on November 7, 1910 totalled 38,
of which 24 were suffered by the Bristol contingent and 10 by the police called in from
Cardiff City and Swansea Borough: the Glamorgan County Police had only 4 men injured. At Llwynypia and Tonypandy on November 8,1910 the total number injured was
80. The brunt fell upon the Cardiff City Police, and the Bristol Mounted men. As before
there were rather smaller numbers than might have been expected of the Glamorgan
police, foot and mounted. At the Powell Duffryn power station in the Aberdare Valley on
November 8th, half-a-dozen of the Glamorgan police reported injuries received.

of the Miners' Federation of Great Britain. When the main business had been disposed of the delegates heard statements from the representatives of Welsh miners. Onions and William Abraham told how, on the previous morning they had interviewed the Home Secretary and that he had promised to avoid the use of the military if at all possible. The delegates reading in their newspapers about the further disturbances of the previous night passed unanimously the following resolution:

That this conference having heard the report of the South Wales representatives regarding the serious situation which has arisen in South Wales, whilst regretting the disturbances which have occurred considers the civil forces sufficient to deal with such disturbances, and will strongly deprecate the employment of the military for such a purpose; and if the military have been sent into the districts affected, asks the Home Secretary at once to recall them. (*9.xi.1910*.)

The letter enclosing this resolution was sent on the same day by Thomas Ashton, as Secretary of the M.F.G.B. But the situation was now different from what it had been the previous morning and Winston Churchill was in a very different mood to that in which he had been so gracious to William Abraham. So the reply came back to Ashton that same evening in a sufficiently sharp tone, as follows:

Dear Sir,

I am desired by the Home Secretary to acknowledge the receipt of your letter and resolution. Mr. Churchill hopes and expects that the strong force of police drafted to the scene of the disorder will be sufficient promptly and effectively to prevent riot. If, however this is not so, we will not hesitate after what has occurred to authorise the employment of the military, and the responsibility for any consequences which may ensue must rest with those who persist in courses of violence.

I am, etc.,
S. W. HARRIS.

Hardly a day had elapsed before the Home Secretary received a protest from the other side. This was from the Monmouthshire and South Wales Coalowners' Association and ran as follows:

Cardiff, November 10, 1910.

Sir,

Yesterday I sent you the following telegram: "The Committee of the Associated Colliery Owners of South Wales in meeting today desire to draw your attention to the absolute necessity of additional military being brought into the District and stationed at those places where the disturbances are occurring. The Owners are thoroughly convinced that the present arrangements are quite inadequate for the protection of life and property." I learn indirectly that additional military and police have been sent into the District under your instructions and your action in this respect is much appreciated by the Owners.

I have been instructed by the Members of this Association to very strongly protest against the delay which occurred in the sending of the troops into the District in the first instance and to say that the Owners attribute the serious rioting which has occurred both in the Rhondda and Aberdare Valleys to the lack of a sufficiently protective force.

As no doubt you are aware the Magistrates at Aberdare on Saturday last and the Magistrates in the Rhondda Valley on Monday pointed out the seriousness of the position and the necessity for the Military being sent at once and the Colliery Owners regret that this course was not followed and so avoid the rioting and consequent damage which took place.

> I am, etc.,
> W. GASCOYNE DALZIEL,
> Secretary.

The Right Hon. Winston Churchill, M.P.

To this letter insisting on the use of the military, the following reply was sent from the Under Secretary to the Home Office:

> Home Office, November 12, 1910.

Sir,
I have laid before the Secretary of State your letter of the 10th instant and I am directed to say for the information of the Monmouthshire and South Wales Coal Owners' Association that he is unable to accept the view that a premature display of military force would have had the effect of preventing the rioting which occurred on Tuesday last. It is not unlikely that it might have had precisely the opposite effect.

I am to add that the Secretary of State received no communication from Aberdare or the Rhondda Valley magistrates either on Saturday or on Monday last.

> I am, etc.,
> EDWARD TROUP.

The Secretary to the Monmouthshire and South Wales Coal Owners' Association, Cardiff, 8.

Winston Churchill from the moment of his first intervention on the morning of Tuesday, November 8th, had perhaps fully expected to be exposed to pressure and criticism from both sides. It was for this reason amongst others that he had taken the unprecedented and, as it seemed to many, the dramatic step of appointing a Major-General to take charge and, because of his rank and prestige, to have a certain overriding influence on all that took place in the Valleys. Churchill and Haldane, at their conference on the Tuesday morning, had obviously considered it better to run the risk implied by their intervention than to have to face the sort of situation that had arisen seventeen years earlier in the shooting down of colliers on strike at Featherstone in Yorkshire. Churchill might be aware that for years afterwards the then Home Secretary (and now his own Prime Minister) Herbert Asquith had been dubbed "Featherstone Asquith" and he would have had no desire to be dubbed "Tonypandy Churchill."

9. THE SCENE IN PARLIAMENT (NOVEMBER 15, 1910)

The Houses of Parliament in the first part of the year 1910 had held even fewer sittings than was usual in those leisured days: and of those sittings a very great number were taken up by formalities. There had been a dissolution of parliament, a general election which lasted from January 14th to February 9th, followed for many days by all the time-honoured and time-consuming ceremonies to inaugurate the Twenty-ninth Parliament of the United Kingdom of Great Britain and Ireland. Then the demise of the crown (the legal phrase for the situation created by the death of a monarch) took place on May 6th. Although there was immediate transfer of the sovereignty with all its attributes and prerogatives, from Edward VII to his heir George V, there were many further days of ceremony, with the royal obsequies attended by the monarchs of Germany and Spain and the nearer northern realms. Then the new monarch sponsored in July the Constitutional Conference whereby the Prime Minister and three of his Liberal colleagues conferred behind closed doors with the leader of the Tory Party and his team of three. These secret meetings, from which the Labour Party[1] and the Irish Nationalists were rigidly excluded, went on throughout summer and autumn of 1910 while open political struggle was suspended and to some extent parliamentary activities languished. The constitutional issue was the curtailment of the powers of the House of Lords, especially on money matters. In their secret conclaves, however, the two "front benches" contrived to get within measurable distance of forming a coalition to carry through measures that would not be popular—such as conscription and an immense increase in the army and navy estimates. In the end, but not until after a quarter of the year had been consumed in these parleys, the Constitutional Conference broke down. The final meeting was on November 10th: at last parliament could meet after an adjournment since August 3rd.

When the House of Commons re-assembled on Tuesday, November 15th, the members were eager to hear what was the nature of the breakdown and also whether some understanding between the two front benches had survived the formal rupture. Chancellor of the Exchequer Lloyd George caused some disappointment by simply moving a further adjournment, in which the Conservative leaders immediately acquiesced. The general atmosphere which had been one of hushed expectancy was ruptured at this point by Keir

[1] At a similar secret meeting of "the two front benches," summoned by H.M. George V at a later date, the cartoonist of the *Daily Herald* showed the Labour Party in the guise of a spaniel, sitting disconsolate on its haunches outside the locked doors of the Conference room.

Hardie, who, having received no satisfaction in response to questions on the coal strike in South Wales, raised the question on the motion for the adjournment and forced two hours of debate upon the Government.

To begin with Keir Hardie turned to the Home Secretary and raised three questions for debate. The first was on an infringement by the police in Tonypandy of the right of peaceful picketing, as set forth in Section 2 of the Trade Disputes Act: and this example of illegal interference by the police was said to have occurred on Sunday, November 6th. Then in accordance with the previous week's decision of the Miners' Federation of Great Britain, he emphasised that "the presence of the military in trade disputes is not a thing to be lightly countenanced," and was able to refer to a 1908 Special Committee of the House, which had reported that "the military shall only be called out in cases of the gravest necessity." Then Keir Hardie gave the point of his complaint as follows:—

The military have been called out in connexion with this dispute in South Wales, not only without any grave necessity, but without any necessity at all. There has not been a kind of disorder or disturbance with which the police force was not amply capable of dealing. If you take what is regarded as the very worst case of all, the Tonypandy window-smashing case, the Home Secretary must know by this time that the number of men taking part in that window-smashing never exceeded a hundred.

Local opinion is practically unanimous in saying that had there been three or four or half a dozen policemen on duty on the streets when the window-smashing commenced, the whole of the disorder might have been stopped. But the whole of the police at this time, with the exception of a few, were at the colliery guarding the owners' property.

Keir Hardie went on to tell how the presence of the military in South Wales was regarded as an insult to law-abiding inhabitants, and might in the end "lead to disorder which would altogether be obviated if the troops were not there." It gave the impression that "the Government is taking side with the employers, and is sending those men into the colliery field to help to intimidate and overawe the strikers, and thereby make success more difficult for them." Keir Hardie in his main criticism protested at unnecessary displays of violence by the police and as examples of this cited incidents in Aberaman and Cwmbach in his own constituency. On two successive days (Sunday, 13th and Monday, November 14th) he had made personal investigations together with the other member for Merthyr, Edgar Jones, who was a Liberal. One after another the two members described the scene of the disturbances and gave accounts, from witnesses (whose evidence had been taken in shorthand), of examples of police brutality.

William Abraham then joined in the request for full inquiry into the conduct of the police. Winston Churchill in his reply was very cautious, and possibly had one eye on the General Election which he knew (although the members as yet had not been informed of it) was not far distant. He was very courteous to Mabon and joined with him in praising "the many virtues of the mining population in South Wales"; looked forward "to the cessation on fair and honourable terms of that labour warfare which has distracted this beautiful valley"; but then went on to say that "he was not convinced by the picture which the hon. Member for Merthyr Tydfil (Mr. Keir Hardie) drew." Finally he declared that "he would be no party to any sort of censure upon the police in this matter" and declined to order the enquiry.

After Churchill had sat down, G. N. Barnes, who had been elected to lead the Labour Party in the sparse sittings of that short parliament of 1910, rose to plead with the Home Secretary for an enquiry. Steve Walsh, member for Ince in Lancashire, speaking with incisiveness, pointed out that the Home Secretary had not given "the slightest reason for keeping the military in these districts": and then raised very seriously the matter of the right of peaceful picketing, and he poured no little scorn upon the "mere expression of a pious opinion" by Churchill. When Hardie divided the House, he and Walsh as "Tellers for the Noes" mustered 41 votes against the Governments' 168 "Ayes". Amongst the "Ayes" there were cast the votes of two steadfast adherents of the Liberal Party Tom Burt and Charles Fenwick.

10. MAJOR-GENERAL MACREADY

The conference in Whitehall of R. B. Haldane and Winston Churchill on the morning of Tuesday, November 8th had been very confident about the need to choose an Army General to be in command of troops and other forces and by this means to convey in the locality, as nothing else could, the authority of the central government. The man of their choice Nevil Macready was an able and ambitious soldier, who had just been made Director of Personal Services at the War Office.[1] He was prepared as a soldier to carry out the orders of his Government without deviation. If anyone could sustain the precepts that the military whilst protecting property must not appear to side either with the employers or the workmen,

[1] Later he was chosen to deal with the Police Union after the Police Strike of August 1918 and for this purpose held the position of Commissioner of Metropolitan Police from 1918 to 1920, until the union had been smashed. A still more onerous post awaited him as Commander-in-Chief in Ireland, from 1920 to 1922, when he was responsible for the activities of the infamous Black-and-Tans. The only peculiarity about his later career was that he was not made a Field Marshal but was retired on half pay in 1923. He died in 1946.

Macready was eminently suited for this task, as may be seen from his reports to the Home Office which form a great part of the Blue Book subsequently published. Macready while open enough about his own anti-socialist views, exhibits some well-bred surprise in finding that coalowners regarded him as being in a sense under their orders. At his first meeting with magistrates and directors of the Cambrian and Powell Duffryn collieries it emerged that they considered the military and police were theirs to be allocated in the numbers they desired to the mid-Rhondda and Aberdare collieries according to their advice. Further, he remarked on a tendency of colliery managers or owners to telephone in with alarmist reports, demanding police protection against marching hordes of strikers, who on investigation turned out to be non-existent. One such example, reported by J. F. Moylan on November 16th originated in the Tonypandy Colliery Office.[1]

Another example, which Macready describes as "a more glaring case," was the Cynon Colliery whither a large force of police had been required, only, reported Macready with some asperity, in order "to enforce the levying of a fine against the men, who had offered to pay at once 80 per cent of the fine, an offer which had been recommended by the manager but refused by the owners."[2]

Certain conditions had been laid down by Macready regarding protection of mines. He had outlined to the managers the circumstances under which troops and police would provide protection for the continuation or restarting of pumping and for imported labour; but he was never free from anxiety lest managers would attempt to circumvent these conditions. In his final memorandum to the Home Office Macready's initial standpoint and his experiences are brought out very clearly. Of the strikers, with whose committee he made direct contact, he says bluntly:

The impression conveyed to my mind in regard to the action of the strikers throughout those disturbances, and the motives for rioting, is that the doctrine of extreme socialism preached by a small but energetic section is entirely responsible for the premeditated attempts to destroy property. This was more particularly the case on Monday, November 7th, the men's minds having been influenced by an address on the previous Sunday afternoon.

The rioting on November 21st had not for its object the destruction of property, but was an ebullition against "blacklegs" and imported police. The men responsible for actual rioting are a small minority, some 30 per cent. of the population at the most, but the situation is invariably complicated by the inability of those whose intentions are not actually hostile to remain indoors.

In a long section on "Police Characteristics" Macready extols

---

[1] See Appendix III to this Chapter.   [2] Ibid.

the superior training and skill of the Metropolitan police while he disparages the county police, for the following reasons:

the mine managing class is looked upon by the local police as having a kind of authority over them, and several instances have occurred where a manager has been consulted, and his opinion taken, where clearly the police officer should have acted on his own responsibility. This curious misconception of duty probably originates from the fact that mine-owners pay for the extra police who are employed on the collieries and in normal times are at their beck and call. When, however, affairs are abnormal this state of affairs should cease, and all orders and responsibility for protection rest with the officer in charge on the spot.

For the behaviour of the military detachments Macready has nothing but praise. About the colliery managers on the other hand, he states:

It appeared to me on arriving in this district that a false impression as to the use of both police and military existed in the minds of the managers. There seemed a general idea that managers were at liberty to carry out any schemes they pleased, such as the importation of "black-legs," or fresh work on pits, in short any measure without consideration as to how it might influence the strikers, and that the military would then be called upon to support such action. Also there was a distinct inclination to direct and apportion the movements and numbers of both police and military, while the information from the managers was in practically every case so exaggerated as to be worthless.

Under the simple heading "newspapers" Macready states in his memorandum.

It is as well to mention that one of the factors that has tended to inflame men's minds and keep up the agitation has been the sensational and inaccurate reports in the local press. In one case the confidential secretary to a manager had formerly been a press reporter, and I was obliged to take both him and his employer severely to task for the exaggerated press reports of which he was the instigator. The strikers fully recognised the baneful effect of the local press, to such an extent that on at least one occasion reporters who attempted to attend a meeting were roughly handled.

Macready, by his clever and astute use of the forces under his command or influence, effectively carried out his mission, to protect both the property and imported labour of the mineowners, with a minimum of friction and without ever resorting to the use of the firearms with which his troops were equipped.

To a large extent he overawed the valleys. An example of his methods was the re-opening of the Gilfach Goch Britannic mine, where the manager on November 15th appealed for help. Without informing the general he had started his fires, and strikers were throwing stones down the smoke-stack. On November 21st Macready reported to the Home Office that D. A. Thomas, M.P., and Leonard

G*

Llewellyn, brought along by the Chief Constable "complained about the inadequacy of protection from the damage which was being done by the strikers. I pointed out to them that it was entirely a matter of numbers, and if the mines must be strongly held, men are not available constantly to patrol the streets. I particularly mentioned the Britannic and Glamorgan collieries as being calculated to absorb the greatest possible number of defenders with the least possible result. I told them that the right course in my opinion, was to reduce the strength of the police garrisons, form local and special reserves, and with strong patrols to move rapidly about the districts, supports being ready at any moment to proceed to any threatened point."

Macready told the Cambrian directors that he would see to the re-opening of the Britannic. This he did four days later, in the manner described in his report of his plans on Thursday, November 24th.

Arranged with the Chief Constable and Major Burnett about the re-opening of the Gilfach Goch (Britannic) Mine to-morrow.

Four officers and one hundred men Royal Munster Fusiliers and a Superintendent and forty police are to leave Pontypridd for Gilfach Goch at 9.35 a.m., arriving at that place at 10.58. 5 troops of cavalry will arrive at Gilfach Goch at the same hour, while Major Freeth from Llwynypia, with half a company Lancashire Fusiliers and half a company West Riding Regiment, will be on the hills between Gilfach Goch and the Rhondda Valley. A magistrate has been warned to be in attendance, and Mr. Llewellyn accompanies the cavalry in order to see to the restarting of the mine.

Directed Major Burnett to call at once for the strike leaders and point out to them that the mine was already damaged by water and it could not be allowed to drown out. If they accepted the situation quietly no more police or military would be left there than were necessary to keep the peace.

Arranged with the Chief Constable that he would be at the Rink during the morning so that in case of disturbances in Tonypandy, or of strikers from Panygraig going to reinforce those at Gilfach Goch, he would be ready with the police to operate against their rear.

All quiet during the night.

During this month of November 1910 the name of Tonypandy became known throughout the Labour Movement; but it was impressed upon far wider circles as well, owing to the exaggerated reports in the press. A later section deals with some of the events after the tenth of November but here it may be as well to wind up briefly the story of General Macready's presence in the Rhondda, which, contrary to the forebodings of Keir Hardie and the older leaders in Westminster, was much less unwelcome to the strikers than many expected. Over half a century later in Tonypandy a

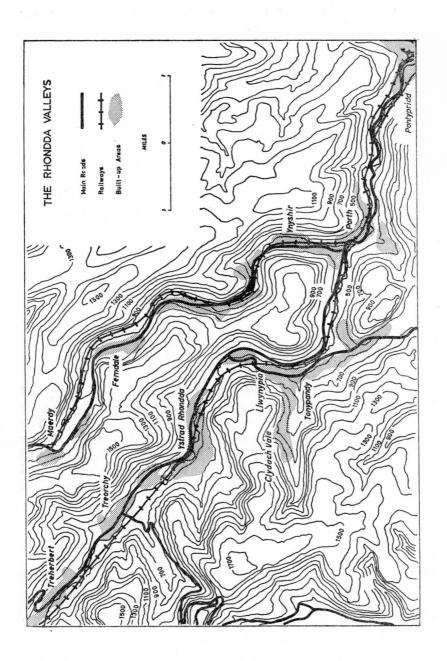

THE RHONDDA VALLEYS

Main Roads
Railways
Built-up Areas

MILES

0

Treherbert
Treorchy
Maerdy
Ferndale
Ystrad Rhondda
Clydach Vale
Llwynypia
Tonypandy
Ynyshir
Porth
Pontypridd

1300
1500
1300
1100
900
1500
1300
1100
1300
900
1100
900
700
700
900
700
500
500
700
900
500
700
900
1100
900
1100
1300
1300
1100
900
1500
1700
700
900
1100
1500
1500
1300

retired miner who had been active in tussles with the hated Glamorganshire police, could recall that "General Macready was the fairest and most straightforward gentleman you could meet": while one of the Cambrian Lodge Committee was emphatic in his statement that "Not one word against the military was ever uttered by the Combine Committee."

There was further rioting in Tonypandy and Penygraig on November 21st occasioned by the efforts of the strikers to stop the arrival of blackleg labour that had been sanctioned by Macready and therefore afforded military protection. Macready shows very clearly his outlook in his report as follows:—

During the rioting that occurred on November 21st throughout the Tonypandy valley, the Metropolitan police while driving the mob before them along the main road were heavily stoned from the side tracks, and suffered severe casualties. In order to counter these tactics on the part of the strikers on the next occasion when trouble was afoot, small bodies of infantry on the higher ground, keeping level with the police on the main road, moved slowly down the side tracks, and by a little gentle persuasion with the bayonet drove the stone throwers into the arms of the police on the lower road. The effect was excellent; no casualties were reported, though it was rumoured that many young men of the valley found that sitting down was accompanied with a certain amount of discomfort for several days. As a general instruction the soldiers had been warned that if obliged to use their bayonets they should only be applied to that portion of the body traditionally held by trainers of youth to be reserved for punishment.

After this, however, the dispute settled down into the long and bitter conflict as we shall recount in the next chapter. By January 5, 1911 Macready had left Pontypridd and returned to London. The troops remained as did a large force of police; and Tonypandy became a generic name for all troubles in the South Wales coalfield in 1910–1911 that recalled to older miners the excitement and indignation caused by the Featherstone shooting a generation earlier.

12. THE WEEK AFTER NOVEMBER 8TH

After the disturbances on November 7th and 8th there followed a calm. On the Thursday, November 10th the Home Office was able to report then "that absolute order had been maintained around all the threatened collieries," and that the "whole situation in the Rhondda Valley is completely under the control of the police." Meanwhile J. F. Moylan, a confidential officer of the Home Office,[1]

[1] HOME OFFICE TO GENERAL MACREADY
(Telegram: Sent at 5.30 p.m. on November 9th)
(A telegram in similar terms, *mutatis mutandis*, was sent to the Chief Constable of Glamorganshire.)
The Home Secretary has sent to Pontypridd by the 3.35 train M. J. F. Moylan a

had arrived and his reports added substantially to their picture of
events. On the same Wednesday, November 9th, Watts Morgan the
District Agent, and other miners' representatives had been up to
London (in response to the Tuesday afternoon message to the miners
from Winston Churchill) to talk with the officials of the Board of
Trade Conciliation Department; but this meeting had no immediate result other than a message to the men about the horses
underground.

But on the day after the Home Office statement the seed of future
troubles was sown by the action of the Glamorgan Coal Company
which had decided to import outside labour to help man the pumps.
They used for this as their agency the Shipping Federation which
either directly or through a "free labour" subsidiary had become
notorious as a supplier of strike breakers. The first contingent of
these reached Llwynypia on Friday, 11th November in the afternoon,
whereupon the following telegram was sent to the Secretary of State
for Home Affairs;

Will you immediately take steps in a matter of life and death? We
the local officials have offered our services in assisting the management at
the Cambrian Combine Collieries to raise and feed the horses.

This has been refused. Blacklegs are introduced. If, indeed, you will
assist us in putting down riots send at once and stop this blacklegging;
otherwise, as local leaders, we refuse to be responsible for what is more
than certain to happen.

Naval Committee, Cambian Combine, Penygraig.

To this the non-committal reply ran: "Your telegram received.
Have communicated it to local authorities. Home Secretary."
That same Friday Macready had convened a small conference
of magistrates and coal owners to explain the policy he proposed
to pursue. In this he was subsequently fortified by a telegram from
the Home Secretary (sent at 9.25 p.m. on November 11th, in reply
to an enquiry made by the General over the telephone) telling him
that he was

entitled in conjunction with Chief Constable to require mine managers
under protection of police and military to inform you beforehand of any
importation of outside labour in order that disturbance may not be un-
expectedly provoked.

Thereafter he was entitled to require

that such labour shall not be imported unless your arrangements for
confidential officer of this department. He has with him a code which will enable you
through him to communicate confidentially with the Home Secretary. The Home
Secretary desires that Mr. Moylan should collect and transmit to him all information
which you or the Chief Constable may be able to communicate, and would be glad if
you would give him every facility in your power for this purpose.—Under Secretary,
Home Office.

maintaining order have reached such a point that safety is in all circumstances assured.

That Friday, November 11th, had been indeed a busy day for Macready. It had begun at one o'clock in the morning when the General, "in response to an enquiry from His Majesty through the Home Secretary" had sent a reply that "the state of the horses in the Tonypandy pits is satisfactory." All had been watered and fed and were in fair condition. Moylan too was finding his way about and keeping the Home Office informed of what he had gleaned. For example his telegram received at 9 p.m. on Friday concluded that "Rioting has been quelled, but there will probably be scattered alarms for some few days," adding his discovery that the "district presents extraordinary difficulties in the way of moving reinforcements about, the different valleys being divided from each other by very steep hills." On the next day, Saturday, November 12th, Moylan's telegram from Tonypandy told how Stipendiary Lleufer Thomas had found the men's leaders disapproved of rioting and would co-operate with magistrates to prevent disorder, "but they cannot undertake to be responsible for anything if 'blacklegs' remain or are imported." The leaders as a first step wanted permission to send four men into Glamorgan Colliery to interview "blacklegs" and try peacefully to persuade them to come out. The telegram continued:

> If this is not allowed by Mr. Llewellyn they wish Home Office to turn out "blacklegs." They do not object to police guarding colliery property but to their protecting "blacklegs." They are also still prepared to meet Mr. Llewellyn and arrange to supply men sufficient to bring up horses and that these men will be trustworthy. They also objected that police were interfering with pickets when peacefully persuading "blacklegs." This is being looked into.

In a message some six hours later that same Saturday, this time from Pontypridd, Moylan wired that the

> Stipendiary had seen Llewellyn "who refuses absolutely to meet Cambrian Combine Committee over question of horses," nor would he allow them to send men into the mine "to interview 'blacklegs'." The Committee however were reported to be taking steps for preservation of order as "indicated in my telegram this afternoon." Police had been instructed as to not interfering with pickets and "it has been arranged that authorised pickets shall all wear white badges."

These meetings were concerned solely with law and order and other such matters arising from the dispute. But what of the dispute itself and any possible early end to it? On this Board of Trade officials had asked if they could meet the coalowners' association. But whereas the miners were summoned to London, the mineowners stipulated that the functionaries of the Board of Trade should travel down to Cardiff—which they did on Saturday, 12th November. At the Engineers' Institute George Askwith, K.C., and Isaac Mitchell met leading owners, viz.

F. L. Davis, Chairman of the owners' side of the Conciliation Board;
Joseph Shaw, and E. M. Hann of the Powell-Duffryn Company;
D. A. Thomas, M.P., and Leonard Llewellyn, of the Cambrian Combine;
Sir Clifford J. Cory, Bart., M.P., Gelli Colliery;
W. J. Heppell, Cwmaman Colliery;
W. H. Mewton, Cilely Colliery; and Gascoyne Dalziel, secretary of the coalowners.

At this interview matters pertaining to the stoppages were fully discussed; but the proceedings were private and no report was given to the press. It is known that the Government representatives were politely informed that they need not hope to mediate until all other miners were back at work and in the case of the Cambrian Combine lockout and strike unless the miners in the Rhondda accepted "the terms of settlement of October 22nd." These were the terms that had been rejected by the miners. The coalowners had no use at this stage for the conciliatory offices of the Government.

Sunday in the valleys was a rest day. No telegrams were exchanged with Westminster. But there were many speeches. At Aberaman Keir Hardie encouraged the strikers, and made caustic reference to the King's concern for pit ponies in a speech which roused some apprehension in the mind of Captain Lindsay whose report to the Home Office on the next day made references to it.

On Tuesday, November 15th, General Macready sent a report to the Home Office, in which he said that he had gone to the Thistle Hotel, Tonypandy, and met eleven of the men's representatives of the Cambrian Committee, to whom he had explained that "I wished to make their acquaintance in order to discuss the present state of affairs from the point of view of protection of life and property." And he had then asked them if they had any complaints they wished "to bring to my notice." One man then described what they claimed to be an assault upon their picket, by the police at Clydach Vale. He said:

the day before yesterday about dawn, he and about fifteen men were on picket a few hundred yards from the colliery entrance; a mine official came along to his work, they questioned him and allowed him to pass on. Presently the sergeant on duty asked what they were doing; they said they were picketing the mine; he said "I will soon shove you out of that", and got together a body of twenty constables and hustled them away. My informant was a man in charge of a picket. He also told me that

Deputy-Chief Constable Cole apologised to him afterwards for the action the police had taken in the matter.

It will be seen that General Macready took up a very diplomatic attitude. He related how another representative said there were no reasons for keeping the horses below, and that it was simply a trick to excite public sympathy. They claimed that their wives and children stood in the same relation to them as the horses did to the Company. The same speaker said that if they could not get their terms their object was to let the mines be flooded to the top.

Having explained that as an official I was quite unbiassed as to the rights of either party, I asked them to inform me at once whenever they had any grievance against the police or military, and told them that the more information of a reliable nature they could give me the more it would possibly tend towards avoiding friction during the present crisis. They promised they would do so and we parted on friendly terms.

A football match between the strikers and the soldiers was played at Tonypandy in which the soldiers were victorious.

On the next day (Wednesday, November 16th) General Macready received the following message in a telegram from Churchill,

You should remember that the owners are within their legal rights in claiming to import labour, but that you are entitled to judge the time, manner and circumstances of such importation in order that no breach of the peace may be unnecessarily provoked, and to ensure that the authorities responsible for keeping order have adequate forces upon the spot. With this leverage you ought to be able to restrain or, at any rate delay injudicious action on the part of owners.

I have no power to veto importation: but if you tell me in any particular case that it cannot be safely done, I shall support you. I have full confidence in your judgement and impartiality, and much can be done in these matters by personal influence.

Two days later a letter was sent to the Home Secretary by the Chief Constable of Glamorgan, who began

Sir,

I regret to say that the strikers are taking advantage of the Trade Disputes Act, 1906, to assemble in localities too numerous to be properly supervised by the police, for the purpose of committing acts of lawlessness, whenever there are not sufficient police to prevent them, or local police to recognise them.

A prompt telegram came in reply, thus:

Your letter of the 18th; you are quite right to act vigorously with your police force against serious riot. A certain amount of minor friction is, however, inseparable from the present situation. Both sides are unreasonable in many ways, and I should recommend you to go gently in small matters.—Churchill.

On the same day, Saturday, November 19th, Macready reported

that pressure was being applied by one of the mine managers. Leonard Llewellyn had written to the Chief Constable and informed him that unless more protection was provided at the Britannic Colliery to enable his officials to work the engines, the colliery would be drowned out and the Company would hold the authorities responsible for any damage that might be done to the colliery in consequence of not being provided with adequate protection. "I may point out," reported Macready, "that it is almost impossible to protect this colliery without holding the tops of the hills which surround it, in order to prevent people rolling stones down the mountain sides into the colliery." Four members of the Cambrian Committee, Clydach Vale, came to see Macready at 8.30 p.m. to whom they complained of undue severity on the part of the police in dealing with pickets, and said they had been told that the police were going to shift all the pickets that night. Macready told them that such was not the case.

The Chief Constable (on Sunday, November 20th) wrote of his fears that "whatever the outcome of the unofficial Conference on Monday the more turbulent spirits may make it a pretext for rioting on Monday night." It is rather remarkable that the Chief Constable should have been so extremely ready for trouble on the next night, and prepared for it, and in advance warn the Home Office of its likelihood—that likelihood being a highly subjective consideration in the mind of the Chief Constable.

13. THE THIRD WEEKEND OF NOVEMBER 1910

When the Members of Parliament came together again on Friday, November 18th, it was to hear what they had been told would be a historic pronouncement from Prime Minister Asquith and so they paid little enough heed to the persistent questioning by Keir Hardie of Winston Churchill and R. B. Haldane on the South Wales Coal Strike. What they heard from the Front Bench was a procedural motion for the speedy winding up of sessional business, since the Cabinet had felt it their duty "to advise the Crown to dissolve Parliament at the earliest possible moment." In the rather formal and indeed somewhat lifeless debate that followed Hilaire Belloc said that the General Election "on which the two Front Benches are determined in conference and by agreement, is not desired by the country" and was imposed on it merely to save the party system to which he gave the following definition:

It means that the Executive of this country consists of men self-appointed, nominally responsible to the House of Commons, but, in reality, when the two halves agree, absolute; and that the very large salaries paid in this commercial country to the heads of the great Executive Departments are shared, turn and turn about in bouts of years for four, five, and sometimes ten years' duration by members of a small clique, largely inter-married, often closely related, and also belonging to one little social circle. (*18.xi.1910.*)

Belloc at the end of his speech intimated that he could no longer be a slave of the Party Whip and therefore would not be sitting in the next parliament but would plunge into journalism, saying "Even the most modest pen in the humblest newspaper is as good as a vote in what has ceased to be a free deliberative Assembly."[1]

Meantime in Glamorgan pressure was being exerted upon the authorities not only by coalowners but also by the Taff Vale Railway Company, who found their stations in the Rhondda Valley heavily picketed and whose officials complained to the Chief Constable that they had difficulties and demanded "that sufficient protection shall be forthwith afforded the Company and the Public using their Railway." One way in which pressure was exercised was not in formal letters or in the skilful use of newspapers but in personal conversation, as is shown in the report to Home Office from General Macready at Pontypridd on Monday, November 21st on how in the early afternoon D. A. Thomas, M.P., and Leonard Llewellyn came to see the Chief Constable "and he brought them to see me." This was the interview which ended with Macready saying:

I told them that in my opinion the policy of giving the strikers as much licence as possible, consistent with the preservation of law and order, was the correct one.

I agreed, however, that we had reached the limit of this policy, and that should any further trouble arise it would be necessary to take measures strictly to interpret the letter of the law. Mr. Llewellyn informed me that he was getting in eleven men from Cardiff in order to keep the Glamorgan mine going at Llwynypia.

These last two sentences, in view of events that were very soon to follow, have a significant sound.

Trouble was expected. How it developed that Monday night and what was the outcome is told in a number of official accounts, including those of General Macready and of the Chief Constable. At once the most vivid and most coherent narrative is that contained in the Memorandum by J. F. Moylan sent to the Home Office on Tuesday, November 22nd. He says:

The strikers had somehow got wind of the fact that Mr. Llewellyn had 12 stokers waiting to come up from Cardiff and they had determined to

---

[1] Five days later when Belloc asked a question on additional inspectors of coal mines, the Home Secretary seized the occasion of his impending retiral from parliament (but not from politics as the Liberal Government were to learn to their cost in the next year) to utter some gracious words of regret: a compliment repaid by the poet and satirist some thirty years later in an unflattering description of Churchill as "a Yankee careerist."

stop them. They lined the railway and beset the stations at Dinas and
Tonypandy. The arrangements made by General Macready and the
Chief Constable for dealing with this interference with railway traffic
came into operation with the 8.10 p.m. train from Pontypridd, which
took on board Inspector Anderson and 10 men of the Metropolitan
Police. On arrival at Dinas they found the station occupied by a noisy
crowd and at once got out and cleared the platform. They then proceeded
with the train to Tonypandy where they found a similar state of affairs.
Inspector Anderson telephoned to the Skating Rink at Tonypandy for
assistance, and Superintendent Williams despatched immediately two
detachments of Metropolitan Police, one to Dinas and the other to
Penygraig.

That same night shortly after eight o'clock the crowd around the
railway station at Tonypandy was perhaps even more numerous
than usual. Presently conflicts developed. The inspector on the spot
telephoned for help to the various places where there were large
numbers of police. At the same time the military were informed.
Large numbers of Metropolitan police converged on the scene of
"trouble." General Macready at 9.50 p.m. despatched Metropolitan
police from Pontypridd to Tonypandy and ordered Major Freeth at
Llwynypia to go at once to Penygraig with a half-company of the
Lancashire Fusiliers: and Major Law at Newport to bring to
Pontypridd two companies of infantry (Royal Munster Fusiliers and
the Devon Regiment): these last arrived at 3 a.m. the following
morning. A squadron of Hussars under Major Haag went by road
from Pontypridd at 11.15 p.m. to Penygraig. The conflicts intensified.
The 50 infantry of the Lancashire Fusiliers arrived at the Pandy Pit
accompanied by a Magistrate.[1]

Moylan's report continues:

There is some conflict of evidence as to how many police were at
Penygraig, but the local Inspector in charge says that after the arrival of
these Metropolitans there were about 40 in all. The police drew up in the
small square of Penygraig, while the crowd took up their position in the
side streets running uphill from the square, and stoned the police. The
volleys were so heavy that the police had to take refuge in doorways, but,
as soon as there was some relaxation, they charged up the hill, and, as the
crowd moved higher up, retreated again to the square. As the police
retreated the crowd descended again and had to be repelled by another
charge. This went on for nearly an hour—the police thinking it unsafe,
with the numbers available, to follow the crowd too far into the narrow
side streets up the hill. As the hills are very steep the police were at a very
great disadvantage, and the uphill charges were very exhausting in their
heavy uniforms.

This awkward situation was relieved by the opportune arrival of
Captain Lindsay with some 70 Metropolitan, Glamorgan and Cardiff

[1] A Magistrate accompanying soldiers at night was a sign that he was ready to read the
Riot Act but usually it would also mean that the soldiers had loaded their rifles with
ball cartridge.

Police. Captain Lindsay had been at Tonypandy in the afternoon arranging for a redistribution of police forces so as to release sufficient men from the collieries to provide patrols. He had returned to Pontypridd about 9.30 p.m., but, hearing on arrival of the disturbances, at once proceeded back to Llwynypia with some of the Metropolitan reserve from here. At Llwynpia he collected some more police from the colliery and some from the street, as he proceeded, and marched to Penygraig, passing on the way through the police at Tonypandy, who were still being stoned, though not heavily, by part of the crowd driven off from Tonypandy Railway Station.

On arrival at Penygraig, Captain Lindsay joined the police in the square and divided his force into four sections. One was left to hold the square, and the other three charged up the hill, to the right and to the left. These charges by the reinforced police drove the crowd off more effectively, and they fled higher up the hill, stoning as they went, and took refuge in houses in the side streets. The police pursued them, and it was in this pursuit that they suffered most heavily. The side streets are very narrow, and the police were met by a cross fire from men and women—especially women—in the doorways and at the windows of the houses on either side. All sorts of missiles were used—stones, bricks, kitchen and chamber utensils, and even ash boxes.

At the very beginning of the pursuit Police Constable Knipe, a Glamorgan constable, who was next to the Chief Constable, had his helmet knocked off with a stone, and the next instant his head cut open with a brick, which severed a main artery. These side streets are not paved, but are only rough roads covered with loose stones which provided the strikers with ample ammunition. The pursuit continued until practically all the strikers had taken refuge in houses, and once the streets were cleared, the police commenced to withdraw, and by 12 midnight the riot was over and the police were retiring to Tonypandy.

By midnight the Chief Constable had the situation "under complete control." The delay in the arrival of the cavalry it is understood was due to the frosty state of the roads. The Lancashire Fusiliers on their way back to Llwynypia "dispersed all the pickets and destroyed the picket camp fires." On the whole affair, the Chief Constable of Glamorgan reported to the Home Office as follows:

The only two alternatives for the police were either to wait until the strikers assumed the aggressive, or to bring on a collision themselves. The strikers were perfectly aware of this, and shaped their tactics accordingly.

I consider, when the inevitable collision occurred on Monday night, the situation was dealt with in a highly satisfactory manner . . .

On the next day (Tuesday, November 22nd) the Home Secretary telegraphed to Macready as follows:

Arrest and prosecution should follow in all cases where evidence is forthcoming against law-breakers. Cases of intimidation clearly going beyond peaceful persuasion, even if they cannot be prevented at the time should be investigated afterwards with a view to the conviction of the offenders. The police should not hesitate to make arrests where *prima facie* cases disclose, and after every incident of disorder police enquiries and detective work should be rigorously prosecuted. This does not mean that pickets should be hustled or the police force be dissipated and exhausted in futile efforts, and must not be brought in conflict with my general advice to the Chief Constable to go gently in small things. Behind the day-to-day maintenance of order which is a matter of judgement and tact, there must be a regular process of bringing offenders, particularly rioters and thieves, to justice. Please impart this to the Chief Constable and take it as a general guide, subject always to your superior knowledge on the spot.—Churchill.

That night of Tuesday, November 22nd, there was a further disturbance, this time in the Aberdare valley at Aberaman at which over a dozen constables reported bruises and other injuries. At Penygraig (and also near Tonypandy) on November 21, 1910, no less than 50 constables had reported casualties. These ran from bruised left leg and sprained right ankle to "main artery severed and severe scalp wound" while others were described as being "struck with stones." Of the 50 casualties nearly 40 were suffered by the Metropolitan police. Less than 10 of the Glamorganshire police appear to have suffered any casualty. There is no record available of casualties, if any, suffered by the soldiers who were so much in evidence high up on the mountainside. But all of these circumstances were fully dealt with later that week in parliament to which we now turn.

14. KEIR HARDIE VERSUS CHURCHILL

The Home Secretary may have thought that he had weathered any storms aroused by his action over the South Wales colliery disturbances and in continuing to exercise a sort of remote control over events in Glamorgan. If so, he was to be undeceived. With bulldog tenacity the Member for Merthyr Tydfil held on to his demand for an inquiry into police conduct and would not let go. Churchill was to find this out both in the last days of the moribund twenty-ninth Parliament of the United Kingdom and in the succeeding year in the thirtieth Parliament that was now soon to be elected.

There was no Government business these last days of the dying Parliament and indeed in that fourth week of November the Members seemed to have come together only to conduct their own parliamentary obsequies. The Prime Minister proposed "That the House, at its rising this day, do adjourn until Monday next at Twelve of the clock" whereupon Keir Hardie prolonged the session by another two hours by starting a debate on a matter arising "out of the great industrial dispute which is now being waged in South Wales." He said: "I claim a public inquiry." Churchill interjected.:

"On what grounds?" Keir Hardie replied: "On the grounds of the charges against the police—charges of having ill-used women and other perfectly unoffending persons, not during a baton charge against a mob, but under circumstances in which revenge could be the only motive."

Keir Hardie, after referring at some length to the events of November 8th and 9th in mid-Rhondda (in the course of which he quoted both from his previous investigations and also from a more recent document[1]), went on to deal with the happenings of that same week:

Now I come to the second riot at Tonypandy, the one which took place on Monday of this week, the 21st. This morning I received the following telephone message which I will read as an introduction to the details which I will give in a minute:
"Mrs. Morgan, 45 John Street, Penygraig, has had her house forcibly entered by police when the whole family were indoors. A most brutal and savage assault was committed on two young men. One of the policemen broke his truncheon, half of which is in possession of Mrs. Morgan."

Hardie furnished details at some length from a series of letters he had received not only from colliers but from local merchants, "from what is practically the Property Owners' Association of the district." There were instances of attacks on peaceful pickets: and Keir Hardie asked the Home Secretary "whether conduct of that kind is either to be sanctioned or tolerated on the part of the police. The pickets are as much entitled to the protection of the police as is the property of the colliery owner or the sacred person of the blackleg."

After some harrowing details in one of the letters which he had read aloud to the House of Commons (his speech occupies ten columns of Hansard) Hardie commented on one eye-witness and said:

He is not a collier, but a merchant in the place, and his description of policemen knocking down solitary individuals, and bludgeoning and kicking them on the ground is surely one of the most serious kind, and one which, coupled with others of a like nature, ought to be sufficient justification for granting the inquiry we are asking.

[1] "I have here a copy of a document sent by the Vicar of Llwynypia, a village near to Tonypandy, the Rev. D. T. R. James, Evan Richards, Congregational minister, M. H. Ellis, Calvinistic Methodist minister, and James Nicholas, Baptist minister. This document, which has been sent to the public Press reads as follows:
'Sir,—The Press reports concerning the street rioting and shop-looting in Tonypandy and Llwynypia have given the reading public the impression that it was carried out by the general body of strikers, whereas the plain truth is that it was the work of a certain small gang of half-drunken, irresponsible persons, many of whom, if not the majority, were from outside the affected district. Earlier in the day, at a mass meeting of the workmen at which the worthy stipendiary of our district received a hearty reception, all the leaders strongly deprecated any form of violence, and urged upon the men that all the demonstrations should be of a peaceful character. This advice was received with applause by all, and they marched in a body 10,000 strong around the district without causing the slightest disturbance whatsoever.' "

At the end of this evidence which he had given Keir Hardie said:

There are the fresh facts which, I submit, justify an inquiry. Much of the disturbance can be laid at the door of Captain Lindsay, who was in charge of the police. This man was responsible for the riot which took place at Tirphil in 1898. On that occasion he caused a number of mounted police to charge into a meeting of colliers which was being held. Naturally the colliers resented this action, and it was called a riot. It is the same man who is again in charge of the police in the strike area, and once more riots follow in his wake.

Winston Churchill, well aware of the General Election eight days ahead, sought at the outset of his reply to be "sweetly reasonable." But towards its conclusion, stung by interjections from Keir Hardie, the Home Secretary could not refrain from making somewhat provocative remarks. He said:

Churchill: I am very sorry I cannot use language which would be gratifying to the hon. Gentleman in this matter. I think that the people of South Wales owe a great debt to the police, for it is the police who have been sent in who alone stand between them and the use of the military.

Keir Hardie: Nonsense.

Churchill: The hon. Gentleman says "nonsense?" Why does he say "nonsense?"

Keir Hardie: The common-sense of the law-abiding inhabitants, of 99 per cent of the people, would have preserved order without either the constabulary or the military.

Churchill: The House will judge of the value of that statement. If it had been left to common-sense, let me tell the hon. Gentleman that there is not a single mine in the whole of that district that would not have been drowned right up to the pit's mouth, filled absolutely with water to the brim, and rendered absolutely impossible to work for five, six, or seven months at a time. In the Britannia Colliery, parts of which are already flooded, undoubtedly, if it were further flooded, some of its workings could never be used again. Then what would become of common-sense, as the hon. Gentleman says?

What is the use of the hon. Gentleman's coming here with the pretence that nothing is going on, when there is in reality a savage war going on between the two forces. I say the people of South Wales owe a great debt of gratitude to the police, who were sent there so that they could stand between them and the military, and who are enabling us, by their fine qualities, to conduct this very grave and serious labour struggle without recourse to the lethal weapons which the troops possess.

I have been greatly blamed for my conduct in this matter, but I am quite ready to defend my action, and I will lay papers, if necessary, before Parliament in support of the course I have taken. I am blamed for not having brought the troops into direct contact with the people. I am quite prepared to meet the attacks upon me.

I am quite prepared to do my utmost to see this matter through with the police, and if I succeed in using the police, and the police alone, though blood may be shed, most of it will be from the nose, which can be subsequently replaced.

I am sorry, but I must deal faithfully with the hon. Gentleman. I do not think that I need have any scruple in speaking plainly to him.

Keir Hardie: There is no love lost between us.

Churchill: I know perfectly well, from every act and speech of his, his life is directed to injuring and assailing the party to which I belong. As he justly says, there is no love lost between us, though I entirely respect the consistency of his career.

He asks me what I am going to do. I will tell him. There are ample forces on the spot to maintain order, and if order is maintained these forces will not be used, no difficulty will occur, and no collisions of any sort will arise between the police and the rioters. If disorder does arise, it will be repressed by the police, if they possibly can do so.

There now came to the support of the Home Secretary Sir John David Rees.[1] Sir John attacked Keir Hardie whose right to deal with the question from an economic point of view he entirely disputed saying:

He appears before the House and talks of a strike as an economic matter—a dispute between capital and labour, when he himself has said, at an International Socialist Conference, that he regards a strike as a weapon of offence, and that he regards an international strike that would paralyse the arms of his country in time of war as a justifiable and proper weapon. (*24.xi.1910.*)

He continued in this strain to an extent that began to embarrass Churchill who more than once made interjections to counter the suggestions or innuendoes of Sir J. D. Rees. The Member for Montgomery, turning again to responsibility for the disturbances, said:

I am bound, and it is my duty, to say what I think: that I attribute those disorders in no small measure, but in a large measure, to the Socialistic preaching of the hon. Member for Merthyr Tydfil, who posed today as the representative of the strikers in this economic dispute. I attribute this lawlessness which has lately crept into these disputes, far more to the pernicious teaching and talk of the hon. Member for Merthyr Tydfil, than to any original sin of the Welsh miner, who, I maintain, has not got a double dose of original sin, and who would have allowed this matter to be settled in the usual manner, were it not for the pernicious doctrines of the hon. Member for Merthyr Tydfil. (*24.xi.1910.*)

After this diatribe he came out in his true colours by asking whether the Government would reconsider the Eight Hours Act "in view of the disastrous results which have followed from its

---

[1] Rees, born in 1854, had a brilliant career in the Indian Civil Service from 1875 to 1901 and had used his opportunities in India to become director of a dozen gold-mining companies and tea estates at a suitably adequate remuneration. After this lucrative career Sir J. D. Rees (quite in the manner of eighteenth century nabobs) decided to seek the suffrages of his fellow citizens in an attempt to enter public life. He began as unsuccessful Conservative candidate for the London County Council in 1901 in Peckham. Then he transferred his attention to the Welsh border county of Montgomeryshire where he stood as Liberal candidate and was successful in the great "landslide" of January 1906.

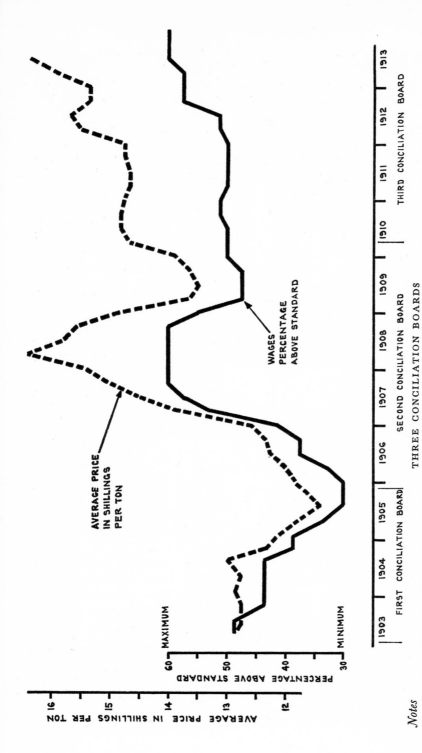

THREE CONCILIATION BOARDS

Notes

(i) The dates of the Conciliation Board Agreements were April 1, 1903; December 11, 1905; and April 8, 1910.
(ii) The average prices are for large coal f.o.b. at Bristol Channel ports as ascertained by quarterly audits; as shown in upper graph.

WAGES
PERCENTAGE
ABOVE STANDARD

AVERAGE PRICE
IN SHILLINGS
PER TON

FIRST CONCILIATION BOARD

SECOND CONCILIATION BOARD

THIRD CONCILIATION BOARD

1903 | 1904 | 1905 | 1906 | 1907 | 1908 | 1909 | 1910 | 1911 | 1912 | 1913

MAXIMUM

MINIMUM

PERCENTAGE ABOVE STANDARD

60 | 50 | 40 | 30

AVERAGE PRICE IN SHILLINGS PER TON

16 | 15 | 14 | 13 | 12

enactment in South Wales?" He further asked the Home Secretary whether he did not think that the "peculiar bitterness" and the difficulties were not "immediately due to that interference with private rights and the proper freedom of employer and employed, which resulted in the passing of the Eight Hours Bill?"—at which point Winston Churchill vigorously dissented. With such support the Home Secretary's case was being considerably worsened.

Sir John Rees was immediately countered by Edgar Jones, the Liberal Member for Merthyr Tydfil, who complained that the Member for Montgomery "makes a pontifical pronouncement as to the origin of the struggle, and declares that the whole thing is due to the Eight Hours Act. I say it is most unfortunate. I do not know whether we have just had the Swan Song of the hon. Member's Liberalism. I suppose we may take it to be such. I can assure him that the miners of the Rhondda Valley, some of whom might have journeyed to Montgomery to vote for him, will be most pleased to regard his intervention as a very welcome Swan Song indeed."

G. N. Barnes, who some twenty years earlier had risen into prominence as secretary to Tom Mann, and who only in 1910 had reached his brief eminence as Leader of the Labour Party (before being superseded by Ramsay MacDonald) now entered the debate and said:

The position taken up by my hon. Friend, as I understand, is that the police have been guilty of certain acts of brutality. The Home Secretary meets that by stating that the police of London are an exceptionally well-behaved body of men. I have no hesitation in associating myself with that testimony.

But he concluded with the words:

I again express my regret that the inquiry has not been granted. At the same time, I associate myself with the junior Member for Merthyr (Mr. E. Jones) in his expression of satisfaction that the Home Secretary is going to keep his mind open with a view, possibly, of granting an inquiry later on. (*24.xi.1910.*)

Thus Barnes' last speech as transient Leader of the Labour Party was in support of the demand that had been initiated by Keir Hardie.

15. STRIFE WITHIN THE FEDERATION

What was the standpoint and what the activity of the Executive Council of the South Wales Miners' Federation in these stormy second and third weeks of November 1910? The miners' agents who very largely constituted the Council had never experienced a situation like it and seem to have been in a quandary again and again throughout the months of the strike. At times they seemed impotent to give a lead themselves while sufficiently established to prevent leadership falling into the hands of others: thus they would refuse to call conferences when it was demanded of them: and later the coalfield conferences which they did call would not accept their recommendations. Reluctantly they would agree to take a ballot vote of the miners: and almost invariably the ballot vote went against their recommendations and their policy. They looked to the Board of Trade to help: but that department of Government trod these paths very gingerly, so long as the coalowners were loath to brook "interference" by the Board of Trade. The Council besought the Miners' Federation of Great Britain to succour them: but though the M.F.G.B. grant of money was taken thankfully, the advice of its officers was not taken, or, if accepted by the Council, was by the men rejected. All the time there was to be strife between the Cambrian Combine Committee and the S.W.M.F. Executive Council; between the young socialists of the Rhondda and adjacent valleys and the older leaders steeped in Liberal traditions and inured to habits that had grown up in the days of the Sliding Scale. Within the Executive Council itself there was strife between the majority and a small minority headed by George Barker (who happened to be not at all young); and this strife was soon to be intensified. To set forth in detail the record of these events and months of vain negotiations while the indomitable men of the mid-Rhondda held out amid growing poverty and extreme distress would take overlong; and the reader must be content with a more summary treatment, which may be preceded here by a brief recapitulation.

The lockout of the 800 workers in the Ely Pit began on September 1st. As a reprisal all the workmen employed by the Cambrian Combine tendered strike notices on October 1st as decided by a coalfield ballot vote on September 27th. The strike began on November 1st. The first disturbances occurred on Monday, November 7th.

On that day the Executive Council at Cardiff were discussing the unauthorised Powell Duffryn stoppage in the Aberdare Valley, which had begun on October 24th. Elsewhere too there were strikes or lockouts, particularly in the Maesteg and Western valleys. The Aberdare dispute was not soon to be settled and it dragged on for many weeks. Meanwhile the lodges in the Aberdare Valley formed a committee which had linked up with the Cambrian Combine Committee. These two bodies, having little faith in the Executive Council, circulated statements through South Wales pleading for a general strike of the coalfield, and later for a national strike of all the coalfields of Britain, to settle what they believed to be a matter of general principle. When the demand of these two bodies for a coalfield conference was refused they took on themselves to call an unofficial conference for Monday, November 21st. This brought decision on November 17th by the Executive Council:

> That it having come to the knowledge of this Council, and this having been confirmed by reports from members of the Council, that the Aberdare miners' representatives, together with the Cambrian Combine Committee are convening an Unofficial Conference for Monday next, this Council strongly urges upon the members of the Federation in the coalfield to disregard invitations to send representatives to such a conference.

But the unofficial conference was held, though not with as great a number of representatives as had been hoped for by those who called it. A week later the Executive Council again discussed the Cambrian Combine dispute, and they decided:

> That any further negotiations for a settlement of this dispute shall be conducted by the General Secretary (Mr. T. Richards, M.P.), Mr. Alfred Onions and Mr. Enoch Morrell with the local Agents and the Workmen. (*24.xi.1910.*)

At this same meeting attention was called to "the injurious effect of an alleged compact" between the two committees and so they decided to ask the Cambrian Combine Workmen's Committee and the Aberdare Strike Committee to meet the Council, "with a view to a meeting being held of the Conciliation Board and a General Conference." Accordingly, on the next day, representatives from each of the two committees attended the Council meeting held in Park Hall, Cardiff. The President, William Abraham, M.P., explained why the meeting had been called and asked the Committees if what had been reported to the Council was true, viz.: "that a compact had been entered into between the two committees that no resumption of work should take place by either of these bodies of workmen until the disputes at the Combine Collieries and the Aberdare Collieries had been satisfactorily settled." Most of the members of the committees denied this: but thereafter there was a difficult situation. The friction between the lesser bodies and the greater body responsible for the Federation as a whole had reached the point that there were two sides as on the Conciliation Board, and a curious simulation of Board procedures. For example, first Tom Richards had stated that the following was the recommendation of the Council:

> That both parties should give up the "Down Tools Policy" which was in contravention of the Conference and the ballot, and that the Council believed that the Down Tools policy will result in failure.
>
> Further that the Council shall have full authority to deal with the Aberdare dispute, with a view of trying to bring about a settlement.

Then Council retired to enable the local committee members to confer together in private. Later, the two committees retired to enable the Council to confer in private. Thereafter it was deadlock. The committees wanted the Council to take over a further unofficial conference which they had intended to call. The Council refused, for while willing to call a conference they were not at all willing to take over the unofficial conference. So the deadlock continued. On Tuesday, November 29th, a further unofficial conference was held. Next day, a meeting of the Executive Council in the Royal Chambers, Cardiff was attended by a deputation of a score of miners from the unofficial conference held the previous day. They were headed by Alderman Fleming, who said: "We are prepared to admit that we have done wrong, in that we have gone behind the leaders to have done some of these things": and he then asked for support for the Aberdare men. The deputation from the unofficial conference and the Executive Council members behaved like two potentially hostile bodies in that they met and retired for consultation. Finally the deputation handed in the following resolution, passed at the unofficial conference in Cory Hall on November 29th,

That this conference request an official conference within six days to discuss the present position of affairs in the affected areas and to form a future policy.

Thereupon the Council resolved unanimously "to call a conference of the coalfield to discuss the general situation." This was to be on Wednesday, December 7th and the agenda was to be

To report upon the various disputes in the coalfield, and to consider the policy proposed by the Executive Council by dealing with the same.

The Special Conference, after much discussion and many propositions, could not reach agreement. The chief agreement at the Conference was on a resolution directed against Winston Churchill, which ran as follows:—

That we condemn the action of the Home Secretary in refusing to grant an inquiry into the conduct of the military and police forces in the Mid-Rhondda and Aberdare Districts, and that we still press any future Home Secretary to hold such an inquiry. (*7.xii.1910.*)

This was passed by 284 delegates representing 152,559 workmen. A week later on December 14th the recommendations of the Council were carried by 1,815 votes to 921. The first was that the Aberdare workmen be advised to return to work (as had been recommended by the Executive Council on November 14th) and

That the Executive Council put forth every endeavour to secure the re-employment of all the workmen, and that the members of the Federation who may not secure immediate employment shall be paid Strike Pay from the Central Fund. (*14.xii.1910.*)

With this conference decision, the Council were able gradually to bring to an end the Aberdare stoppage. But as the end came nearer they bethought themselves that a precedent might have been created for defiance of rules. A later minute under the heading of "Grants" runs:

The Council having considered the many Grants recently made, which were not strictly in accordance with the Rules of the Federation, hereby RESOLVES—"That the Council will not in future take the responsibility of granting financial assistance to any Workmen not warranted by the Rules of the Federation." (*22.xii.1910.*)

It was at this stage that, as we saw, the disturbances were regarded by General Macready as having completely quietened down.

The decision on the situation of the twelve thousand Cambrian Combine workmen was:

That having failed to receive a satisfactory settlement of the dispute of the Cambrian Combine Collieries, the Federation members be urged to pay their levies promptly in support of these Workmen and that an appeal be made to the Federation of Great Britain to render us assistance in fighting this battle. (Adopted *14.xii.1910.*)

The Special Conference delegates (148 in number,) brought the reports of Lodge decisions on the Council's recommendations. Before they dispersed they passed two additional resolutions:

(i) That the Executive Council be instructed to ask for a national conference to consider the question of Minimum Wage.
(ii) That this conference press forward in accordance with the decision of the Edinburgh Conference, the questions of Working in Abnormal Places, and Lower-Paid Workmen. (*14.xii.1910.*)

These decisions held in their wording the real kernel of the dispute that had begun with the Ely Pit lockout. It was on these questions that not only the Cambrian workmen but many others felt there was a deep grievance. These two decisions were not new in South Wales: but their reaffirmation at this mid-December conference while the General Election was in progress had much significance for the struggles of the next fifteen months.

THE CAMBRIAN COMBINE

Naval Colliery Co. (1897) Ltd.

Name of Colliery							No. employed in 1910	No. employed in 1912
Ely (S)	..	..	..	..	..	..	939	925
Nant gwyn (S)	..	..	..	..	..	..	821	1,030
Anthony and Pandy (S)	..	..	..	..	..	340	685
Adare (H) (level)	..	..	..	..	..	..	44	42
					Total	..	2,144	2,682

Cambrian Collieries Limited:
General Manager, Leonard W. Llewellyn

Cambrian Navigation I (S)	..	..	..	..	..		701	731
Cambrian Navigation II (S)	..	..	..	..		1,498	1,613
Cambrian Navigation III (S)	..	..	..	..		1,855	1,961
					Total	..	4,054	4,305

Glamorgan Coal Co. Ltd.
General Manager, Leonard W. Llewellyn

Gilfach (H.C.)	..	..	..	..	..		46	90
Llwynypia No. 1 (S)	..	..	..	..	..		1,712	1,015
Llwynypia No. 2 (S)	..	..	..	..	..		1,539	1,265
Llwynypia No. 6 (S)	..	..	..	..	..		656	795
Sherwood (H.C.)	..	..	..	..	..		537	500
					Total	..	3,950	3,665

Britannic Merthyr Coal Co. Ltd.

Britannic	..	..	..	..	..	..	—	697

Appended to the name of each colliery above is an alphabetic letter to indicate the kind of coal produced, viz:—C coking; H household; S steam.

Source: *The South Wales Coal Annual* for 1909–1910, pp. 110 to 125.

TOM MANN'S ARTICLE
written on 7.xi.1910
and excerpted from *Justice* 12.xi.1910

THE STRIKE OF TWELVE THOUSAND MEN AT THE CAMBRIAN COMBINE COLLIERIES
Eight thousand in procession at five o'clock in the morning

The Cambrian Combine consists of three groups of mines, known as the Cambrian, the Glamorgan and the Naval Collieries at each of which group there is, roughly about 4,000 men employed. Besides these in the Rhondda the Combine also control the Britannic Merthyr at Gilfach Goch.

The Managing Director of the Combine is Mr. D. A. Thomas, M.P. for Cardiff. The General Manager is Mr. Leonard W. Llewellyn.

Scores of disputes exist in the South Wales Coalfield, many of which are due entirely to the Managers fixing prices for getting coal at so low a figure that it is impossible for the men to make an ordinary wage. As the men work on tonnage rates the method is for the management to fix the price of each seam in conjunction with the Lodge Committee and failing this the matter is referred to arbitration. In practice in many instances the fixing of prices is done arbitrarily by the owners' representatives and this is enforced by them where they can. Such an instance occurred at the Ely Pit about 3 months ago, one of the Cambrian Group, where 70 men working a new seam found it impossible to get a wage under the terms fixed by the owners, and refused to work under them; at this the owners gave notice to all the other men in the mine to terminate their contracts—that is, they locked out all the other men at the pit to enforce the price they had decided upon. The present strike of 11,500 men is in direct protest against this locking out business of the bosses to reduce the men's wages. This is the direct and sole cause of the strike in the Rhondda at the Cambrian Combine Mines. It is a most serious matter to the men, as new prices are continually being fixed and the invariable practice is to lower them.

Before striking the whole case was dealt with by a conference of delegates of the South Wales Miners' Federation and afterwards by a vote of the miners themselves, throughout South Wales. It was agreed to support the Cambrian men financially but not to help by a general stoppage. Accordingly all the Cambrian men gave their notices in and these terminated last week.

Now comes the difficulty. Besides those who belong to the Miners' Federation there are members of three other unions whose co-operation is of utmost importance to successful action. These are the Winding Enginemen's Union,—i.e., those who drive the hoist engines for the shafts —also the Enginemen's and Stokers and Craftsmen's Union—i.e., those who drive the hauling engines to bring the trams to bottom of shaft from the workings—and the Firemen or Stokers. These being in sectional Unions although the miners may act unanimously, it still leaves the men unaffected. A working agreement between these theoretically exists, but like all such arrangements it only works when the responsible men are actuated by the true principle of solidarity, and it is easy to find stumbling blocks. Winding men being under a separate agreement, they were not prepared to make common cause unless the action should be taken by the miners to give them sufficient reason. This meant that in each of the three groups of mines there have been about 300 officials, ostlers, enginemen, stokers, etc., or, roughly about 1,000 people in all, keeping the mines in order so that the company's property should not deteriorate. From a class struggle standpoint this is not the way. Class solidarity by ALL leaving, and let the capitalists look after their property, or let it go to blazes, is the only sensible fighting policy. To intercept the sections referred to, it was decided that all miners should demonstrate near their respective mines at 5 a.m. in the morning. At 6 o'clock there was a procession at the Cambrian group of 2,500 in one line that marched along

12
COMMITTEE OF
LADY HELPERS,
1912

GATHERING
COAL FROM
SLAG HEAP

STREET SCENE, DOWLAIS,
1875

13 BARGOED. MINERS UNDERGROUND WAITING THEIR TURN

FIRST COMPOUND WINDING ENGINE IN SOUTH WALES, 1893

the main street, near to a point adjacent to the company's property, and back again. In addition, about ten squads of fifty strong were along various routes and on the mountain sides to meet those who would be leaving night shift or starting day shift. The rain fell very heavily at intervals, but many women were in the procession, a number with infants. Choruses were sung, and occasional excitement caused as a group of officials would be met, or a few enginemen or stokers. Mounted police were patrolling good humouredly, but at 6.25 two enginemen were slyly making their way towards the pit; they were recognised, and some of the women talked to them in pretty emphatic Welsh, which I could not understand. Immediately a crowd gathered, and mounted police for the moment dropped the steady kindly attitude they had previously shown and charged. It was said some women were knocked down. I did not see the women down being some half dozen yards behind the horses, but it angered the crowd who immediately showed a disposition to effectively resent any rough behaviour and at least one policeman got a nasty knock. In a $\frac{1}{4}$ of an hour this had subsided; but the processionists kept at it, their numbers serving as the reserve force from which to draw contingents for special work.

By 8 o'clock, as far as one could judge not more than half-a-dozen got to the mines out of 300: and reports came from the Glamorgan group that the demonstrators had been very successful; some hustling had taken place, but officers and enginemen did not reach the mine.

This is the first time during the 40 years history of mining here that a general fight of this kind has been conducted by the miners and it is the best lesson as to the need for solidarity that the men have had and it will not be lost.

At Aberdare where Charlie Stanton is the Agent, 10,000 men are out, chiefly the men of the Powell Duffryn Mines and those in sympathy with them. To-day the miners' council meet to decide what support shall be given to the Aberdare men. As yet they have not been granted any support, and thus there is a great difference between the fight in Aberdare and this in the Rhondda. In the latter, as previously stated, the 12,000 have the backing of the whole of the South Wales Miners' Federation. It is to be hoped that the Aberdare men will get it too!

TOM MANN
Tonypandy, Rhondda Valley, South Wales
Monday, November 7, 1910.

APPENDIX III TO CHAPTER SEVEN

EXCERPTS FROM HOME OFFICE BLUE BOOK
Colliery Strike Disturbances in South Wales—
Correspondence and Report: November 1910.
(Cd.5568)

Mr. Moylan to Home Office
(Memorandum: Sent on Wednesday, November 16.)

The Cynon Colliery men in the Avon Valley having resumed work this morning, the strike is now confined to the Rhondda and Aberdare districts, except for the small pit of the Coytrahen Park Company at Tondu, where an early settlement of the dispute is confidently anticipated.

In the Rhondda Valley three meetings of the men were held during the day, and they are reported to have decided that their present strike tactics were a failure, and that the best course was to arrange with the men of the Aberdare Valley to call a conference of men's representatives from the whole of the South Wales Coalfield and endeavour to bring about a general strike.

At 11.40 a.m. a telephone message was received at Tonypandy Police Station from the Clerk at the Tonypandy Colliery Office of the Cambrian Combine, that a body of 400 armed strikers was marching over the hills in the direction of Nantgwyn Colliery, and that the manager desired police protection. Forty Metropolitan Police were despatched in great haste, and arrived breathless on top of a steep slope to find that the armed strikers were the Lancashire Fusiliers taking their walk. This fact could have been ascertained by the manager with very little trouble in a few minutes; instead he had the police telephoned for! The same manager asked if he could have a line of sentries on the hill tops! The General and the Chief Constable have given instructions that if any mine manager wants police reinforcements he must first satisfy the police officer in charge on the spot, and send his requisition through him.

Difficulties continue with regard to picketing. Several complaints have been made to-day by men who have been stopped by pickets from going to work. They allege that they have been threatened and intimidated, and that pickets of 12 men have stood in a line across the road and prevented their further passage. These complaints are being investigated.

The instructions to the police as regards importation of "blacklegs" are that no escort is to be given to them without authority from the Chief Constable, and the mine managers have been told that, if they wish to introduce further labour, they must inform the authorities in the first place.

The weather has turned extremely cold and the hills are covered with snow.

J. F. MOYLAN.

No. 54.   Mr. Moylan to Home Office.
           (Memorandum: Sent on Sunday, November 13.)

To-day I accompanied Colonel Edwards and Major Burnett, commanding 18th Hussars, in a motor car to the two valleys further west to which detachments of the Metropolitan Police were sent on Friday and Saturday, namely, (1) the valley which runs up from Bridgend and (2) the Avon valley which runs up from Port Talbot.

As the crow flies (2), the furthest valley, is about 17 miles from Pontypridd, but by road it is more than 60.

In (1), the first valley, is the Brynmenin Colliery of the Coytrahen Park Colliery Company at Tondu, which applied for assistance on Friday night and received 30 Metropolitan Police. On investigation, we found that the case for such assistance was very slight. The colliery is a very small one employing about 250 men, who were out on strike. Some threats had been made publicly, but had also subsequently been publicly withdrawn at mass meetings of the men. The Manager said he feared men would come down from other collieries and attack him, but, as far as we could judge, these fears were somewhat remote, and no attempt had been made to put the colliery in any state of defence.

In (2), the second valley, are the Duffryn Rhondda Pit (employing 1,500 men), the Cynon Pit (employing 800 men), and the old Cynon Pit (employing 600 men), all under the same control. They are situated high up the valley, where it is an extremely narrow and deep glen. A rough road runs up, but the easiest approach is by the track of the Rhondda and Swansea Bay Railway. 50 Metropolitan Police and 46 Carmarthen Police were sent there on Friday in circumstances which, on investigation to-day, appeared to be most unfortunate. The men in the Cynon Pit came out about a month ago (but went back shortly after), without giving notice, and were sued for damages. Before the case came on they were offered the chance of settling the damages on the same terms as the Duffryn Rhondda men had settled a similar dispute some time ago, but refused. The Court ordered 19s. to be deducted from the wages of each of the 60 men sued, the deduction to be made from their wages last Friday. After the decision the men apparently expressed willingness to accept the easier terms previously offered and the colliery Manager advised the owners to agree to this, but, after considering it for some time, they decided on Thursday to refuse and make the deduction ordered by the Court. The men threatened to retaliate by acts of violence. The Manager, in view of these threats, urgently requisitioned and obtained, on Friday, the police now there, the Metropolitan Police arriving early in the afternoon and standing by while the men's wages were paid. The men held a meeting and decided to go out on strike, and, after making some small demonstration against the Metropolitan Police, proceeded by train to their homes at Pontrhydyfen and Cwmavon. The police are en-camped in sheds and outhouses high up on the mountain side and have remained there since Friday.

It will be seen from this short account of the facts that these Police were sent for solely in order to enable the deduction from wages to be made, and that the effect of their arrival has been to send the men out on strike! If there had been no large force of Police here to draw on, the Manager admitted that the deduction would not have been made and there would have been no strike.

The presence of such a large force of police and military here has undoubtedly given Colliery Managers the impression that they can obtain unlimited supplies of them on any pretext. This unfortunate impression has now been removed to some extent. A demand was actually made for the despatch of cavalry to the Avon Valley, where they could only have proceeded up or down by way of the railway track! The military are preferred partly on account of their small cost to the colliery owner.

J. F. MOYLAN.

No. 61.

Monmouthshire and South Wales Coal Owners' Association to
Home Secretary
(Answered by No. 62: See also Nos. 63 and 64)

Cardiff, November 14, 1910.
Dear Sir,
I enclose a statement which was placed before the owners' side of the Conciliation Board of South Wales to-day by the Manager of the Cynon

Colliery, Aberavon, where a strike is now taking place, in reference to certain circumstances connected with the introduction of the military for the protection of the colliery and the workpeople. The owners' side wish me to see you upon this matter as it was thought desirable that the subject should be enquired into.

Yours, &c.,

FRED L. DAVIS, President

The Right Hon. Winston Churchill, M.P.

Enclosure in No. 61

Yesterday at 1.30 p.m. I received a message from the Aberavon Police Station saying that some officers were coming up and wished to go round the Cynon Colliery. They were informed that I was at the house, and I arranged to meet them at the Walnut Tree Hotel later. I met them at the hotel at about 3.30 and introduced myself. Colonel Edwards, who I understand is a Chief Constable of one of the Metropolitan Divisions, told me that they could not discuss anything until they had had something to eat. At the same moment an Inspector came into the room and told him to withdraw for the time being.

Colonel Edwards asked me if all this trouble was not brought about for a sum of £50. I replied that the amount in question at the moment was £50, which had been awarded us by the Court, and which we were entitled to deduct, and that it was not a question of the damages, but that it was the precedent of the whole thing involved.

He then stated that in his opinion it was most absurd that all these police are to be brought into the district to protect us in carrying out this stoppage. He further stated that in his mind there was no need for any extra police or military, and that he did not see that they were called upon to protect the owners against the workmen.

I stated the position of affairs in the coal-field, and he said that that was only one side of the question.

After this he went out and spoke to Inspector Canton, and after stating his case before him, Inspector Canton asked him if they were going to protect my house and the residents.

He suggested to the Inspector that I and my family should immediately clear out of the district.

During the conversation he suggested that no extra police ought to have been asked for until some damage had actually been done. I asked him whether I as a British subject with investments in this country was not entitled to protection. He did not concur in this view. I immediately retorted that probably he was a gentleman who had not a halfpenny at stake, or else he would not have made such a remark.

I think it right to bring this before the coal owners in order to show the class of men who are put in charge to protect us.

Colonel Edwards told me that he was not going to allow his men to be kept in the district indefinitely, and that it was quite open to him to withdraw them at any moment. I pointed out to him that these men were now sworn constables for Glamorganshire, and that I had made a special requisition for their services and that they were employees of mine as long as I wished.

November 14, 1910.   PERCY JACOB.

No. 62.

Home Office to Monmouthshire and South Wales Coal Owners' Association.
(In reply to No. 61: See also Nos. 63 and 64).

Whitehall, November 18, 1910.

Sir,

I have laid before the Secretary of State your letter of the 14th instant, in which you enclose a statement which was placed before the Owners' side of the Conciliation Board by the Manager of the Cynon Colliery, Aberavon, and ask him to see you with regard to the matter described in the statement.

In reply I am to say that the Secretary of State is at the present moment much pressed by other engagements and he does not think it is necessary to see you in this matter as it is clear that the manager's statement is based on a complete misconception of the position of the police in reference to mine owners. The concluding sentence of the statement is, "I pointed out to him that these men were now sworn constables for Glamorganshire and that I had made a special requisition for their services *and that they were employees of mine as long as I wished.*" It seems to Mr. Churchill surprising that the owners should have placed before him any document containing such a proposition. The owners must be aware that the police occupy an absolutely impartial position and that they are no more the employees of the mine owners than they are the employees of the strikers. They are there solely for the purposes of maintaining order and to protect each party in the dispute from violence or illegality on the part of the other, and any pretension on the part of the coal owners to control their movements or to direct their action must be repelled as strongly as any similar pretension on the part of the strikers. It is entirely in the discretion of the Police and the Military Authorities to say where and when, and in what circumstances, the constables can be most usefully employed to maintain order and to protect life and property: and the Secretary of State will support the Officers in command in refusing to be influenced by managers or owners who may share this manager's misapprehension as to his position and powers.

On the remainder of the manager's statement the Secretary of State thinks it hardly necessary to comment. The account which it gives of his interview with Colonel Edwards, who was sent down by the Secretary of State to assist in carrying out the arrangements for the distribution and accommodation of the Metropolitan Police, is full of inaccuracies and mistakes, and gives a wholly wrong impression as to their conversation. It is, however, perfectly true that Colonel Edwards raised—and properly raised—the question on whether the authorities of that colliery had had adequate reason for applying for police protection. On Thursday the 10th instant an urgent application was made, in response to which a force of nearly one hundred constables was sent to the district, who, on arrival, found that the sole occasion for their presence was that the management of the Cynon Colliery proposed on paying their men to deduct from their wages certain sums which had been awarded to the Company by a Court of Law. Whether in the face of the Truck Acts and the decision of the House of Lords in the case of *Williams v. North's Navigation Collieries* the management had legal justification for this procedure, the Secretary of State cannot say without further information; but, even assuming that the course taken was within their legal powers, he cannot think that they chose a happy moment for exacting their rights to the full, especially as the men were ready to submit without protest to the greater part of the deduction; and, in his opinion, it was clearly their duty to have informed the police beforehand of the precise nature of the occasion on which their services were required. In the present disturbed condition of Glamorganshire, when the services of the police are urgently required to deal with difficulties arising in many different places, such an incident as this shows that it is imperatively necessary that, before responding to similar appeals, the Police and Military Officers should make rigorous inquiries as to whether the applications which they receive for assistance are really well-founded; and, if in any case these inquiries should lead to delay, it is the owners who countenance such action as that taken by the management of the Cynon Colliery who would be responsible for any untoward results that might ensue.

The Secretary of State begs that you will strongly impress on the owners whom you represent that the Police and Military Authorities have full discretion under present conditions to say where and when the forces at their disposal are most urgently required in the interests of peace and order, and that owners should carefully refrain from actions of a provocative character and should not apply for police protection except when a real and urgent necessity exists. It is only if the owners will in this way co-operate loyally with the police and military that they can hope to surmount the existing difficulties without further disturbance.

I am, &c.,

EDWARD TROUP.

Fred L. Davis, Esq.,
President of the Owners' Representatives
on the Conciliation Board of South Wales,
Cardiff.

No. 63.

Monmouthshire and South Wales Coal Owners' Association
to Home Office.

(Answered by No. 64: See also Nos. 61 and 62)

Cardiff, November 29, 1910.

Sir,

I am instructed by Mr. Fred L. Davis to acknowledge receipt of your letter to him of the 18th instant in reference to the statement made by the Manager of the Cynon Colliery, Aberavon, which was forwarded to the Home Secretary at the request of the Owners' Representatives on the Conciliation Board for the South Wales Coal Trade.

Mr. Davis does not see any advantage to be derived from going further into the details, nor from dealing with the several points raised by the Home Secretary, beyond saying that the Home Secretary's observations evade the main question, viz., the absolute necessity for the introduction of the military, the proof of which was furnished by the actual events which occurred at the colliery on the occasion referred to.

I am, &c.,

W. GASCOYNE DALZIEL,
Secretary.

Sir Edward Troup, K.C.B.,
Under Secretary of State, Home Office.

No. 64.

Home Office to Monmouthshire and South Wales Coal Owners' Association

(In reply to No. 63)

Whitehall, December 10, 1910.

Sir,

I am directed by the Secretary of State to say, with reference to your letter of the 29th ultimo, that he has again perused the statement made by the Manager of the Cynon Colliery, which was forwarded to him by Mr. Davis at the request of the Owners' Representatives on the Conciliation Board, but that he does not find that what you describe as "the main question, namely, the absolute necessity for the introduction of the military," is raised in any way in that statement. If it had been raised, he believes his previous reply sufficiently indicates what his answer to that question would have been.

He thinks Mr. Davis is well advised in not wishing to carry the correspondence further, but he would again urge that what is said in the last paragraph of his letter of 18th ultimo should have the earnest attention of the owners.

I am, &c.,

EDWARD TROUP.

The Secretary to the Monmouth and South Wales
    Coal Owners' Association, Cardiff.

CHAPTER EIGHT

THE CAMBRIAN DISPUTE—1911

I. THE PARLIAMENTARY DUEL RESUMED

THE General Election which had taken place from December 2 to 19, 1910, was productive of hardly any change in the Party composition of the House of Commons and to this extent seemed to justify in its result the strictures uttered by Hilaire Belloc and by various Labour Members on the Liberal and Tory leaders whose behaviour throughout the summer and autumn of 1910 had brought upon the country the vain and ineffectual turmoil of a General Election. The Tories who, as a result of the January–February Election of 1910 had won 273 seats, were now as a result of the December General Election of 1910 to hold 272 seats. The Liberals, who in the January–February Election of 1910 had held 275 seats, now returned with exactly the same number as the Conservatives. Labour began the year with 40 seats and ended it with 42. The Irish Nationalists began with 82 seats and ended it with 84. Both the Labour Party and the Irish Nationalist Party on practically every issue supported the Liberal Government against the Tories. The total result of all the turmoil was "no change." It had all been unnecessary from the point of view of the interests either of the nation as a whole or of any of the classes inside it.

The absence of public interest in these contrived electoral convulsions was shown by a very significant fact. The first was that although the electorate had increased from 7·6 million to 7·7 million in ten months, the number who cast their votes fell from 6·6 million to 5·2 million. The total number of elected M.P.s continued to be 670: while the antiquated procedures under which they met and debated in the Palace of Westminster continued to be the same as it had been for many generations. For example, day after day passed in antique procedures from Tuesday, January 31st, until February 6th when "His Majesty's most gracious speech" was read by Mr. Speaker to the House and a member wearing Court dress rose to move "That a humble address of thanks be presented to His Majesty." The debate on the address then lasted right on until February 15th. Any topic at all could be raised in relation to the administration. The ball was opened by Arthur James Balfour, the former Prime Minister, who after 1905 had been driven from constituency after constituency until he found an abiding place as representative of the City of London.

Out of all the branches of the administration Balfour fastened first upon the Home Office. The Secretary of State (Churchill) had "succeeded in attracting the gaze of the civilised world," partly by his behaviour in connection with the "deplorable disturbances in parts of South Wales": for, said Balfour, "had he not held back the military and not shown some doubt and hesitation at a critical moment, much destruction of property, many unhappy incidents, and many circumstances which all, whatever their opinions, must look upon as a great blot on the procedure of civilised society, might have been wholly avoided."

It was not, however, until late on the second day of the debate on the address that an Amendment[1] on the question of the police could be spoken to. The Rt. Hon. William Abraham (he had the previous month been made a Member of the Privy Council) rose in his place to ask for an inquiry into the charges made against the police "in that portion of South Wales known as Mid-Rhondda, or better known in London as Tonypandy." Mabon said:

I do not want to find fault unduly with the police. They probably pursued what they thought to be their duty, amid many difficulties, and perhaps under some provocation.

But we who have taken the trouble to make inquiries in our own behalf, and on behalf of the men we represent, are strongly convinced that the police did many things which they ought not to have done, and that they treated very severely some of the men even when they were only attempting that which as pickets they had a perfect right under the law to do.

I have been a representative of these men for thirty-five years. I have had the honour to represent them in this House for fully twenty-five years. You will understand then that their interests are dear to me. I have been recognised as the leader of these men. I have represented them in their conferences with the employers, doing what I could for them. During that time we have had strikes and lock-outs; but disturbances like this, never! And I cannot believe that the men I represent are the creators of this trouble. Hence the House will bear with me when I am pleading for this inquiry in order to know who the guilty parties are.

Although I do not do justice to this matter with my Welsh tongue, I appeal earnestly that justice may be done in the interests of the men whom I represent, in the interests of peace and righteousness, in the interests of the police, and in the interest of the Government itself . . .

Keir Hardie, to whose initiative in mid-November the whole question of a proposed inquiry into the conduct of the police was

[1] "And further, we humbly desire to express our regret that Your Majesty's advisers have not seen fit to recommend the appointment of a special committee or commission to inquire into the charges made against the police in connection with the recent trouble in a portion of the South Wales coalfield, and the question of liability for personal injuries sustained in connection therewith."

H*

due, now rose to "associate myself with the pathetic appeal made by my Rt. Hon. friend." He was able to put the matter in a rather more searching way.

Keir Hardie ended by saying: "If the same kind of thing goes on unchallenged, as has happened in South Wales, the working section of the public will lose confidence in the authority and will regard the police as acting in the interests of the masters and helping to keep the men in subjection." (*7.ii.1911.*)

Another Liberal, the fellow Member of Keir Hardie in the double-barrelled constituency of Merthyr Tydfil, Edgar Jones, joined once more in the request for an inquiry, the result of which he was sure would be to "re-establish these people in the eyes of the country, and put an end to the slanders which had been cast upon them by the exercise of the imagination of London pressmen who went down there in a hurry."

William Brace, the Member for South Glamorgan, rose to point out that both William Abraham and Keir Hardie had raised the question because they were instructed to do so by their constituents as well as by the vote of the South Wales Miners' Federation. He said:

I represent the colliers. I am kept by them. I am paid by them, and they are a body whom I am proud to represent. I do not for one moment think that they are guilty of the charges levelled against them, and, in common honesty, we are entitled to ask in their name for the fullest investigation.

Winston Churchill, who then represented Dundee, replied to the debate with a very long speech. He began mildly enough but very soon passed over to a counter offensive against Keir Hardie whom he clearly realised as his most dangerous opponent. He took the opportunity at the same time, in reply to the criticism by the Leader of the Opposition as given above, to give a summary account of what had happened in South Wales. It was at the same time, naturally, an attempt to vindicate his own conduct as Home Secretary against the suggestion by the Tory leader that there had been "a horrible outbreak of barbarism" or "a blot upon the procedure of civilised society." He then turned to the defence of the conduct of the Metropolitan Police and of them only ("I am not responsible for what was done by the Bristol Police or the Cardiff Police or the Glamorganshire Police.") Here he took a leaf out of Keir Hardie's book. Keir Hardie had read some very damaging statements to supplement the series of statements made on the adjournment debates of November 15th and November 24th. These sworn statements from witnesses, buttressed by the presence of a Liberal Member of Parliament, had put Churchill in rather a difficulty in the November debates. Consequently he now produced some counter-statements "made by credible, substantial and reputable persons." He then laid stress on the casualties suffered by the Metropolitan Police and concluded that no case had been made out for an inquiry into police conduct in general. Having thus exonerated the Metropolitan Police, who were directly under his command, Churchill went on to exonerate the mining population of South Wales in the following peroration:

In my opinion the riots were largely caused by rowdy youths and roughs from outside, foreign to the district, and I think it only just to place that on record in fairness to the miners of South Wales, who have been attacked in a general way by people who know nothing at all about the matter.

Local authorities and private employers are very ready sometimes, and from insufficient cause, to call for troops. Troops cost them nothing, police cost money to the local authorities.

Law and order must be preserved, but I am confident that the House will agree with me that it is a great object of public policy to avoid a collision between soldiers and crowds of persons engaged in industrial disputes. All such collisions attended, as they must be, by loss of life and by the use of firearms, do great harm to the Army, which is a volunteer Army, and whose relation with the civil forces of the country must be carefully safeguarded, and they also cause feuds and resentments which last for a generation.

For soldiers to fire on the people would be a catastrophe in our national life. Alone among the nations, or almost alone, we have avoided for a great many years that melancholy and unnatural experience. And it is well worth while, I venture to think, for the Minister who is responsible to run some risk of broken heads or broken windows, to incur expense and an amount of inconvenience in the police arrangements, and to accept direct responsibility in order that the shedding of British blood by British soldiers may be averted, as, thank God, it has been successfully averted in South Wales.

So ended Churchill's third speech for the defence in the matter of the police and against the demand for an inquiry. But, as will be seen, his rhetoric did not convince either Keir Hardie or those for whom Hardie spoke including the miners in every coalfield and a large proportion of the working people of the whole country.

2. A THREE CORNERED DEBATE

Keir Hardie's pertinacity, and Winston Churchill's unyielding attitude, were shown a month later in a debate on Supplementary Estimates. Keir Hardie once more called attention to "the action of the Home Office in refusing to grant an inquiry into the allegation made against the police in connection with the recent strike in South Wales." After preliminary points Hardie said:

In raising this question for the fourth time I would remind the Committee and the Home Office that I am not acting on my own initiative. This question came to me first of all on behalf of the men, women, and children who claim to have been assaulted. Since then the matter has been taken up by the Executive of the South Wales Miners' Federation. My hon. Friends the Members for Rhondda, South Glamorgan and West Monmouth, are absent to-night in connection with miners' business, but I am speaking for them as well as myself when I again press for an inquiry into this matter. (*6.iii.1911.*)

Hardie went on to point out that if an inquiry took place it must not be a sham inquiry but must be undertaken on the spot and persons complaining must have the right to be represented by Counsel. Churchill in reply counter-attacked instead of answering in the placable manner expected from cabinet ministers on such occasions. Churchill overdid it—as he was prone to do both then and later. The result was unexpected by the Labour Members. Tory Members of Parliament seized the opportunity to attack the Home Secretary from an entirely different point of view and the Deputy Chairman of Committees, J. H. Whitley, found himself presiding at a debate that went on for nearly three hours and in which, presumably through lack of experience, he allowed extraneous matters to be brought in.

Alfred Lyttelton who had in October, 1903, succeeded the famous Joseph Chamberlain as Colonial Secretary in the Tory Government of 1900 to 1905, came of a famous cricketing family (Gentleman not Player). Lyttelton sharply enough raised the question "whether the Home Secretary was justified in sending the Metropolitan Police there at all in place of the soldiers" and asked under what powers he had taken a step "displacing the authority of the Secretary for War and the local authorities," who, in case of disturbances, "in the opinion of every candid man would be the best judge of what degree of force is necessary." Lyttelton ended: "I ask again by what authority the Home Secretary sent Metropolitan police at all?"

Churchill, no doubt somewhat to his chagrin, had to reply in a speech almost as long as that in which he had thought to have dealt summarily with Keir Hardie. He was stung into admitting that it was the Secretary of State for War "who first actually arrested the movement of troops." He told how Haldane "came over to me, and we discussed the matter together, and decided definitely—as a matter of public policy—to send Metropolitan Police instead."

The Member for Cambridge University, J. F. P. Rawlinson, now took a hand in baiting Churchill who had once more to make an explanation. But now Churchill's cavalier treatment of the question raised by Keir Hardie rebounded on his own head. W. F. Roche, a Liberal Member for Pembroke, confessed that he was "rather disappointed" that the Home Secretary had not seen his way to grant an inquiry into the conduct of the police in this matter. In the course of his reply to the two Tory speakers Churchill, as the new "Rupert of debate," made a sally against the Conservative leader. This now brought down on him a lengthy counter-attack from A. J. Balfour who ended by saying:

The Chief Constable wanted soldiers. He could have got soldiers long before the looting began on the Tuesday night. He got neither soldiers nor police . . . It was the deliberate action of the Minister for War and the Home Secretary, who decided that they had much better keep the soldiers at Swindon for four or five hours doing nothing, so that when the cavalry did arrive on the scene rioting had begun and they were too late.

Consequently the Secretary of State for War, R. B. Haldane, was now involved in an attempt to clear the matter up by giving a detailed account of what had happened on November 7 and 8, 1910. After Page Croft, the Member for Christchurch, had referred to the Home Secretary's telegram to the strikers as "one of the most ill-advised concoctions which ever went from a Government office," Thomas Richardson, Labour Member for Whitehaven, described Churchill's reply to Keir Hardie as "not only unsympathetic, but provocative." He then went on to say:

The Executive Committee of the South Wales Miners' Association— who surely represent the official view of the workmen—have through the person of the junior Member for Merthyr, asked the House to enter upon an inquiry, not only to free the miners as an industrial class from the stigma which has been laid upon them, but to do a bare act of justice to defenceless women and innocent children. (6.iii.1911.)

Lord Hugh Cecil, the Conservative Member for Oxford University, was so opposed to Keir Hardie's request for an inquiry that he rose to warn his fellow Conservatives about how they should vote if it came to a division. At this point Keir Hardie received rather remarkable support from a Member of Parliament who had formally seconded him at the beginning of the debate. This was Walter Stowe Bright McLaren, a coal and iron master who might have been expected to be utterly opposed to Keir Hardie on this and other questions, especially in view of his family connections and interests. McLaren said:

I intervene in this debate because for many years I have been a member of the South Wales Conciliation Board, and I am also connected with one of the largest collieries in South Wales. I am convinced that it is a necessary step at the present time to adopt a conciliatory attitude, and to endeavour to smooth over the painful feelings which have been left owing to these riots. I am certain that if the Home Secretary had adopted a more conciliatory attitude, and had consented to the inquiry asked for, it would have brought peace in South Wales.

Without going further into the details, I only again, as one who wishes conciliation, and whose duty in South Wales has been to promote conciliation between employers and men, appeal to the Committee to vote in favour of this inquiry, but not with a view to censuring the police, but in the interests of peace, harmony, and good feeling in South Wales, where it is desired this inquiry should take place.

Keir Hardie winding up his side of the debate made answer to some of the points raised. But the debate was continued by some of the hereditary legislators who largely made up the elected House of Commons. The first of these was Lord Ninian Crichton-Stuart, Conservative Member for Cardiff, a city largely owned by his father the Marquis of Bute. Lord Ninian raised a question about the refusal of the Glamorganshire authority to pay the expenses of the Metropolitan Police.[1] Churchill admitted this was true but said:

It is quite true that the Standing Joint Committee of the County Council of Glamorganshire have refused, but it is also true that the Chief Constable, upon whose requisition the police were sent, signed an undertaking on their behalf that the sum in question should be paid. I understand that the Glamorganshire Standing Joint Committee now repudiate the signature of their officers, although they were very glad to avail themselves of the services of the police. (*6.iii.1911.*)

Finally, George Lansbury, Labour Member for Tower Hamlets (Bow and Bromley Division), defended Keir Hardie saying:

I want to protest, before I sit down, against the bloodthirsty sort of doctrine enunciated on the other side. It seems to me their only regret is that soldiers did not go down, and that the Home Secretary did not tell them, as was told to other men on a memorable occasion, "Don't hesitate to shoot." I at least am very glad that policemen were there instead of soldiers.

On a division being called there voted for Keir Hardie, who had McLaren as his co-teller, 23 Members in the Aye Lobby. The Noes numbered over ten times as many in the Liberal Lobby.

3. APPEAL TO THE MINERS' FEDERATION OF GREAT BRITAIN

Meantime, while the November events in the mid-Rhondda had thus become the subject of repeated parliamentary duelling and had therefore come to be discussed throughout the country in those days when debates in the House of Commons were much more fully reported in the newspapers than in later decades, there were further

[1] See Appendix I to this chapter for details of the police brought into the coalfield.

developments in the course of this Cambrian Combine dispute. The Executive Committee of the Miners' Federation, meeting early in January at the Midland Hotel in Derby, had before it a request from South Wales to call a conference "with a view to rendering financial assistance": and thereupon decided to call a conference three weeks later when they would also consider "payments in abnormal places, and the low rate paid to daywagemen."

When the three days conference began on Tuesday, January 24, 1911, the delegates from Monmouth and South Wales were almost a quarter of the 142 delegates present: and indeed would have been more than a quarter but for a disaster the previous day on the Taff Vale Railway at Hopkinstown in which three members of the South Wales Executive Council lost their lives. The three Rhondda members were: W. H. Morgan of Treherbert, Tom Harris of Pontygwaith, and Tom George of Ferndale. William Abraham, who earlier that month had been made a Privy Councillor, spoke as follows:

Although they are but three men, yet from our Executive and cause in South Wales we are losing not only three dear friends, three men of sterling merit, three men of the best, three whose counsels were always acceptable, three of the moderate, temperate, wise members of the Federation. In fact, three of the pillars of the Welsh Federation were taken away at a moment's notice. One cannot speak. Silence is the best way of expressing ourselves this morning.

In their place on the Executive Council there were elected a little later in the year three members of the Cambrian Combine Committee, namely, Tom Smith, John Hopla and Noah Rees. In place of Tom Evans, who had resigned earlier, Noah Ablett, checkweigher in Mardy, was elected.

The conference opened with W. E. Harvey, M.P., of the Derbyshire Miners' Association in the Chair. The Vice-President of the S.W.M.F., William Brace, M.P., put the case for assistance to the men on strike with all his customary lucidity of utterance. Questions were asked. To John Wilson, M.P., of the Durham Miners' Association, who had raised the question of payments made to men out on strike against the rules of the Union, Tom Richards gave an explanation both of the Cambrian Combine dispute and of what had happened in Aberdare where the Council had been "refusing to support these men from the funds from the time they were out contrary to rule." But in one case the pit had stopped altogether. Therefore, he said, "When they were prepared to go back to work they could not have it, and they could not get work anywhere else. We should have been wanting in human sympathy if we did not say, 'We will relieve you until you can get work.' " Later, when a question had been asked about "the settlement" alleged to exist by the employers, Tom Richards again spoke:

We are peculiarly situated in South Wales; we have a good deal of Home Rule there. Every agent is a Czar in his own district more or less, and no one else dares interfere with him. It happens to be in Mabon's district where this great difficulty has taken place.

They secured the best possible terms they could at the moment, and Mabon and his colleague (*Mr. Watts Morgan*), who were agents for the district—it had not come before our Council in those negotiations at that moment—took these terms to the workmen. . . . They put it to the workmen, in face of the looming stoppage and the time of year, mid winter, and proposed that those men ought to give those terms a trial rather than stop. There is no doubt about that.

The workmen unanimously decided not to accept these terms, and the representatives of this district who were parties to these negotiations took part with our Council in considering the whole matter and decided to finance the workmen against accepting those terms. That is the truth, the whole truth and nothing but the truth. (*24.i.1911.*)

Before the debate ended there came the following speech from Tom Smith, one of the Cambrian Combine Committee and soon to be elected on to the South Wales Executive Council. He said:

I represent the area affected. I am one of those who have come out of the fire myself and can speak on this matter with knowledge.

Perhaps some of you think that the men were unreasonable in refusing the terms offered. Let me say in defence of our leaders that they never did say that those terms were right or were in any way satisfactory. Our leaders have studied it, and have denounced it from beginning to end.

It was only in the face of the rigours of winter, and they did not know exactly what was the spirit of unity among the men. They did not want to go into a battle if they thought for one moment that our forces were divided, but when they saw the spirit of determination and unity among the men our Executive took no objection to our going against those terms. (*24.i.1911.*)

The speaker from Aberdare, C. B. Stanton, took occasion to say that

the man who is at the head of this, the great engineer Mr. D. A. Thomas of the Cambrian Combine, is a man whom the workmen themselves dragged along in his carriage at election time. That man is out today to smash the Federation since he left his business here at Westminster, waiting for a peerage which will come without a doubt.[1]

He is out to smash this Federation, and he is doing it. He has got these men out, and our funds are flowing out at the rate of £6,000 or £7,000 a week.

There was no real doubt as to the outcome of the debate and at the end of the first day the Executive Committee sat down to work

[1] The peerage did come: but seven years later, when Thomas took the style of Lord Rhondda.

out recommendations for decision on the morrow. The first of these was:

That the Miners' Federation of Great Britain contribute to the South Wales Federation the sum of £3,000 per week to be called by a levy of 3d. per member per call.

This was to be sent on to the General Secretary of the Miners' Federation, "for the purpose of assisting the South Wales Federation to pay its members who are out in accordance with rule."

It was also agreed that a statement be got out in circular form and issued to the districts giving particulars of the dispute: while with regard to the examination of books, etc., in South Wales the matter was left to Thomas Ashton to call in what assistance he might require. Then it was resolved: "That Mr. Ashton and Mr. Harvey assist the South Wales Miners' Federation to bring about a satisfactory settlement of the dispute, if possible." Then, after a little discussion, a resolution "with one dissentient" was carried "urging upon members of the South Wales Miners' Federation the advisability of increasing their monthly contribution so as to provide a stronger defence for them against any similar attack that may be made upon them in the future, and to secure uniformity in the payment of members of this Federation." (*25.i.1911.*)

After the vote was taken at the beginning of the second day Vernon Hartshorn of the Welsh delegation expressed "a very high appreciation of the splendid and generous disposition that has been displayed." Thereupon Noah Ablett "very pleased and delighted" said he had "very great pleasure in seconding the resolution, from the point of view of solidarity, the idea that we are one as miners in fighting our battles." Whereupon the Chairman said dryly: "We cannot very well thank ourselves. We will take it that South Wales is very grateful. What has been said is on the notes."

4. ABNORMAL WORKING PLACES

The Cambrian Combine lockout and strike came to be inextricably mingled in the outlook of the strikers with the question of abnormal places and minimum wage. To this question the second and third days of the January 1911, Special Conference of the M.F.G.B. were devoted. The 142 delegates, including 14 Members of Parliament, decided as follows:

That in order to carry out the resolutions passed at the Annual Conference held at Edinburgh in October last,[1] be it an instruction of this

[1] "That the miners of Scotland, England and Wales be requested to meet their respective employers and demand a fair living wage to be paid to all miners working in abnormal places, failing to get which, that a national conference be called with a view of further dealing with the matter." (Edinburgh, Thursday, October 6, 1910.)

conference to all districts in the Federation, to immediately press for the average or minimum wage in each district to apply to all workmen engaged in abnormal places; and should any district fail at the end of three months from this date to obtain this the members of this Federation be recommended to consider the advisability of taking national action to endeavour to enforce it. That a conference be called by the President and Secretary at the expiration of its term and receive reports and decide what action shall be taken. (*26.i.1911.*)

On the question of "the rate of wages at present paid to daywage-men, including surfacemen," the delegates decided that this in-formation should be got from each district and then submitted to a later conference. On these two questions, especially on abnormal places, the delegates from South Wales had an interest that was as acute as that of any other district, if not more so. This was shown in the speech of Brace who said that the trouble with their em-ployers was that, while saying

"We are prepared to pay for fair services," in actuality they reserve to themselves the right every time of making their officials the final and sole tribunal to say whether a place is unfair and whether a place has been working fairly. That, gentlemen, is a condition of affairs which we in Wales cannot allow to go on longer than we are actually bound to.

Brace then said that they would have moved on the matter in Wales had it not been for the annual conference decision. He went on to say:

I have resented with a strong resentment this continuous statement of the employers that immediately a man gets into an abnormal place where he cannot make a living, his whole character changes, and that from an honourable man he becomes a dishonourable man; from a man who can be trusted to work hard and fairly by the ton, he cannot be trusted to work by the day.

Jack McGurk of Lancashire associated himself "with the remarks of Mr. Brace," and after citing examples from Lancashire went on to say:

Now what have we noticed lately? Not long ago we had the gutter, yellow press vilifying our men for coming out on strike and starving women and children. Whenever they come out on strike they are an evil class—they are out to do no good, they are out for wrong.
But at the back end of last year, what did we find? The same cynical scribes describing our men as heroes of the mine after a disaster such as we have had in Lancashire at the Hulton Colliery. Seeing that public opinion is such that a number of our men have to be slaughtered before we can get public opinion ripe and with us, then it is a very difficult matter indeed to convince the public that we have a just cause.
Now after what has happened during the last two years, I am fully con-vinced that if this Federation will say that at least we are going to have a day's wage for every man who goes down the mine, or make it such as

the Government will have to take hold of the mines of this country, then I feel sure it will be the best thing this Federation has done.

John Cairns for Northumberland told of how there a joint committee set up in 1872 handled these difficult questions and was able to overcome the difficulties. To this George Barker said in reply that "We in Wales" had made an application for a committee such as Cairns had told about but had met with an absolute negative from the owners. He went on:

They refused to appoint a Committee; they refused to recognise our claims for wages in abnormal places in any sense whatever.

The owners have refused absolutely to deal with us with reference to this matter. Only on the 20th of this month we had another interview with the owners, and the furthest we could get with them was this: That there were all degrees of abnormality in a place.

Then after giving examples of what the owners had said Barker went on to say:

Now, this is the position in Wales. We have got probably thousands of men who are working in abnormal places. During the last six months we have had figures presented to our Executive, and there are men in some of the districts that have not had a shilling a day after they had paid for their help.

When they go to the employer he tells them that the firm is not a charity organisation society, and if they do not like the wages offered they can go elsewhere. Now that is the position. We find we are unable ourselves to grapple with this position and we come now and we ask you to give us the power of this great organisation. Our men are expecting this. We can give you the detailed information upon this. The owners are killing our organisation piecemeal in Wales.

Only think what we have gone through since we were up here last March! We have had Wales on the verge of insurrection; we have had misery unspeakable down there, and we have got it today; and we have got a callous body of men who are deaf to all our appeals. There is nothing can be done with those men but force. We shall have put force against force. The only force that we can exercise is through the means of this great national organisation.

He ended by saying that it was necessary to organise a strike nationally "at some particular date specified so that we can have a general battle right along the line."

One after another on the second day of the conference delegates from the various coalfields gave their experiences. But when Edmund Harvey, M.P., of Derbyshire read out a draft resolution by which the Conference would "call upon all districts to carry out" the Edinburgh resolution, there was considerable impatience manifested. To Alfred Onions it seemed "merely a repetition"; and in his mild manner he upbraided the other districts for not being in a position to carry the matter a step farther.

Noah Ablett then spoke as follows:

In South Wales at least I can say that for the last ten years the price of coal has gone up something like six shillings per ton. There has been a decrease with regard to the cost of trans-shipment, and the cost of working in many respects. From the financial and monetary side, anything that can be got from the owners should be got now.

We must take into account economic conditions and human nature, it is said. The economic conditions are of such a character that throughout the coalfield there is an unrest which has never been manifest before in our history. The people are ripe now for any definite move that may be made.

There has been a constant rise in the price of living and in the price of commodities. The mining industry is quite unique. It is unique in the first place in the fact that it is virtually a monopoly. Taking the profits which the coalowners get from the men's labour there is the probability of us having a part of that and still allowing the capital the same interest which it would obtain in any other industry.

The solution to this problem does not lie in deciding the question of the daywagemen and the men in abnormal working places. I think the time has now come to propagate the idea that we must rise to the fullness of the situation that our powers will give to us. I am thoroughly convinced that it is in the powers of the Miners' Federation to secure a minimum wage tomorrow if they wanted it, and the only "famine" that exists is that we do not want it. We can get it for the reason that I believe we are the largest organisation in this country.

If I believed Mr. Wadsworth's statement I should be very pessimistic indeed. I refer to the statement that he made that we shall never get what we want through the "down tools" policy. There is nothing else. There is no other way by which it is possible to beat the employers who are arrogant and insolent in regard to our demands for the minimum wage. I deprecate the phrase "daywagemen" and so on in connection with an association like our own. I firmly believe we should organise all these men into our Federation; if we take craftsmen and the men on the top of the pit wherever they are, into our Federation, we should use our power to get the wages for the very lowest of the men that are there to be equal to ours. We ought not as the premier body in the world at this time of day to allow ourselves to consider that we should get a different pay for these men than for ourselves . . .

Noah ended by saying:

I think what we ought to declare for is a minimum wage on a basis of 8s. for every man who is organised in the Federation. (*25.i.1911.*)

This speech of Noah Ablett has been cited at some length as typical of the newer standpoint that was developing in South Wales amongst the miners on strike. But in one respect, in the demand for equal pay for all grades, it is to be doubted if this represented the views of more than a very small minority.

5. ASHTON AND HARVEY PUT THEIR OAR IN

The same day (Wednesday, January 25, 1911) that the National Conference agreed on support to South Wales, W. E. Harvey, M.P., and Thomas Ashton with Richards and Onions and three of the Combine Workmen's Committee, attended at the Board of Trade. There G. R. Askwith, K.C., read them a letter he had written on January 10th to D. A. Thomas on the "assurances" that might be given to the men and Thomas's reply thereto.

In this reply there was given "a definite assurance that we have no desire or intention to reduce the general level of wages at the Naval Collieries." This was communicated to Tom Richards on January 20th in view of the approaching M.F.G.B. conference on Tuesday, January 24th: and after the meeting at the Board of Trade on the next day Askwith, on January 27th, wrote to Tom Richards suggesting that in view of these "definite assurances" a ballot might now be taken of the men locked-out or on strike.

A week later at the invitation of the South Wales officials, Ashton and Harvey attended the Executive Council meeting in Cardiff, where there was a prolonged discussion about these letters and the interpretation thereof. It was thought that much hinged on this, as was explained to the deputation of ten representatives of the Cambrian Combine workmen "then invited into the room." So the decision was that the deputation dealing with these negotiations, and Messrs. W. E. Harvey, M.P., and Thomas Ashton, should interview the Naval Collieries Directors "for the purpose of ascertaining the definite meaning and value of the offer contained in the correspondence between Mr. G. R. Askwith, K.C., and Mr. D. A. Thomas." (*3.ii.1911.*)

That night Tom Richards wrote to G. R. Askwith asking him to arrange such an interview. The suggested meeting was called by the Board of Trade in the Engineers' Institute in Cardiff. On Saturday, February 11, 1911, G. R. Askwith (accompanied by Isaac Mitchell) took the Chair, read the correspondence which had led up to the meeting and asked W. Brace, M.P., to continue the discussion. After a lengthy meeting lasting three hours certain explanations were put into writing and counter-signed by the chairman as the outcome of the meeting. They were as follows:

Upon questions being asked with reference to assurances proposed by Mr. D. A. Thomas, it was stated by Mr. Llewellyn that, as regards the new seam in the Ely Pit, alike in cases where a man is in an abnormal place, or is wanting allowances, those allowances will be settled between the manager and the particular man, but Mr. Llewellyn said that:

"If the men who work the seam are not satisfied with the wages which they earn, whether the place is normal or abnormal, I will take the matter in hand myself and let the Miners' Agent come down and settle the matter with me in the place itself. Where we find that the man has done a fair day's work, I will pay him a fair day's wage."

Any such agreement shall be made in writing.

He added he had no objection to seeing that the same procedure would apply in other pits in the Naval collieries by the managers of those pits meeting miners' agents. He agreed that any bargain arrived at between any managers and the men would be accepted as final.

G. R. Askwith, February 11, 1911.

Later, in reply to Brace, Leonard Llewellyn stated that the same procedure would be followed in the Cambrian, Glamorgan, and Britannic collieries.

So much is taken from the official press notice by G. R. Askwith: it was enough for the owners, meeting four days later, to pass a resolution objecting to Llewellyn's offer. But the transcript of the notes of the proceedings shows that the associated owners had no cause for their anxiety as is made clear by the following exchange:

Mr. Brace: Supposing the average wage in the past has been 7s. 6d. per day and when the new price list is tried, and the man earns below 7s. 6d. would the Company make the man up to 7s. 6d.?

Mr. Llewellyn: That is not the intention at all.

Mr. Brace: Am I right in assuming that the assurances mean that if there is a fall in a man's wages below the past average of say 7s. 6d. that the man is to be made up to that amount?

Mr. Llewellyn: There is no doubt that it does not mean that. The Company cannot agree to a minimum wage, and the Company cannot give the men what they are now asking for. When a man has an abnormal place and cannot earn his wages on the list the Company will assist him by giving allowances, but the Company cannot agree to any standard wage as it is out of their hands. It is not the intention of the Company to reduce the general earnings of the man. . . . Every case will be dealt with on its own merits.

The next week when the news of the effort at conciliation by Messrs. Askwith and Mitchell had sped through the valleys it was clear that it found favour with neither side. The associated owners at Cardiff on Wednesday, February 19th, passed a resolution, as we have seen, censuring the directors of the Naval Collieries for having made the apparent concession as counter-signed by G. R. Askwith.

On Thursday, February 16th, there was held a meeting of the Executive Council of the South Wales Miners' Federation at which once more W. E. Harvey, M.P., and Thomas Ashton, J.P., were present on behalf of the Miners' Federation of Great Britain. The dozen representatives of the workmen who had been present at the negotiations in Cardiff were also invited in. The representatives of the workmen made it unmistakably clear that they did not accept these terms and could not possibly recommend to the workmen that they should be accepted. Then they withdrew. Messrs. Harvey and Ashton, however, were of a contrary opinion, particularly as regards the ballot vote suggested by G. R. Askwith. The minute of the meeting runs as follows:

Mr. W. E. Harvey, M.P., stated that Mr. Ashton and himself considered that the proposed terms of settlement should be submitted to a ballot of the workmen for acceptance or rejection giving detailed reasons why they had arrived at that conclusion.

In their report subsequently to the Executive Committee of the Miners' Federation of Great Britain, the two emissaries gave the further reason that "the terms were the outcome of much correspondence and many meetings arranged by the Board of Trade."

The South Wales Council, however, did not accept the advice of Messrs. Harvey and Ashton and after further long discussion unanimously adopted a resolution regretting that "the absence of mutual trust and confidence between the managers and workmen at these collieries, render it impossible for them to accept terms that leave the wages of the workmen so absolutely dependent upon the decision of the managers of the mines." Then, after recalling that the origin of the dispute lay with the owners who had locked out "800 of their workmen" in the Ely Pit, the Executive Council went on to propose four methods of settlement, any one of which, if accepted by the owners, would "bring this dispute to an end." These terms, communicated to the owners through the Board of Trade, were emphatically (and argumentatively) rejected on February 24th by the Naval Colliery proprietors. With this outright rejection of the Executive Council's new proposals there was a complete breakdown in negotiations. The lockout and strike were to go on, with no end in sight; the lockout now in its sixth month, the strike in its fourth month. That same day, February 24th, the Executive Council decided to double the monthly shilling levy. It was resolved:

That another shilling levy per member per month be called to meet the present strike pay liabilities, and that a circular be sent to the lodges explaining the necessity for this. (*24.ii.1911.*)

This may be regarded as the end of the February intervention of the Board of Trade and of the Miners' Federation of Great Britain.

6. THE MARCH INTERVENTION AND BALLOT

In the last paragraph of his letter of January 27th, G. R. Askwith had suggested a vote of the men. The coal owners for years had been opposed to such "votes of the men" on the ground that the negotiators should have full power to settle. Now at any rate as far as the Board of Trade were concerned there was a swing of opinion. It may be that it was felt or believed that the Cambrian Strike Committee did not fully represent the men. A month later coal-owner Callaghan seems to have shared the Board of Trade standpoint when he told Askwith of his vain hope that the leaders of the men would have acted "on the suggestion made by you that the opinions of the men concerned should be ascertained by ballot." The views of Ashton and Harvey, as we have seen, also chimed in with this suggestion, which Tom Richards had ignored from the beginning of the correspondence.

Messrs. Ashton and Harvey, however disappointed they might be at the rejection of their advice to hold a ballot, were convinced that it should be held. They reported in this sense on March 2nd to the M.F.G.B. Executive Committee, by whom they were instructed to continue their efforts and to meet once again the South Wales Council.

The renewed attempt at a settlement lasted altogether less than three weeks. Before it began there was another kind of intervention, in the shape of a deputation, representative of local inhabitants and interests, to both masters and men. Trade, local government, religion and the magistracy were all concerned to urge the S.W.M.F. Executive Council to re-open negotiations so that the Cambrian Combine dispute might be brought to an end.

Rhys Williams of Miskin Manor (Deputy Chairman of the Glamorgan Quarter Session), addressed the Council on behalf of the Mid-Rhondda Chamber of Trade. The strike had now lasted for nearly six months and "it had come to their knowledge that a good deal of poverty and misery existed in the district." The lull in the negotiations made them think it a favourable time to approach the Council in the interest of the workmen, the tradesmen and all concerned. A large number of tradesmen who had done their best by giving credit, as long as it was possible to do so, "were now on the verge of ruin." This was their justification for approaching the Council: and they proposed waiting upon the coal owners as well.

On behalf of Rhondda Urban District, W. P. Nicholas, Solicitor, said that although the District Council were naturally sufferers in their rateable value by having such a large industry at a standstill, that was not the reason why they joined this deputation: but that they were aware of great suffering and poverty in the district, and that a large number of workmen and their wives and children were "entirely dependent upon charity, not being in receipt of strike pay from the Federation." He was sure that the Council would leave nothing undone to bring about a reopening of negotiations.

The Reverend Ambrose Williams from the Rhondda Distress Committee asked for a little financial assistance to enable them to carry on the work of dispensing food, and in some instances, clothing and boots. They had accomplished this for a long time, "thanks to the kindness of gentlemen in the Rhondda and various other places," but there appeared to be a falling off in their income, while their liabilities were increasing day by day. He begged "in the name of humanity and Christianity" that the Council should, if possible, make them a grant, in order to enable them to continue "to dispense at least bread."

The minute of the Executive Council records that first of all Abraham and after him Brace thanked the deputation who were given a promise that the Council would carefully consider the matter of assistance. (*6.iii.1911.*)

The next day W. E. Harvey, M.P., and T. Ashton attended the Council meeting in the Royal Chambers, Cardiff. Ashton read the report given by himself and his colleague on March 2nd to the M.F.G.B. Executive Committee, where they had recommended that the South Wales Council be asked to re-open the matter of taking a ballot of the workmen. That report had been accepted by the M.F.G.B. Executive Committee: hence their presence that day in Cardiff. Then Ashton stated that he considered "it was only fair that the workmen who had been out on strike for a long time should have a voice in deciding whether they should continue after the negotiations had completed certain terms."

W. E. Harvey, M.P., confirmed Ashton's statement and then went further. He was in favour of the terms; and said: "When the manager agreed to deal with the Bute Seam as a whole, with the other assurances, members of the committee thought that these terms were better than obtained in almost any colliery in the Federation." This all led to a long discussion which ended with the following resolution being adopted, with two voting against:

That we request Mr. G. R. Askwith, K.C., to convene a further meeting of the parties to the negotiations upon the matters in dispute. (*7.iii.1911.*)

The next day again Tom Richards began a further correspondence in which he suggested that the Board of Trade should become the arbiter in the person of G. R. Askwith, K.C., after which a ballot would be taken. This proposal, sent on to the coal owners, brought an immediate reaction. The coal owners on March 14th unanimously (and telegraphically) rejected arbitration. The correspondence ended with Askwith's letter of March 20th conveying that with the decision of the Coal Owners' Association there was no point in the Union trying further along that line.

This correspondence, when read out to the Council meeting, was followed by a long discussion. Finally it was proposed:

That a ballot of the workmen of the Cambrian Combine collieries be taken upon the question of resuming work upon the terms contained in the price list arranged on October 22nd last, together with the assurances of Mr. D. A. Thomas, Mr. T. J. Callaghan, and Mr. Leonard Llewellyn, of the 13th January, 1911, and the 11th February, 1911, given to Mr. G. R. Askwith, K.C. representing the Board of Trade. The price list to be given a fair trial for twelve months, the list to continue in force thereafter, subject to one month's notice on either side. (*21.iii.1911.*)

Now the division in the Council revealed itself. An amendment was moved that a ballot of the workmen should not be taken but that the Council should decide whether these terms could be accepted or not. Five voted for the amendment and eleven against. Thereafter twelve voted for the proposal and four against. Whereupon it was decided "That the foregoing decision be conveyed to the Cambrian Combine Committee, Messrs. T. Richards, M.P., W. E. Harvey, M.P., T. Ashton and Alfred Onions be asked to attend." (*21.iii.1911.*)

The Cambrian Combine collieries ballot was held on Saturday, March 25, 1911. The ballot paper set out the proposed terms of settlement together with the assurances including the letters from D. A. Thomas of January 13th and the February 11th assurances by Mr. Leonard Llewellyn. The ballot paper also contained the statement:

Mr. Askwith, K.C., Messrs. Harvey and Ashton, and the members of the Council, consider that the workmen directly affected by this prolonged strike should be given the opportunity of deciding by a ballot vote whether these terms for the resumption of work should be accepted.

Then the ballot paper was simply "I am in favour . . ." or "I am against . . ." The vote was overwhelming. Those against were 7,041. Those for were 309. The majority was 6,732. It was a majority of over twenty-two to one. It revealed the determination of the men to reject the terms as their chosen representatives in the Cambrian Combine Committee had rejected them.

We have now to see what happened on the day after the S.W.M.F. Executive Council (on March 21st) had passed the resolution for a ballot vote and when the appointed persons had gone to Mid-Rhondda to "convey the decision" to the Strike Committee.

First let us have the account given by Thomas Ashton himself in a pamphlet he published ten weeks later. In this he tells how the Council meeting of the South Wales Federation on March 21st decided by a large majority that a ballot vote of the men on strike should be taken "on the terms approved of by the Executive Committee of the Federation of Great Britain" and then he goes on to say:

"When we arrived at Tonypandy the streets were full of men and youths who to our surprise shouted out: "No ballot." "Go back to England." "Keep your £3,000." "Give us the twentieth rule." We got through to the meeting room and met the committee, a number of whom showed a spirit of hostility both to myself and Mr. Harvey. After we had left, Mr. Richards still remaining, the meeting agreed that the ballot should take place. Mr. Harvey and myself were escorted to the railway station through a by-path by two of the men who left the meeting and who had some influence on the waiting crowd of men and youths outside the schoolroom gate. Before we arrived at the station we were again in the main street amidst the shouting crowd. The two men were still with us, and policemen following behind, who came on to the station. A ballot of the men was taken on the Saturday following, but what a fiasco. We reported to the Executive Committee of Great Britain and the matter was left over until the special conference which was held at Caxton Hall, London, on the 26th April.

In an interview given at that time and appearing in the press W. E. Harvey, M.P., gave an even more lurid account of the events of March 22nd in Tonypandy.

Three weeks later at the first meeting of the Council after the events of the 22nd that preceded the ballot vote, the minute records the following resolution:

That the Council expresses its sincere regret that the representatives from the Miners' Federation of Great Britain were subjected to discourteous treatment when visiting the Rhondda Valley in connection with the Cambrian Combine dispute, and strongly disapproves of such conduct on the part of those indulging in it. (*10.iv.1911.*)

That night there were disturbances in Clydach Vale and Blaenclydach and casualties such as "injury to ankle" and "cut on side of nose" were recorded in the case of five constables. The next day (Thursday, 23rd) the disturbances continued. At Blaenclydach on March 23rd there were recorded 17 casualties to constables, mainly of the Monmouthshire Police Force.

At the Annual Conference held Monday to Wednesday, March 27th to 29th, in the Cory Memorial Hall following the presidential address (from William Brace, M.P.) the matter of the importation of the police and military into the Rhondda Valley was also raised: and the following resolution of protest was adopted:

That this Conference protests against the action of Mr. Clement Edwards, M.P., for opposing in the House of Commons a demand for an enquiry into the action of the police and military forces, in connection with the Rhondda and Aberdare strike, inasmuch as this enquiry was asked for in accordance with a resolution passed by a South Wales Miners' Conference. (*27.iii.1911.*)

Later, under the heading "Financial Position," Alfred Onions, the General Treasurer, gave a statement as to the financial position; and after a general discussion the following resolution was unanimously passed:

That this Conference, after careful consideration of the failure of the negotiations for a settlement of the matters in dispute at the Cambrian Combine collieries, and the decisive declaration by a ballot vote of the workmen that the terms offered by the employers are unsatisfactory, calls upon the members of the Federation to regularly pay the levies called by the Executive Council in support of these workmen, and that every district be requested to send on from their district fund pending the collection from their members the whole of the arrears owing of the Cambrian collieries' levies. (*27.iii.1911.*)

With this ballot and Cory Hall Conference resolution there ended the March intervention. There was nothing further but the continuation of the strike and the lockout.

7. M.F.G.B. CONFERENCE WANTS ARBITRATION

Nothing happened for four weeks: and nothing was said. Then in the Caxton Hall, Westminster, on April 26th, the M.F.G.B. President, Enoch Edwards, made a suggestion to the special conference originally called for the discussion of the Mines Regulation Bill. His proposal was "to submit this dispute to a tribunal of arbitration to settle it." Many from South Wales spoke in favour of this proposal. None objected. Tom Smith for the strike committee said: "If ever there was intense heroism manifested it has been by the women and children in this struggle. I take it if arbitration is offered by this great Federation, and is refused, then you are not going to allow us to starve any longer." Then, after a sagacious and encouraging speech by Vice-President Robert Smillie the resolution was carried unanimously as follows:

That in the opinion of this Conference the matters in dispute in the Bute Seam at the Ely Pit of the Cambrian Combine should at once be submitted to arbitration, and this Conference relegates to the Executive Committee of this Federation the taking of immediate steps in the matter. (*26.iv.1911.*)

The South Wales coal-owners, on "fundamental principle," refused arbitration: but were willing to meet to discuss the dispute. By mid-May three meetings had resulted in a set of terms being signed by four coal-owners' and four workmen's representatives. The latter four were the South Wales President and Secretary and the President and Secretary of the Miners' Federation of Great Britain which was thus made directly responsible for the proposed settlement.

The terms were: (1) that for a trial period of twelve months the company would pay a cutting rate of 2s. 1⅗d. per ton on the Upper Five Foot seam of the Ely pit (being the amount previously negotiated by Abraham on October 23, 1910) and that elsewhere work would be resumed as soon as places were ready in the pits; (2) that the assurances of January and February, 1911, by D. A. Thomas and others (believed by Ashton to be worth 6s. 9d. a shift) would be carried out; (3) that a committee of the Conciliation Board or, should they fail to agree, the Independent Chairman thereof should decide whether or not in any particular case these assurances in fact were being carried out. The M.F.G.B. Executive three days later approved this.

But the terms got anything but a welcome reception in South Wales. Enoch Edwards in his later report to the M.F.G.B. Executive said only that at the South Wales council meeting of May 20th, "Mr. Ashton and myself were not received very graciously." Enoch put it very mildly. But Ashton was deeply hurt. A letter from him the next day (May 21st) to Tom Richards showed this:

We have obtained all in the terms of the agreement that we set out for and fully carried out the instructions of the Special Conference, and yet we are told that we have jockeyed and sold the men. I have worked for the miners 45 years. I have attended on thousands of deputations and assisted in settling hundreds of large and important disputes. Some of these settlements have not always been satisfactory to myself, but no man has ever said I sold them before yesterday. (*21.v.1911.*)

Subsequently, in a widely publicised statement, Ashton furnished details of what had occurred on the Saturday (May 20th) when Edwards and he attended the S.W.M.F. Council. Edwards had explained the whole proceedings of the negotiations with the coal-owners and the proposed final settlement arrived at; and then:

Two or three representatives from the strike district who have recently been appointed on the Council were grossly insulting. They said that the men had been sold—jockeyed and sold: that the case had been in the hands of Mr. Ashton, who knew nothing about the case, and of Mr. Edwards who knew less. They were asked to withdraw these words but they refused.

The Council meeting had concluded with the proposition: "That the Cambrian Combine workmen be strongly recommended to accept the arranged terms and the representatives be thanked for securing the principle of finality in the settlement of any dispute that may arise." As soon as Edwards and Ashton had left the meeting in high dudgeon further consideration had been adjourned to the Monday, May 22, 1911. On the Monday the discussion was continued and revealed a sharp division of opinion. There were present twenty-seven, half of whom spoke. Charles Edwards spoke for recommending the terms to the workmen for acceptance, as did Alfred Onions, James Manning, Watts Morgan, William Vyce, C. B. Stanton, and, finally, from the chair, Mabon. Vernon Hartshorn moved that the terms be sent to the workmen without recommendation: and this was supported by George Barker. It was agreed that a conference be called: and the motion "that the Conference be advised to recommend the Cambrian Combine workmen to accept the arranged terms of settlement" received eleven votes against seven: but Noah Ablett, Tom Smith, Noah Rees and John Hopla left the room, refusing to take part in this vote. The opposition to the policy of the Chairman (and, at this point, of the M.F.G.B. also) had grown to the point where William Abraham could muster only half the Council in his support. The terms presented made "very little if any improvement" (as Hartshorn had pointed out) upon the terms that had already been rejected by an overwhelming ballot vote of the Cambrian Combine workmen. The question now was: how would the conference of the whole coalfield look upon these terms?

8. WELSH CONFERENCE REJECTS MID-MAY TERMS

The Cambrian Combine Committee, to whom the proposed terms were utterly repugnant, now went a step further. Within a couple of days they brought out a manifesto[1] which was sent to every lodge in the coalfield.

In this they taunted their President and Secretary with having been for the second time "palpably fooled," referred to the "spoof assurances" and recounted the cause and course of the lockout and strike. In one part the manifesto said:

We have been deliberately and foully misrepresented by a large section of the public press. We have been bludgeoned by the police. One of our comrades lost his life in contending with the police. Two comrades, in the stress of the struggle in illness and privation, committed suicide. Many of our fellows have suffered imprisonment. Some are now in prison who have foully had their liberty sworn away, and are as innocent of any crime as any reader of this appeal.

If we could only tabulate even a part of the suffering and misery endured by our women and children, we feel sure that you will agree with us that the fight has gone too far and the suffering too great that we should now be handed over to the mercy of the D. A. Thomas Combine.

We ask you to say, friends, that the time has arrived when the surrender policy of our apologetic leaders must stop.

It concluded with advice as to what policy should be pursued at

[1] See Appendix II to this chapter.

the forthcoming coalfield conference three days later and also at the national conference called for mid-June. This it was clear would have an immediate effect on the delegates to the special conference in Cardiff called for Saturday, May 27th.

As a counter to this manifesto the officials in their opening statements at the conference did their utmost to persuade the delegates to accept the terms of May 15th. But Mabon's eloquence was in vain. The temper of the delegates had been shown at the very beginning by a decision (on a card vote) to exclude the journalists who were there in number. To Mabon's arguments they turned a deaf ear. He said he was astonished that they were being criticised and condemned: for the solution offered was finality in their local disputes, so that they were getting what they had been trying to secure for 25 years: but they were now told it would cripple their Federation. To him the course now proposed to be taken was the most dangerous ever adopted.

The General Secretary submitted a full report of the proceedings in the negotiations with a justification of his policy: and Vice-President Brace gave further explanation of what had taken place: but their speeches could not deflect the delegates from a judgment that had been ripening in the lodges. It hardly needed the arguments of Tom Smith to convince them that the men who acted in these last negotiations "ran away from the resolution of the conference" of a month earlier which had sought for arbitration. "Why," asked Tom Smith, "were the workmen's representatives, who had been in this dispute from the beginning, not called in? If that course had been pursued these terms would not be before the conference this day. The terms were exactly the same terms as had been offered and rejected by the Council and ballot of the workmen."

Thereupon it was proposed and seconded that the terms be rejected: and with the same unanimity the adjourned conference on Monday, May 29th, passed a resolution recommending the lodges to reconsider "the sectional strike policy hitherto adopted" and to ask the Miners' Federation of Great Britain at its conference on June 14, 1911 "to make common cause with the workmen by declaring a general stoppage throughout the Federation for the purpose of securing for all colliery workmen a definite guaranteed Minimum Wage"; and, "failing this national action," that the South Wales Miners' Federation declare a stoppage to secure this end.

9. AN INCREASE OF TENSION

The unanimous decision to reject the May terms had flouted the advice of Abraham and Richards, dishonoured their signatures and left sore feelings behind. Indeed the battle was now joined between the officials and their Council majority and those who were described as "the opposition of the socialist members of the conference." The tension was increased within the next few days. Mabon now launched a denunciation in the press of the policy adopted as one "of despair and starvation."[1] His articles brought immediate replies, and amongst the sharpest of them, one from Vernon Hartshorn. The spectacle was presented of the leading members of the Executive Council at loggerheads.

Furthermore, Thomas Ashton on June 2nd issued his own manifesto in which he wholeheartedly denounced the strike leaders in the Rhondda. This in turn came up in the Executive Council where after an angry discussion it was agreed "that we disassociate ourselves entirely from the manifestos." This applied both to Ashton's and to that "of the Naval workmen."

On the same day Noah Ablett, who was now beginning to develop a programme, gave two notices of motion. The first was "That the whole of the workmen engaged in the mining industry be organised into one organisation: that immediate steps be taken to bring this about: that all previous resolutions on this subject contrary to this be rescinded." The second was that the Executive Council should recommend to the next available conferences of the South Wales Miners' Federation and of the Miners' Federation of Great Britain, that "the time has now arrived when we agitate and use all our power to secure a minimum wage of 8s. per day for every workman organised into the Miners' Federation of Great Britain." (*8.vi.1911.*)

The checkweighman from Mardy, only six months a member of the Executive Council, was putting forward successively the tenets of industrial unionism.

Meanwhile the lodges were considering these matters and instructing their delegates for the special conference on Monday, June 12th, in Cardiff, where William Brace, M.P., was in the Chair. This confirmed the previous decision to press for a national stoppage but rejected action by South Wales alone by 188 votes to 86. Instead the delegates were instructed "to support national action" upon the question of abnormal places and lower paid wage men if the London conference were to refuse to take "national action" upon the minimum wage. It was a stormy conference: and the feelings aroused were shown by a somewhat startling resolution put forward by the business committee; namely

That this conference asks Mabon to resign his position as President of the South Wales Miners' Federation.

---

[1] *South Wales Daily News*, June 3, 1911.

14   SIRHOWY. SINKING THE PIT, MARKHAM COLLIERY, 1911

15 BALLOTING ON COAL STRIKE, JANUARY 1912

STRIKERS GETTING BACK PAY AT CILFYNYDD, 1912

Brace, however, from the Chair ruled this out of order as well as another recommending that "all Executive members" stand for election in their respective districts, "after the Combine dispute is settled." But the 300 delegates, representing 142,396 members, sternly resolved:

That this conference is of the opinion that all controversies of the present or any other crises should cease to be discussed through the press. That as a conference we also condemn the action of Mr. Ashton in issuing a circular referring to the Cambrian Combine workmen. (*12.vi.1911.*)

These decisions had immediate repercussions. That same evening in London a pre-conference meeting of the M.F.G.B. Executive Committee heard what had happened that day, and also in the preceding three weeks. They may have been distressed at the news but they were not dismayed: nor would they yield an inch to the Welshmen. Instead they laid their plans to thwart any attempt to bring the South Wales motion up at the special three-day conference called for the consideration of (1) the Cambrian Combine dispute, (2) the new Mines Bill, (3) the question of abnormal places. These plans they set out in three resolutions[1] carried against the vote of the four South Wales representatives.

10. M.F.G.B. SPECIAL CONFERENCE
JUNE 13 TO 15, 1911

It was a very large conference that met in the Westminster Palace Hotel on Tuesday, June 13th with 178 present. Out of the 159 delegates on the floor 51 came from South Wales. It was bound to be a stormy conference after the denunciation of the local strike leaders by Thomas Ashton on June 2nd and the vote of censure upon this by a conference which covered over a fifth of the M.F.G.B. membership. The chairman of the conference, Enoch Edwards, M.P., was in a sense a party to the dispute: and although he disclaimed any intention of making remarks that might cause discord he could not have the same soothing effect as was usual. It was not long before there was a heated altercation between Ashton and a member of the S.W.M.F. Executive Council. Tom Smith, speaking as "a man at the

---

[1] 1. "That we confirm our previous resolution and accept the terms of settlement, and also recommend the conference to accept the same."

2. "That the subject to be discussed in conference tomorrow (Tuesday, 13th) be the Cambrian Combine dispute and that our president make it clear to conference that the national subject for payment in abnormal places will not be considered until Thursday (15th)."

3. "That having learned the character of the resolution to be moved by the representatives from South Wales, this Executive Committee desire to inform the conference that such a resolution is outside the province of this conference and only the subjects named in the circular calling the conference can be in order." (M.F.G.B. E.C. *12.vi.1911.*)

I

face, a collier," riddled "the assurances" given by D. A. Thomas. ("He can look you in the face with a bland smile, that cunning smile so characteristic of the man who says: 'I have no desire to reduce the general average of wages,' but at the same time does so. We have had some of it; we know him.") He ended his speech with an eloquent appeal.

> We are here on the 43rd week of our strike fighting for a fair wage. You know what the backbone of this fight is. . . . It is the heroism, the self-sacrifice of the women—women who have stood up by their husbands and said: "Die, rather than give in." You can withdraw the £3,000 a week from us. If we know that our end will be buried in confusion, and smoke and blood, it shall go down to posterity that the men of the Cambrian died fighting while you with the power to be our saviours trample us under your feet. Do it if you will. The Cambrian men are determined they will fight the greatest despot in South Wales and will not go down that pit until they have got a guarantee of their wage.

The eloquence of Tom Smith stirred many of the delegates; but when the chairman called upon Alderman W. House of Durham it was clear that the influence of the district that came next in size to South Wales would be thrown into the balance right away.

The older leaders of the county associations, especially those which still sent Liberal Members to parliament, were shocked that one district, though by far the largest, should have unanimously resolved to condemn the revered national secretary: and the speaker for the Northumberland Miners' Mutual Confidence Association urged upon the Welsh delegates that "your safeguard is the agreement signed by Mr. Edwards as President of this great Federation, Mr. Ashton, Mr. Abraham and Richards, all honourable men with an honourable service behind them." These were men "who have spent their best blood, brain and muscle in the service of the miners of their country."

Vernon Hartshorn, in a reasoned and forceful speech, endeavoured to compose the emotional atmosphere that had been generated in the conference. He steered clear of the points on which Ashton had sought to generalise the causes of difference into a conflict between "the principles of trade unionism or anarchy." He stressed the belief of the South Wales men that the settlement would not yield the results claimed. On the other hand, he sought to generalise the dispute in a different way and to raise it to the level of a national question of abnormal places and a minimum wage:

> We think first of all the conference resolution has not been carried out. We think the assurances are not such as will justify us in recommending the men to return to work. There is one statement in the circular which I think, in fairness to Wales, should be made clear. He says, in his final

remarks, that "all along they have been crying for the 20th rule to be put in operation" and he goes on to say: "It was never intended to be used to assist a district to fix prices in a seam at a colliery, or in any case where less than 80 men are directly affected" (Hear, hear; certainly, and we say amen. I will challenge Mr. Ashton or any other man in this conference to produce a statement which has ever been made by a responsible leader in South Wales, that we have contended that there should be national action on the question of a price list.

What we have contended for in this dispute is that we should establish a minimum wage. That is a dispute which is common to all the coal-fields of the United Kingdom. Here we have got a price list which will not meet the normal conditions of the seam. We say that this 2s. 1$\frac{3}{10}$d. will not enable men to make a wage under normal conditions. Then the only alternative is to get a guaranteed wage for all the miners who go into the mine. That is common to the whole of the coalfields of the kingdom; that is something which would benefit the whole community, and which, if the Federation went for, would embrace this combine dispute, and enable them to go back and try the price list for 12 months. We say that the Federation ought to take national action for settling the minimum wage for all men. It is a matter of common interest and common importance, and we should take united action on it.

Thomas Ashton followed with a speech defending himself from criticism and reiterating what he had written in his pamphlet. It was his first speech in open meeting for nearly a score of years. Then came a fateful resolution that "In the opinion of this conference, the object sought for at the special conference at the Caxton Hall on the April 26th is secured in the proposed terms"; together with the corollary that "this conference now agrees to accept no further responsibility in this dispute."

William Brace rose to plead for the holding back of the resolution, the meaning of which was that "our Cambrian men must accept the terms submitted to them for settlement, and if they do not accept, the three thousand pounds a week which the Federation has been paying to us to support these men in their fight, will be discontinued."

Our men, not the Cambrian men alone, but the whole of our coalfield unanimously rejected those terms. As a leader of the Welshmen I am therefore in this position, that while I accept the responsibility of re-commending that the terms be accepted, that immediately the coalfield rejected those terms their decision is my decision.

Brace concluded by saying:

Don't let it go forth to the coal-owners tomorrow that you are against us in this matter . . . I make an appeal to the conference, as earnest as any man can, to delay coming to any decision if you cannot see your way to support us further in the future.

William Brace for some years had had the ear of the M.F.G.B. conferences, perhaps more than any other leader from Wales: and there may have been a hope amongst the Welshmen that his speech would bring some shift of opinions. Such hopes if they existed were dashed when W. E. Harvey of Derbyshire rose to speak. He, together with Ashton, had been the target for obloquy at Tonypandy at the end of March, and though he had kept quiet and restrained at the April 26th conference his tongue was now unloosed, and to such purpose that delegates from South Wales were rising one after another to protest.

The Chairman intervened to say: "Don't let us make the situation worse by irritating language." But tempers had risen. One after another leaders of the English coalfield spoke against South Wales. Dr. John Wilson, M.P., General Secretary of the Durham Miners, taunted the men from South Wales that they had gone about the coalfields, "solicited alms like beggars" and that they had not paid their levies fully for their own men on strike "with 140,000 working in the district," he said, "a levy of 1s. per man per week would have kept the Cambrian men from poverty." . . .

"If the men in South Wales had believed in this strike they would have levied themselves not a 1s. a week but 2s. 6d. a week." This statement provoked noise and disorder which prevented the speaker from continuing on that theme. In the end the result was a foregone conclusion. The resolution was carried by 465,000 to 137,000. The result left South Wales isolated from the other coalfields. As soon as the conference was over (there were two days further discussion on other questions) the M.F.G.B. Executive Committee took the following decision: "That the grant of £3,000 per week to the South Wales Federation in support of the Cambrian Combine Collieries workmen be paid this week and two more payments beyond this week." (*16.vi.1911.*)

To any hostile critic it might appear that the M.F.G.B. Executive Committee had contracted into the dispute at a weekly price and that they were now contracting out of it, when they found they could not control the issue of events.

11. "ONCE MORE UNTO THE BREACH"

No sooner had the Miners' Federation of Great Britain withdrawn support than the chief owner of the Cambrian Combine made a declaration. D. A. Thomas, M.P., stated "there is nothing in the assurance which can legitimately be construed into a guarantee of a minimum of 6s. 9d. per day." (*15.vi.1911.*)

Meanwhile Thomas Ashton, on his return to Manchester, decided to make a further intervention. Emboldened perhaps by the warm support given to his previous statement of June 2nd and its undoubted effect in the coalfields, he now on June 20th sent out a circular to the coalfields in the strange form of an open letter to Tom Richards, M.P. In this he asserted that the terms of settlement meant 6s. 9d. a day or more: and that if any attempt were made to pay less, then the workmen could appeal to the Miners' Federation of Great Britain. Apparently Ashton was totally unaware of D. A. Thomas's statement of June 15th. Certainly Ashton could hardly have chosen a worse occasion for his doubtless well-meant effort.

The effect was very different to what had been anticipated. Before seven days were out the fat was in the fire. An angry meeting of the South Wales Miners' Federation Executive Council on Monday, June 26th, took a series of decisions. The first was to approach the Miners' Federation of Great Britain in view of D. A. Thomas's denial of Ashton's interpretation (6s. 9d. per day) and to ask that the grant of £3,000 a week be continued. They also resolved on a general conference of the South Wales coalfield: and for a statement on the Cambrian Combine dispute to be drawn up for presentation to the Miners' Federation of Great Britain.[1]

On Friday, June 30th, the M.F.G.B. Executive Committee refused. Earlier that week, on Wednesday, June 28th, Ashton began what turned out to be a lengthy enough correspondence with D. A. Thomas and Mark Harcombe as well as with the coal owners' Secretary.

Back in Cardiff, at the conference of July 1st, the Right Hon. William Abraham, sorrowfully brought the news of the refusal. D. A. Thomas, he thought, had timed his intervention so as to create "the present chaotic position."

William Brace thought the fight must go on until the coal owners accept either the interpretation of Mr. D. A. Thomas or Mr. T. Ashton. Endeavour should be made to raise the matter again at the conference on July 28th. He hoped that the suggestion to send missionaries into the other coalfields would not be acted upon, as that would be unconstitutional and the beginning of civil war, and he must not be held to be a party to it.

A general discussion took place with a fighting speech from Brace. They resolved to press for national action on the minimum wage question and for the Cambrian Combine dispute to be dealt with at the M.F.G.B. conference of July 28th, or at a special conference called for that purpose. The Executive Council were to call the necessary levies. Finally, by an overwhelming majority of the 218 delegates they resolved:

[1] See Appendix III to this chapter.

That this conference takes the responsibility of issuing a manifesto to the English and Scots coalfields explaining the position in South Wales and that the missionaries be sent to place them in the hands of the English and Scots miners. (*1.vii.1911.*)

Whereas the circular sent out earlier that week had been sent to the secretaries of the coalfields for distribution, the further step was now being taken of going direct to the men themselves in meetings or in whatever manner they could make contact with them.

Although Brace objected that this was unconstitutional the Executive Council thereupon resolved: "That the sub-committee be empowered to engage twenty representatives to distribute the manifesto in the various coalfields." This was plunging into missionary activity with a vengeance.

It may here be noted that already some three weeks earlier at the Council meeting of Monday, June 19th, "Mr. D. Watts Morgan called attention to the fact that the Cambrian Combine officials are visiting various collieries with a view of securing the dismissal of workmen who, prior to their employment there, had been in employment at the Cambrian Combine collieries. Thereafter it was resolved: 'That full particulars be obtained and laid before Mr. Nicholas, Solicitor, and that he be invited to attend the next meeting of the Council.'"

The Council meeting on July 6th decided to levy the members of the South Wales Miners' Federation at the rate of 3s. per month. Edward Gill and Noah Ablett with the General Secretary were to prepare the manifesto and a quarter of a million copies were to be printed. Finally, Tom Richards was to write asking that the resolution of May 29th should come up at the conference on July 28, 1911.

So on July 6, 1911, the letter went from Royal Chambers, Cardiff:

Dear Mr. Ashton,

I am instructed by my Committee to write you calling your attention to the resolution of our conference passed on the 29th May last and forwarded to you asking that the question of a definite guaranteed minimum wage for all colliery workmen should be considered at the national conference upon June 14th, 1911.

You will remember the Chairman stated that it could not be considered at that conference, intimating it could be discussed at a future conference. Therefore the Council are surprised that the matter is not upon the agenda to be considered at the conference to be held upon the 28th inst. and request that you will issue a supplementary agenda that the following question may be dealt with:

To consider the advisability of declaring a general stoppage throughout the Federation for the purpose of securing for all colliery workmen a definite guaranteed minimum wage.

Yours faithfully,

THOMAS RICHARDS.

925 Ashton Old Road,
Manchester.
July 7, 1911.

Dear Mr. Richards,

I have received your letter of yesterday.

The subject to be discussed at the special conference on the 28th of this month is not one for the purpose of securing to every colliery workman a definite minimum guaranteed wage as stated in the resolution passed at your Council meeting.

The subject to be discussed is to press for the average or minimum wage in each district to apply to all workmen when engaged in working abnormal places. I do not remember the Chairman saying that a resolution such as you suggest could be considered at the special conference, but I hope to see Mr. Edwards next week and will consult with him before considering your proposal to issue a supplementary agenda.

I think your resolution would be in order to appear on the agenda for the Annual Conference.

Yours truly,

THOS. ASHTON.

T. Richards,
Royal Chambers, Cardiff.

These two letters were laid before the M.F.G.B. Executive Committee on July 21st, the circular calling the Conference was then read. The President said that it was strictly in accordance with the resolution passed at the last conference.

In the meanwhile the South Wales Council met again and it was reported that the M.F.G.B. Executive Committee had refused to issue a supplementary agenda for the conference on July 28th to enable the question of a minimum wage for all colliery workmen to be discussed. So it was resolved that at the conference the following motion be moved on behalf of the South Wales District: "In the opinion of this conference this problem can best be solved by the securing of a minimum wage for all colliery workmen in the mines of the United Kingdom. Mr. Brace to propose and Mr. Hartshorn to second."

Though it was decided that the resolution from South Wales would not be in order to appear upon the agenda, the pressure from Cardiff was beginning to have an effect of a kind. At the conference of June 15th on the question of abnormal places a resolution for a further adjournment to await reports was carried by 95 votes against 55, many of which minority were undoubtedly from South Wales. It ran:

That having heard the reports from Districts on this question, and seeing that those reports are incomplete and negotiations with the coalowners are still proceeding, this conference be adjourned until July 28, at 10 a.m. to complete the reports and negotiations in the respective districts and also to decide what action shall be taken.

When it came to July 28th, the following decision was carried:

After having heard the reports from the districts on the abnormal places question, this conference instructs the officials of this Federation to arrange with the coal-owners of the United Kingdom for a joint meeting to consider the question of paying a district minimum rate for working abnormal places.

Failing to get satisfaction on this question a conference be called without delay to decide on a ballot of all members of this Federation to ascertain if they are in favour of ceasing work until a district minimum wage is obtained. (*29.viii.1911.*)

12. RETREAT AND RETROSPECT

When Thomas Ashton had written his unusual "open letter" to Tom Richards, it would seem that he had perhaps even contributed by his midsummer intervention to the prolonging of a dispute he was anxious to bring to an end. The effect of it all can be seen in the decisions taken in South Wales Executive Council first in July and thereafter in August. With all doors locked and bolted and barred, the Cambrian Combine miners had to find some way out of their now really desperate situation. Moreover, the coalfield levy as a method of sustaining the strike was falling out of favour in quite a number of lodges: some protested against the Council's decision for "another shilling levy without a ballot": (*31.vii.1911.*) in the Monmouthshire Western Valleys a mass meeting protested against continuing the levy and favoured a general South Wales stoppage. So the Council resolved to send a deputation (Vernon Hartshorn, James Winstone and Enoch Morrell) to attend the meeting of the Cambrian Joint Committee "with a view of having a general discussion upon the whole situation." (*31.vii.1911.*) Later that week Vernon Hartshorn gave a report: the Cambrian Combine Joint Committee were not in favour of continuing the struggle on the present lines; nor were they in favour of "Down Tools in this coalfield."

The prevailing opinion in the committee, so Hartshorn reported, was that "they ought to go to the men and tell them they were beaten": but he and the other two representatives of the Executive Council were opposed to this. Failing a meeting of the Conciliation Board with Cambrian workmen and Cambrian owners "to try to agree upon terms" the men would go back on October 22, 1910, terms "and will adopt guerilla warfare." Thereupon the Councils having heard and considered the report of their representatives "sent by this Council to consult with the Cambrian Combine Joint Committee" instructed their secretary to arrange for an early meeting of the Conciliation Board to discuss "the matters in dispute

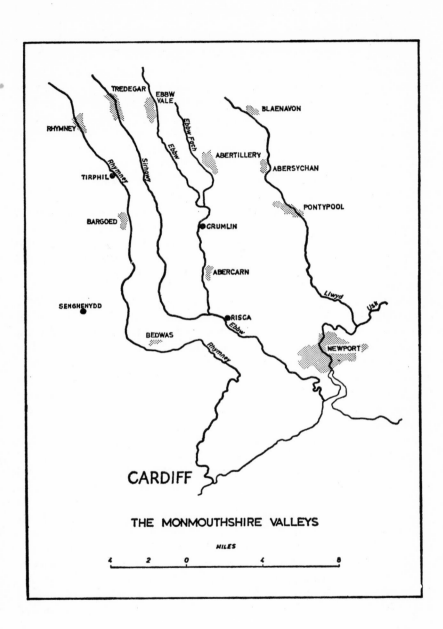

THE MONMOUTHSHIRE VALLEYS

MILES

4   2   0   4   8

CARDIFF

I*

at the Ely Pit with a view to a satisfactory agreement being arrived at." (*4.viii.1911.*)

Before the Board met on Wednesday, August 9th, the Council assembled at the Engineers' Institute, found there awaiting them Mark Harcombe and John Hughes "as a deputation from a mass meeting of the Cambrian Combine workmen." They stated that eight workmen had received summonses for unlawful assembly, assaults, etc. and thought "there ought not to be any negotiations until they were withdrawn, as they are likely to prejudice any good that might result from the negotiations": and what steps could the Council take to get these summonses withdrawn?

A fortnight earlier the last of the "colliery disturbances" had taken place at Penygraig where on Tuesday, July 25th, thirty-seven police casualties were reported, itemised as bruises, abrasions, injuries, etc. The fact that for the first time the majority of these casualties were of the Glamorgan police, with only a few from neighbouring counties, seems to indicate that Captain Lindsay felt that with his own men he could now cope with any fiery embers amongst the starving villages of mid-Rhondda.

Meantime the Council, having resolved that the President (Mabon), D. Watts Morgan, and Alderman John Thomas seek an interview with the authorities about the summonses, decided on a table of three proposals any one of which might end the dispute. But the owners would have none of it: no such proposition was permissible: one or other of the "settlements" of May or of October 1910, must be accepted without any variation. This implacable answer left the miners no option: to extend the strike or to end the strike—that was now the question. The Council sat throughout Saturday, August 12th, with a very full attendance together with a deputation[1] from the Cambrian Combine Joint Committee.

The discussion was minuted in such a way that the standpoint of each speaker was clearly shown, and was circulated to the lodges. The decision was made to close the dispute, after a proposal for "down tools" was defeated by 12 to 2. The choice of either the October or May terms of settlement was left to the workmen who in a mass meeting accepted the latter. There was some few days' delay in resuming work, as the workmen insisted that all of the pits must start at the same time, but by the end of August it was minuted that "they are ready to start the Naval Pits: a mass meeting is to be held today when it is thought a general return to work will be agreed upon." (Thursday, August 31, 1911.)

[1] Of these the following took part in discussion:

Owen Buckley	Mark Harcombe
Edward Hughes	John Hughes
Will John	D. Jones
W. H. Mainwaring	

It was in August that the strike began to end, amid great suffering and misery. It was not until the beginning of October that work was being resumed, and even so, places could not be found for some 3,000 of the men. The Executive Committee of the M.F.G.B., informed of this on October 4th, granted £2,000 in aid of those men. At the end of December, Ashton, on behalf of the M.F.G.B., enquired whether the agreement in the Ely Pit was being carried out by the management and especially whether any man working at the coalface had received less than 6s. 9d. per day since the resumption of work. The reply was that no case was known of a collier who had received less than 6s. 9d. a day in the Ely Pit and that "most of the men since they resumed work had earned big wages at the tonnage rate."

The Cambrian Combine men had been forced to accept the original terms of settlement of October 1910 as regards the 2s. 1$\frac{3}{10}$d. cutting price for the Bute Seam in the Ely Pit of the Naval Collieries. Nevertheless, in the course of their struggle they had raised the question of abnormal places to be a national mining issue and in the later stages had carried this still farther to the issue of a National Minimum Wage. To this they had converted the whole of the South Wales coalfield and were presently to convert the whole of the miners of the United Kingdom. They had lost their local dispute; they had won the desired national movement to settle the wider question. The strike with all its bitter hardship and suffering had not been in vain.

So ended the Cambrian Combine strike: and so also ended the Ely Pit lockout. They had been out for ten months and twelve months respectively. They had been defeated, with great loss: but out of their dangers and tribulations there was to come a nationwide struggle on the broader principle of the minimum wage. The Cambrian Combine miners had been made "to eat the leek": but their tears had watered the growth of a much greater leek which in less than a twelvemonth the owners were forced to chew upon and then to swallow.

How did the miners themselves weigh up the conduct of the strike by their leaders? The answer to this was given just before the October 1911 Annual Conference of the Miners' Federation of Great Britain. On its Executive Committee three seats allocated to South Wales had been held for years by three of their officials— Tom Richards, M.P., Secretary, William Brace, M.P., Vice-President, and Alfred Onions, Treasurer. These three were now displaced by the socialist opponents as a result of the ballot given overleaf:

Result of Ballot in Order of Votes Cast

Vernon Hartshorn	20,543
C. B. Stanton	20,497
George Barker	20,181
Wm. Brace, M.P.	18,244
Tom Richards, M.P.	12,987
James Winstone	12,802
Alfred Onions	11,834

There was that same September another significant vote. The sitting member of the Executive Committee of the International Miners' Federation was the Right Hon. Wm. Abraham, M.P. He received only 13,450 votes from South Wales against C. B. Stanton who received 27,008. Thus a most overwhelming defeat by a two to one majority was inflicted upon Mabon, who had for twelve years held the presidency of the Federation and before the Federation for nearly a quarter of a century had been the best known amongst the Welsh miners' leaders. All recognised (and he himself stated it) that this was the definite defeat not so much of a man as of a policy. Only a few months were to pass before Abraham ceased to be the leader of the miners of South Wales. Notice had been given him by that vote and he made up his mind to go on grounds of impaired health. William Brace similarly understood the significance of the September ballot, and wrote to the Western Valley, Monmouthshire (of which since 1890 he had been the advisory agent) offering his resignation. The valley council, meeting on November 20, 1911, decided by 17 votes to 8 not to accept the resignation. So, too, it was with the other leaders who for so many years had maintained a liberal standpoint in politics and a corresponding conciliatory outlook on the industrial arena. Henceforth they had to follow where once they had led.

PARTICULARS OF POLICE IMPORTED INTO RHONDDA AND ABERDARE VALLEYS

Mr. Pointer (for Mr. Keir Hardie) asked the Home Secretary whether he can state the total number of police imported into the Rhondda and Aberdare Valleys in connection with the recent trade dispute therein, the districts from which they were drafted, and the number from each?

Mr. Churchill: The total number of police sent into the Rhondda and Aberdare Valleys from other districts at different times during the strike amounted to 1,499, drawn from the following eleven forces:—

Name of Force					Number
Metropolitan	..	..	..	..	902
Glamorganshire	..	..	..	..	216
Carmarthenshire	..	..	..	..	45
Monmouthshire	..	..	..	..	41
Gloucestershire	..	..	..	..	26
Breconshire	..	..	..	..	11
Cardiff City	..	..	..	..	101
Bristol City	..	..	..	..	63
Swansea	..	..	..	..	43
Merthyr Tydfil	..	..	..	..	31
Newport	..	..	..	..	20
			Total	..	1,499

Of this total, the highest number engaged on duty at any one time was 1,301, on November 15th and 16th. The number at present on duty is 312. (*16.ii.1911.*)

MANIFESTO BY THE CAMBRIAN COMBINE WORKMEN
Cardiff Conference, on Saturday, May 27, 1911.

TO OUR FELLOW WORKERS IN THE MINES OF SOUTH WALES

COMRADES,

We issue this Manifesto in the form of an Appeal; but it will probably be a bitter Appeal, because it issues from sore hearts.

On Saturday next, you will be expected to send a delegate from every lodge in the coalfield to the Conference at Cardiff. You will further be asked to authorise your delegate to vote at that Conference in favour of recommending the Cambrian workmen to accept the proffered terms.

Fellow-workers, for our sakes, for your own sakes, for the sakes of all those who are dear to you, we ask you NOT TO DO THIS, and we will try to give you SOME REASONS WHY YOU SHOULD NOT.

We confidently hope that when you have considered the matter you will agree with us that THE TERMS OFFERED ARE WORSE THAN DEFEAT. Remember that we have fought a hard fight against tremendous odds, and we would like to impress upon you that THE METHOD OF

FIGHTING WAS NOT OF OUR SEEKING. You decided that for us, for by your ballot vote you told us that MID RHONDDA WAS TO BE THE COCKPIT OF THE FIGHT. We accepted the position with misgivings, but manfully entered on the fight, and we think you will give us the credit for having fought well, and we are not beaten—far from it! With your assistance (and we ask you to look at the position fairly and dispassionately), we will not only win out, but win something substantial for you as well.

(*There follows the passage which is quoted above in Section 8.*)

We ask you to say friends that the time has arrived when the surrender policy of our apologetic leaders must stop. They have not realised what it means to us in suffering. We know what questionable use Mr. F. L. Davis and other employers have made of the fact that Mabon and Mr. D. Watts Morgan recommended the terms rather than face the rigours of winter. But this is no excuse for the childlike way that Mabon and Mr. Tom Richards have allowed Mr. Llewellyn (the General Manager of the Combine) for the SECOND TIME TO FOOL THEM SO PALPABLY. It is reported that Mr. Llewellyn seemed to be the happiest man of the group on the evening of May 15th when the proposed settlement was arrived at. This might well be so. Under this agreement he will get his full pound of flesh; but we after all our suffering, get ABSOLUTELY NO SECURITY.

We, at some of Cambrian Pits, know something of the working of these precious Boards. At Clydach Vale, in 1901, after a five and a-half months' strike, a Conciliation Board was formed for the Cambrian alone, with the late Judge Owen as independent chairman. The working of that Board was the worst thing the Clydach Vale men ever knew. Under it the WORKING CONDITIONS WERE WHITTLED DOWN WITH A VENGEANCE. Mabon and Mr. Tom Richards knew all about this, yet seemed to have conveniently forgotten the matter in the present negotiations. It was this Board that made the reputation of Mr. Leonard W. Llewellyn, and laid the foundation of the present Combine. From 1901 to March 1905, the conditions of these men became so evil and the men SO DISORGANISED, that the pits were NOT EXAMINED BY THE WORKMEN in their own interests for some 18 months prior to the explosion that occurred in the No. 1 Pit in March 1905. We have a bitter experience of these tying-up Boards.

The terms now offered have been twice rejected, once through a ballot, now they are again offered with A MOST OBJECTIONABLE ADDITION to them.

We ask you, fellow-workmen, to note that the Executive Council are evenly divided on the question of recommending these terms. 11 voted for the terms, 7 against; and 4 LEFT THE ROOM rather than take part in the recommendation.

When the Executive decided to confine the fight to the Combine area, Mr. D. A. Thomas said that this put him and his company on velvet. In these negotiations, Mr. Llewellyn has undoubtedly had our leaders on toast. The employers (represented by four of the keenest men in the country, in the persons of Messrs Davis, Griffiths, Heppel, and Dalziel), felt it incumbent upon them to call in for consultation Messrs Callaghan, Pullin, and Llewellyn. But our benighted representatives thought they were more than a match for the seven, hence the present debacle.

We ask you fellow-workmen to examine the present terms offered. You will find there is absolutely no bottom to these SPOOF ASSURANCES. See clause 3 of agreement and you will find that the independent chairman HAS ABSOLUTELY NO TANGIBLE BASIS to work upon. Mr. F. L. Davis is very anxious that nothing shall enter into the Cambrian settlement that will imperil the Conciliation Board. Small wonder! The present agreement under the Board is admittedly 15 per cent worse than the worst sliding scale we ever had.

We know something, too, of the difficulties of the rest of the coalfield. We have a shrewd idea of what Mr. D. A. Thomas meant when he said, "He would readily give an undertaking to supplement low wages by allowances as is customary throughout the coalfield!" We know also that your position has not been better but rather worse since we've been out. We know that you find our levies burdensome. But are you willing to have paid all these levies for less than nothing; that we should be worse off and you no better? Would you not far rather that we should win out and you also to get an assured wage when you've worked for it?

Well, fellow-workmen! there is A SURE AND A CERTAIN WAY and that is not by voting us back to work and STARVATION AND EVERY INDIGNITY as was and is unfortunately the lot of the Aberdare men through no fault of theirs because we know they fought valiantly.

For your manhood's sake DO NOT SEEK TO AVOID YOUR LEVIES BY THIS METHOD. See rather that you send a mandate to Cardiff not to hound us back against our will but with a solid mandate that SOUTH WALES SHOULD GO UNITEDLY TO THE CONFERENCE OF JUNE 14 AT LONDON AND DEMAND THAT NATIONAL ACTION be taken on the resolution now before that conference for an 8s minimum for all colliers and 5s for all unskilled labourers below that point. By these means and these only can you save us, save the Aberdare men and save yourselves.

If you send us back then the national minimum wage may be shelved for years. But if on the other hand (as we ask you in all sincerity) you do not send us back then the Federation must take national action for the 8s minimum for Wales, England and Scotland or they must put up the shutters. A Federation that cannot or will not support us is not worth supporting.

Finally, avail yourselves of this opportunity on Saturday next at Cardiff or it may be many years before we again get such a golden opportunity.

Yours on behalf of the Cambrian Combine workmen.

WM. JOHN.	J. IVINS.
N. REES.	J. HOPLA.
M. HARCOMBE.	T. SMITH.

APPENDIX III TO CHAPTER EIGHT

S.W.M.F. MANIFESTO OF JULY 8, 1911

TO THE MEMBERS OF THE MINERS' FEDERATION OF GREAT BRITAIN

Fellow Workmen,

The Workmen of the South Wales Coalfield, in open Conference, have instructed us to place our position as a Coalfield before you, in the belief that your Conference decision on our appeals had been based on an imperfect knowledge of our very desperate situation. We therefore place before you the following brief account:

DISPUTES AND THEIR CAUSES.

There are at the present moment 11,000 men engaged in Disputes— on Strike and Locked Out—and each depends for settlement on the recognition of the principle of security of pay for work done. Bottomless Price Lists, a Decreasing Wage; together with unfavourable judgements in the Law Courts, where, unfortunately, too much of our time and money are spent—have left us in a pitiable predicament. These conditions can only be changed, in our opinion by the establishment of a Minimum Wage.

A DISMAL DILEMMA

To meet the necessities arising out of the Disputes, the Executive Council of the South Wales Miners have called upon the members to pay a Contribution of 4s. per month, and that in the face of a decrease in wage. On the other hand, the Coalowners, by simply paying one penny half-penny per ton indemnity, are enabled to hand over to the Cambrian Combine alone, the handsome sum of £26,000 per month. Thus the pressure exerted by the Herculean efforts of the men are rendered comparatively insignificant, and, if it were simply a question of holding out, the employers, could stay for many years without seriously feeling the pinch. We are now faced with the following dilemma. If the Cambrian men are forced back to work without obtaining a substantial concession, it cannot fail to seriously injure our Federation. If we decide to continue supporting them without hope of settlement, we must still further increase our Contributions, and it is quite certain that Demoralisation will follow unless the 20th Rule, in defence of a Fair Wage Rate, is applied soon.

ABNORMAL WAGE CLAUSE AND MINIMUM WAGE

The South Wales miners have, in common with the Yorkshire Miners, appealed for the 20th Rule on the Question of a Minimum Wage for all Colliery Workmen. It must be admitted that the South Wales Miners' Federation is responsible for bringing the question of what has been called "The Abnormal Places Clause" before the notice of the Miners' Federation of Great Britain, but our long experience of this matter, the actual insertion of these Clauses, in individual Price Lists, the negotiations with the Owners, and the decisions of the Courts, have convinced us that the cleverest scheme for trying the Secure Payment in Abnormal Places is so grievously defective, that we can no longer hold up such a policy as a remedy for the prime evils of the present. At two large representative Conferences of the South Wales Miners, it has been decided, practically unanimously, to strenuously agitate for a Minimum Wage in preference to the "Abnormal Places" policy. Notice of our intention was given at the Miners' Federation of Great Britain Conference, June 15th, but we were there not able to discuss the matter because the reports of the various Districts of the Miners' Federation of Great Britain were incomplete, and the Conference was adjourned to July 28th. Steps have been taken, however, to have the Motion placed on the Agenda of that Conference.

AN APPEAL FOR SOLIDARITY.

Fellow Workmen,

We have tried briefly to outline our desperate position. Never in our history have we been faced with so terrible a crisis. We cannot but feel that it is the absence of a Minimum Wage Clause in our present Conciliation Board Agreement, which was accepted upon the recommendation of the Miners' Federation of Great Britain, that is the root cause of our trouble. The Strikes affect all the Workmen in the Coalfield who are thus prevented from putting up the same fight as formerly; the Strikers are Boycotted; Colliery Officials are patrolling the Collieries in the capacity of Private Detectives, and, as a result, many cases of extreme hardship have been reported to us. Men who have migrated from the strike area, and obtained work elsewhere and have brought their families and their scanty stock of worldly goods with them, have suddenly been dismissed, with the consequence that unless help was immediately forthcoming, would be stranded among strangers. We have no desire to harrow your feelings with the pathos and tragedy of the Strike. Most of you know what a Strike is, and can realise what a ten month strike on 10s. a week entails. If it continues without relief, the Workmen may lose faith in their organisation. The South Wales workmen have a profound belief in the sympathetic comradeship of their English and Scotch fellow-workmen, and will always give a hearty response to any appeal that is emanated from them. Do not let the Welshmen lose that precious faith—the one most essential to Solidarity and the most formidable weapon against our oppressors. On July 28th, this question will be raised at the National Conference by the Welsh Delegation, and we appeal for United and Simultaneous action from all Sections of the Federation.

(Signed) THOMAS RICHARDS,
General Secretary

APPENDIX IV TO CHAPTER EIGHT

In *The Rhondda Valleys* by Dr. E. D. Lewis a footnote on page 176 gives the following as the *Cambrian Strike Manifesto* of June 16, 1911.

> "Through all the long dark night of years,
> The people's cry ascendeth,
> And earth is wet with blood and tears
> But our meek sufferance endeth.
> The few shall not for ever sway
> The many toil in sorrow.
> The powers of Hell are strong today
> Our kingdom comes tomorrow.

Fellow workers, we need your support in this strenuous struggle and the support of every man and woman who is prepared to make his or her sacrifice to put an end to Capitalistic Despotism and to do battle for the cause of Industrial Freedom."

On behalf of the Cambrian Combine strikers:

WILLIAM JOHN:	*Chairman*
COUNCILLOR NOAH REES:	*Vice-Chairman*
JAMES IVINS:	*Treasurer*
COUNCILLOR MARK HARCOMBE:	*Secretary*

CHAPTER NINE

THE MINIMUM WAGE DISPUTE

I. FROM ABNORMAL PLACES TO MINIMUM WAGE

DURING all these many anxious months of 1910 and 1911 in South
Wales the Miners' Federation of Great Britain was on the move,
almost with the gradualness of a geological process, surmounting
one obstacle after another, both external and within its own ranks.
In all coalfields the "missionaries" from the Rhondda and other
valleys had found a response: within the solid structure the molecules
were astir. The question of "abnormal places" (where a collier might
toil all day and, because of difficulties in the strata, be unable to win
either the coal or a reasonable payment for his effort) had first come
up for national consideration from South Wales in the Spring of
1910. Six months later at the instance of South Wales, the M.F.G.B.
Annual Conference decided that "the miners of Scotland, England
and Wales be requested to meet their respective employers and
demand a fair living wage to be paid to all miners working in
abnormal places." (6.x.1910.) Throughout the year 1911 special
conferences were held until on September 29th a joint meeting was
held with representatives of the coal owners who, however, would do
nothing nationally but referred the miners back again to the districts.
So this approach to the owners brought no satisfaction. After twelve
months the patience of the miners was exhausted: and the Annual
Conference decided:

> That the Federation take immediate steps to secure an individual
> district minimum wage for all men and boys working in the mines in the
> area of the Federation without any reference to the working places being
> abnormal. In the event of the employers refusing to agree to this then
> the amended 21st Rule[1] of the Federation be put into operation to demand
> the same. (6.x.1911.)

The decision was unanimous. The grievances of South Wales,
found also in other coalfields, had at last been put in the very
forefront of the British miners' policy; and for this principle of the

[1] The 21st rule, previously the famous "twentieth rule," amended on the proposal of
South Wales, henceforward ran as follows:
"That whenever any Federation or District is attacked on the wages question or the
conditions of labour, or with the approval of the Conference specially called for that
purpose has tendered notice to improve the conditions of labour or to obtain an advance
in wages a conference shall be called to consider the advisability of joint action being
taken." (6.x.1911).

minimum wage, all were prepared, if need be, to stop the wheels. The amendment of the strike rule, giving "power to move in an aggressive manner as well as defensive" had been put forward from South Wales. Tom Richards, M.P., explained "the genesis of the resolution" from "some severe conflicts in South Wales," arising out of negotiations early in 1910 on the new Wage Agreement. "We carried on these negotiations," said treasurer Alfred Onions, "until we failed to agree. We then applied to the Miners' Federation of Great Britain to assist us, by putting the twentieth rule (now twenty-first) into operation. The reply to that proposal on behalf of the Federation was that the twentieth rule did not exist for that purpose. It seems to be merely a defensive rule." (*6.x.1912.*)

Once these momentous decisions had been taken the course of events rolled slowly onward with unhurrying pace for the next hundred days until a strike ballot in January 1912 showed over half a million miners determined upon a national stoppage. Then the pace quickened: and within twenty five days the Prime Minister and his chief lieutenants intervened in the dispute. But their intervention was of no avail. The greatest strike till then of a whole industry in any country began on March 1, 1912.

Nothing could avert the stoppage willed by the millionfold mining community to surmount the obstacle in their path. The obstacle proved to be an "immovable object"; for the mine owners too (and perhaps especially the South Wales owners) felt that they had right on their side, as well as "the immutable laws of political economy." Where right is claimed on both sides, only might can decide. Which would be the more powerful? Which could hold out the longer? Loss of earnings, loss of livelihood, actual privation *versus* loss of trade and loss of profits? But naked alternatives such as these exist only in logic, not in life. The intervention of the onlookers, especially through the machinery of the State including an Act of Parliament (when all conciliatory efforts of the ministry had come to nothing) settled the question—and settled it against the will of the miners' representatives.

The whole train of events from the Annual Conference to the end of the strike lasted over six months. Through all this period there is scarcely any separate history of the South Wales Miners' Federation, as there had been before and would be once again. They were a contingent, albeit the most numerous, of a great army defending or advancing the livelihood of a mining community that numbered between three and four millions.

The story of the minimum wage and of the great strike of 1912 has been told fully elsewhere in[1] its national aspect: and here only the

---

[1] See *The Miners: Years of Struggle*, Chapters 3, 4, and 5.

aspect as it presented itself to the miners of the South Wales coalfield need be narrated. This aspect, mainly one of unity, if not
unanimity, had some facets, as revealed in successive national
conferences at monthly intervals, that bring out the distinctive
position of the South Wales Miners' Federation.

In the debates of these national conferences in the last quarter of
1911 the speakers from South Wales were often to the fore in urging
a stiff attitude to the employers. Some of them used arguments of a
kind which the delegates had been more accustomed in the previous
fifteen years to hear from the mouths of Scottish Socialist delegates.
Arguments such as these, expressing a keen sense of class antagonism,
did not accord particularly well with the Liberal attitude of delegates
such as Dr. John Wilson, M.P., General Secretary of the Durham
Miners' Association or Rt. Hon. Thomas Burt, M.P., who twenty
years earlier had been a minister in Gladstone's last administration.
Yet it was from Thomas Burt's Northumbrian delegation that a
resolution was moved for an immediate strike ballot. In support,
George Barker of Abertillery made a forceful plea for immediate
action, citing the position of the lower paid miner "the colliery
labourer with a standard of three shillings per day plus fifty per cent
or 4s. 6d. per shift," and saying:

This makes for a full week's work 27 shillings. But he does not work
full. There is the slack time, trade, and general holidays to be taken into
account, which will reduce the average from six days to five-and-a-half
per week and reduces his average wages from 27s. to 24/9d. per week.

Barker then gave the family budget which, for a family of six
persons would work out at about 14s. 6d. per week for rent and rates,
heating and lighting, clothing and footwear, leaving ten shillings
and threepence "to feed six persons for a week," and concluded:

Allow a bare three meals per day, in all eighteen meals per week—one
hundred and twenty-six meals—with one hundred and twenty-three
pence to pay for them, or less than one penny per meal per head.

Have we overstated the case? No, if anything it is understated. There
are thousands in this movement that are existing for less than one penny
per meal per head. (15.xi.1911.)

The speech of James Winstone in support of the minimum wage
resolution at the Annual Conference had been an example of the
more general argument from Wales. Winstone said that although a
man of peace he was not "a man of peace at the price the workmen
had now to pay for it." He believed in negotiation but there must
be reciprocity and "when we meet the employers we are usually met
with a blank 'No.' " He concluded by saying:

Even after we have declared for the minimum wage, after we have won
the minimum wage, we are only taking a mere part of the wealth produced by these men from time to time. I shall not rest satisfied Sir, until

this Federation declares that the whole of the wealth produced shall belong to the wealth producers.

So far as I am concerned, and speaking for myself personally, if the Chairman will pardon me for a moment, there can be no mutual interests between the exploited masses and the exploiting classes either economically or politically. (*6.x.1911.*)

Meantime, in most districts there had been negotiations with employers. Of these full reports were given at the Caxton Hall Conference on November 14th before the main debate began. William Brace told of the meeting three weeks earlier with the Monmouthshire and South Wales Coal Owners' Association. The owners, he reported, had been obdurate, as had been made absolutely clear by their spokesman Fred Davis. They would not recognise the principle of a minimum wage: they had no alternative proposals to make: and it was their intention to adhere strictly to the third Conciliation Board agreement—which would not expire before April, 1915.

It was no surprise that Barker followed by Hartshorn and Brace should support the proposal made for an immediate strike ballot.

But meantime the employers on the English Conciliation Board had conceded "the principle of the Minimum Wage." An amendment was carried to welcome this concession and to adjourn "to a further date so that further efforts may be made to bring about a satisfactory settlement." (*15.xi.1911.*)

The amendment was carried by 376,000 to 238,000 votes coming from five districts. South Wales was one of the minority.

At this point the Scots delegates intimated that they wished to move a further resolution. The South Wales delegates, all of them at once, strongly objected: it was not in order to move a resolution at that point: and as they heard the terms of the resolution they were all the more offended. However, the Chairman ruled that the resolution was in order and the discussion began. One after another the delegates from South Wales argued not so much against the Scottish proposals as a whole but against a phrase suggesting it could be done within the existing agreements. This, of course, was quite impossible for South Wales where they could not go ahead with the minimum wage demand within the ambit of the existing agreement. That agreement tied them hand and foot. Whereas the Scots took a legalistic point of view the Welsh were not going to be so trammelled up—and possibly prevented from having any effective result to all their activities. There was a storm in the conference.

There was one Scots delegate, David Gilmour, whose way of speaking had often made his hearers restive. Gilmour, unlike Robert Burns' "Holy Willie," was not specially sanctimonious: but censorious he undoubtedly was, in this going far beyond the habits of speech of the nonconformists south of the border. The two dozen and more Welsh delegates at these conferences clearly felt that they had had enough to put up with in the occasional obtuseness (as it seemed to them) of their English colleagues without having to endure advice from the Scots. So the Welsh socialists interrupted the Scottish socialists with a sort of nationalistic fervour, the agent from Aberdare breaking in on an argument by Bob Smillie with the shouted remark: "Mr. Gilmour has insulted Wales every time he has spoken." It reached the point that Enoch Edwards, M.P., had to speak from the chair saying: "I do not think this continual bickering between Wales and Scotland is going to help this movement . . . never mind either Wales or Scotland, but address yourself to the question before us." (*15.xi.1911.*) Smillie made concessions. The offending clauses were taken out: and the two-day debate concluded with an agreed resolution to negotiate nationally (but not to interfere with district negotiations) and to receive final reports on December 20th.

A few days before Christmas the delegates assembled at Caxton Hall, Westminster, where, after being upbraided by the chairman both for unpunctuality and for leakages to the press,[1] they learned that their resolution of November 15th had been completely ineffective. The Executive Committee had not been able to be in contact with the British coalowners, who the previous week had decided that "no good purpose can be served" by such a meeting. Then came the reports from the delegates. These were conclusive. In no district would the employers agree to an individual minimum wage. Vice-president Robert Smillie rose and drew the conclusion that the time for district negotiation had gone, and that negotiations in connection with the question must be taken on national lines, saying:

The owners have been humbugging us when they tell us they think no good can come out of a national meeting so long as local negotiations are going on. That seems to me to be an attempt to humbug us and blindfold us.

I say that the action of the employers is an insult to the Miners' Federation of Great Britain. We should make it clear that the mine owners are responsible for any crisis that arises, and not the miners or their leaders, who I think have done their best in this matter. (*20.xii.1911.*)

[1] "If you can tell me a man taking reports that are likely to find their way into the papers, as they did at the last conference here—if you will tell me I am going to name him, and he is going through that door.

"This is a private conference, and it is unfair for anybody else to supply reports as to what has taken place here. There are crowds of reporters, and of course they are paid to get information." (*20.xii.1911.*)

Conference, in a series of resolutions, decided on a strike ballot,[1] results to be available "not later than January 16, 1912." It was also moved by the Executive Committee "That in case the ballot results in favour of a national stoppage, notice be given in every district, so as to terminate by the end of February, 1912." An amendment of a two-thirds majority vote, was moved by Dr. John Wilson, M.P.

"That in case the ballot results in a two-thirds majority in favour of a national stoppage, notice be given in every district, so as to terminate at the end of February 1912." (*21.xii.1911.*)

It was strongly urged by Charles Fenwick, M.P. for Morpeth who in the 'nineties had been for a little while Secretary of the Trades Union Congress. Like Wilson he would have nothing to do with the Labour Party. These two as well as Steve Walsh, M.P., for the Lancashire and Cheshire Miners' Federation, gave sufficient reasons for the delegates (in spite of the opposition of Scotland and most of South Wales) to accept the amendment by 82 votes to 78.

Finally it was agreed to hold in four weeks time another national conference at which a report would be given by the M.F.G.B. Executive Committee on the tabulated statements which each district was asked to send in, showing "what is desired to be its minimum wage." Then delegates left for their Christmas holiday.

2. STRIKE NOTICES AND SCHEDULES

When the delegates, 160 in number, assembled amid hard weather at the New Central Hall, Birmingham, on the afternoon of Thursday, January 18, 1912, they heard from Thomas Ashton that the results of the ballot vote[2] had been 445,801 for and 115,921 against.

[1] Conference approved the ballot paper as drafted by the Committee:
MINERS' FEDERATION OF GREAT BRITAIN
BALLOT VOTE ON MINIMUM WAGE
Are you in favour of giving notice to establish the principle of an individual minimum wage for every man and boy working underground in every district in Great Britain?

[2] *Result of Ballot Vote on Minimum Wage*

District				For	Against
Yorkshire	..	..	..	63,736	10,477
Lancashire and Cheshire	..	..	50,517	11,393
Midland Federation		..	..	26,069	5,275
Derbyshire	..	..	..	17,999	6,816
Nottinghamshire	..	..	..	17,086	5,386
Leicestershire	..	..	..	3,681	907
South Derbyshire	..	..	..	2,178	593
North Wales ..	..	..	..	7,327	1,566
Cumberland ..	..	..	..	4,918	813
Bristol	..	..	..	1,084	342
Somerset	..	..	..	3,378	370
Scotland	..	..	..	60,611	12,035
South Wales ..	..	..	..	103,526	18,419
Northumberland	..	..	..	22,595	7,557
Durham	..	..	..	57,490	28,504
Cleveland	..	..	..	2,021	5,225
Forest of Dean	..	..	..	1,585	243
		Total	..	445,801	115,921

This ballot was decisive. It had shown not only the requisite majority of two-thirds that was now necessary but a nearly four to one majority, while some of the larger districts, such as South Wales, voted in a proportion of over 5 to 1. The support from the members of the Federation was even more massive than had been supposed.

The next business was the tabulation of the minimum wage for each district. South Wales was one that had set out the claim three months earlier, as Brace had reported to the November national conference. The S.W.M.F. Executive Council, meeting in Cardiff, in October had prepared, and sent on to their employers, a schedule of wages, as follows:

Minimum Wage (Monmouth and South Wales)

1. That the following rate of wages shall be fixed as minimum rates inclusive of fifty per cent above the standard rates of 1879, any increase in the percentages above fifty per cent to be added to these rates:

	per day	
	s.	d.
Colliers	8	0
Timber men and rippers	8	0
Assistant timber men and rippers	6	6
Underground blocklayers and road men	7	0
Hauliers, 18 years of age and above	7	0
Riders, ropemen, and traffic men 18 years of age and above	7	0
Hitchers	7	0
Banksmen	7	0
Assistant Banksmen	6	6
Tippers	5	6
Screenmen	5	0
Labourers	5	0

2. Wages of boys and others not provided for in the foregoing to be graded according to age and other conditions.

3. All workmen employed night or on the traffic shift to be paid at the rate of six turns for five nights worked, this payment to be made at the rate of a turn and one-fifth of a turn per shift worked.[1]

4. These rates not to interfere with any higher rates paid to any of the foregoing grades of workmen. (*23.x.1911.*)

Meantime the Executive Committee, after long and anxious meeting, studying the schedules of the rates sent in from each district, had not been able to formulate a resolution. In most cases an advance in wages was being sought. This was the crux. It was here that Davie Gilmour had been insisting that no advance should be incorporated

---

[1] Peculiar to South Wales was the following practice: "At the majority of the collieries the man who works nights and also the man who works in the afternoon (called the traffic shift) gets paid six turns for five shifts worked."

At a number of collieries this principle was not in operation and the demand was to have it uniform all over the coalfield. Secondly, as Brace said on November 10th, "Instead of taking the extra shift, we have divided it into five parts, and each shift to be paid at the rate of a turn and one fifth of a turn per shift worked."

in any claim to be put forward. Eventually the committee of nineteen men, amongst whom were six members of parliament, decided:

That this committee tabulate for each district separately the individual minimum wage for piece workers, such minimum to be as near as can be ascertained the present rate of wages. (*18.i.1912.*)

but this decision they decided not to put to the conference. It was not any easy matter: it was not without much heart-searching that the minority inside the Executive Committee were overruled or won over to reduce their claims to the extent suggested by the majority.

Meantime in the conference on behalf of the committee a resolution was moved

That an intimation be made to the employers that the workmen's representatives are prepared to meet them to continue negotiations in districts, and nationally with a view to arriving at a satisfactory settlement. (*19.i.1912.*)

When this resolution was read out it caused a feeling of dismay: protests were voiced. Foremost among the protesters were William Brace, M.P., Tom Richards, M.P., and Alfred Onions, the three from Wales who in the autumn had been knocked off the National Executive Committee. "The Committee," complained Tom Richards, "has simply evaded their responsibilities"; to which a delegate from Yorkshire unkindly retorted: "They said the same thing when you were on the Committee." At length the chairman, nettled by the critical remarks ("Mr. Richards has said we were seeking to evade something: I do not care to be charged that I am evading anything: Mr. Richards had had a long experience of the Committee, and I think he might have spared some of us that expression"), rose to explain why the Committee had not tabled a definitive resolution. Some districts held that the minimum rate might mean (or even should mean) an advance in wages—which they "were justly entitled to ask." Others, the Scots being the most vocal among them, held they were not entitled to ask for an advance in wages. The Committee, Enoch Edwards claimed, had not been evading the issue but had been busy trying to reconcile these two interests. This did not satisfy all the delegates, though it silenced the ex-members of the Committee. An amendment simply for adjournment was moved but then a shrewd and short reply to the discussion was made by Alderman William House of Durham who said:

We have a great public to deal with outside, and if we can show negotiations on this great question have been abruptly terminated by the owners and we can put the onus on the owners, that is surely a sufficient policy in itself: it is logical and business-like tactics, and added that no terms could be settled in any district until the whole of the settlements had gone before a conference of the Federation. Thereafter the amendment was defeated by 133 votes to 15: and the resolution was carried. Four weeks later, when the delegates assembled in Westminster on Thursday, February 1st, their first business was an emergency resolution, which had a bearing upon the troubles of the past year in South Wales: it was unanimously agreed

That this conference strongly urges upon the Home Secretary to take into his consideration the sentence passed upon the miners at the late Cardiff Assizes, with a view to obtaining their early release. (*1.ii.1912.*)

Thereafter Enoch Edwards, M.P., told the delegates that the schedules sent in from districts were so varied, and involved so many intricate changes and increase of rates, that the Committee "have had to find a solution on other lines." There had been no unanimity upon how to interpret the Southport resolution on which they were charged to act. "Of course" said Edwards "no one disputes, I think, at a crisis like this, that the Committee and this conference would be entitled to overhaul the list sent in from a district which sought a considerable increase upon their rates." So, after some further expositions, he read the following resolution agreed to by the Committee.

That in accordance with the resolutions agreed upon at the last meeting of this Committee, held in Birmingham, and based upon the resolution passed at a conference, held in London, on November 15th last, the following claims be formulated for an individual minimum wage in each district for piece workers.

The claims from seventeen districts varied from 7s. 6d. (for Yorkshire and Nottinghamshire) to 7s. for Lancashire, 6s. for Scotland, down to the low rate, 4s. 6½d., for Bristol and Somerset. South Wales was set down at from 7s. 1½d. to 7s. 6d.

To this resolution an amendment was moved by W. Brace, M.P., seconded by Tom Richards, M.P., "to adjourn the final vote upon the respective schedules for each district to a date to be fixed by the officials so as to give an opportunity to delegates to report to their districts and receive their instructions thereon." (*2.ii.1912.*) The amendment was defeated by 101 votes to 37.

What was the cause of this amendment and this division? First, in the M.F.G.B. committee meetings of the last three days of January, the South Wales representatives had contended that the schedules should not be revised. But the decision went against them, as the majority felt that the minimum wage demand should not be mixed up with an attempt to secure an advance in wages. So, as we have seen, the South Wales figure was reduced from 8s. to between

7s. 1½d. and 7s. 6d. per day. Secondly, the thirty-one South Wales delegates, apprised of this at their meeting in London, instructed Brace and Richards (who were no longer on the national committee) to move the above-quoted amendment on February 2nd with the result given above. It was a set-back to all their hopes, and particularly to Noah Ablett who had tacked on the wage advance as part and parcel of his revolutionary policy. The South Wales Council were anything but pleased: and at their meeting the next week resolved:

That we deplore the action of the Miners' Federation of Great Britain in reducing our schedule of rates, and no further revision should take place without first consulting the workmen; and, further, that no final agreement be entered into without being ratified by a ballot of the workmen. (*6.ii.1912*.)

3. THE CONFRONTATION

Once more there was a meeting in London, this time a national joint conference of coal owners' and miners' representatives in Westminster. There Enoch Edwards, M.P., put forward to the assembled representatives of the coal owners the proposal for a minimum wage, and all the details connected with the application. There was no excuse, he maintained, for a man going home without his money after working a whole day in the pit: and he said that "the time has come when, as in all conceivable trades, we should in some way or other have a fixed bottom." (*7.ii.1912*.) In answer to questions Enoch Edwards said: "I admit at once frankly there are no agreements for a fixed minimum wage: and to that extent it may be suggested that we are treating the agreements with scant courtesy." Presently the coal owners' chairman asked the 36 miners' representatives (the Executive Committee, plus seventeen additional representatives) to retire as the coal owners were the more numerous body. Indeed it was in much the same proportion as at the previous meeting on September 29th when there were 46 coal owners present, among them six from South Wales, namely:

F. L. Davis	D. A. Thomas
Thomas Griffiths	T. H. Deacon
Evan Williams	W. Gascoyne Dalziel

When, after three-quarters of an hour, the joint meeting resumed, the owners' chairman said: "at this resumed conference, I am sorry to say, we have not the representatives from South Wales present with us. They felt so strongly with reference to the remarks passed as to existing agreements that they were forced to withdraw from our meeting, and they have since sent in the following statement which they wish put upon our proceedings":

Mr. Edwards stated that there are no agreements for a fixed minimum wage, and that to that extent the workmen's representatives are rather treating the existing agreements with scant courtesy. He further intimated that while the workmen's representatives would be prepared to accept any suggestions, the acceptance of this minimum wage is the point upon which the workmen will cease work until it is conceded. This being an intimation of the men's intention to tear up existing agreements, the South Wales coal owners are unable to take any further part in the proceedings. (*7.ii.1912*.)

Enoch Edwards placably replied, saying that he would be very sorry "if any observation of mine has led to the withdrawal of South Wales," for he would not wish to say anything "that would add to the strained relations between the interests in South Wales, and it is far from me to do anything at all in that direction."

There were then further retirals, first by the owners and then by the miners' representatives, who tabled their reply as follows:

That we express our regret the coal owners have refused to accept the principle of an individual minimum wage for all men and boys employed underground, as we know there can be no settlement of the present dispute unless this principle is agreed to. In view of the fact, however, that we have no desire for a serious rupture in the coal trade of the country, we are willing to meet the coal owners at any time to further discuss the matter, if the coal owners express a desire to do so. (*7.ii.1912*.)

The joint conference ended amid expressions of mutual goodwill which were joined in the more easily as the six gentlemen from South Wales were no longer there.

Three weeks of February elapsed, during which time notices were running out. A strike was approaching of a magnitude hitherto unknown in British history. Previous lockouts or strikes had affected only a section of British industry. But if all the miners in the United Kingdom were no longer to go down each day into darkness and there win the essential daily fuel, then the effects would not only be on a greater scale than anything hitherto, but of an entirely different kind. Nearly all the inanimate sources of energy in Britain, such as waterwheels, or windmills, had long been superseded by the steam engine. Coal had no rivals except in transport: and even there, apart from recently introduced fuel oil in some oceanic liners and warships, it was only a matter of coastwise sailing vessels and horsedrawn barges on the waterways. On the unimproved roadways, horse-carriages and waggons were still far more frequent than the dust-smothered petrol-driven automobiles. In these circumstances of the first years of the twentieth century a coal stoppage meant a creeping paralysis of the whole of the industrial life of Great Britain. This was widely appreciated, both at home and abroad.

As far as the continent of Europe was concerned, the first sign of an understanding of the effect of such a stoppage was a meeting in

Westminster on February 21st and 22nd of the Committee of the International Miners' Federation. After an explanation of the dispute by vice-president Robert Smillie, Thomas Ashton outlined policy for "the continental delegates," who were not to be asked to come out "in a sympathetic strike" but who could best help by "keeping their coal out of every part of the island." "Not one pound of their coal," said Ashton, "should come into any part of Great Britain or go to any of the British markets abroad." He concluded that, if they worked one day less per week, that "would go a long way towards assisting us." Thereafter a resolution passed by the international committee recommended that during the strike in Great Britain "the miners on the Continent curtail the output of coal as far as possible." (*22.ii.1912.*)

4. THE GOVERNMENT INTERVENES

Meantime an invitation came from the Prime Minister "to meet me and some of my colleagues" on February 22nd, in order to find "some means of averting the disaster of a national stoppage." On the date appointed the four officials of the Miners' Federation of Great Britain went to the Foreign Office where they were met by Prime Minister Asquith, Foreign Secretary Sir Edward Grey, Chancellor of the Exchequer Lloyd George, and the President of the Board of Trade Sidney Buxton. The leading members of the Government were told of the grievances of the miners, and of how these might be remedied. But there was no discussion: for only the full Committee and conference were empowered to do this. Thereupon the Prime Minister extended his invitation not only to the twenty members of the Executive Committee but also to the 150 delegates who would be attending the special conference called for Tuesday, February 27th.

Public interest was now fully aroused. The coalfields had ceased to be remote. Scores of letters were sent to the Federation officers. One was from the Lord Mayor of London, who had been meeting Lord Mayors and Lord Provosts and other civic heads. Others came from ministers of religion, praying that some way might be found to avert the coming strike and all its consequences. By Monday, February 26th, it was clear that the Prime Minister and his leading colleagues, meeting the mine-owners over the weekend, had encountered difficulties in that quarter. Alarm was manifested in parliament, and questions were asked that day in the House of Commons.

The next day the activity of the newspaper press, as a whole very hostile to the miners, was considerably stepped up. In the van was

The Times which a quarter of a century earlier had gained itself lasting notoriety by the forgeries in its articles on "Parnellism and Crime" which sought to link the Irish Nationalist Party with criminal conspiracies. On this occasion *The Times* set itself to show that the aim of socialist revolution lay behind the policy of the miners. This object it sought to achieve by extensive quotations not from handwritten letters (as happened in 1887 with their Piggott forgeries) but from the printed text of a pamphlet issued a little while before by propagandists in the Rhondda Valley and called *The Miners' Next Step*. It was in the Rhondda in the late autumn of 1910 that Tom Mann had been carrying on his "syndicalist" agitation: and the word "syndicalism" was now widely sown in the British newspaper press which soon treated it as a "bad" word. The harvest of these dragons' teeth was later to be reaped by members of parliament as well as by union leaders and Labour Party chiefs.

On this Tuesday, February 27th, however, there was as yet no sign of such a harvest. The Prime Minister did not seem to be aware that he was confronted by a revolutionary conspiracy: and persisted in treating the matter simply as an extensive industrial dispute— as indeed it was. For when the scores of delegates came at noon that day from the special conference at the Westminster Palace Hotel to the Foreign Office in Downing Street, Premier Asquith treated their basic demand as just in principle and consistent "with the best interests of the community."

All this was very pleasant news for the assembled century and a half of delegates, who rejoiced when Asquith said: "We do not intend that the resistance of what I hope is a dwindling minority, but what at this moment is obviously a minority of the employers of labour, should indefinitely delay the attainment of an object which we believe you have properly put before yourselves and which we have satisfied ourselves is consistent with justice and with the best interests of the community". (*27.ii.1912.*) They were further gratified when the Prime Minister added that "one of the most satisfactory features" of the whole of the dispute "consisted in this that it was an unselfish demand on the part of the great bulk of the miners," most of whom were already getting more than the minimum wage. But once these things had been said, the Prime Minister in the remainder of his speech sought to persuade the miners to alter their claims for an individual minimum wage in each of seventeen districts. On this matter, he asked again and again, could there not be "a reasonable latitude of discussion and consideration?" His audience were impressed by the skill with which he had marshalled his arguments and brought them to bear on the case. After all, he was the esteemed leader of the Liberal Party to which most of those

present had belonged for many years. But the delegates, though
impressed, were not won over. When, next day, they heard from the
lips of the chairman the four propositions[1] made by the Government
for the purpose of a settlement they discussed the matter and then
carried the following resolution unanimously:

> That we agree to reaffirm the resolution passed on the 7th instant in this
> hotel by the Executive Committee and the seventeen additional re-
> presentatives from districts and we repeat that there can be no settlement
> of the present dispute unless the principle of an individual wage for all
> men and boys employed underground is agreed to by the colliery owners.
> We are still willing to meet the colliery owners at any time they desire
> to discuss the minimum wage rates of each district as agreed upon at a
> special conference of this Federation. (*28.ii.1912.*)

These last days of February from Tuesday, 27th, to Thursday,
29th, were full of meetings, discussions, conferences, questions in
the House of Commons, answers in the House of Commons, all
against the background of feverish and not always well informed
press comment. On Tuesday, February 27th the delegates heard the
address of Mr. Asquith. The next day they discussed it and gave
power to the Executive to continue further explanations and,
within limits set by the conference and the preceding ballot vote,
to conduct negotiations.

When the four propositions were put to the employers the reception varied from district to district. The great majority in districts of
the English Conciliation Board had proved amenable to the reason-
ing of the three leading members of the British Cabinet,[2] and
accepted the four propositions. The Durham owners grudgingly
accepted. The owners in Northumberland turned the proposals
down by a majority but changed their mind the next day. There
was some ambiguity in the Scottish owners' resolutions but Scotland
was regarded as having entered a refusal. There was no ambiguity
at all in the case of South Wales, whose representatives had stormed
out of the joint meeting of owners and trade unionists on February
7th. They resolved that:

[1]. His Majesty's Government are satisfied after careful consideration that there are
cases in which underground employees cannot earn a reasonable minimum wage from
causes over which they have no control.

2. They are further satisfied that the power to earn such a wage should be secured by
arrangements suitable to the special circumstances of each district. Adequate safeguards
to be provided to protect the employers against abuse.

3. His Majesty's Government are prepared to confer with the parties as to the best
method of giving practical effect to these conclusions, by means of district conferences
between the parties, a representative appointed by the Government being present.

4. In the event of any of the conferences failing to arrive at a complete settlement within
a reasonable time the representatives appointed by His Majesty's Government to decide
jointly any outstanding points for the purpose of giving effect in that district to the above
principles. (*27.ii.1912.*)

[2] See Chapter IV of *The Miners: Years of Struggle* by R. Page Arnot.

The coal owners of South Wales adhere strictly to their present agree-ment, which terminates by notice at the earliest date on March 31, 1916. After most careful consideration they are unanimous in stating that they cannot agree to the Government's proposals. (*29.ii.1912.*)

This was the situation that confronted the miners' conference on the last day of February. Enoch Edwards, dealing with the attitude of the various groups of owners, said:

I do not think that it is a piece of astonishing news to this conference that South Wales has absolutely refused, they have been refusing all along:

and, with some bitterness, added:

I think all the correspondence, all the arguments, and all the state-ments, in opposition to the course we are taking comes very largely from people who are very fortunate in their collieries, and who have, in their lifetime or their father's, been very little removed from the days of clogs, and that these are the people who have shown the most bitter hostility to our general application for a minimum wage. (*29.ii.1912.*)

Then after discussion the conference of 150 delegates carried unanimously a resolution as follows:

That the Conference maintain the position taken up from the first, viz. that no terms can be accepted unless they include the schedule of rates for each district for an individual minimum wage as already laid before the coal owners of the United Kingdom, also the Prime Minister. (*29.ii.1912.*)

Having thus decided to stick to their guns the conference delegates went to the Foreign Office and at 3 o'clock heard a second address by the Prime Minister. The miners' chairman, like others, was very impressed by the manner and the whole behaviour of the Prime Minister. But in one phrase of the Prime Minister, several delegates had detected a possible snag, when he said that ministers would fight for the scheduled rates—provided they could "satisfy themselves upon the soundness of these figures." The chairman, back at the resumed conference at 4 o'clock that afternoon, said: "Well now, you have heard the speech from the Prime Minister. I can quite believe lots of men will remember that speech for many days to come. It has certainly marked a turning point upon industrial questions, an important turning point, after all our efforts to secure a minimum wage and after we found ourselves in a complete block with a certain class of the community because they refused to listen. I suppose that South Wales has not come along because they have refused up to now to have anything to do with the minimum. Well, the Prime Minister, if they can satisfy themselves on these figures, has given an undertaking that they intend to force them."

The conference adjourned: and when it met again that evening was informed by Enoch Edwards of the intervening discussions, in which he had repeated again to the Cabinet quartet that "we are bound by the resolutions here to those rates" and concluded: "We have made it clear to them that we cannot be a party to going before the employers to prove these rates if the final judgement is to be left in the hands of somebody else, with power to decide these rates against us." (*29.ii.1912.*)

In these last hours of February the efforts of the Government to avert the stoppage failed. The next day dawned, the conference assembled and then dispersed to their districts leaving matters in the hands of the Committee in the following terms:

That the matter be relegated to the Executive Committee to continue any further negotiations that may be advisable and with full authority to call a conference together whenever necessary. (*1.iii.1912.*)

That afternoon of Friday, March 1st as the wheels ceased to turn in the coalfields of Britain the Prime Minister informed the House of Commons that the Government's proposals had been declined both by a section of the coal owners and by the miners. It was deadlock in the negotiations. It was a complete stoppage in the coalfields.

K

CHAPTER TEN

THE GREAT STRIKE OF 1912

1. THE LIBERAL DILEMMA

ON Friday, March 1st, the majority of the miners of Great Britain came out on strike. The number was somewhere near a million. The Home Office gave the figures of the number employed as at December 31, 1911: 878,759 underground workers, and 210,331 surface workers, making a total of 1,089,090. Apart from "safety men" whose continued employment had been sanctioned by conference resolution no miners were at work. No coal was being hewn, no coal was being wound to the surface. Such a thing had never happened before throughout the seven centuries of the coal trade. Indeed, the strike was of a magnitude that had never occurred in any single industry in any country of the world. It was a situation unparalleled, unprecedented and without any motivation of the kind which in past years would have given the excuse for a Government to use measures of coercion in order to avert it.

Indeed, the Liberal Government were in a considerable quandary. The newspapers, headed by the threepenny *Times*, followed by the halfpenny *Daily Mail*, were alleging an almost treasonable conspiracy against the established order. In somewhat more polished language this was also being put forward in the House of Commons by hereditary legislators such as the Cecils. But however welcome such explanations might be to intransigent coal owners and to the sensationmongers in the newspaper press (as well of course as to the vocal circles of the older universities, remote from a real acquaintance with the life of the working people and always prone to nurse abstractions), nevertheless the Cabinet could not adopt this. The nature of their quandary was quite different. They did not want to take active steps upon a path that might lead towards an ultimate nationalisation of coalmines. On the other hand they knew well from personal experience that to yield to the more intractable sections of the coalowners would bring them a harvest of further troubles.

Asquith had also a particular series of considerations to bear in mind as to the position in the House of Commons. The General Election of December 1910 had left the two main parties evenly balanced. Consequently the Liberal Cabinet of 1911 onwards had to rely on receiving the votes of the Labour Party (now two score in number) and the Irish Nationalist Party which was twice as large. The Irish Nationalists supported the Liberal Cabinet on the understanding that sooner or later the administration would bring in a measure of Home Rule for Ireland: but this did not mean that the Nationalist members had anything like the same social outlook as the trade unionists of the Labour Party. Whatever kindliness Asquith and his chief colleagues Edward Grey and Lloyd George might feel towards these humbler members of their party in the Commons who had for years been somewhat opprobriously termed the "Lib-Labs" (and now for the most part were in the ranks of the Labour Party) and however this might be reciprocated, no undue strain must be put upon it. True, there were some amongst his audience of 170 delegates at the Foreign Office who were still steadfast in their adherence to the Liberal Party. Indeed, as he surveyed the delegates he could recognise many more who had been in the Liberal ranks and had duly accepted the Liberal Whip for several years. Amongst those were the mining members from Wales.

There was, however, another side to it. From the middle of February onwards the Government had been in touch with leading coal owners. Here, too, a party question was bound to enter in. In the composition of the Liberal Party from its formation in 1852, sixty years earlier, up to 1912 there had been, apart from Liberal principles, a certain apportioning as it were of party sympathies with particular interests. For example, it was believed that the main body of the landed gentry as well as the whole of the liquor trade, would never support any party other than the Conservatives. Similarly, shipping interests were in the main taken to be Liberal. It was believed that the City of London was traditionally Tory, at any rate ever since mid-Victorian times: but this was not entirely true. The change to free trade by Sir Robert Peel in the 'forties of the nineteenth century had been so fully accepted by many of the banks as well as by discount houses and merchant bankers as to bring with it steady adherence of some leading bankers and financiers to the Liberal Party—though the greater majority of lesser City interests were traditionally and indeed fanatically Tory.

Some industries were divided. In coalmining, representatives of the newer and more advanced capital investments were often staunch Liberals, as opposed to the older landed interests which took part in mining, such as those of the Marquess of Londonderry, or the Marquess of Bute.

The Prime Minister had been long enough in parliament to know how much both party allegiances and party funds depended on support to Liberalism from modern coal owners. Amongst these was

D. A. Thomas, who was one of the largest coal owners and one of those most bitterly opposed to any legislation that seemed to him or to his colleagues to interfere with the smooth and profitable development of their industry.

Religious, or rather, ecclesiastical interests were also sharply divided. However many bishops with a Liberal tendency might be appointed by the Prime Minister, those could not in the seven years since 1905 affect the ingrained conservatism of the vast majority of the Anglican clergy, whose influence on the side of the Tories was fully predictable. Equally, the influence of Dissent, gathered in a dozen different churches, was cast in the main on the Liberal side. In Scotland the established Presbyterian Church tended to give its support to the Conservatives while the dissenting Presbyterians, together of course with the Methodists, Independents and Quakers, were staunch supporters of Liberalism.

This was even more the case in Wales where the established church was the Church of England, the Anglican confession, and where the overwhelming majority of the population in the late eighteenth and throughout the nineteenth century had shown themselves to be firm adherents of the Chapel, that is, the nonconformist or dissenting bodies such as Independents, Baptists, Methodists of four kinds, Salvationists and many others.

Besides these there were the adherents of Catholicism, growing in number in each part of the island, and on the whole appearing, so far as the facts are known, to take a standpoint according to their class position in society. The "old Catholics" tended to be Conservative, as did also well-to-do Catholics and professional men and women of that faith: while the wage-earners, certainly in the coalfields, tended to have either a Liberal or a Labour outlook. In South Wales the adherents of the Church of England and of the Roman Catholic Church were relatively few in number: while most miners were or had been supporters of one or other of the dozen nonconformist bodies and sects.

There was, however, still another consideration. This was the faithful support of the Liberal Party that came from nationalist as well as religious feeling in South Wales and often seemed to cut across class divisions. With all these considerations there was a pretty kettle of fish for the Liberal Cabinet and the three chief Ministers.

There was, however, one final consideration. Asquith might be willing in his administration from 1908 onwards to adopt welfare legislation as urged and carried through by his more advanced colleagues such as Lloyd George (and Lloyd George's then very radical lieutenant Winston Churchill) but he would never agree to anything which seemed to imperil the existing framework of society or the undisputed private ownership and control of the staple trades of the country.

For all these reasons it may be understood how in spite of his eloquence Asquith was unable to convince the miners to adopt the standpoint which the overwhelming majority of the mineowners now shared with him. One who was closely in touch with events at that time recounted to the author some fifty years ago how Enoch Edwards, brought up in the Liberal tradition and all his life (until his Union had voted to join the Labour Representation Committee) an adherent of the Liberal Party, looked on and listened almost adoringly while his former revered leader urged "the four principles" of the Liberal Cabinet. Nevertheless each time, unweariedly, Enoch Edwards, when it came to his turn to reply, would simply pull out of his coat pocket a sheet of paper and say how much he was affected by what the Prime Minister had said but that for his part he must adhere to the following figures which he would then proceed once more to recount.

2. IN THE HOUSE OF COMMONS

Within less than a week the effects of the strike began to make themselves felt. The chief railways, with the exception of the Great Eastern, began measures to suspend express trains and to curtail their services. The price of coal began to rise considerably: and soon to such an extent that a debate on coal prices was initiated in parliament. But there was as yet no general debate on the strike itself. At the close of parliamentary questions on Monday, March 4th, the Prime Minister lucidly set forth what had happened after the Government had decided that it had a duty to intervene, and the outcome of their intervention in the four propositions already disclosed to Parliament six days earlier. These proposals had now been accepted by some 65 per cent of the owners but not by the coal-owners of Scotland or of South Wales. The propositions had also commended themselves to the miners' representatives who, however, insisted that acceptance of the principle of a minimum wage varying from district to district was not enough but that the actual figures (the irreducible minima set forth in the M.F.G.B. resolutions of February 2nd) should also be accepted. This was their reservation.

Asquith then told the Commons of his second address to the 170 delegates at the Foreign Office on Thursday, February 29th (published in the press on Friday, March 1st) and waxed indignant at the allegations in some newspapers that he had conceded the principle of a minimum wage for all industries. "I am not in the habit," he said, "of engaging in sly flirtations of this kind with socialism and then trying to conceal from the public the manner in which I have been employing my time." Asquith explained that the Government had not thought it possible to coerce the coalowners "to accept, not merely the principle, but the very figures which had been dictated by the men without inquiry, without negotiation, without any machinery for arriving at an equitable determination." He had put that argument to the men, and out of all the many cases he had had to present in the course of his life "it has never been my good fortune to present a case which seemed to me so irresistible from the point of reason, justice, and common sense. And as I watched these men, the very flower of the mining industry of this country, while I was speaking—I was over-sanguine—I flattered myself, and I think some of my right hon. friends shared my opinion, that I had almost persuaded them. Well, I did not." (*4.iii.1912.*)

So the negotiations had come not to a breakdown but to a deadlock. The leader of the Conservative opposition at once said they would do nothing to embarrass the Government and disclaimed any desire for a discussion from which "no possible good could be gained." This did not prevent a number of his followers from raising very provocative questions day after day in March. Some of them kept asking questions, such as whether there had not been prevention of blacklegging at this or that mine, whether there had been assaults on policemen who protected them, whether the Government would please enforce law and order and so forth. To such as these the Home Secretary made reply that, "considering the extent and magnitude of the strike, it is remarkable how few and insignificant have been the disturbances accompanying it. Perhaps I may be allowed to take this opportunity of recognising the assistance which the leaders of the miners have rendered by their speeches and influence in the maintenance of law and order." (*18.iii.1912.*)

But while the Home Secretary kept pouring oil on troubled waters and giving smooth answers that suggested an absence of repressive measures (about which there had been more than enough publicity in the case of the suffragettes) actually the officials of the Home Office were in process of preparing drastic steps. They were in close touch with the chief constables who the previous autumn had received messages from the Home Office about the strengthening of their forces including enrolment of special constables in view of any impending strike. In addition there were the law officers of the Crown, of whom the senior at this time was Attorney-General Sir Rufus Isaacs, who afterwards jumped from the post of Lord Chief Justice to become Viceroy of India where he was noted for his repressive measures. Whatever the Home Secretary might choose to say in answer to parliamentary questions, it was clear that the machinery was ready to be set in motion to take any repressive measures that might be thought necessary or desirable. The movement of troops into the coalfields was contemplated, and here the first measure of repression was prepared. This took the form of a series of arrests and state prosecutions.

This in turn caused considerable disquietude amongst socialists (including the half-dozen socialists in the two-score strong parliamentary Labour Party) and still more in the small Radical wing of the Liberal Party. It was one of these last, Josiah Wedgwood, member for Stoke-upon-Trent, who first raised the matter. Vigilant for "the freedom of the press," Josiah Wedgwood asked about proceedings that were being taken against newspapers and their printers and others responsible for distributing an appeal to soldiers not to shoot down men on strike.

To this, as well as to questions put by George Lansbury, the Attorney-General sought refuge behind "the public interest" from the responsibility of giving a direct answer. But the members of parliament felt this to be an evasion and were pertinacious enough with their questions. They dragged the required information bit by bit out of the ministers responsible, until at length the prosecutions culminated in the arrest and trial of Tom Mann, who had been in the van of revolutionary trade union agitations, not only in Clydach Vale and Tonypandy on November 7, 1910, but in the transport and railways wage disputes of summer 1911. To many at the time it seemed clear that by gaoling Tom Mann (for twenty-five years one of the best known socialist leaders in Britain and in Europe), the Government hoped to strike terror into the rank-and-file of the miners' associations.

If the Members of the House of Commons were content to leave the issues of the coal strike in the hands of the Government, it was not the attitude of the newspaper press. The metropolitan and the provincial papers in England as well as the Scottish and Welsh press were in general quite unrestrained in their hostility to the strike: but it was from the largely trustified press of London's Fleet Street, where the Harmsworth family held so much from the *Daily Mail* and its pup the *Evening News* upwards to the recently acquired majority ownership of *The Times*, that there came the most venomous attacks on the miners. The reports in the news columns were often found to be unsubstantiated, while baseless local rumours were picked up and spread in a million-fold circulation. The sensationalism which had been very much on the increase since the beginning of the century was given free rein. By the end of the first seven days of March the members of the M.F.G.B. Executive Committee felt themselves compelled to utter a protest on the reports that had appeared, particularly "in the London news-papers."

They expressed strongly "their indignation at a certain portion of the Press," which they accused of "deliberately misleading" the public. After refuting several false allegations, they spoke of the ill effect that could result from "many false statements" that were being circulated. In particular they spoke of "the absolute unanimity amongst the members of the Miners' Executive" and described the attempt to suggest to the public and the miners' that it was otherwise as "a disgrace to journalism."

3. GOVERNMENT RESUMES MEDIATION

After the prolonged efforts in the last week of February by the Prime Minister and his three chief colleagues, the Government seemed for the best part of a week to be resting on their oars. But on Thursday, March 7th, they resumed direct negotiations with the M.F.G.B. Executive Committee. The Premier asked them in Downing Street if there was any change. Did the Federation still stand to an irreducible minimum? Enoch Edwards replied that there could be no interference with the rates submitted, which are considered to be the rates that a collier would be working at, if he were getting coal by daywage. When ministers asked if the actual daywage rate could be accepted as a principle, Vernon Hartshorn replied that a number of their old price lists were obsolete, and the managers ignored them and paid much higher rates. The Premier said that those rates would be paper rates only. Hartshorn then said that generally the rate in South Wales was 7s. 1½d. but there were some 7s. 6d. After this there was again a pause until new proposals requiring the summoning of the miners' national conference were brought forward. When the thirty-six from South Wales joined their fellow delegates in Westminster, it was in a palatial chamber of the Foreign Office "very freely offered" when no room was found for them in their customary inn. There they learned that on the previous Friday the Prime Minister had handed over a written invitation for a joint discussion with the coal owners. This was a matter for a special conference to decide: and that was why it had been summoned. With complete unanimity the conference decided:

That we recommend

the conference to accept the invitation of His Majesty's Government to meet them with the colliery owners jointly in conference without prejudice, with a view to a free discussion of the whole situation, with the understanding that the principle of the minimum wage is excluded from the discussion. (*11.iii.1912.*)

Under the chairmanship of the Prime Minister the joint meeting of the owners' and the miners' committee began next day and went on for two more days.

The conference, reassembled on Wednesday, March 13th, learned that "there is no evidence forthcoming that they are prepared to accept our terms as yet." This was the report from Enoch Edwards who at the end of the joint meeting had been informed by Fred L. Davis and other coalowners from South Wales ("and they were very emphatic about it") that what we were seeking to do was "simply to bring 75 per cent of their collieries into bankruptcy." Enoch could not refrain from exhibiting to the delegates his scepticism when told "by the chairman of a conciliation board" that 75 per cent of "these immensely wealthy firms are going to smash up if they accept our claims."

But there was also a question from the Prime Minister: whether, if three of the miners' five claims were agreed to, the miners would go back to work, leaving two to be settled afterwards. This hypothetical sort of questioning was not to the liking of the committee who felt that they could not promise to advise a resumption of work until there was a definite settlement.

Tom Richards, M.P., for the past six months no longer a member of the Executive Committee on which he had sat for over seven years, was now on occasion likely to be a formidable critic. On the resolution which had been elaborated the night before by the Committee and was in the hands of delegates, Tom Richards made some characteristic remarks. The resolution ran:

> That we express regret that the mine owners have not shown any disposition to concede the rates of wages claimed by the workmen, and this Conference cannot advise a resumption of work until a minimum wage is agreed to for the various grades of underground workers. We are, however, willing to enter into negotiations at once with the mine owners in the various districts for the purpose of securing a settlement of all points of dispute, at the earliest possible moment. (*13.iii.1912.*)

Tom Richards commented:

I am not going to move the resolution, or say anything against it. There can be no harm in eliciting, so far as we can, information in order that we can understand exactly where we are.

First of all, I understand the position of the Prime Minister is, in putting these questions, whether he has a right to do this as pointed out by the Vice-President or not. We must always remember we are the aggressors in this matter, and questions must be put to us rather than to the other side. We are fighting the employers on this occasion, we are the aggressive force because we have a grievance, and we are trying to get it remedied.

The Prime Minister is asking us if our schedule of rates for colliers or
K*

hewers is accepted; if the 5s. minimum for datallers is accepted by the owners; if the 2s. minimum for boys starting is accepted by the owners; are we prepared upon that acceptance to recommend a resumption of work whilst the other matters which we ourselves agree are somewhat complicated, are attempted to be arranged by districts?

If these three things are agreed to, the question seems plain and simple. If these things are agreed to, are you prepared to resume work while you try to settle up the other matters in dispute? What is your reply to that? We do not attempt to reply to that question in the resolution, we simply stand where we were. We simply say, no, our demands, whole demands before we go back to work, that is the position, let us understand it now. Personally I say again that so far as manœuvring for position it appears to me to be a worse thing every time that a body of men could do.

James Winstone, agent for the Eastern Valleys of Monmouthshire, at once disagreed "with my friend Mr. Richards" and rallied to the defence of the Executive Committee on which Barker, Hartshorn and Stanton now held the three South Wales seats. "Personally," he said, "I have absolute confidence in the wisdom of the Executive Committee, I have not the slightest hesitation in declaring that I stand by their integrity and I believe that they have done this morning the wisest possible thing in the interest of the men whom we have the honour to represent, and I do sincerely hope their recommendations will be carried without a solitary dissentient."

Thereafter the Committee, armed with the resolution, which was carried unanimously, went off to meet the owners again. While these negotiations were going on, the conference met in the late afternoon and in the evening, only to adjourn on each occasion.

6. A CRUCIAL DAY

On opening the conference on Thursday, March 14th, Enoch Edwards, M.P. said:

Yesterday we were asked, not for the first time, to explain upon what principle the rates we are asking for in our Number One Schedule are based. How were they ascertained? Why the rates should vary from 7s. 6d. to 4s. 11d. according to districts? And what reasons could we give for this difference in rates, and how has it been ascertained?

The Prime Minister is anxious to get a clear distinct understanding for himself, how we have arrived at them.

Particular collieries had come up in the discussion which had lasted a very long time. At the end Asquith had made the following suggestions:

1. That a neutral person be present in the event of local negotiations simply to assist discussion.
2. That there should be some provision if there were a deadlock in such negotiations for someone with power to decide.

3. The need to split up the next day into sub-committees so that knotty points could be discussed by those who had special knowledge of them.

After discussion the conference passed two resolutions in one of which they left present matters in the hands of their national committee. The other dealt with the possibility of local negotiations.

Delegates were particularly anxious not to accord any power or arbitration to the proposed "neutral person": but, once satisfied on this, they carried the resolution unanimously but for one single vote, as follows:

That at meetings to be held in the districts to consider the points provided for in Resolutions 3 and 4, we agree to the proposal of the Prime Minister that some neutral person might attend to help to guide the discussion to facilitate an agreement. (*14.iii.1912.*)

Thereafter on points of order statements were made with reference to earlier remarks by Enoch Edwards. From South Wales, Tom Richards, M.P., referred to the statement that "75 per cent of the pits in South Wales would be closed if these minimum wages were conceded." He went on:

In order that the Committee may not be frightened by this statement (no doubt it is made to have a prejudicial effect) I may say we have some small properties like any other coalfield but let me point out I was going through some figures yesterday and there are 28 firms in South Wales employing 100,000 men for the last 10 or 12 years, who have had the whole of their capital returned. The average dividend has been enormous, therefore, I do not think you need be afraid of closing the South Wales coalfield. (*14.iii.1912.*)

That Thursday afternoon the Prime Minister and his chief colleagues had a separate meeting with the coalowners' consultative committee. Then came the miners' representatives. The coal owners had just left the room: and it was clear that negotiations were at an end. The Government had decided to bring in their Bill, which would contain the stipulations for district settlements and for arbitration which he had in vain sought to wring out of the M.F.G.B. Executive Committee and the conference delegates.

When at ten o'clock in the morning of Friday, March 15th, the conference resumed, the chairman told how pressing Asquith had been upon the questions of determination of issues by districts and finally by arbitration. Were they prepared, if there was failure to agree to have "some neutral person to decide for us?" George Barker added:

Before we left the Prime Minister last night the very last words he said on leaving him was, bring me an answer upon this question. Now, in my opinion a great deal depends upon the answer to the Prime Minister. . . .

I think in accordance with the traditions of this Federation we should not submit a vital question of this kind, especially upon the principle of a minimum wage, to a third party. (*15.iii.1912.*)

Finally, the conference agreed unanimously:

That this Conference hereby re-affirms the decision arrived at yesterday.

and thereafter adjourned till the evening.

When the miners' conference resumed at 7.35 in the evening, the chairman and members of their Executive Committee, somewhat exhausted after "a lengthy day at the Foreign Office," informed them of the upshot: how "Mr. Asquith has told us that they shall bring in a Bill to compel the owners to pay a minimum wage. That Bill will be introduced into the House of Commons on Tuesday. In framing the Bill they have invited the co-operation of both parties, and it will be the business of the Committee when we meet to appoint someone on our behalf to watch and to suggest from our side what we should like in the Bill. Mr. Asquith put that position before us. We had on adjourning to talk the matter over among ourselves, and we have submitted a few points to the Government." . . . "Mr. Asquith has impressed upon us rather strongly more than once that it is desirable that we do not precede this Bill by passing resolutions that are going to make it difficult for the Government. Well, now, it is no part of my business to stand as spokesman for the Government by any means. We have got our own interests as a Miners' Federation to safeguard. In the interests of them, however, we have not got to a point where we can afford to quarrel with the Government that is taking up this work for us that we are unable to do for ourselves. Human society is so constituted that the people who have the most brass get a good deal of their own way, and we cannot have a fair square fight simply because of that." (*15.iii.1912.*)

Then Enoch Edwards made a reference to the "painful aspect" of the effect of the strike on workers in other industries as follows:

Not only does it include, as between the colliery owners and ourselves, but other large interests of the working class people are involved, and that for the moment is rather a painful aspect of this case, because it is a very painful aspect in localities where other industries are dependent upon us, and we have thrown these industries idle. The men, women, and children have to suffer. However, this is part of the warfare in this world, and it is very difficult to separate it. (*15.iii.1912.*)

Finally he read the following five points which "our deputation" handed to the Premier and his colleagues:

No resumption of work until the provision of the Bill becomes an Act of Parliament.

A time limit of one month to settle the details after the passing of the Act.

The rates to be paid in each district to be retrospective from the date of resumption of work.

The 5s. for adult workers and the 2s. for boys' minimum, to be provided for in the Bill.

A minimum rate of wages to be paid in each district; a district to be considered each or any of the seventeen districts of the Federation of Great Britain. (*15.iii.1912.*)

The vice-chairman and Vernon Hartshorn amplified the explanations, the latter saying that the Government could not put the scheduled rates into a Bill. Why? Because, said he:

They have not the technical knowledge which would justify them in making themselves responsible without inquiry for every item in the schedule, and they say that to go through the length of inquiry that would be necessary in order to possess themselves of the requisite information would require very much time; and they say the nation is in such a condition that the Government cannot afford to spend that time in making that inquiry, and without that knowledge they are not going to make themselves responsible for every item in our schedule. They say they have not time.

Then, like the previous speakers, Hartshorn paid a tribute to the Liberal Ministers:

I want to endorse what Mr. Smillie has said with reference to the attitude of the Government. Whatever may develop before the end, we at any rate have no cause to complain, as workmen's representatives. I think Mr. Lloyd George has shown special anxiety that we should come out of this, at any rate, the miners shall come out of this in a favourable light. (*15.iii.1912.*)

Then it was agreed that a report be given to the press and they adjourned till Wednesday, March 20th, when the Bill would be fully available. The report stated simply that—

The Committee reported that the negotiations with the colliery owners were broken off, that the Government decided to introduce a Bill to secure a minimum wage for all grades of underground men and boys: and the Conference decided that the Committee should have full power to consider the Bill with the intention of safeguarding the interests of the workmen. The Conference was especially emphatic they could not advise any resumption of work until the Bill became an Act of Parliament, or till it was seen what final shape the Act of Parliament would take.

7. A BILL IN PARLIAMENT

On one and the same day the Government arrested Tom Mann and introduced their Minimum Wage Bill in the lower House. Even while remedial legislation was brought in by the one hand, law-and-order was to be sternly maintained by the other. The latter policy, however likely or unlikely to intimidate the men on strike, at once swelled the protest that had already been voiced in parliamentary questions as well as outside and was soon to bring on a debate in the House of Commons.

In tabling the Bill the Prime Minister explained how more than two weeks of endeavour to bring an agreed solution had proved to have been in vain and that now on March 19th the proposed measure would embody the four government propositions of February 28th. The new leader of the Tory opposition, Andrew Bonar Law, then spoke: he would do nothing to embarrass the government. After Ramsay MacDonald, leader of the forty-odd Labour members, had welcomed this remark, the debate began to settle down into a series of arguments of a somewhat technical kind, mainly between mining members and coalowning members. Suddenly the discussion was brought away from this concrete level by a speech from Lord Robert Cecil. The strike, he said, was "part of a great conspiracy" and, to build up his proof of this accusation, he went back to the publication in September, 1910, of the *Industrial Syndicalist*. Thereafter two themes ran through the debates, one on the provisions of the Bill, the other on the red salmon of syndicalism.

The first reading of the Bill was agreed but the second reading two days later was opposed. A. J. Balfour, recently deposed from leadership of the Conservative Party, moved total rejection and was followed immediately by the Prime Minister. The debate, thus launched, went on for eight hours till midnight. Enoch Edwards was third and said: "I stand here, almost a wreck, after six months' hard work, in the interests of peace in a great struggle to settle this question." The next was Viscount Helmsley[1] who came from rural Yorkshire and was in a state of alarm about syndicalism. He was countered immediately by Sir Alfred Mond[2] who said that "the Noble Lord seems rather upset by the terrors of syndicalism and the hysterical condition in which the Conservative Party finds itself."

Mond, concerned to pour cold water on the heated imaginations of Conservative members for rural constituencies, referred scornfully

---

[1] Charles William Reginald Duncombe (1879–1916) was first cousin thrice removed of Thomas Slingsby Duncombe (1796–1861) the Radical advocate of Chartism in an earlier parliament. As Viscount Helmsley he represented the Thirsk-and-Malton division of the North Riding of Yorkshire from 1906 to 1915 when he succeeded his grandfather as second Earl of Feversham.

[2] Alfred Moritz Mond (1868–1930) chief founder of Imperial Chemical Industries, sat in the Liberal interest for Chester from 1908 to 1910 (when he became a baronet), for Swansea from 1910 to 1923, for Carmarthen 1924 to 1928 when he was elevated to the House of Lords as Baron Melchett of Landford. In 1916 he entered the Lloyd George coalition government as First Commissioner of Works (1916–1921) and Minister of Health (1921–1922). After the first world war Mond developed his interests in nickel on an international scale and also in the anthracite industry of South Wales.

to those opposite who unnecessarily "read every ridiculous pamphlet published by every ridiculous person in the country." He believed that the Commons in its debates might rule out "these mysterious people behind the scenes who are pulling unknown strings" and then said:

It seems difficult for a great many people to realise this is not a great conspiracy against the State, but an attempt by a certain section of workmen to improve their industrial condition, a thing they have been trying to do for a long time, and a thing they have failed to do because the coalowners have refused to agree to their terms.

When I hear of labour holding up the trade of the country I think it might be justly retorted that the coal owners are holding up the trade of the country. I am not saying that either side is wrong, but, as far as the result to the country is concerned, the country would be quite happy if the coalowners would accede to the men's terms, so that the men could go back to work on Monday. The country would certainly be pleased, though the coalowners might not. (*21.iii.1912.*)

Then he turned to argue particularly against the contention of the South Wales coal owners, saying:

We have been told, with much emphasis, that the agreement made in South Wales in 1910 has not been kept. I have obtained a copy of that agreement and I have studied it, and I have failed to find any clause in it, and no one has yet pointed out to me any clause, which debars the miners of South Wales in any way from asking for a minimum wage. If I make an agreement with anybody, and we do not come to terms on a particular clause and leave it out, that does not debar me from raising that point. It actually gives me liberty to raise it.

It seems to me, as I read the agreement—and one who was not a party to the negotiations can only deal with the document itself—there has been no breach of agreement, nor can I see any counsel advising that there was a ground of action if the owners wanted to bring one for damages. I do not think it is fair to say there has been a deliberate breach of agreement. (*21.iii.1912.*)

This was a significant speech on questions of the coal industry by one who was afterwards to play such an important part not only in South Wales but in the question of industrial relations generally. Nor was it the only speech in favour of the Bill by members who themselves were coalowners. The debate otherwise soon turned into the usual party exchanges, with the leaders of the Tory opposition blaming the leaders of the Liberal Party while eschewing the subject of "syndicalism" which so fascinated and horrified their less experienced followers. Amongst the coal owners in Parliament next in the debate was the Liberal, Sir Joseph Walton (1849–1923). He was a coalowner who had been in favour of the miners' Eight Hour Bill when at the Barnsley by-election of 1897 he received the support of the leaders of the Yorkshire Miners' Association against the Socialist candidate who was backed by Keir Hardie, Tom Mann and Robert Smillie. Sir Joseph Walton had travelled extensively in all the habitable continents and had written a work in 1900 entitled "China and the Present Crisis." Now this coal owner found the proposals of the Government were "most moderate in their character," was "amazed" at the line taken by the Opposition and said:

Do we not in this House enjoy a minimum wage of £400 a year which we voted for ourselves? We do not even compel the members as a condition of receiving that amount to work with "regularity and efficiency," as is provided in this Minimum Wage Bill. (*21.iii.1912*.)

After ten o'clock in the evening, Austen Chamberlain (1863–1937), who the previous year had not attained the leadership of the Tory Party as the ardent Protectionists had hoped, rose to make the closing speech for the Opposition. His argument was on very general grounds (for example, he blamed electioneering speeches of Lloyd George for the sort of situation that had arisen or could arise) but he made no mention of either socialism or syndicalism on which some of his followers had laid such stress. The Government answer was given by the Secretary of State for Foreign Affairs, Sir Edward Grey (1862–1933) who, with Lloyd George and Asquith, had been devoting all his time for the previous three weeks and more to the mining problem and to such an extent that his permanent officials believed that urgent questions of foreign affairs were being ignored or neglected. Grey skilfully restated the case for the Bill.

Division was now expected: but Sir Arthur Markham (1866–1916) who sat as a Liberal for the Mansfield Division of Nottinghamshire since 1900, rose to put arguments in favour of the minimum wage which he as a coalowner had advocated "ten years ago—and since," and had actually paid in his own pits. He was greeted from the Tory benches with much hostility and frequent shouts and interjections until he turned on his interrupters "who are jeering at me," accused them of ignorance and prejudice and concluded the first portion of his speech with words that may have sounded paradoxical from the lips of a prosperous mineowner.

After all, the origin of this dispute may be traced to one fact and one fact only. The miners labour in a most dangerous calling in which three men are killed daily and 500 are injured daily, and not one miner but thousands go home weekly with not more than 2s. or 3s. a day after a hard week's work. Are these men not entitled to strike for a decent living wage? (*21.iii.1912*.)

When the Division was called at midnight, the second reading was carried by 348 votes for the Ayes to 225 votes for the Noes: and the Bill was thereupon "committed to a Committee of the whole House for tomorrow." (*21.iii.1912*.)

8. THE BILL IN COMMITTEE OF THE WHOLE HOUSE

The miners' conference meeting on Wednesday, March 20th, had not been at all pleased with the government measure, in which their vice-president descried "the hand of the coalowners written largely over this Bill." So they passed a resolution that no Act of Parliament without "a minimum wage of not less than 5s. per day for all adult workers other than piece workers, and 2s. per day for boys of fourteen "would be acceptable to the workmen. In a second resolution apparently to stiffen up the standpoint of the Committee, and after a debate in which mistrust of two leading members of the Labour Party (P. Snowden and G. N. Barnes) was voiced, the Conference recorded its opinion that "the Bill must contain the schedule rates for hewers in each separate district." Further it called upon the Labour Party to move an amendment to the Bill "for the inclusion of these rates."

Eventually the conference adjourned till Friday, 22nd, after it had decided unanimously to relegate further consideration of the Bill to the Executive Committee "supplemented by Members of Parliament representing the Federation, for the purpose of drafting such amendments as will bring the Bill into harmony with the decisions of the Federation." (*20.iii.1912.*)

The delegates, reassembled on Friday, March 22nd, had little more than an hour for discussion before the House of Commons would go into committee on the Bill. The chairman sought to cheer them, saying:

I think we have got an understanding that the 2s. rate and the 5s. rate (although there is terrific opposition to the 5s.) shall be inserted in the Bill.

The delegates found this a modicum of comfort amid their dismay at the uncompromising manner in which Sir Edward Grey the night before had ruled out the schedules from the Bill. This was mentioned by Vernon Hartshorn and by George Barker, both members of the national executive committee. Barker said:

I think everybody who was in the House last night must have been convinced of the fact that the Government did not intend to incorporate the hewers' schedules in the Bill. Sir Edward Grey emphasised upon the fact that no great assembly was going to be intimidated by an outside agency.

I want to say then, if this Conference is not going to intimidate or influence Parliament, we must take care that we do not let Parliament intimidate or influence this Conference. What is this great Parliament to whom we have entrusted our liberties composed of? It consists of six hundred and seventy men. Six hundred and thirty men who were capitalists and landowners, and it will be the death knell to the liberties of this movement if we hand them over to a body of this character, therefore I say we cannot hope to get much from those who represent those great interests of the country. I say that we must hold the sovereign power in our own hands.

Mr. Walsh has said if this Bill is passed we shall be compelled to accept it. I think that is very problematical because even if you get an Act of Parliament you cannot make men go into a pit if they do not want to go down.

Enoch Edwards then found it necessary to make quite clear from the chair the nature of the Government's proffered bargain: "If the 5s. and 2s. were put in the Bill, should we be prepared then to say that the men would go to work?"

The House of Commons met at noon and the discussion on a long series of amendments to the Bill went on without intermission for over thirteen hours. In the midst of the debate, J. Ramsay Mac-Donald, leader of the Labour Party, put forward suggestions which, when taken up very seriously by the Prime Minister, seemed as though they might lead to an early settlement. Their first result was to effect a complete alteration of the parliamentary time-table. Instead of the Bill being rushed through report stage and then third reading on the Saturday (a day on which the House never met in normal circumstances) the debates were suspended while agreement between the parties on the 5s. and the 2s. was ardently sought by the Prime Minister and his colleagues.

9. THE BILL IS HUNG UP

Enoch Edwards, in opening the miners' conference on Saturday morning, referred to what had taken place in the Commons on the previous day and asked:

"Shall we accept the invitation of the Premier to again meet the owners and go into this question on Monday morning, that is, the 5s. and the 2s.?" (*23.iii.1912.*)

In the discussion Tom Richards, M.P., after stressing a little the fact that he was now outside the circle of negotiators, said: "I have arrived at this conclusion that the Prime Minister is either fully convinced he can persuade the coalowners to agree to the 5s. and 2s., or that he will put it in the Bill. That is how I read the appeal." He concluded with the following remarks on the five shillings:

This point ought to be pressed on the Prime Minister that they need have no apprehension or fears as to the damage to the South Wales collieries on account of the poorer collieries. It is the big combines who refuse to pay, because we can always compel the little, poor collieries to pay, and therefore there is no fear as to the damage to the South Wales coal trade if this were put in the Bill.

After further discussion it was decided: "That the invitation of the Prime Minister to meet the employers be accepted." (*23.iii.1912*.)

When the 128 delegates assembled at one o'clock in the afternoon of Monday, March 25th, to meet the dozen and a half members of their committee, they learned from the chairman that no meetings with the owners had as yet taken place: and that their committee had been waiting in the Foreign Office until the Prime Minister, busy most of that morning with the owners, would be able to meet them. So the conference adjourned till five o'clock and then until eight o'clock, to be told that their committee was not in a position to report as yet. It was the same on the next day. They met at noon when the chairman told them that there was "very little fresh" to say to them.

That evening at six the delegates learned from the chairman that "The Government refuse to put in the 5s. and 2s.; the owners refuse to concede; the Bill is being debated in the House."[1]

Enoch Edwards told of his own shattered illusions in some revealing remarks: "I am sorry that we have no better news. I am sorry for many reasons because we did expect at any rate that a Liberal Government would have taken their courage in their hands and have accepted the 5s. and 2s."

Third Reading was coming up that night. So the motion was passed: "That the Labour Party be advised from this conference to vote against the Bill." (*26.iii.1912*.)

Parliamentary proceedings that Tuesday afternoon were indeed as inimical to the miners' hopes as their chairman had stated. All day the negotiations outside Parliament were still going on until after four o'clock when the Prime Minister entered the Chamber to take charge of the Bill. He was "speaking with profound emotion," according to contemporary accounts: and indeed Asquith said: "I speak under the stress of very strong feeling." The die had been cast against the miners' last hopes. The debate on the report stage went on for another nine hours, in a House that was hostile to the miners' claims. In the early hours of the morning, without pause, it was moved "that the Bill be now read the third time." When Ramsay MacDonald stated that the Bill without the 5s. and 2s. amendments was mere words, had given nothing to the miners that

[1] Sir Arthur Markham, M.P., who had an immense influence in Chesterfield and surrounding parts, in the debate on the 5s. and 2s. said:

"I understand that it is said that if Mr. D. A. Thomas, whom the House must not regard as an extreme man, had not joined the Coal Owners' Association, we should have had no strike in South Wales at all. The fact is (that)it is the South Wales Coal Owners who have forced this on, because they wanted a fight and were not satisfied until they could get one. All this has arisen out of the Cambrian strike. Mr. Thomas wanted at that time to refer the whole question to arbitration but the coal owners would not allow him to do so. In fact South Wales owners have built up a stone-wall attitude on this question; they have declared they intend to fight it out and that is the spirit in which the negotiations have been carried on. (*26.iii.1912*)

would settle the dispute and was therefore such that the Labour Party would vote against, he was bitterly assailed by Lloyd George for his statements. Keir Hardie, speaking in support of the miners' contention was frequently interrupted. James O'Grady, the Member for Leeds East, after claiming "I represent the most poverty-stricken constituency in the country and most of them poor Irish labourers," voiced that local opinion of men who would starve "rather than allow the Government to sell the pass on the miners": and ended by stating bluntly:

I claim that the Government have simply backed up the capitalists, as they always have done in labour measures. Members on both sides of the House have urged the bringing out of troops to intimidate us and to drive the miners back. You can carry laws, carry resolutions, and bring your troops out, but, thank God, the men will starve rather than go back on dishonourable terms. I hope the House will reject the Bill. (*26.iii.1912.*)

The effect of O'Grady's speech was diminished when Steve Walsh, M.P., made it clear in his final remark that once the Bill was passed he would recommend a return to work: for he was "a citizen first and a trade unionist afterwards."

Then the vote was taken at 2.40 a.m.: Ayes, 213; Noes, 48.

The Bill now went to the House of Lords, where Second Reading was moved and debated throughout the afternoon and early evening of Wednesday, March 27th: while late that same evening, the House of Commons was debating a motion on Syndicalism. On Thursday, March 28th, the Bill was in Committee of the Upper Chamber and, after amendments were accepted, passed its Third Reading. The Bill, with amendments, thus passed through the House of Lords and was returned to the Commons, who the same evening in the hour before midnight accepted "That this House doth agree with the Lords in the said Amendment." Twelve hours later the Royal Assent was reported: so that on Friday, March 29th, the Bill had become law.

10. THE BALLOT AND ITS OUTCOME

The miners' delegates did not wait for all the parliamentary processes to be completed: but on the morning of Wednesday, March 27th, they met and in short order adopted a series of resolutions that their committee had prepared. The first was unanimous, as follows:

That the best thanks of this Conference be conveyed to Mr. MacDonald and the Labour Party for the great help they have rendered this Federation in their endeavour to improve the Minimum Wage Bill. (*27.iii.1912.*)

The next resolution was carried with only the three votes of Bristol and Somerset against: "That a ballot vote of the men be taken."

Whether there should be a recommendation from conference as to how the ballot should be cast was raised and discussed: but when the matter was put to a vote there were only four in favour of such a course, while 127 voted for the committee's resolution which ran:

That the following be placed on the ballot paper: Are you in favour of resuming work pending settlement of the minimum rates of wages in the various grades by the District Boards to be appointed under the Mines Minimum Wage Act?

In the afternoon the following resolutions were carried unanimously:

That Mr. Ashton get a copy of the ballot paper printed, and send one to each district, and then for each district to get their own ballot papers and send out.

That the result of the ballot be sent to Mr. Ashton not later than Wednesday next week, April 3, 1912.

That Mr. Ashton be instructed to send copies of the Act to each district.

That the best thanks of this conference be given to Mr. Edwards for the splendid way in which he has conducted the work for this Federation during this week.

The following resolution was moved:

That this conference does not advise but leaves the ballot paper as agreed to decide for itself.

For this resolution .. .. .. 98 delegates voted.
Against resolution .. .. .. 31 delegates voted.

The chairman remarked to the delegates:

That vote has tied you up. You have agreed to it by a majority, and district officials should not unduly emphasise, let me say, either one way of another. It is left there for the men to say what their views are upon this question. I will leave it there.

Well now, Mr. Richards has raised the question as to whether there should be another conference following upon this. Well, now is the time to say that your General Secretary should be instructed to put the figures before the committee, and leave the responsibility with the committee and the officials to call a conference, if necessary. You can do that by resolution.

Tom Richards thereupon moved "that the matter be left with the Committee", remarking that "the figures will speak for themselves and decide our action." Then he said that it was important for them to be in their districts (rather than conferring in London) and added:

The men like guidance in these matters, and the next week and the week after will become more crucial than ever, and it is highly important

I speak for South Wales. These men who are here I know are the men to guide the workmen in South Wales.

So in every coalfield they awaited the results of the ballot. It turned out to be very different from what some of the leaders had expected: and entirely confounding for those others who held that a handful of men had engineered a national strike of men who were all looking for a means to return to work. The figures were 201,013 for resumption of work and 244,011 against it.

When on Thursday, April 4th, the national committee met to consider the ballot they found themselves in somewhat of a dilemma. There was a division of opinion, partly reflecting the absence of any uniformity in the response from the various coalfields, partly because of hesitations about any apparent infringement of the usual under-standing of majority rule. Finally, the committee sought to resolve their dilemma by a resolution as follows:

Seeing that there is no provision in the rules or regulations of the Federation to guide this committee as to the majority required to continue the strike, except the resolution passed at the conference held December 21, 1911, that a two-thirds majority was required to declare a national strike, we agree that the same majority be required to continue the strike; and seeing that a two-thirds majority is not in favour of the continuance of the strike, and acting upon that vote, we advise the resumption of work. (*4.iv.1912.*)

The conference two days later with only 113 present (97 delegates and 16 members of committee) was opened by an exhausted Enoch Edwards with brief remarks. He pointed out the reduction in the total poll (from 561,722 to 445,024); and that the total of those for continuance of the strike (244,011) was much less than the "For" votes (445,801) of mid-January; and stressed the significance of the very large number who had not taken part one way or another in this April ballot. He recalled that at their conference of December 21st it had been decided by 82 votes to 78 that a two-thirds majority would be requisite for this national strike: and called on Smillie to move the committee's resolution.

Two big delegations (Yorkshire and Lancashire) had come mandated to vote against the committee's resolution and for con-tinuance of the strike. Finally, however, only those two districts cast their votes against the resolution, which was carried by 449,500 votes against 125,000. Four small districts were not present at the conference.

The men in several of the smaller districts: in the Midland Federation (Cannock Chase, Pelsall, Warwickshire); in the Forest of Dean and Bristol were already at work when the conference met on April 6th. By Monday, April 8th, most of the coalfields resumed work; but at a large number of collieries in Lancashire the men did not return to work for several days after that. For most of the miners the strike lasted about forty days during which time they and their families had no certain resources other than the strike pay which even in the best cases was somewhat meagre.

At the conference on April 6th there was no discussion, no reference even to peculiarities in the figures of the ballot vote other than the reference to the fall in the total poll. But in the coalfields and even amongst the general public there was discussion, about the total figures[1] and about those of South Wales.

The peculiarity in the detail of the vote was that whereas South Wales, by far the largest district, had voted overwhelmingly by over a five to one majority in January for a strike, now in April by a two to one majority they were for resumption of work. Many at the time sought for an explanation of so huge a turnover. Those who had been foremost in the agitation within the national body for action on the minimum wage were now least to the fore in resistance to the Government's solution. Many reasons were adduced, some of them based on a consideration of national characteristics. This apparently alluring avenue of approach has to be shunned by the researcher into human affairs. More materialistic considerations are likely to furnish a clue to the behaviour of a mining community that, together with their families, amounted to a population of nearly a million persons.

The South Wales miners had given way sooner than other large districts for the simple reason that their resources were so much less. In this respect their weakness was rooted in the organisational weakness native to any federal alliance, such as was the Miners'

[1]BALLOT VOTE ON THE MINIMUM WAGE ACT

	For resumption	Against
Lancashire and Cheshire	11,334	29,840
Yorkshire	13,267	43,914
Derbyshire	8,080	13,428
Nottinghamshire	8,187	8,213
Midland Federation	18,168	11,278
Cumberland	2,980	4,877
South Wales	62,538	31,127
Durham	24,511	48,828
Northumberland	10,674	14,195
Scotland	23,186	30,473
Bristol	772	326
Somerset	2,130	1,220
Cleveland	4,919	908
North Wales	7,446	1,190
South Derby	1,626	1,090
Leicester	1,195	2,104
Forest of Dean	No Ballot	
Totals	201,013	244,011

Federation of Great Britain. Why were the resources less in South Wales? Firstly their funds were less at the beginning of 1912 and this for three reasons:

(a) their basic contribution of three pence a week was half that of most mining associations;

(b) their system of strike levies, designed to meet lodge or valley needs, proved a broken reed if all were brought out on strike;

(c) the frequent levies in the previous years 1910 and 1911 to maintain the Cambrian Combine strike and lockout had drained the valleys dry.

For all these reasons the South Wales Miners' Federation was the section of the Miners' Federation of Great Britain least equipped to maintain a prolonged struggle on a nationwide scale. Secondly, the miners in Monmouth and South Wales were at a disadvantage compared to such big coalfields as Yorkshire or Lancashire in that there was no other source of income than the breadwinning male members of the family. In other counties there were light industries such as textiles where women could be at work, or other alternative sources of employment. Not so in Glamorgan whose valleys when they ceased to nourish shepherds could sustain in those days only the coal mining industry.

Thirdly and lastly, the decision of the national conference to make no recommendation had left the agents unfettered, if they chose to disregard the advice of Enoch Edwards: and disregard it they did. In most cases, though not all, they recommended a return to work.

Noah Ablett and his supporters might bitterly reflect on the old proverb "You can bring a horse to the water, but you cannot make him drink." They had won their battle for a forward policy and an advanced theory within the South Wales Miners' Federation council and coalfield conference. They had electrified parliamentary debate at Westminster. They had even voted the old leading officials off the national executive in London. But in the end the Council was made up mainly of agents: and these they had not been able to shift nor was there any regular system of elections by which they might have been shifted. The old agents took their opportunity: and if they did not feel that they were taking their revenge on Ablett and his fellows, nevertheless their action had a similar effect. Indeed, it had a wider effect, for it introduced an element of weakness into the whole national organisation: and it disbanded to a certain extent the solidarity of the miners' struggle. But it brought lessons for the future.

LENIN'S CONTEMPORARY COMMENTS

What was the result of the five to six weeks' strike? Here one answer can be given in the words of V. I. Lenin who had been closely watching the struggle that March of 1912 from across the channel in Paris, and who made a whole series of instructive comments. Writing in retrospect some nine months later in No. 1. of *Pravda* of the year 1913, Lenin stated:

"The most outstanding event in the past year has been the miners' strike. If the railway strike in 1911 displayed the 'new spirit' of the British workers, the miners' strike certainly marks a new epoch.

"In spite of all the preparations of the ruling classes for 'war,' in spite of the strenuous effort of the bourgeoisie to crush the resistance of the disobedient slaves of capital, the strike was a success. The state of organisation of the miners was exemplary. There was not a trace of blacklegging. Coalmining by soldiers or inexperienced labourers was out of the question. And after a six weeks' struggle the bourgeois government of Britain realised that the country's entire industrial life was coming to a standstill and that the words of the workers' song, 'All wheels cease to whir when thy hand wills it,' were coming true.

"The government yielded.

"The British Government which usually feeds its workers with promises of reform 'some day,' now worked at top speed. *In five days* a new law was rushed through Parliament, introducing a *minimum* wage, i.e. regulations establishing rates of pay *below* which wages cannot be reduced.

"It is true that this law, like all bourgeois reforms, is a miserable half measure and in part merely a deception of the workers, because though fixing the lowest rate of pay, the employers grind their wage slaves down all the same. Those who know the British Labour movement, however, assert that since the coal strike the British proletariat *is no longer the same*. The workers have learned to fight. They have discovered the *path* that will lead them to victory. They have become aware of their power. They have ceased to be the meek lambs they so long seemed to be to the satisfaction of all the champions and extollers of wage slavery.

"In Britain a change has taken place in the relation of social forces, a change which cannot be expressed in figures but which everyone feels.

"Unfortunately, not much progress is being made in Party affairs in Britain. The split between the British Socialist Party (formerly the S.-D. Federation), and the Independent (of socialism) Labour Party continues. The opportunist conduct of the M.P.s belonging to the latter party is giving rise, as is always the case, to *syndicalist* tendencies among the workers. Happily these are not strong.

"The British trade unions are slowly but surely turning towards socialism, in spite of many Labour members of Parliament who stubbornly champion the old line of Liberal Labour policy. But it is beyond the power of these last of the Mohicans to retain the old!"

Pravda, January 1, 1913.

Five months earlier, in August 1912, Lenin had dealt with this new content in the British Labour Movement, writing:

"The labour movement in Britain is becoming stronger and stronger. Strikes are assuming a mass character; moreover, they are ceasing to be purely economic and are turning into political strikes.

"Robert Smillie, the leader of the Scottish miners who recently displayed such strength in mass struggle, declared that in their next big fight the miners will demand the transfer of the mines to the state. And this next big fight is inexorably approaching, because all the miners of Britain perfectly well realise the impotence of the notorious Minimum Wage Act to bring about any real improvement in their conditions."

Pravda, August 12, 1912.

CHAPTER ELEVEN

COAL MINES (MINIMUM WAGE) ACT, 1912 AND AFTER

I. THE PROVISIONS OF THE ACT

THE Act which the miners had rejected did little more than lay down in legal terms the principle of the individual minimum wage and establish machinery for subsequent settlement. The Act, which was to last for three years, had only six sections of which the two last were mainly formal. The first section begins with the statement that:

it shall be an implied term of every contract for the employment of a workman underground in a coal mine that the employer shall pay to that workman wages at not less than the minimum rate settled under this Act and applicable to that workman, unless it is certified in manner provided by the district rules that the workman is a person excluded under the district rules from the operation of this provision, or that the workman has forfeited the right to wages at the minimum rate by reason of his failure to comply with the conditions with respect to the regularity or efficiency of the work to be performed by workmen laid down by those rules; and any agreement for the payment of wages in so far as it is in contravention of this provision shall be void.

As they read and re-read the elaborate phraseology devised by parliamentary draughtsmen in the firm belief that without it no Act would be watertight, many leaders of the miners may well have longed for the terse wording of the ten commandments they had learned from the Holy Bible in their youth. But the effect of the section could be spelled out without too much difficulty: the minimum was not absolute but conditional, and some workmen would be altogether exempted: everything depended on the "district rules." These district rules, it is provided in the second clause of this section, "shall lay down conditions" respecting "regularity and efficiency" of the work, and the time for which a workman is to be paid in the event of any interruption of work "due to an emergency." If these conditions were not complied with, the workman would forfeit his right to the minimum wage—except in cases over which he had no control. The rules would decide. Whatever payment of wages would be made at a minimum rate, so the third clause of the first section stated, would date back to the passing of the Act.

The second section provides for the settlement of minimum rates of wages and district rules by joint district boards, to be set up in a score of coalfields. All was to be without prejudice to existing agreements or customs for wages higher than the minimum. Moreover, in settling any minimum rate of wages the joint district board "shall have regard to the average daily rate of wages" paid to the workmen of the class for which the minimum rate is to be settled. The phrase quoted, being imprecise, was likely to be productive of much trouble, as was recognised in a contemporary comment:

> The words "have regard to" are delightfully vague, and rather savour of the lawyer throwing dust in the eyes of the anxious trade unionist who wanted to bind the independent chairmen of the district boards to fix the minimum nearly as high as the average for each class of workmen.[1]

The third section made provision for variations both in the minimum rates of wages and the district rules: and the fourth section stipulated that if a joint district board failed to settle within three weeks (or within an agreed "specified period longer than three weeks") then the independent chairman would settle. The Act of Parliament, it is clear, was thus a skeleton structure to be clothed with flesh by the joint district board in each coalfield. A great deal turned upon the man chosen (or appointed by the Board of Trade) to be independent chairman.

2. DECISIONS TAKEN IN SOUTH WALES

The ballot papers in the vote for or against continuance of the national strike had to be in the hands of Tom Richards by Tuesday, April 2nd. That same day a special conference was held in the Cory Memorial Hall in Cardiff. The 273 delegates, representing 121,701 members, may well have been aware not only of the trend of the voting in their valleys for ending the strike but also of the fact that in some places the men were ready and willing to return to work without waiting for the outcome of the ballot in Great Britain as a whole. Their first resolution ran:

> That this Conference desires all workmen to refrain from resuming work until the result of the ballot throughout the Miners' Federation of Great Britain is ascertained and the decision of the National Executive thereon has been received. (*2.iv.1912.*)

The Executive Council were authorised to act as the representatives of the workmen upon the Joint District Board "as required by Clause 2 of Sub-section 1 of the Coal Mines (Minimum Wage) Act." The Conference had now its first opportunity to take up the arrest of Tom Mann, persecuted for their sake as they thought, and to

[1] Professor H. S. Jevons, *The British Coal Trade* (Kegan Paul, Trench Truebner & Co. 1915), page 574.

plead for other captives. So the delegates resolved "that we protest against the arrest of Mr. Tom Mann and the imprisonment of the printers connected with the same matter." (*2.iv.1912.*)

When the next Special Conference assembled Tom Mann was already imprisoned in Strangeways Gaol in Manchester: so by resolution the Conference expressed "its sympathy with Mr. Tom Mann in the unjust sentence that has been passed upon him." (*11.v.1912.*)

A second resolution of the April Conference had called upon their Executive Council to take immediate steps "either by way of deputation or some other form, in order to give effect to the petitions already presented to the Home Secretary for release of, or a very substantial reduction in the sentences now being served by the workmen who were connected with the recent colliery disturbances in South Wales." (*2.iv.1912.*)

This had some effect for two weeks later the following letter was received from the Home Secretary:

Dear Mr. Richards,
    Before receiving your letter I had the cases of Messrs. William John and John Hopla under my consideration. In view of the complete absence of disturbance in South Wales during the recent strike, and the manifest determination of the miners to preserve order, I have thought the occasion proper for clemency in respect to these two prisoners.
    I have accordingly advised a reduction of their sentences from 12 to 8 months.
                                    Yours very truly,
                                    REGINALD McKENNA.

Both John Hopla, a member of the Executive Council, and William John, chairman of the Cambrian Combine Committee, had received severe sentences. William John was to be elected to the post of miners' agent at Tonypandy while he was yet in prison and was soon to join Hopla on the Executive Council.

3. TROUBLE WITH THE ENGINEMEN

After the instruction to return to work had been given by a national conference in London on April 6th, a considerable number of pits remained idle in South Wales, due to the enginemen's strike. The Executive Council on April 9th invited representatives of the enginemen's union to discuss the matter. This union was the Monmouthshire and South Wales Colliery Enginemen, Stokers and Surface Craftsmen's General Association which had seceded from the South Wales Miners' Federation in 1903. Thereafter, as happens in the case of a breakaway, relations were not good for a while.

Later, however, there had been an improvement to the extent that each had signed a document of "Mutual Working Arrangements"[1] on February 5, 1910. By the end of 1910 the enginemen's union had 64 branches and 9,367 members.

Mutual Working Arrangements had led to discussions on amalgamation but these had been broken off a few months before the great strike. The enginemen too had given in strike notices on February 1st to the colliery owners: and their standpoint was that they would not go back until some of their demands were met; nor would they yield to the arguments put forward by the Executive Council, at the meeting on April 10th, that all should go back together. After the enginemen's representatives had gone the S.W.M.F. Executive Council resolved on a manifesto to their own members. In this they stated that surface workers had grievances which the Council would take up "in the immediate future" with the colliery owners and that, failing agreement in this, the matter would be brought up before the Miners' Federation of Great Britain with a view to national action: but at the same time the instructions were repeated for all members of the Federation "both underground and surface workmen to return to work forthwith." This manifesto angered the enginemen whose conference on Monday, April 15th passed a resolution very critical of the miners' union. To this a rejoinder was given in a resolution of the Council two days later. Eventually the matter was settled for the time being and the pits all resumed working. Later, relations between the two unions improved, proposals for amalgamation were once more discussed and, as will be seen, they were eventually agreed upon.

4. JOINT DISTRICT BOARD

When it came to the setting up of the Joint District Board there was no initial difficulty, either in its constitution or in the choice of chairman. "Our board is rather large because the coalfield is large," reported Brace some weeks later, "about fifty-two members representative of the employers and ourselves. It is our old conciliation board. The independent chairman is the chairman of our conciliation board, and we mutually agreed to ask him to take the position."

But five weeks later Brace was telling a London conference of the snags encountered. Simply on the question of the 5s. for adult underground workers "we have met for ten days" with Lord St. Aldwyn and the outcome was such that his colleagues wished the independent chairman to resign. But that he would not do. Indeed, there had

[1] See Appendix I to this chapter.

been so little agreement that the joint district board failed to settle the first minimum rates of wages and district rules within three weeks after the time (*April 18th*) at which it was recognised by the Board of Trade. Thereupon it was agreed to substitute the "specified period of ten weeks" which would take them up to the beginning of July to reach an agreed settlement. Similar difficulties had been encountered in other coalfields: but the time taken in South Wales to settle the district rules, as well as the minimum rates, was to prove abnormally long. In the meantime there was held a Miners' Federation of Great Britain special conference in London at which Brace reported for South Wales. The upshot was a unanimous resolution of "strongest protest" against "awards which fix the minimum rates for underground workmen at less than" what the Prime Minister had declared should be "a reasonable living wage."

The Conference instructed the Executive Committee to ask for an interview with the Government, and "that a further Conference be held without delay to receive the report of the deputation."

The interview was requested immediately but the Prime Minister at that time was away from Downing Street. On his return he suggested the interview might be left over until all the joint district boards under the Minimum Wage Act had completed their work. This as it turned out was not until after July 5th. By that date Viscount St. Aldwyn in South Wales had made his award.

There were two schedules to the award. The second of these contained the district rules.

Throughout the country there was considerable diversity in the district rules that were drawn up. Those settled for South Wales had some peculiar features as will be seen from the detailed text as given in Appendix II to this chapter. Amongst the peculiarities was the statement that in order to qualify for the minimum a miner must have worked five sixths of the week. In many other coalfields the Joint District Board decision was for four fifths of the week. It was clear that some of the normal weekly events in a coal pit might easily prevent the hewer from being able to attend. In that case there was no possibility of his attending the five sixths if he were to lose only one day. Some of these questions came up for discussion in the next year. Another peculiarity of South Wales was that the minimum rates as fixed were subject to the same conditions as the rates fixed by the conciliation board, in this respect, that if there was a percentage addition payable under the conciliation board agreement of December 1910, then that addition would be put also upon the minimum wage. This was in sharp contrast to the Joint District Board for Yorkshire where the failure to insert any such provision was to result in a prolonged and difficult strike in the Yorkshire coalfield in the summer of 1914.

The onus was upon the workman to prove his right to the minimum wage; and some of the rules laying down what conditions had to be met before the right was held to be established were considered at the time to be harsher than they ought to be. In some cases the South Wales miners took the matter to law to find whether some of the rules as imposed by Lord St. Aldwyn were against the provisions in the Minimum Wage Act and were therefore *ultra vires*. Their lawsuits had varying success: some they lost and some they won.

5. THE DEPUTATION TO THE PRIME MINISTER

When by mid-July all the awards under the Act had been made the time was ripe for the Prime Minister to meet the twenty miners' representatives. Their spokesmen, Smillie, Straker and Hartshorn, voiced the dissatisfaction felt in the districts with the working of the Act.

Smillie ended by saying that they had not come there to tell the Prime Minister that the Act was an absolute failure. Neither, however, were they there to say that it had been an enormous boon to the colliers or that it would give peace to the mining districts, but "we are here to say that we shall give the Act a fair trial but we think its working requires to be watched in the interests of the men." Hartshorn then spoke as follows:

In the spring, earlier, it has been pointed out in South Wales there were between ten and twenty thousand men whose wages were below the 5s. That unquestionably had been one of the causes of the trouble. Unfortunately we are left with that grievance still, though in a somewhat modified form. The South Wales award fixes the rate of certain classes of men below 3s., the award being fixed at 3s. plus percentages in some cases, and 3s. 2d. plus percentage in others. That meant that at the present time some will get 4s. 6d. and others 4s. 9d., but even that is subject to a reduction of 15 per cent., so that the actual minimum will be 4s. 0·6d. to 4s. 3·3d. The matter I refer to is a very small one, and really ought to be rectified in its entirety. The South Wales award has not added more than 2s. per ton to the cost of production, and to rectify the matter complained of will not increase that by more than a farthing per ton at the outside.

The Premier: "You have done very well in South Wales."

Mr. Hartshorn: "We have done fairly well."

The Premier: "I see my old friend Mr. Barker. He told us when we met before that 'We're out for cash.' You have got a good lot of cash out of this."

Mr. Hartshorn: "Yes, a good deal, but there are the matters referred to, and 2d. a ton would put them right."

16 SENGHENYDD COLLIERY

SENGHENYDD. OCTOBER 14, 1913

The Premier: "That is one way to put it. That is what it would cost the employer or the consumer."

Mr. Hartshorn: "This extra cost of not more than a farthing would raise the wages to the 5s. and we hope sincerely you will see your way to give us some assistance. (*15.vii.1912.*)

Asquith in his reply said that, as was inevitable with emergency legislation, there had no doubt been misunderstandings and instances of friction. On the whole, however, he gathered from the deputation that the statutory bodies had not done too badly. He was certain that the miners had derived an enormous boon from the Act: and he did not believe that either owners or consumers would suffer in consequence of it.

The results of this interview with H. H. Asquith was laid before a conference a month later together with reports from the districts. When the delegates who had dispersed to enjoy the sea breezes of Blackpool in the August sunshine came back to the Art Gallery they passed a resolution which expressed their "strong dissatisfaction" with the working of the Minimum Wage Act, especially in regard to the following:

(*a*) the fact that with few exceptions no award has provided for the paying of 5s. per day to the low paid wage workmen,

(*b*) in many instances the Independent Chairmen have not had reasonable regard to the average wages of the piece-workers in fixing the minimum wage,

(*c*) these awards which require 100 per cent of attendances at work to qualify for the minimum wage,

(*d*) the serious delay of many owners in paying the arrears of wages due under the awards, and

(*e*) further strongly condemns the action of those owners who are coercing or bribing workmen to contract out of the provisions of the Act, either by promising or refusing them work or by offering increased tonnage rates or percentages. (*16.viii.1912.*)

The resolution instructed districts to supply the necessary information: and it empowered the Executive Committee to convene another Conference to deal with any difficulties that might exist.

Meantime the Executive Committee was to render all possible assistance to any district resisting "any attempt on the part of the owners to violate or evade the provisions of the Act."

6. CENTRALISATION

The climax of the great strike had been reached and passed. The long struggle that had begun nearly three years earlier was over. It had its consequences. Mabon, whose policy had been unmistakably rejected, chose this moment to make his final departure from the

L

scene where he had been dominant for nearly forty years. At the annual conference held in the Cory Memorial Hall on June 5 and 6, 1912, Mabon, in a voice trembling with emotion, delivered his farewell speech as president. Thereupon it was resolved: "That Mabon be elected an honorary member of the Executive Council."

Indeed, it was high time for Mabon to go. He himself had recognised this nine months earlier when the vote taken in the autumn on 1911 had shown that he had lost the confidence of the South Wales miners. At that time his closest associates, the Vice-President, the Secretary and the Treasurer (Brace, Richards and Onions) had all been replaced by the ballot for the Executive Committee of the Miners' Federation of Great Britain. In its editorial the *Merthyr Pioneer* had commented: "The defeat of Brace, Richards and Onions is an incident of the greatest significance. It says that the Welsh coalfield has grown tired of trying to face two ways; has turned its back upon the past, and has begun in earnest to march forward to the goal of economic freedom. The three defeated leaders belonged to the half-way house order of Liberal-Labour; the three men elected are militant socialists and active members of the Independent Labour Party."

In his favourite organ, the *South Wales Daily News*, Mabon regretfully reached a similar conclusion. He wrote:

Had I been in their places those who voted them out of the position would have voted me out also. Not only that, but my policy—the policy of conciliation and arbitration failing conciliation—a policy that I have lived for forty years to carry out, and also to serve to the best of my ability in the interest of my fellow-workmen—has been rejected unmistakably. (*10.x.1911*.)

What Mabon called conciliation was beginning to be given another name by this time. The younger men were already using such terms as "class-collaboration" to define the policy of Mabon.

After the affecting scene of Mabon's valedictory speech the conference resolved "That the conference agenda in future be printed in English and Welsh." Then at the end of their business of the audit there was a general discussion upon the question of centralisation with a card vote. The result was 1,148 votes for centralisation and 896 votes against. It was not a new question. It had come up several times. Indeed, as often as some critical situation brought home to a number of the miners the inadequacy for effective working of their original highly federal constitution of 1898 there were proposals put forward for centralisation. These were as regularly unsuccessful even when they began with a considerable impetus for achieving their object. Now once more an annual conference decided for centralisation though by only a small majority.

When the conference re-assembled on the next day William Brace reported that at a Council meeting the matter of framing a scheme of centralisation upon the lines laid down by the conference the previous day was considered. The Council found it impossible in the time at their disposal to do this, and as the Council would for the next few weeks be continually engaged in the work of the District Board, they recommended that six members of the Council and six to be nominated by the conference should at once proceed to prepare a scheme to submit to another conference. This was agreed and the following six representatives elected: Messrs. Frank Hodges, George Davies, William Hancock, Albert Thomas, Thomas Langley and David Thomas.

Annual conference then passed a series of resolutions which presumably were intended as instructions to the sub-committee. One resolution, however, was not carried. It ran:

"To consider the expediency of separating the political and industrial duties of officials of the Federation, with a view to allotting to each set of representatives their separate tasks." For the proposition—938 votes. Against the proposition—1,286 votes. The proposition was defeated. (*6.vi.1912.*)

The following officers were appointed: President, Mr. William Brace, M.P.; Vice-President, Mr. James Winstone, C.C.; General Treasurer, Mr. Alfred Onions, J.P., C.C.

A month later the Executive Council were discussing the question of reorganisation with the Drafting Committee and again on July 15th, when it was agreed to adopt the recommendation of the Drafting Committee "that the members of the Executive Council under the scheme be elected by a ballot vote of the whole of the members of the Federation." (*15.vii.1912.*)

At the end of July at a special conference, Brace gave an outline of the method adopted in drafting the reorganisation scheme. Straight away it was moved that the scheme be rejected. This received 1,194 votes. The move to accept the scheme received 1,255 votes. In parliamentary language the scheme had received Second Reading. But it was also decided "that the present districts should be retained," by a vote of 1,178 against 1,130; similarly, the proposal for a Council of 24 members was carried by 1,258 votes to 886 for a Council of twelve.

The conference had already carried other resolutions and was going on dutifully to discuss several more when it was realised that the decision to retain the existing districts had wrecked the scheme. There was no point in going on any further until salvage operations had been put through. So they decided to refer the whole scheme back to the drafting committee to redraft it upon the basis of retention of the existing districts. That evening there was a joint meeting of the Executive Council and of the drafting committee held at the close of the conference of July 29, 1912. The committee considered the decision of the conference and resolved as follows:

That conference be informed that the committee is of the opinion that the workmen cannot have centralisation and the retention of the districts, as at present. That a ballot be taken to find out whether the workmen are prepared to abolish the districts. (*29.vii.1912.*)

The next day this proposal was agreed to. The ballot was to be taken on September 5th/6th and the following form of ballot paper was agreed to:

Shall we abolish all districts and centralise the Federation both financially and administratively?

This ballot, duly taken in the first week of August, was reported to the Council meeting of September 11th as follows:

Ballot "for" and "against" the abolition of districts and the centralisation of funds and administration:

Votes "for"	47,688
Votes "against"	37,348
Majority "for" ..	10,340

Thereafter it was decided to submit the scheme once more to a conference. In the meantime on October 14th at the Council meeting the following motion was moved:

That in view of the Anthracite District having decided to sever its connection with the Federation if the centralisation scheme is adopted without districts retaining their present administrative powers, the Council decide to recommend to the conference the abandonment of the scheme.

Upon a vote being taken this proposition was defeated.

Finally the redrafted scheme came up before a special conference held in the Cory Memorial Hall on November 11, 12 and 13, 1912. There were 200 delegates present representing only 89,510 members. Numerous amendments were made to the 45 rules submitted. On the third day of the conference it was decided that the complete scheme should be submitted to a ballot vote of the members; that a copy of the scheme be supplied to each member and that 10,000 of the copies be printed in Welsh. It was to be in the hands of the members two weeks before the ballot was taken. These decisions, of course, meant that the ballot was deferred to the new year.

Meantime at a Council meeting on December 2, 1912, "Mr. Tom Smith gave a report of the meeting of the Anthracite District which he and Messrs. Vernon Hartshorn and William Jenkins attended on behalf of the Council on Saturday last. The deputation urged upon them not to sever the connection with the Federation. He did not believe this movement was due to the centralisation scheme, as they believed that if they severed their connection with the central body they can have a wage board at Swansea and that they can become connected with the M.F.G.B. as a district."

After discussing this report, the Executive Council resolved:

That the General Secretary write the officials of the district intimating that it is the desire of the Council that the officials attend their next district meeting, with a view of informing them of the difficulties surrounding their proposal to secede from the Federation. (*2.xii.1912.*)

After all efforts had been made to get a scheme of centralisation, after the three-day November conference the proposals were now to be submitted in their finalised form to the membership for ballot vote, at the end of January in the new year. But the new year had not run six weeks when the result was known. The South Wales Miners' Federation membership had overwhelmingly rejected the scheme for centralisation or, as it was finally called, the scheme for reorganisation.[1]

7. THE DEFEAT OF REORGANISATION

The overwhelming defeat of reorganisation was a very great disappointment to those inside the Federation who had been urging it for several years. The figures were beyond cavil or questioning. By a nearly two to one majority the members rejected it by 43,508 votes against 24,106. It was a serious setback. It was not for another twenty years and more that success would be fully attained for reorganisation. What had been the cause? Many of those who had aimed at reorganisation were sure that the Executive majority had out-manoeuvred them. They had framed various parts of the scheme and had them accepted by the coalfield conference in the full knowledge that the miners in their lodges would not accept it. This was the standpoint of quite a few of those who were coming to be called "the rebels." Certainly there was one feature inside the proposals which it might have been thought would certainly ensure their defeat as a whole. With the proposals for centralisation there was linked a proposal to double the contributions from 6d. to 1s. per fortnight. This doubling of contributions had been rejected the previous summer at the same time as there had been a considerable majority for reorganisation as a general principle. So it was firmly believed that the way in which the scheme had been propounded had brought about its inevitable rejection; for certain proposals were

---

[1] See Appendix III to this chapter.

liable to raise a very large degree of hesitation both amongst lodge officials and district committees, and a maximum degree of hesitation in the minds of the agents. The agents would no longer hold their positions for life but would be subject to re-election every three years. Moreover, they would be controlled by the Executive Council on which they might or might not have a seat. This and other items were a very far cry from the practically unlimited autonomy of each valley in the federal structure of the South Wales Miners' Federation. The lesson was reinforced that constitutional questions and problems of reorganisation provided the most formidable obstacles to re-formers.

The reformers had been there for only a few years and with the exception of George Barker, agent for Abertillery, were young men. Several of them, endowed by the union, had gone to Ruskin College. There the disturbances had culminated first in the formation of the Plebs League run by the students and then in the famous strike of March 1909. Noah Ablett in the very first number of the *Plebs* magazine appearing in February 1909 had set forth the aims of independent working class education. But he had done more. He had begun that series of educational classes inspired by Marxist teaching, for the first years at any rate, that were to have such an effect throughout the coalfields of Britain and in other industries. He had also plunged into the politics of the coalfield. It was a startling change from the devout, religious and Chapel student who had gone up to Ruskin and the agitator who was now to urge complete reform of the organisation and policy of the South Wales miners.

Ablett was not the first of the Ruskin rebels, even if he was amongst the most prominent upon his return. His senior Rees, not so vocal as Ablett and never pushing himself forward, had a much longer experience of trade union administration and a more immediate grasp of what key measures could reconstitute the Federation. As secretary of the 4,000-strong Cambrian Lodge he had played a leading part in the wider Cambrian Combine Committee: and in the spring of 1911 had been one of its three members elected to the Executive Council where they replaced the supporters of Mabon after their untimely deaths.

The long drawn out Cambrian lockout and strike had left little opportunity for formal organisation of those who were opposed to Mabon and his policy. But as time wore on there came into activity "the unofficial reform committee," the secretary of which was W. H. Mainwaring of Clydach Vale, the little valley running off the Rhondda Fawr. It was this body which produced that autumn of 1911 two very big results. For the first they were to some extent responsible. This was the overwhelming ballot vote against the leaders in the choice of representatives upon the Miners' Federation of Great Britain Executive Committee. For the second they were wholly responsible. This was the preparation of a pamphlet, afterwards to be so famous, entitled *The Miners' Next Step*.[1] Copies were sent around to prominent "leftwingers" in the coalfield. One draft after another was made; finally it was submitted to an unofficial conference at Cardiff. This was the pamphlet which had such an unexplained reception, such a blaze of horrified publicity first in the *Western Mail*, then in *The Times* and then in the other press (one of which—the *Morning Post*—continued year after year to quote it and to gloat over it with the anticipatory leers and shudders of the Fat Boy in *Pickwick Papers*). The publicity was further expanded during the debates on the Minimum Wage Bill in the House of Commons and in the House of Lords. Lastly, there was a special discussion in the House of Commons. With the horrific reputation thus bestowed upon the pamphlet in the press and in Parliament, its effect in the coalfields of Britain, and particularly that February in the valleys of Monmouth and South Wales, was that for a while *The Miners' Next Step* became a household word. But the effect of it was not so lasting as writers in the newspapers were wont to imagine in the months and years that followed. Not only Labour M.P.s but their own miners' M.P.s like Mabon and Brace, Richards, and Williams and even socialists like Keir Hardie and Snowden fervently voiced their opposition to syndicalism: and syndicalism that year in the newspapers was equated with *The Miners' Next Step*.[2]

[1] Its full title was *The Miners' Next Step: being a suggested scheme for the Reorganisation of the Federation* (Issued by the Unofficial Reform Committee). Its contents were set out as follows: "Chapter 1 Examines our Methods and Policy in the Past; Chapter 2 Is a Criticism of our Present Position; Chapter 3 Outlines the Goal we should strive for; Chapter 4 Lays down the Constitution we Need; Chapter 5 Deals with the Policy of the New Organisation."

Its authorship was shared by half-a-dozen of the reformers: part was by Noah Ablett and C. L. Gibbons; part (on the constitution) by W. H. Mainwaring and Noah Rees; part by George Dolling of Ynyshir; and part by Will Hay.

[2] It was republished in November 1964 by the South Wales Area of the National Union of Mineworkers.

MUTUAL WORKING ARRANGEMENTS WITH THE MONMOUTHSHIRE AND SOUTH WALES COLLIERY ENGINEMEN, STOKERS, AND CRAFTSMEN'S ASSOCIATION

For the purposes of a mutual understanding in matters affecting the interests of the Members of the above Organisations, and in order to more satisfactorily and effectively carry out the work of organising the workmen in the Coalfield, and with a view of rendering all moral support when disputes arise from time to time between the members of the respective Organisations and their employers, the following provisions are hereby agreed to as a basis of a working agreement between the two Organisations:—

(1) That the Enginemen, Stokers, and Craftsmen's Association pay to the Miners' Federation a recognition fee of 1½d. per member per quarter towards the expenses incurred in the administration of the General Wage Agreement.

(2) That when matters of general interest are under consideration, Joint Committees shall be held. Neither party shall tender notice at any Colliery until the matter in dispute has been previously considered by the Board.

(3) A Committee consisting of an equal number of members of both Associations shall constitute a Joint Board, who shall have full power to deal with any dispute arising in connection with the enrolment or transfer of members from one organisation to another, or any other dispute arising from time to time affecting the mutual interest of either Association.

(4) That the entrance fees and contributions shall be the same in both Associations.

(5) That each Association pay the expenses of their own members when attending Board Meetings. Such meetings to be convened jointly by the Secretaries of the respective Organisations. All other expenses incidental shall be equally divided.

(6) That each Association shall have entire freedom in the management of their own affairs, except as varied by this Agreement.

THOMAS EVANS,
E. MORRELL,
WILLIAM HARRIS,
JOHN D. MORGAN,
THOMAS LUCAS.

February 5, 1910.

Signed on behalf of The Monmouthshire and South Wales Colliery Enginemen, Stokers, and Craftsmen's Association—

TOM STROUD,
WILLIAM HOPKINS,
THOMAS WARBURTON,
WILLIAM WOOSNAM,
WILLIAM DAVIES.

February 5, 1910.

APPENDIX II TO CHAPTER ELEVEN

THE MINIMUM RATES IN SOUTH WALES

Whereas at joint meetings held at Cardiff, on April 3, 1912, of the representatives of the colliery owners of South Wales and Monmouthshire and the representatives of the workmen employed at the collieries, a Joint District Board was constituted for the purpose of the Coal Mines (Minimum Wage) Act, 1912; and I, Viscount St. Aldwyn, was appointed Chairman of such Board; and whereas on April 18, 1912, such Board was duly recognised by the Board of Trade as the Joint District Board for the District of South Wales (including Monmouth); and

Whereas the Joint District Board failed to settle the first minimum rates of wages and district rules within three weeks after the time at which it was recognised, and the members of the Board representing the workmen, and the members representing the employers, agreed to substitute the specified period of ten weeks for three weeks, for the purpose of Subsection (2) Section 4 of the Coal Mines (Minimum Wage) Act, 1912; and

Whereas rules of procedure for the conduct of the business of the Board, and a classification of the workmen to whom the Act applies, were agreed to by the Board; and

Whereas it was agreed to by the Board that the standard rates of December, 1879, or the equivalent as provided by Clause 10 of the Conciliation Board agreement of December, 1910, should be taken as a basis for the general minimum rates of wages, plus the percentage additions from time to time payable under the said agreement, and that special district minimum rates less than the general district rates should be applicable to coal mines in Pembrokeshire; and

Whereas it was decided by my casting vote that a standard rate of 3s. should be taken as the basis for the minimum day wage rate of labourers over 18 years of age, and it was subsequently decided by my casting vote that the age for an adult workman of every class, except haulier trammers and riders, should be 21 instead of 18, and that on this understanding the minimum day wage rate of labourers should be reconsidered; and

Whereas the Board has failed to settle the first general minimum rates of wages and district rules, and the first special minimum rates of wages for Pembrokeshire, within the aforesaid period of ten weeks;

Now I, as Chairman of the Board, in pursuance of the terms of the Coal Mines (Minimum Wage) Act, 1912, having heard the parties, do hereby settle the said rates, rules and special rates, as follows, viz:— . . .

L*

SCHEDULE I

Part I
General District Minimum Rates of Wages

The general rates of wages shall be the standard rate hereinafter fixed for each class of underground workmen, to which is to be added the percentage from time to time payable under the Conciliation Board agreement of December 1910.

Class 1.—Workmen over 21 Years of Age

	Standard rate of day wage
	s. d.
1. Collier in charge of a working place, who is a regular pieceworker, and is prevented from earning piecework wages by a fault in the seam or other cause arising in the colliery and beyond his own control, or by a request from the management to work away from his place on more than seven days during a period of three months	4 7
(In any other case the minimum day wage rate of such a collier working at day wages away from his working place shall be the minimum day wage rate applicable to the class in which he is working.)	
2. Collier in charge of a working place who is not a worker at piecework (subject to the above rule)..	4 3
3. Colliers' helpers	3 4
4. Timbermen, and repairers or rippers doing timbering work —regular pieceworkers	4 7
Day wage men	4 3
5. Rippers (not doing timbering work)	4 0
6. Assistant timbermen and assistant rippers	3 4
7. Roadmen	3 7
8. Hitchers (leading)	3 10
(ordinary)	3 6
9. Ostlers and labourers	3 2
10. Underground hauling engineers, electric, steam and compressed air main haulage	3 4
Subsidiary haulage	3 2
11. Underground pumpmen, electric, steam and compressed air—main pumps	3 4
Small pumps	3 2
12. Fitters if employed entirely underground	3 4
13. Electricians if employed entirely underground	3 5
14. Rope splicers if employed entirely underground	3 10
15. Masons and pitmen if employed entirely underground ..	4 2
16. Cog cutters	3 5
17. Timber drawers and airway men	3 10
18. Shacklers and spragmen and watermen	3 2
19. Lamplockers, lamplighters, oilers	3 0
20. Coal-cutter men	4 3

Class 2.

	Standard rate of day wage
	s. d.
Boys under 15 years of age	1 6
Boys over 15 and under 16	1 9
,, ,, 16 ,, ,, 17	2 0
,, ,, 17 ,, ,, 18	2 3
,, ,, 18 ,, ,, 19	2 6
,, ,, 19 ,, ,, 20	2 9
,, ,, 20 ,, ,, 21	3 0

Class 3.

	s. d.
Hauliers above 18 years of age—	
(1) Day hauliers	3 11
(2) Night hauliers	3 8
Tonnage hauliers, above 18 years of age, for hauling coal ..	4 2
Riders above 18 years of age	3 9
Trammers above 18 years of age	3 3

In collieries where night hauliers are now paid day hauling rates that practice shall continue.

Part II

Special District Minimum Rates of Day Wage for Coal Mines in Pembrokeshire

Class 1.—Mines East of the River Claddau

The rates fixed are standard rates of December 1879, to which is to be added the percentage from time to time payable under the Conciliation Board agreement of December 1910.

	s. d.
1. Coal hewers	3 0
2. Underground enginemen	2 7
3. Hitchers and banksmen	2 7
4. Roadmen, repairers, hauliers, riders and beam-men ..	2 6
5. Trammers over 16 years of age	2 2
6. Boys under 15 years (increasing by a standard rate of 2d. with each year of age until placed in one of the above classes)	1 0

Class 2.—Mines West of the River Claddau

The minimum rates of day wages shall be the following nett rates:
Cutters and repairers, 3s.; assistant cutters, assistant repairers and hitchers, 2s. 9d.; trammers, beam-men and unskilled labourers, 2s. 6d.; boys under 16, 1s.; from 16 to 18, 1s. 6d.; from 18 to 20, 2s.; after 20, their class rate.

Part III

The several scales applicable to boys in this schedule shall apply to boys who have started underground work at 14, and have continued to work underground. A boy starting underground work at a later age than 14 to be paid the minimum provided for the age a year below his actual age, until he has had a year's experience of underground work. Afterwards the minimum applicable to his age shall apply.

The minimum wages fixed by this schedule shall be free from any deductions for explosives.

All customs, usages, practices or conditions for the payment of extra or additional wages, or for the supply of fuel, now existing at the respective coal mines to which the minimum wages fixed in this schedule are to apply, shall remain in full force and virtue notwithstanding anything contained in this schedule, except that the minimum day wage fixed for workmen doing hauliers' work is to include payment for dooring.

APPENDIX III TO CHAPTER ELEVEN

RE-ORGANISATION SCHEME: FINAL BALLOT, 1913

District	Voting in Ballot on Re-organisation Scheme	
	For	Against
Aberdare	1,297	1,739
Afan Valley	692	1,193
Blaina	829	2,280
Dowlais	77	343
East Glamorgan	934	1,590
Ebbw Vale	457	3,102
Eastern Valley	1,114	2,691
Garw	1,310	1,489
Merthyr	606	1,919
Maesteg	901	4,371
Mon. Western Valley	2,645	4,995
Ogmore and Gilfach	847	860
Pontypridd and Rhondda	1,237	792
Rhondda No. 1	4,928	5,775
Rhymney Valley	1,096	2,404
Saundersfoot	55	211
Taff and Cynon	520	995
Tredegar Valley	1,472	4,876
Western	2,999	1,883
Totals ..	24,016	43,508

CHAPTER TWELVE

YEAR OF THE GREAT DISASTER

I. SMALL STEPS TO BETTER ORGANISATION

THE ballot votes of the beginning of February had been decisive:
the structure of the South Wales Miners' Federation was not to be
changed. As it had begun in 1898, so it was to continue. After all the
repeated attempts at a different constitution, all summed up by the
slogan word "centralisation," after the programme for thorough-
going change put forward by the "unofficial reform committee," the
old organisation of the separate valley districts, each with its own
sovereign "tsar" was to remain—and was to persist for another
score of years. It was darkly hinted at the time (and repeated a
quarter of a century later by one of the younger agents) that the
old Lib-Labs of the Executive Council had wrecked the scheme, that
they had cunningly thrown a monkey-wrench into the proposed new
machinery of administration (accepted in provisional form in
September 1912) in the shape of a proposal to double the existing
Union contribution. This may or may not have been so: but it was
widely believed at the time by the aggrieved young leaders of the
minority.

But though centralisation was thus defeated, and rejected for a
generation, some changes began to show themselves both in personnel
and in organisation. The election on June 6, 1912, of the outspoken
socialist James Winstone as vice-president was a sign of change.[1]
The four officers had always been Lib-Labs since 1898: but now one
of the four was a close associate and follower and namesake of James
Keir Hardie. By the end of June, 1912, a new agent for the Garw

[1] The election of James Winstone to vice-presidency when Mabon vacated the presidency twenty months earlier was a sign of that change in the outlook of the delegates from
the standpoint of the first ten years of the South Wales Miners' Federation. It was not
simply the choice of a veteran member of the Executive then entering his fiftieth year,
nor was it the recourse to yet another stalwart from Monmouthshire like the other three
officers of the Federation. For Winstone had been singled out much earlier as one of the
more advanced members not only by his attitude on Federation policy but by his outspoken socialist standpoint. But he went far beyond Brace in his political standpoint.
He was a member of the Independent Labour Party, a close associate of Keir Hardie, and
a determined fighter in local elections. After many struggles he was elected to one position
in local government after another. As a member of the Risca Urban District Council he
was responsible for the move to adopt there the Housing of Working Classes Act. Later
he was elected to the Abersychan Council. He was also on the Pontypool Board of
Guardians. Later he was to be elected chairman of the Monmouthshire County Council.
In Monmouthshire he was the vice-chairman of the Education Committee and represented the Council both on the County Councils Association and on the governing body of
the University of Wales.

district, Frank Hodges, a Ruskin College "striker," had taken his seat on the Executive Council. Henceforward, the brood of Ruskin and the Central Labour College began to appear more and more in key positions as lodge delegates or lodge secretaries; and they were also to be found in other official posts—checkweighers, Executive Council members, or agents.

On August 29, 1912, the Executive Council, hitherto meeting usually in Royal Chambers in Park Place, met for the first time at 22 St. Andrew's Crescent, Cardiff. By the spring of 1913 proposals for the equipment of the new office with a full personnel were put to the annual conference (on March 31st) and duly carried. Thus, after fifteen years of somewhat makeshift arrangements the Federation had at last permanent headquarters; their general secretary, Tom Richards, M.P., had become "a full-time officer" and his brother-in-law, Evan Thomas, Assistant Secretary "at a salary of £150 per annum." Tom Bateman of Dowlais was appointed to be "the clerk" at £100 per annum.

A further step forward was taken at the 1913 Annual Conference on March 31st when the 215 delegates (representing 109,462 members) now began to bring forward policies for their conference which were designed to stimulate the M.F.G.B. on specific questions. These were such as amendments to the Coal Mines (Minimum Wage) Act and to the Eight Hours Act (to include surface workers). The Nightmen's Bonus Turn, a New Standard Rate and Co-operative Action of Trade Unions were the headings of resolutions. The conference also began to press the Labour Party to be more insistent on behalf of "the education of the children of the working class" and also for housing by public authorities. Other resolutions, of considerable importance, dealt with electoral policy and with "non-union men." For this last resolution a day was fixed when non-unionists had to be "brought into compliance."

For several years the number who paid no union dues had been on the increase. Indeed, the proportion organised in the Federation had fallen very low, and this throughout years of rapid growth in the total manpower. In 1900 there were 148,000 employed in the South Wales coalfield and of these the proportion enrolled in the South Wales Miners' Federation[1] was nearly 87 per cent. Twelve years later there were 225,000 employed of whom only 50 per cent were in the Federation. Membership, fluctuating up and down, had been at its lowest in 1905 with 110,000; and at its peak with 144,000 in 1908: but then, and precisely in the years of growing "industrial unrest," there had been a great falling away.

This was in the sharpest contrast to the general tendency, not only

[1] Boys were half-members and counted as such.

in the coal mining industry but in all British industries, where between the end of the year 1905 and the end of 1911 the membership of all trade unions increased from just under two millions to just over three millions. In coal mining and quarrying nearly half a million organised in trade unions in 1905 had become three-quarters of a million by the end of 1911: and this 50 per cent increase applied to nearly every coalfield other than South Wales.

There were discussions at the time as to why the South Wales coalfield had reached this exceptional situation. One obvious reason was that the very rapid influx of labour in these years came mainly from rural Wales or from the nearest English counties such as Hereford, Gloucestershire and Somerset—areas in which wages were extremely low and trade unionism largely unknown. On the other hand there may have been a small proportion of "non-union men" who had ceased to pay their union dues because of dissatisfaction with the relatively meagre results that had come from the union's activity on the Conciliation Board and otherwise. In a particular year such as 1911 the strain imposed by the Cambrian Combine dispute with its recourse to high levies may have to be reckoned as a factor.

Both in the Executive as a whole and in each valley organisation it was now felt that the situation was becoming rather serious. The first steps, however, were taken not by the separate valleys but by collieries in various places stopping work in February, 1913. Indeed, it had begun in the winter: it was reported that collieries in the Garw Valley on December 2, 1912, were idle on the question of non-unionism, there being 2,500 men affected. Again, the Cwm Dare collieries were idle owing to "non-unionism trouble," 1,000 being affected on February 1st. On February 3rd the Gwaun-cae-gurwen collieries stopped work because of "non-unionism trouble," and, by the middle of the month many collieries had stopped on this question. On February 17, 1913, the Western District decided to give a month's notice on March 1st on the problem of non-unionism. A few days later the Rhondda District and the Rhymney Valley District each gave a month's notice on the question. If all these were to have taken action simultaneously it would have been a strike of greater dimensions than that of the Cambrian Combine two years earlier. There was therefore reason enough for the Annual Conference on April 1st to take its decision fixing a day "when all workmen employed at the collieries are expected to become members of the Federation." This was followed immediately by a letter to all lodge secretaries from Thomas Richards, in the following terms:

That Thursday, the 1st of May (Labour Day), is to be observed as a General Holiday by all colliery workmen throughout the coalfield, and that prior to that day all workmen are expected to become members of the Federation.

The letter stipulated that "Simultaneous show cards" during this month were to be organised at all collieries "at which there are at present non-union men employed," and that the general result would be considered "at mass meetings to be held upon May 1st." A further decision was that workmen employed "at all the collieries reported to be free from non-union men shall return to work" on Friday, May 2nd.

Following their annual conference the Executive Council invited representatives of the Enginemen to come to their meeting on April 2nd. It was just under a twelve month since the sharp difference between the two unions at the time of the ending of the Minimum Wage strike. Brace welcomed the visitors and said it was the desire of the Federation that all workmen employed at the collieries should belong to the same organisation. The enginemen's representatives agreed to work out "proposals for amalgamation"; and these they submitted by the end of May 1913. To these the Executive Council put forward amendments "in the direction of making provision for the merging of this Association in the Federation, rather than upon a system of amalgamation, as proposed by the Enginemen's Association." (*16.vi.1913.*) At the joint meeting that afternoon much discussion ensued. Speeches and counter-speeches were delivered at some length until an adjournment was made, after which W. Hopkins stated that they now desired to substitute an annual conference for a quarterly conference, and that their connection with the national union should be continued until Whitsuntide 1914, when they would be prepared to sever their connection. William Brace replied that no separate conference could be accepted, but they accepted the proposal for national association. The following proposal was made on behalf of the Federation Council:

That the lodges of the Enginemen, Stokers and Surface Craftsmen at present in existence shall continue and connect direct with the various Federation districts in which they are situated.

That the workmen eligible to join these lodges shall be confined to workmen who are solely engaged in the working or maintenance of the colliery machinery.

Any lodge at any time not having 40 members, or when mutually decided, shall be disbanded, and the members transferred to the miners' lodge.

The Enginemen's lodges shall be entitled to representation at district meetings and conferences, in accordance with rule.

The Executive Council minute of this joint meeting concludes:

It being understood that the foregoing conditions for "merge" were agreed upon, a sub-committee was appointed to draw up the detail terms. (*16.vi.1913.*)

It seemed that at last "a marriage had been arranged": but in the event it was to be a long time ahead before the solemnisation of the nuptials which had been so devoutly desired by the Executive Council and particularly by the band of unofficial reformers headed by Noah Rees, Hodges and Noah Ablett.

2. SAFETY

All mining whether it be for gold or silver or uranium is arduous and dangerous. When vapours of a noxious kind ooze from minerals such as cinnabar or coal, there is a double danger. Only "they that go down to the sea in ships" are in greater peril of life and limb than those who go down the mine to get coal. Wives and mothers walk at all times in the shadow of calamity. This has been true of every coalfield of Europe: and of none more than of the coalmining valleys of Monmouthshire and Glamorgan. On the average four miners suffered death each day in the British coalfields. But though the total number of deaths actually increased from 1900 to 1920 there had been a steep fall in the rate of fatal accidents throughout the previous fifty years. From 1850, when the number of deaths per hundred thousand employed underground was 514·9, there was a gradual fall to 1885 when the figure was 252·3 and from that to a rate of 144·5 in 1900. There was a rise to 151·9 in 1905 and 191·7 in 1910. This fatal accident rate was due to falls of ground to a much greater extent than to any other cause—far greater than shaft accidents, haulage accidents or accidents of other kinds, and greater, too, than explosions. But amongst all the other causes of deaths underground the public attention was chiefly caught by the explosions of firedamp or coaldust which involved the loss of very many lives at once.

In these multitudinous sudden deaths South Wales holds a melancholy eminence from the story of its past no matter how far back the statistics carry us in our search. The output of the South Wales coalfield between 1851 and 1871 was only an eighth to a ninth of the total output of coal in the United Kingdom: while by the early eighties it was about a seventh, with manpower rising in a roughly corresponding proportion. But the proportion of fatal accidents was higher by whatever measurement was used: and the proportionate number of principal[1] disasters caused by explosion was very much higher. Between 1851 and 1860 the toll of principal disasters in the South Wales coalfield was one third of the United

[1] Principal disasters are "those involving a loss of ten lives or more."

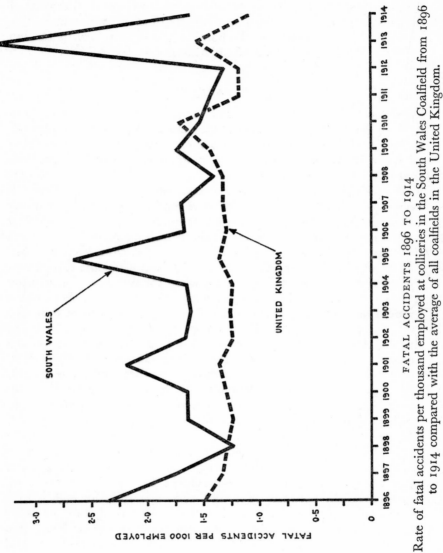

FATAL ACCIDENTS 1896 TO 1914

Rate of fatal accidents per thousand employed at collieries in the South Wales Coalfield from 1896 to 1914 compared with the average of all coalfields in the United Kingdom.

Kingdom total at a time when the South Wales output was only one ninth of the whole: and so it went on decade after decade. Over the whole of the seventy years up to 1920 the South Wales figures of death in principal disasters added up to 3,179 compared with a British total of 8,520. Of all the coal wound to the surface in Britain, South Wales furnished from one ninth in the fifties to a fifth in the second decade of the twentieth century: but it always cost about a third of the total deaths. How frequently explosions were located in the South Wales coalfield is shown by the list of 27 British disasters from 1890 up to 1913; no less than thirteen were in this one coal-field.[1]

From the very beginning of mining trade unionism the question of safety played a very big part in their concerns. No less than three of the original seven objects of the M.F.G.B. bore upon this question. The sixth object, for example, was: "To deal with and watch all inquests upon persons killed in the mines where more than three persons are killed by any one accident." So soon as the South Wales miners in the course of the year 1899 were received into the M.F.G.B. this rule was applied. Out of 24 such inquiries in the eight years

[1] *Principal Colliery Disasters*
Caused by Explosion of Fire-damp or Coal Dust
in the Years 1890 to 1913

Year	Date		Name of Colliery	County	No. of Killed
1890	February	6	Llanerch	Monmouth	176
	March	10	Morfa	Glamorgan	87
1891	April	2	Apedale, Sladderhill Pit	Stafford	10
	August	31	Malago Vale	Somerset	10
1892	August	26	Nth. Navigation, Park Slip	Glamorgan	112
1893	July	4	Combs	York	139
1894	June	23	Albion, Cilfynydd	Glamorgan	290
1895	April	26	Quarter	Stirling	13
1896	January	26	Tylorstown	Glamorgan	57
	April	13	Brancepeth	Durham	20
	April	30	Micklefield	York	63
1899	August	18	Llest, Garw	Glamorgan	19
1901	May	24	Universal (Senghenydd)	Glamorgan	81
1902	September	3	McLaren No. 1 Pit, Tredegar	Monmouth	16
1905	January	21	Elba, Gowertown.	Glamorgan	11
	March	10	Cambrian, Clydach Vale	Glamorgan	33
	July	11	National, Wattstown	Glamorgan	119
1906	October	10	Wingate Grange	Durham	25
1908	February	20	Washington, "Glebe"	Durham	14
	April	9	Norton Hill	Somerset	10
	August	18	Maypole	Lancaster	75
1909	February	16	West Stanley	Durham	168
	October	29	Darran	Glamorgan	27*
1910	May	11	Whitehaven, Wellington Pit	Cumberland	136
	December	21	Hulton, No. 3 Bank Pit	Lancaster	344
1912	July	9	Cadeby Main	York	88†
1913	October	14	Senghenydd	Glamorgan	439

* Including five persons killed during rescue operations.
† There were two explosions on the same day. As a result of the first 35 persons were killed, the second explosion causing the loss of 53 members of the rescue parties.

between 1899 and 1907, no less than 16 out of the 24 dealt with disasters in South Wales.[1] When the Garw disaster occurred on August 18, 1899, the Executive Committee of the M.F.G.B. were prompt to give what aid they could to their Welsh comrades. They sent down Ben Pickard, M.P., President of the M.F.G.B. and Treasurer Enoch Edwards. In the Garw disaster 19 men met their death at the Llest Pit, suffocated as the result of an explosion of gas. The gas accumulated "in the stall of Abednego Williams": and was ignited by the introduction of naked lights. It was a fiery mine: the Government inspector had warned the manager of the danger of working the colliery with naked lights; but nevertheless the manager had continued the practice with the result that "19 persons lost their lives in consequence thereof." He had not merely acted against advice of Government inspectors, but also against General Rule No. 8 of the Mines Act of 1887 which stipulated that if locked safety lamps had to be used then naked lights must not be used in the same district of the mine. In their report Ben Pickard, M.P. and E. Edwards stated that the enquiry was "in some respects unique in its character. We not only had the ordinary court with its various officials, but the interpreter": and they went on to recount how—

Although some of the witnesses could speak English they elected to give their evidence in Welsh. This gave the witness a splendid opportunity to take time before answering questions and to give his evidence much more leisurely and with much advantage. He first of all understood the question in English, then had the question again put to him in Welsh, thereby giving him ample time to reply to the question either evasively, ambiguously, or in an indirect form. There is no need to say that this was fully taken advantage of by the said witnesses.

On the other hand a light was thrown on the difficulty encountered in eliciting the facts at such inquests because of the risk of unemployment run by any of the miners who were willing to give evidence that told against their employers. In the opinion of Pickard and Edwards "The witnesses produced by the men did fairly well, and stuck to their brief with manly courage, considering their position and the general opinion of those by whom they were surrounded."

The M.F.G.B. president and treasurer said that the mining experts gave evidence which was "discreditable and unwarrantable under the circumstances."

They criticised also the Mines Inspectors for not pushing more firmly for the suppression of naked lights and they ended by saying that "the verdict was certainly against the weight of evidence."

[1] M.F.G.B. Reports of Inquiries into Explosions 1890/1908, page 44.

The verdict ran:

The jury regrets that safety lamps were not in use in this colliery previous to the explosion, and consider that the management unfortunately committed an error of judgment in not introducing them.

3. THE ROYAL COMMISSION ON MINES

On June 7, 1906 there was appointed a Royal Commission on Mines particularly to deal with the health and safety of miners. This meant an inquiry into the administration of the Mines Acts. It also was to inquire into the existing system of investigation and inquiry into accidents, this last being a matter on which the miners' leaders in South Wales held very definite views. They held the view that inspection could not be considered adequate. Inspection took place "by sample." Tom Richards, M.P., giving evidence from South Wales, told the Royal Commission:

We have several seams being worked in the same mine and it is possible for things to be alright in one seam, whereas they might be quite contrary in the other. I think it gives a false sense of security to both workmen and owners that Inspectors should visit a colliery in this way, because they may base their calculations that everything is alright on the inspection, whereas the Inspector is only inspecting a very small portion of the colliery.

Some seven years later these arguments were once more put forward by William Brace, M.P., as president of the South Wales Miners' Federation in a deputation to Reginald McKenna who was then Home Secretary:

A system of inspection by sample must lead people to live in a fool's paradise. A pit is peculiar to itself. You may have a great colliery in perfect condition save and except one small portion, but that small portion is enough, not only to devastate the mine, but to destroy all the lives in the pit. In face of that foundation of fact, to suggest that a system of inspection (which I will call inspection by sample) which in no case permits, unless it be in very small collieries, the whole of the mine to be inspected by your staff of nine Inspectors, is adequate, is to lead us into a feeling of security when there is no security. (*4.ii.1914.*)

At the Royal Commission on Mines representative owners and managers had been of the view that this inspection "by sample" was the only practicable method and was sufficiently effective. To them it appeared also to be the cheapest method, and the one that interfered least with the ordinary routine working of the pit. On the other hand those who spoke for the Miners' Federation of Great Britain had proposed that the French system of inspection should be adopted in Britain. This was the system by which workmen inspectors, or safety delegates, were elected from the workmen employed for a longer or shorter period, usually for several years, and during this period these workmen inspectors were paid directly by the Government out of monies contributed by the French mine-owners.

To adopt such a course would obviously have made it possible to increase to an adequate amount the total of inspection carried out throughout the coalfields of the United Kingdom. The three representatives of the miners, on the Royal Commission (W. Abraham, M.P., E. Edwards, M.P. and Robert Smillie) were in favour of this. The majority were against them. But the Royal Commission recommended a considerable increase in the staff of governmental inspectors and an improvement in their qualifications. The number was raised from a total staff of three dozen inspectors to nearly four score shortly after their report was published. The miners' representatives, however, could not be satisfied with this, con-siderable improvement though it was bound to be. Again and again they raised the question of workmen inspectors. Once more it was William Brace, M.P., who (in the same interview with the Home Secretary) made the proposition on behalf of South Wales, "the greatest coalfield in this Kingdom and the most disastrous coalfield, with a record so tragic that it frightens me when I think about it."

Brace said:

My proposition is that there should be a new set of inspectors created altogether, a staff of inspectors selected by the workmen but paid by the State. Those inspectors ought to be sufficiently numerous not to have more than a total of 5,000 men to look after, and, instead of their time being taken up by railway travelling, they should be placed in an area easily get-at-able so that they can give the whole of their time to their particular work. I suggest that these inspectors should be selected by a ballot of the workmen, in the same manner as the checkweighers are selected. (*14.ii.1914.*)

He went on to suggest that the amount required in salary would be about £7,000 a year for South Wales and about £40,000 a year for the United Kingdom. The Home Secretary at this point intervened and asked: "But how would your inspectors differ from the inspectors now appointed?" Brace replied bluntly "that the workmen instead of the Home Office would appoint them, but the Home Office would pay them." The Home Secretary asked: "How would they differ from the workmen's inspectors appointed under Section 16 of the Act of 1911?" In reply it was said that they would be the same class, their functions would be the same but, "they would be independent of the employers." "They are now," said the puzzled McKenna. Brace explained to him that the degree of independence was limited, saying: "They make an inspection of the mine today and tomorrow they will be at work; they have to earn their bread at that colliery under that employer." But no steps were taken to go beyond those that were to appear under Section 16 of the Act: it was a matter on which always thereafter particular stress was laid by the South Wales Miners' Federation.

4. COAL MINES ACT, 1911

The Report of the Royal Commission published in 1909, was not immediately followed by legislation. In the winter of 1910–11 the Executive Committee of the Miners' Federation of Great Britain more than once went on deputation to the Home Secretary to see if matters could be speeded up. Eventually a Bill was brought forward and passed its Second Reading on March 17, 1911. Three special conferences of the Miners' Federation were held in March, April and June on the Bill, clause by clause. The Executive Committee spent hour after hour upon it working out detailed amendments. There were meetings with the Home Secretary and joint meetings with the coalowners.

The trade union amendments were moved down on the Order Paper in the House of Commons by the mining Members of Parliament. The Bill with its 127 Sections and series of schedules was before the Standing Committee on twenty-three separate days and received a further three days' discussion before a Third Reading in the House of Commons on December 5, 1911. It passed without delay through the House of Lords and so on to the stage of Royal Assent, given on December 16, 1911. The Bill was to come into force two hundred days later on the July 1, 1912.

The key section read as follows:

Inspections on Behalf of Workmen

16—(1) The workmen employed in a mine may, at their own cost, appoint two of their number or any two persons, not being mining engineers, who are or who have been practical working miners and have had not less than five years' experience of underground work, to inspect the mine, and the persons so appointed shall be allowed once at least in every month, accompanied, if the owner, agent, or manager of the mine thinks fit, by himself or one or more officials of the mine, to go to every part of the mine, and to inspect the shafts, roads, levels, workings, airways, ventilating apparatus, old workings, and machinery, and shall, where an accident has occurred in a mine of which notice is required under this Act to be given, be allowed to go together with any person acting as legal adviser to the workmen, or with a mining or electrical engineer selected by the workmen, accompanied as aforesaid, to the place where the accident occurred, and to make such inspection as may be necessary for ascertaining the cause of the accident, subject, however, to the provisions of this Act requiring the place where an accident has occurred to be left as it was immediately after the accident.

This Coal Mines Act 1911 was perhaps the fullest example of that type of positive legislation which had been on the increase in the nineteenth century. Whereas previous statutes for some 700 years had mainly dealt out prohibitions, positive legislation of this kind developed largely with the growth of a new form of industry and a new working class. In taking care for the health and safety of the people or any sections of it, positive laws may be said to contain more provisions for "thou shalt" in contradistinction to the thousands of years of legislation from Khammurabi or the Mosaic Ten Commandments when the main stipulation of most statutes has run in the form of "thou shalt not."

An example may be cited from Part II of the Act which contains provisions as to safety in no less than 47 sections.[1]

Included in Section 71 is the stipulation that a barometer as well as a thermometer and hygrometer should be placed in conspicuous positions and regular readings entered in a book by the qualified officials. The reason, of course, for this particular provision was that under circumstances of low barometric pressure fire-damp (mainly made up of methane or marsh gas) would seep or ooze out of the coal seams in greater amounts than at times of high barometric pressure and would therefore materially add to the risks run by the workmen. Furthermore, the use of certain methods of ventilation was prescribed: and Section 31 (Clause 3) ran as follows:

> After the first day of January, nineteen hundred and thirteen, or such later date as, in view of the circumstances of the mine, may be fixed by the inspector of the division, there shall, in every mine in which a mechanical contrivance for ventilation is used, be provided and maintained in a condition to be put into immediate operation adequate means for reversing the air current.

5. SENGHENYDD

The Coal Mines Act, after the Royal Commission on Mines of 1906 to 1909, had been debated throughout the year 1911 and passed into law in the early winter of that year. Two years later there came the Senghenydd disaster. The explosion which in loss of life was "the greatest disaster in the annals of British mining" happened on Tuesday, October 14, 1913: the number who met their death was 439. It was a new pit, but one with a bad record because of the gaseous nature of the seams. On May 21, 1901, some five years after they had begun to wind coal from this relatively new pit, a disastrous

---

[1] These cover the following main headings: ventilation; safety lamps; shafts and windings; travelling roads and haulage; support of roof and sides; signalling; provisions as to machinery; electricity; explosives; prevention of coal dust; inspections as to safety; withdrawal of workmen in case of danger; and certain miscellaneous provisions.

explosion, by which 81 lives were lost, devastated the whole of the mine, only one man being saved alive. As late as 1910 there had been an outburst of gas that was not brought under control for four days and it had been necessary to withdraw the men from the pit. It was thus known to be among the more dangerous coal mines in Britain.

The Universal Colliery of Senghenydd lies at the head of the Aber Valley, a mile above Abertridwr and about eleven miles as the crow flies north/north-west of Cardiff. The seams worked were three in number. The underground workings were in two main divisions, the West side and the East side. The seams worked were won by two shafts, namely, the Lancaster (downcast) and the York (upcast) both 18½ feet in diameter and both sunk to a depth of nearly 2,000 feet. The West side (the scene of the explosion) was divided into six districts, namely, the West York, Pretoria, Mafeking, Kimberley, Ladysmith and Bottanic. The system of working was the long wall system, the width of the stalls being eleven yards "centre to centre." The output of coal was about 1,800 tons a day.

The village of Senghenydd had grown up with the colliery which was the source of livelihood for some two thousand families. That autumn morning men and boys had gone to work, but children had not yet gone off to school. It was 8.10 a.m. when the shock was heard and felt. Trevor Evans,[1] then a little lad, remembered it well: "I ran out into the street. The shock was terrible. We thought it was an earthquake."

What was the nature of this event, 800 fathoms deep, that could so shake the ground in the Aber Valley? The answer could not be given in full till five months later; then it could be found, at any rate to a considerable extent, in a narrative compiled by H.M. Chief Inspector of Mines from answers to questions that had been put to Edward Shaw, for twelve years the manager of the colliery. There were two under-managers, one for the East and one for the West side. Acting under the latter on the West side there were three over-men, one for the Ladysmith and Kimberley districts, one for Mafeking and one for Pretoria. Under them again were fourteen firemen, of whom seven on the day shift would be in charge that morning of about 430 to 440 men on the West side.

This then is the narrative as derived from the answers to questions given by Edward Shaw:

When the explosion occurred, Mr. Shaw, the Manager, was in the lamp room at the surface. At ten minutes past eight o'clock he heard a report and at once went over to the Lancaster pit and saw that the surface in the immediate vicinity was wrecked, that the banksman was

[1] Afterwards for many years chief industrial correspondent of the *Daily Express* at the peak of its four million a day circulation: and now Sir Trevor.

killed and the assistant banksman injured. After visiting the fan and finding everything right there, and having given order to a mechanic about taking out the broken cage at the top of the downcast shaft and repairing the planking over the pit head, he was joined by D. R. Thomas, the overman, and together they got into the cage at the top of the upcast shaft, examined the air for a distance of fifty yards and found it foul with smoke and fumes. Signals were being sent up from below, so being joined by others, they descended the shaft. When halfway down they saw the body of a man in a tram in the upcoming cage with his legs hanging on the crossbars. This man had been practically blown into the tub in the cage at the pit bottom. They signalled to stop the cage, crossed into the other, and pulled in the body and then continued their descent. . . .

The overman, D. R. Thomas, who gave a clear and graphic account of his movements, said that when he got into the Main West Level and worked along towards the West, "it was exactly like looking into a furnace." There were no stones lying about on the road, a point of importance when discussing the probable point of origin of the explosion. Thomas was then told by the Manager to go to the East side with a party of men, while he, with one other man, remained on the West side.

Mr. Shaw proceeded along the Main West Level for a distance of forty yards to where the hauling engine was situated, and found the planking of the engine beginning to blaze. He and the man with him knocked down the planking and extinguished the fire. Then they went on to the crab engine, and the timber there was on fire "and all the timber, so far as I could see from there on was all ablaze. . . . Every collar blazing in front of me for twenty or thirty yards." No falls of any magnitude had as yet taken place there and for a distance of thirty or forty yards, "but the laggings were just beginning to break down."

These quotations are sufficient to show the nature of the explosion as it first appeared to those who went down to investigate and to help. In giving in some detail the remainder of these attempted rescue operations, the Chief Inspector of Mines, who for the Inquiry was appointed Commissioner, incidentally made some criticisms. For example, on page 22 of his report, paragraph 73, he said:

Mr. Shaw stated that within the hour he had men at work connecting the pipes to the column in the downcast shaft and bringing water through the first cross-cut on the West side, but that they were greatly hindered in their work by smoke and fumes, and that it was not until the arrival of breathing apparatus from the Porth Rescue Station—about eight miles distant—that a proper connection was made. As this was not until 11 o'clock—word not having been received at the Rescue Station until 10 o'clock—much valuable time was lost. There were trained rescue brigade men at the colliery, but no breathing apparatus was kept on the premises.

Secondly, the Commissioner commented adversely on the water supply as follows:

In my opinion the insufficiency of the water supply was a most regrettable incident. Of course, there is always the risk of pipes in shafts or underground being broken by the force of an explosion, but the time lost in repairing them would be much less than that absorbed by having to instal a complete column.

At the Inquiry I asked Mr. Shaw whether, in view of the previous disaster—though, as a matter of fact, there was no fire on that occasion—he did not think it would have been advisable to have made arrangements for conveying more water into the mine to meet the case of a possible fire in the future, and he replied, "Well, looking back on what has happened I agree it would have been advisable." At that we must leave it.

The narrative continued by saying:

When Dr. Atkinson and myself arrived on the scene on Tuesday afternoon at 5.30 p.m. the fire was being fought with water and fire extinguishers. No actual fire was then visible, it being buried beneath falls, and it was arranged to fill away and send to the surface as much of the heated debris as possible, and so advance against the fire. Shifts were arranged to carry out this work, each shift acting under a colliery official or mining engineer and each shift working for six hours. (Para. 77.)

The speed of the fan was slackened the day after the explosion.

A Committee of mining engineers and others was appointed on Wednesday midday to control the rescue operations.

6. ACTION OF THE UNION

When the mournful tidings spread through the coalfield a special session of the Executive Council of the South Wales Miners' Federation was summoned to meet on the spot. There in the Gwernymilwr Hotel of Senghenydd, after passing a vote of sympathy and condolence with the relatives of those who were killed, they resolved: "That the Home Secretary be requested to hold a full and independent Enquiry into the circumstances of the disaster at Senghenydd Colliery." (*16.x.1913*.) How was the stricken village of Senghenydd to be relieved? On this it was resolved:

That this Executive Council of the South Wales Miners' Federation forthwith appeal to the public for funds to relieve the great distress which arises as a result of the terrible disaster, and further that the Officials of the Federation at once interview the Lord Mayors of the Cities of London and Cardiff, with a view to funds being opened for them.

The officials were authorised to inform the Lord Mayors that the Federation would be prepared, at a later date, to confer with them on any proposals which might be suggested "for the amalgamation of the funds and for the administration thereof."

The meeting had been convened at the scene of the disaster in the Aber Valley as so many of the Council members were already there, giving a helping hand. On the surface they were busy with others, at whatever had to be done. Beneath was still an inferno of stench and flames and noxious vapours. Those who went down to rescue the entombed men found themselves fire-fighting and exploring a chaos.

Men there "on behalf of the Federation" were formed into a party, with Vice-president James Winstone charged to give any necessary instructions. Four days after the explosion, there was still gas in the main intake "immediately over the fire"; but, according to a message from Winstone to his colleagues meeting on the Saturday in Cardiff, they had "made considerable progress in abating the raging fire" (*18.x.1913.*), while on the surface "they ought to have money to relieve the distress." The Council recommended all the lodges to call a levy in support of the Relief Fund: and also to ask the employers "to deduct a levy in the offices if they are requested by the lodges to do so." (*20.x.1913.*) This the owners agreed to do.

Back at the Gwernymilwr Hotel in Senghenydd on Saturday, October 25th, the Executive Council was concerned chiefly with the distress and poverty consequent on the explosion. How was financial support to be given? They took the decision to call a conference in the Cory Hall to raise funds to relieve the distress caused by the Senghenydd disaster and "to further consider the provision of funds for unemployment generally." (*25.x.1913.*) At the opening of the Conference thus hurriedly called, the delegates heard the following telephone message received from their Vice-President Winstone at Senghenydd:

We have been able to explore the Ladysmith District to a point 1,654 yards from the bottom of the pit, which leaves us 454 yards from the face, which we hope to reach to-day. We have recovered 80 bodies from the pit. We have been greatly impeded by large falls and accumulations of gas and have just gone over a fall 100 yards in length. (*31.x.1913.*)

In a vote of condolence, "this conference of the whole of the miners of South Wales" tended to the sorrowing relatives the "heartfelt sympathy and condolence of the 200,000 workmen who were united with them by many tender ties and associations, and who day by day are still exposed to the terrible dangers entailed in the production of coal." (*31.x.1913.*)

7. EXPEDIENCY AT THE HOME OFFICE

The resolution of the Cardiff Conference at the end of October had strongly supported the application for an inquiry made by the officials of the Miners' Federation of Great Britain. These together with W. Brace, M.P., had been instructed by their Executive Committee, meeting on the ninth day after the Senghenydd disaster, to seek an interview with the Home Secretary. They were to request the appointment of a special court of inquiry, "to consist of three persons representing respectively the Government, the colliery proprietors and the workmen." The Coal Mines Act 1911, had laid it down that, if in any mine an accident had caused "loss of life or personal injury to any person," the Home Secretary might call for a special report from an inspector, but in more serious cases a court of inquiry was allowed for and expected.[1] The Act of Parliament which conferred on the Home Secretary these new powers to take action, if thought "expedient" had come into operation after the end of June 1912: but October 1913 found the Home Secretary reluctant to exercise them. October came to an end: and the first ten days of November had passed. In all the coalfields there was mounting anxiety: with 439 miners burned to death or suffocated, surely the law would soon be put into force.

Meantime in London there was no sign of movement in the Home Office. At an Executive Committee in Southport President Smillie told how the officials, with William Brace, had met Home Secretary McKenna, who had expressed a considerable amount of sympathy with their application and said that he thought a special Court should be appointed. He had stated, however, that he would have to "consult the other side" and also go into the legal position. "He had also gone so far as to say that he thought no colliery owner could be found to serve on the Court, in which event he would be helpless." Thereupon the Miners' Federation of Great Britain Executive Committee resolved:

That we express our disappointment and dissatisfaction with the position taken up by the Home Secretary, and that we appoint the deputation to again meet him and urge upon him the necessity of appointing such a Court as the deputation who waited upon him on Monday, October 27, 1913, asked for. (*11.xi.1913.*)

A fortnight later the Executive Committee heard the report from Robert Smillie that "they had met the Home Secretary, but he was afraid they had got very little further than at their last interview with him. Mr. McKenna said that they had been trying to get over the difficulty in which they found themselves, and in the result he was

[1] Section 83 of the Act, dealing with courts of inquiry, opened with the following words:
"83—(1) Where it appears to the Secretary of State that a formal investigation of any accident and of its causes and circumstances is expedient, the Secretary of State may direct such investigation to be held, and with respect to any such investigation the following provisions shall have effect:—
(a) The Secretary of State may appoint a competent person to hold the investigation, and may appoint any person or persons possessing legal or special knowledge to act as assessor or assessors in holding the investigation:
(b) The person or persons so appointed (hereinafter called the court) shall hold the investigation in open court, in such manner and under such conditions as the court may think most effectual for ascertaining the causes and circumstances of the accident, and enabling the court to make the report in this section mentioned."

forced to the conclusion that the only person likely to take part in the court on the owners' side was the President of the South Wales Coal Owners' Association." After some discussion it was resolved:

That this Executive Committee, after full consideration of the report of the officials on their interview with the Home Secretary, hereby decide that this Federation will not be satisfied unless a court of three persons be appointed to inquire into the cause of the explosion at Senghenydd Colliery, and we instruct our Secretary to send a copy of this resolution to the Home Secretary. (*25.xi.1913.*)

Nearly three more weeks elapsed. Still there had been no reply from the Home Secretary as to the appointment of a Court of Inquiry into "the real cause of the explosion," whereupon the Secretary was instructed "to write the Home Secretary for a definite reply on this matter, and if the reply is not satisfactory this Committee must be called together again." (*12.xii.1913.*)

It was not until December 18th, or nine weeks after the disaster, that the Home Office consented to set up an Inquiry.

8. INQUEST AND HOME OFFICE INQUIRY

The inquest which by ancient law must be held in a Coroner's Court to find the cause of sudden death could take precedence over any other Court of Inquiry, whether criminal or civil, or, as in this case, one specially set up by the Secretary of State. Consequently although the opening sittings of this last were held in the Law Courts at Cardiff on Friday and Saturday, January 2 and 3, 1914, the proceedings had then to be adjourned for three weeks owing to the timing of the Coroner's Inquest. It might have seemed unnecessary for this overlapping of these two inquiries to take place, entailing a repetition of evidence and the attendance twice over of those most concerned. But these were two separate jurisdictions: and the Coroner whose office had existed for untold centuries was not obliged to defer to any other authority. The Commissioner appointed by the Home Secretary to hold the statutory Inquiry had finally to yield though not without making public protest at the inconvenience caused.

The inquest, held at Senghenydd on Monday, January 5, 1914, and on seven following days before David Rees the Coroner, had ended with a verdict of "accidental death." The more expert and also more thorough Inquiry came from a Warrant of Appointment issued by the Home Secretary on December 28, 1913, in the following terms:

In pursuance of Section 83 of the Coal Mines Act, 1911, I hereby appoint Mr. R. A. S. Redmayne, Chief Inspector of Mines, to hold a

formal investigation of the causes and circumstances of the disaster which
occurred at the Universal Colliery, Senghenydd, Glamorganshire, on
October 14, 1913.

And I further appoint Mr. Evan Williams and Mr. Robert Smillie to
act as Assessors in holding the investigation.

The sittings after a gap of over three weeks were resumed on
January 27, and continued on the following days for over three weeks
until February 21st. The inquiry was extensive (as may be seen from
the two massive volumes of the evidence) and thorough: altogether 52
witnesses were asked 21,837 questions. The different interests
represented at the Inquiry were:

The Lewis Merthyr Consolidated Collieries Limited (the owners
of the Senghenydd Colliery), and the Agent and Manager of the
Senghenydd Colliery: By Mr. John Sankey, K.C., and with him
The Hon. Trevor Lewis (instructed by Messrs. C. and W. Kenshole,
Aberdare).

A number of the bereaved families: By Mr. Clement Edwards,
M.P.

The Miners' Federation of Great Britain, and the Monmouthshire
and South Wales Colliery Enginemen, Stokers, and Surface Crafts-
man's Association: By Mr. W. P. Nicholas (of Messrs. Walter
Morgan, Bruce and Nicholas, Pontypridd) and with him Mr. W. E.
Harvey, M.P., and Mr. Edward Hughes.

The South Wales Miners' Federation, and the Senghenydd work-
men: By Mr. William Brace, M.P., with him Mr. Thomas
Richards, M.P., Messrs. Alfred Onions, James Winstone, Hubert
Jenkins, and D. Watts Morgan.

The General Association of Firemen and Deputies: By Mr. E.
Williams.

The investigation was painstaking. Edward Shaw, Agent and
Manager, was examined for three whole days: and some witnesses,
including James Winstone, were recalled again and again. But was it
comprehensive? There was one significant omission to which at the
close of the Inquiry Clement Edwards, M.P., drew attention: apart
from Edward Shaw, nobody came to represent the owners. This,
commented Clement Edwards, was an "extraordinary fact" that
no director of the company had put in an appearance "to show that
they took reasonable steps, as proprietors of this colliery, to see that
the Act was not broken, that there were no breaches of the Act, and
that there was no non-compliance with the Act or with the Regulations." (*20.iii.1914.*)

An answer to this was furnished by the solicitor for the Lewis
Merthyr Consolidated Collieries Company Limited, who said that
he was at a loss to understand why Clement Edwards had found fault

with the fact that "there was no director here to give evidence."
"The Inquiry," he said, was called "for the purpose of inquiring into
the causes of this explosion and also into the circumstances surrounding it": and he asked:

What possible assistance, if I had called a director before this Court,
could he have been? The directors, as we know, have no practical knowledge of the working of the mine, and so to have expected us to have
called either Lord Merthyr or any other director, I am certain you will
agree with me, would have been wasting the time of the Court.

Lord Merthyr: This was no other than the former Sir William
Lewis, founder of the Sliding Scale and of the Monmouthshire and
South Wales Coal Owners' Association, who had been the President
of the Mining Association of Great Britain, of the Institution of
Mining Engineers, and of the University College at Cardiff: he was
Chairman of the Monmouth and South Wales Board of Examination
for Mining Certificates. As a most representative coal owner he had
been chosen to serve on a series of Royal Commissions on Coal Mines,
on Royalties, on Labour; on the Action of Coal Dust in Mines; on
Coal Supplies; on Shipping Rings and on Trade Disputes. This
iron-master and coal owner, a Conservative in politics, had been
showered with honours. When he reached his 75th year there was
added to his knighthood and his baronetcy the honour of a barony;
and, with what his family must afterwards have regarded as an
unfortunate coincidence, their sire chose to be styled the first Baron
Merthyr of Senghenydd. He had hastened to the colliery that he
owned (and after which he was named) on the day of the disaster and,
it might have been thought, was therefore in a position to give useful
evidence. Lord Merthyr of Senghenydd was not summoned to the
Court of Inquiry.

Clement Edwards, M.P., had gone on to launch very serious
strictures on the conduct of the mine. He said: "A more amazing,
more flagrant, more culpable violation of an Act of Parliament I do
not recall." It was flagrant ignoring of the provisions of the Act
which was "pre-eminently a code of provisions and regulations for
securing the safety of the life and limb of those who work below
ground" . . . "arrived at as the solemn determination of Parliament
after the most exhaustive methods of inquiry" . . . "by differently
constituted bodies and experts."

It contains a whole set of provisions for avoiding the dangers of an
explosion, being initiated, and for avoiding the dangers of an explosion,
when initiated, extending to a calamitous length. But there is not a
single important provision contained in that Act for dealing with the
different factors, that go both to the initiation and to the promulgation of

an explosion, which has not, in part, been violated by the management of the Senghenydd Colliery.

Clement Edwards went on to say:

I am not going to travel in detail over every one of the breaches, but there have been breaches in regard to ventilation; there have been breaches in regard to gas tests; there have been breaches in regard to the reporting of gas; there have been breaches in regard to electric sparking; there have been breaches in regard to the dusting of roads. There have been, as far as I can analyse the evidence, something like twelve to fourteen specific breaches of the Act, and most of those breaches appertain to one aspect or another of the provisions which have been instituted for dealing with and preventing explosions. (*20.ii.1914.*)

Charles Kenshole, apart from his justification of the shielding of Lord Merthyr and other directors, as quoted above, did not attempt seriously to contest that there had been breaches of the Act. These, however, can best be dealt with in a consideration of the contents of the Report rather than from an examination of the voluminous pages of the minutes of proceedings of the 15-day long Inquiry.

9. THE COMMISSIONER'S REPORT

The reports to the Home Secretary, completed in April 1914, on the *Causes of and Circumstances attending the Explosion which occurred at the Senghenydd Colliery on Tuesday, October 14, 1913*, were by the Commissioner R. A. S. Redmayne and the two Assessors. Of these the main report including tables, appendices, maps and diagrams was in five parts: (1) Description of the Colliery; (2) The Condition of the Mine precedent to and at the time of the Explosion; (3) Narrative of the Explosion and of the Rescue Operations; (4) The Point of Origin and Cause of the Explosion; (5) Summary of Conclusions and Recommendations.

The first part of the report gave the description of the mine under such headings as electric signalling, ventilation, measurement of air currents, in which it was noted that:

The book in which the air measurements were entered was not in the form prescribed by the Secretary of State, and was not countersigned by the Manager and Under-manager. The management had, therefore, contravened Section 24 (1) and (2) of the Coal Mines Act, 1911. The requirement (c) contained in General Regulation 77 had not been carried out either in respect of the East or West Side prior to the Explosion.

The Commissioner therefore found himself unable to say what was the volume of air current traversing the working faces. Under the heading "Volume of inflammable gas generated" a table showed that this "amounted to about 1,200 cubic feet per minute," and the
M

comment was added that: The mine was in this "respect typical of the more 'fiery' mines in the steam coal area of the South Wales coalfield." It was, therefore, a mine "in which the best method of ventilation should be adopted, and as to the carrying out of which the greatest care should be exercised." Moreover the mine was in places liable to sudden outbursts of gas. In October 1910, on the occurrence of a large fall on the Mafeking Level "there was a heavy discharge of gas which continued to be delivered for four days after the fall was cleared. On this occasion the men were withdrawn from the mine."

Under the heading "Coal Dust" the Commissioner reported that though the roads were cleaned, this cleaning was not done every 24 hours and he added: "The roof and sides were not cleaned at all": and he concluded consequently that "the requirements of Section 62 (3) of the Coal Mines Act, 1911, were not fully observed." Subsequently under the heading "Arrangements for watering the mine," on which he had criticisms to make he also made the remark: "From my inspection of the mine, subsequent to the explosion, I have no doubt whatever that coal dust existed on the roof, sides and timber in dangerous quantity." Attention was drawn to the fact that in the disaster a dozen years earlier (under the same manager) where 81 persons lost their lives, Mr. S. T. Evans, K.C., M.P. (afterwards Sir Samuel Evans, one of H.M. Judges) in his report said that provisions should be made "for preventing the accumulation of coal dust, and for the regular and efficient watering of the roads, roofs, and sides in the main haulage and travelling ways in mines which are dry and dusty."

Again, in paragraph 36 the Commissioners stated: "The manner, too, of reporting the presence of gas was unsatisfactory in some instances." The same descriptive section had mentioned a series of infractions of the rules and regulations under which a coal mine had to be conducted. It is noticeable that at the time a Cardiff Professor[1] of Economics and Political Science was first to comment that, in this fiery mine and after the 1910 outburst of gas which was not got under control for four days, yet "in spite of this fire the manager, who was also the agent of the owners, had apparently not taken any special precautions. He did not even take any steps to carry into effect a large number of the provisions of the Coal Mines Act 1911."

As for the remainder of the report it would perhaps be fitting if mention is made of these infractions with which it was "bristling." In Part II, which dealt with the condition of the mine prior to and

[1] Herbert Stanley Jevons (1875–1955), geologist and economist, was professor at Cardiff till 1911. From then until 1914 (when he went to India) he was engaged in housing reform in the South Wales coalfield.

at the time of the explosion, the first point made was that the requirement in Section 71 (2) of the Act "That the barometer and hygrometer shall be read and recorded at such intervals and by such persons as may be prescribed by General Regulation" had not been carried out. Fortunately a barograph obtained from nearby Aberdare showed that on the day of the explosion and on the previous day there was no abnormal depression, that is, "there was no diminution in atmospheric pressure as would account for abnormal emissions of gas." Other causes had to be sought. But since nearly all the persons employed on the West side on the morning shift had been killed by the explosion, the Commissioner found it "very difficult to determine definitely what was the state of that side of the mine on the morning of October 14th."

Part III of the Commissioner's Report gave a narrative of the explosion and of the rescue operations. It is clear that the explosion and the disaster had three features—blast, fire and finally the after-damp (the name for the poisonous gases, largely carbon monoxide, after an explosion).

Another incidental criticism made by the Commissioner was on the mistake of those mining engineers called together by Lord Merthyr in that they ruled out the shutting off of air by means of sandbags. It was not until three days later that sandbags were procured and finally it was not until the second week of November that the fire was finally damped off so that exploration of the workings could be undertaken. The relevant passage is:

That the mining engineers and management anticipated successfully combating the fire within a short time is supported by the fact that when a suggestion was made that sand could be used for this purpose it was overruled as unnecessary. Ultimately, but not until October 17th, sandbags were procured from Cardiff. Mr. Clement Edwards put the following question to Mr. T. Greenland Davies, Junior Inspector of Mines: "I think you were present at an earlier stage when the Chief Inspector asked if there was a shortage of a supply of water, and they seriously considered the question of using sand, and Mr. Leonard Llewellyn said it was not a sandy district, and I said if it were a question of sand I could get a hundred volunteers, get the railway company to run a train, and we could have sand in a few hours from Penarth, and Mr. Llewellyn said they would have the fire out before they could get back," answered, "My impression is that that happened the next day" (*Wednesday*). Mr. Edwards: "You do remember what I have described?" Answer: "Yes."

Part V deals with the point of origin and cause of the explosion and the different theories put forward to account for it. There were two main views. One was that of the mining engineers called by those representing the owners and the management: and their theory was supported, to some extent, by the representatives of the men who gave evidence and who were themselves, as we know, agents; and also by one junior inspector of mines. The other main theory, that the explosion originated somewhere on the Mafeking incline, was put forward by Dr. W. N. Atkinson, H.M. Inspector of Mines for the South Wales Division, who in this opinion was supported by the Senior Inspector of Mines and by the Junior Inspector. Great weight had to be attached to the theory of Dr. Atkinson who was one of the most experienced technical experts of the whole inspectorate and, as such, had been lent by the British Government to the French Government at the time of the Courrières disaster in 1906. His theory was accepted by the Commissioner himself and also by the assessor Robert Smillie and by the two representatives present of the Miners' Federation of the Great Britain.

I find myself unable to accept the theory advanced by the owners to account for the explosion,

wrote the Commissioner who concluded that the weight of evidence was in favour of the theory of Dr. Atkinson.

10. THE COMMISSIONER'S CONCLUSIONS

The conclusions reached by R. A. S. Redmayne, H.M. Chief Inspector of Mines in his function as Commissioner were set out in part five of his report (Cd. 7346) under some half-dozen headings. On the probable site of the origin and possible cause of the explosion, he wrote:

After carefully weighing the facts revealed by the evidence of the various witnesses and from my own personal investigations underground at the Senghenydd Colliery, I have come to the conclusion that there is strong probability of the explosion having originated on the Mafeking Incline, and that it was preceded by an occurrence similar to that which took place further outbye in the Mafeking Return in October 1910, namely, by heavy falls liberating a large volume of gas.

These heavy falls exposed seams of coal and beds of hard rock, and an outburst of gas may have come away at one of them. The only apparent means of ignition would be sparks from the electric signalling apparatus, or from rocks brought down from the fall, and we know that explosions have been originated by both these causes.

The only other possible means of ignition were safety lamps or matches. The difficulty in regard to the former is that no lamp was found in the place, and even were a broken lamp found under a fall there would be the inference that it may have been broken by the fall. There were, however, lamps lower down the hard heading, but there is no evidence pointing to any of them having been the igniting cause of the explosion. In respect of matches, as has already been stated, a rigorous search of the persons descending the mine was being carried out daily, and the possibility of a match being the igniting cause is, in my opinion, remote.

After citing two General Regulations (118 and 132) which give the precautions to be taken to avoid "open sparking" from electrical wires and apparatus in mines with inflammable gas, he wrote:

Undoubtedly, therefore, electrical signalling was being used in a part of the mine in which there was likely to be inflammable gas in quantity sufficient to be indicative of danger.

It was argued by counsel appearing on behalf of the owners and management, and evidence was called to show, that the sparks caused by bringing the wires together, or in the ringing of the bells, were not of sufficient intensity to ignite gas—in effect that there was no "open sparking." In this connection I can only regret that the safer plan of excluding sparks altogether was not adopted.

It is all the more astonishing that the management should have faced the risk that the sparks produced *might* have ignited gas in view of the Bedwas Colliery explosion, which occurred on March 27, 1912, and which was proved beyond reasonable doubt to have been caused by the sparks from an electric bell. The attention of owners of mines throughout South Wales was called to this explosion in a circular letter sent out by Dr. Atkinson, dated August 28, 1912.

The Commissioner then drew further conclusions from the account of the rescue operations given in part three of his report and added some recommendations:

I incline to the belief that if rescue apparatus had been kept at the colliery, and men equipped with breathing apparatus and carrying with them a lighter form of apparatus, had at once penetrated the West York by the return and the Bottanic District a few more lives might have been saved.

I am convinced that had there been available at that time an adequate water supply, and had brigades of rescuers attacked the three fires (i.e. at the two cross-cuts and that on the Main West Level) simultaneously, the fires might have been extinguished in a comparatively short time.

I should have thought, in view of the fact that the colliery was such a gassy one, and as it had already been devastated by an explosion, that the management would have made arrangements for a supply of water adequate to meet an emergency of the kind that actually occurred.

On the state of the mine before the explosion the Commissioner chiefly dealt with the fact that the roof and sides had not been cleared of coal dust (a breach of the Act) which showed that "the mine was not in a satisfactory condition." He recommended either covered trams or thorough wetting of the coal ("I see no practical difficulty in the way of effecting either remedy"—para. 124). Then he wrote of "the desirability of stone dusting in mines" and added:

I know that apprehension exists in some quarters as to whether such a remedy would not be worse than the disease, the idea being that the introduction of stone dusting might be conducive to miners' phthisis, but I would point to the fact that dust derived from argillaceous shale has existed naturally in many mines in the United Kingdom for long past without, so far as I know, injurious effects resulting to the workmen employed therein.

"Miners' phthisis" was the term then used to describe a variety of lung diseases of which some were later to be known just as silicosis and then more comprehensively as pneumokoniosis.

After noting other infractions or failures to meet requirements laid down by law, the Commissioner listed a number of the more serious defects as follows in paragraph 133:

I have alluded in the body of the Report to several breaches of the Coal Mines Act, 1911, and the Regulations made under that Act, namely, failure to provide means for the immediate reversal of the air (breach of Section 31 (3)), failure to measure the air in each ventilating district, at, or as near as practicable to, a point 100 yards back from the first working place at the working face which the air enters (breach of General Regulation 77 (c)), failure to record the measurements of the air current in a book in the form prescribed by the Secretary of State and omission of manager and under-manager to countersign (breach of Section 24 (1) and (2)), failure by persons on whom responsible duties are imposed with respect to the ventilation underground to record the reading of the baro-meter immediately before going into the mine and after coming out of the mine (breach of Section 71 (2)) and failure to remove, as far as practicable, coal dust from the roof and sides (breach of Section 62 (3)).

Further breaches of the Coal Mines Act, 1911, referred to in the body of the Report are Section 34 (1) (iii), page 9, Section 64 (1), page 11, and in respect of General Regulation 60, page 12.

His general conclusion about the management was given in paragraph 134 as follows:

Some of these breaches, compared with those to which I have already given especial prominence may appear trivial, but taken in the aggregate they point to a disquieting laxity in the management of the mine.

I regret exceedingly to have to say this because Mr. Shaw impressed me as an honest, industrious, and in many respects, an active manager, and he gave his evidence in a clear and straightforward manner and assisted in the Inquiry to the utmost of his power.

The Commissioner also had a good word to say for the manager's behaviour on the fatal Tuesday, October 14th:

It would be invidious, where all the mining engineers and miners en-gaged in attempted rescue operations worked so hard in endeavouring to get past the fire into the workings with the object of saving life, to commend individuals by name, but I think a particular meed of praise is due to Mr. Shaw and to the small band of workers who accompanied him underground immediately after the explosion.

II. THE ASSESSORS THINK DIFFERENTLY

Though the foregoing report was signed by the Commissioner alone, he, together with two assessors, made up the Court. The assessors had played an active part, not only in the examination and cross-examination of witnesses but in other ways including inspections underground of the scene of the disaster. Frequent and extensive inspections of course had been carried out before the investigation began by R. A. S. Redmayne in his capacity as H.M. Chief Inspector of Mines. When it came to the conclusions neither assessor agreed completely with the Commission; but whereas Robert Smillie put his differences in the form of a memorandum, the other assessor submitted an entirely separate report. In his memorandum Smillie began by stating that while he was "in general agreement" with the main body of the report, he had observations to make on points which were "of importance as contributing a higher death roll than might otherwise have been recorded." Of these points, five in all, the most important was the question of the reversal of the air current; "and on this point," wrote Smillie, "I differ most strongly from my two colleagues." The situation in the Senghenydd Pit was that Section 31 (3) of the Act, dealing with ventilation had not been complied with, a grave offence, as the Commissioner pointed out: but, in Smillie's view, an offence that cost many of the lives that were lost. The Act insisted on adequate means for immediate reversal of the air current. This requirement became operative on January 1, 1913. It had not been complied with in Senghenydd. Moreover, up to April 1913, "nothing seems to have been done." Smillie expressed his surprise that up to April "no action had evidently been taken" by the Inspector of Mines for South Wales Division to see that this provision of the Act was carried out. "It is evident," wrote Smillie, "that it was only in April that any application was made by the owners for an extension of time to enable them to make structural alterations with the view to putting themselves in a position to reverse the air current."

This extension of time was granted by the Inspector of the Division, in accordance with the powers given him under the Act. The extended period came to an end on September 16, 1913. By that date the "adequate means" was still not provided. Fourteen days grace was then given of the termination of the exemption—up to September 30, 1913. Still the "adequate means" was not provided. Two weeks later 439 men lost their lives.

In his report the Commissioner forbore to enter into the question (raised by Smillie) as to why his own staff of the inspectorate in South Wales had allowed three months to elapse from the end of

1912 during which time the Act was not being enforced by one of the most important colliery companies in the coalfield. On the culpability of the manager, however, the Commissioner's report, in paragraph 13, is quite explicit:

> In that adequate means for reversing the ventilation which could be put into "immediate operation" were not provided on the date of the explosion, the owners and Manager, as their counsel, Mr. Trevor Lewis, frankly admitted, were guilty of a contravention of Section 31(3) of the Coal Mines Act, 1911.

Further he says, in paragraph 83, "I have the manager's own confession" that, because of his failure fully to carry out the Act, "it would have taken two hours to have put the means of reversal into operation." Then he adds:

> Had the means at the surface been available for *immediate* reversal it would not have taken long to have effectively stopped off the West side cross-cut and so carried the reversal of the air current underground. I think it probable that as a result of this the men in the West York District would have been saved, but that those in the Bottanic District would have been adversely affected by the reversal. In fact, I incline to the belief that it would in all probability have resulted in the death of these persons.

It is on this point that Smillie is seen in his memorandum to "differ most strongly" from both his colleagues when he wrote:

> Surely this was a case in which immediate reversing of the air current ought to have taken place, because the manager and those acting with him must have known that all the fumes coming from a very serious fire of the nature described by him were being carried into the workings of the mine.
>
> I think it would be admitted by everyone who took part in the Inquiry that the reversing of the air current would have meant the saving of the lives of all of the men in the West York district. Most of those men had found their way to within a short distance of the York pit when they were overcome by the fumes.

This led Smillie to draw his damnatory conclusion, a very definite expression of his feelings, as against the more sophisticated chain of considerations ("I incline to think . . ." etc.) of the Commissioner:

> I understand that a discussion took place more than once on the afternoon of the day of the explosion regarding the advisability or otherwise of reversing the air current. I feel that this step was not taken, not because it would not have been wise to have taken it, but because it was found impossible, as provision for reversing the air current had not been made.

As far as the more knowledgeable members of the public were concerned, it was Smillie's conclusion that seems to have been accepted, as in the case of the already cited contemporary book of Professor H. S. Jevons, which runs:

The report of the Enquiry bristles with evidence of infractions of the Act, and if many of them, like failing to appoint officers in writing, were more or less technical, others like the failure to provide apparatus for reversing the current of air, and failing to deal properly with coal dust, are of the greatest moment, and are most probably responsible for a large proportion of the deaths.

12. EVAN WILLIAMS AS THE OWNERS' CHAMPION

The other assessor was Evan Williams who was to earn the admiration of his fellow coal owners for the skill and tenacity with which he defended their interests. He was the elder son (born in 1871) of Thomas Williams of Llwyn Gwern, Pontardulais, who had founded Thomas Williams & Sons (Llangennech) Ltd., a colliery company employing at their four pits little more than a thousand men in 1913; and less thereafter. His father sent him to the small but expensive Christ College of Brecon, a school that dated from the Tudor dynasty, whence he passed into Clare College, Cambridge. Having got the degree of Master of Arts he returned to enter his father's business which he and his younger brother conducted for a long time as sole directors. Though in after years he was to spread his wings more widely and range far beyond the confines of Carmarthenshire, so far he was known chiefly as a member of the Conciliation Board for the Coal Trade where his standing amongst his fellow owners won him the chairmanship for 1913–14 of the Monmouthshire and South Wales Coal Owners' Association.

As assessor, he did not disappoint those who had put their trust in him. He took the rather unusual course of submitting a separate report. It began as follows:

I regret I am unable to subscribe to Mr. Redmayne's report owing to my differing from him in greater or less degree upon several material points, and I therefore beg respectfully to submit to you separately my observations and conclusions upon those questions on which I am not in agreement with either or both of my colleagues.

Evan Williams, with considerable argumentative skill and in great detail, gave his own description of the class of coal mine to which Senghenydd belonged: and then paid particular attention to those points on which it appeared to so many others that there had been breaches of the Act, or laxity in administration of the colliery. He wrote:

With regard to the management I consider that the colliery was well and efficiently staffed and neither in the number of officials nor in the provision of labour, materials, or any arrangements necessary for the safe working of the mine was there evidence of any expense having been spared, but quite the contrary, and we have it from the evidence of the

M*

Inspector of Mines that he found on his visits that the general state of the colliery was excellent.

On the accumulation of coal dust he argued at length and reached the conclusion: "I consider that Section 62 (3) was complied with as fully as possible." On the theories put forward by witnesses as to the cause of the explosion Williams referred to Redmayne's report— "but", he wrote "I regret I am unable to accept his conclusions." Williams held that the cause was "an open light in the lamp cabin," and drew the lesson that no open lights should be permitted underground in this type of mine. Finally, his winding-up paragraph ran:

I am of opinion that the explosion was not consequent upon any breach of the Act or Regulations, nor due to any lack of precaution of a kind not required by law, other than that which may be attached to the position of the relighting station, and while there were some contraventions of the statute, they were all, with the exception of the failure to complete the means for immediately reversing the ventilation, of the nature of neglect to comply with formalities of no importance in themselves.

To few can this assessor's report have been more gratifying than to the agent and directors of Lewis Merthyr Consolidated Collieries Ltd., particularly to the venerable Lord Merthyr of Senghenydd whose reputation, acquired over a period of more than forty years, might now seem to be at stake. To the Liberal Home Secretary, to whom it was addressed, it might seem to contain a warning from the Chairman of the Coal Owners in South Wales that any criminal proceedings to follow the Inquiry would be unfavourably regarded: and the Welsh coal interest in all its facets was one that the Liberal government could not afford to ignore. Nevertheless, they did decide to prosecute with results to be told later; for now we must turn once more to recount the attitude of the South Wales Miners' Federation on all matters arising from the Senghenydd disaster.

13. SAFETY PROPOSALS OF SOUTH WALES MINERS' FEDERATION

The men who met their death underground at Senghenydd had died blasted by the force of the explosion, or burnt alive by the fire in the workings, or stifled by its fumes, or choked by the deadly afterdamp. That autumn day they had suffered a brief or a protracted agony. In less than one day, in a few hours, it was all over. But days and weeks and months were to pass before the sharpness of grief was assuaged at the head of the valley or before the mingled feelings of pity and horror throughout all the valleys were dulled.

Anxiety mounted in families whose' men had to go down the pit as morning and evening, from mid-October to the darkest days of December, the tidings spread of what was being found below by the explorers in the dismal subterranean chaos of the Universal Colliery.

With the New Year, 1914, came the grim items each day of the evidence given at the Coroner's inquest, to be followed by the harrowing details of conditions as told by witnesses at the still more searching investigation which went on from the last week of January. The common solidarity of mankind in the face of disaster, nowhere more strongly manifested than amongst miners, was heightened. All the feeling aroused in the mining community by such a catastrophe was thus kept at a pitch of intensity for week after week: and was deepened by the magnitude of the disaster into a common apprehension of what the future might hold in store for each family. The old saying of the Roman poet, repeated in antiquity and in the medieval centuries in times of personal crisis till it seemed like a biblical text, the Latin syllables that were hissed in the ear of Abelard when he witnessed the trial of another, were now being uttered in Welsh that winter throughout many a valley of the coalfield.[1]

Something had to be done—this was the universal demand—and men looked to the Federation to do it. Already, as we have seen, the Executive Council had sent a group of the most capable agents to be at Senghenydd under the leadership of Vice-President James Winstone. Besides calling a special conference (which took the decisions on relief of distress as told earlier in this chapter), back in Cardiff another conference was to be called even before the end of the Home Office Inquiry, at which all the explorers of Senghenydd as well as the President and the Secretary and other Agents were present. They had heard and they had learned enough for the delegates to be able without waiting to make up their minds on urgent measures for safety in mines. The response had to be given without delay to the mounting anxiety in the coalfield.

William Brace, M.P., addressed the coalfield special conference on the agenda before them, especially the safety proposals which was their main business that Monday. Science, as he pointed out, had accomplished such marvellous things in connecting continent with continent until people in the Far East were our near neighbours and with the machinery and other methods adopted in the production of coal there had been an enormous increase in output. But it was appalling to them that neither the application of science nor anything else appeared to have been able to cope with the terrible disasters in

---

[1] "Thine own fate is at stake when flames engulf a neighbour's roof."
(*Nam tua res agitur, paries cum proximus ardet*)

the coalfield and the series of accidents to workmen that were taking place in the mines. It was his wish to impress not only on the conference but upon everyone else that something must be done by the Government in maintaining the law, so as to provide further protective measures. He recalled that during 1912 there had been twelve explosions causing the death of 461 persons; 591 accidents, caused by fall of roof and sides, had been responsible for 664; 73 shaft accidents had resulted in 96 deaths; and 384 miscellaneous accidents had been responsible for 400 fatalities.

It was clear that it was expected from the conference to make a big step forward.

In his cross-examination of witnesses at the Government Inquiry up till then, Brace had used a somewhat different method from other Counsel. He had sought to broaden the scope of the Inquiry in such a way as to lay a basis for further remedial legislation. Again and again he had endeavoured to bring out amongst the possible causes of the explosion such facts as would apply to other pits as well as Senghenydd; and against which precautions could be taken and indeed laid down by an amending Act of Parliament. In short, Brace in all his cross-examination had very much an eye to the future while others had been more immediately concerned with the past and what had happened in October 1913. For example, Brace had sought to have it admitted by witnesses that "overhead rollers or sheaves" were a possible cause of sparks and hence of explosions.

The result of this special conference in Cardiff was that the delegates, after discussing for the best part of two days the sort of safety proposals that had been thus adumbrated or elaborated by Brace and others of the Executive Council, took a series of decisions, and formulated a number of safety proposals.[1]

14. PROSECUTION AND RESULTS

The formal investigation had ended on February 21, 1914: and conclusions to be reached were eagerly awaited. But they did not immediately appear. After six weeks there was a growing impatience voiced in the following resolution.

That this Council expresses its disappointment that the Home Office Commission has not issued its report. In view of the existing law limiting the period of prosecution to six months after the explosion for instituting prosecutions, and that this period will expire on April 14th, the Council urge upon the Home Secretary to at once institute prosecutions for the breaches of the Mines Act alleged to have occurred at this colliery, and that a deputation wait upon the Home Secretary for this purpose. (*30.iii.1914.*)

[1] See Appendix I to this chapter.

By mid-April the necessary steps had been taken by the Home Office on behalf of which the Division Mines Inspector for Wales instituted a prosecution against the manager of the Senghenydd Colliery and another against the owners, Lewis Merthyr Consolidated Collieries Limited. Thereupon the Executive Council resolved "That the officials of the Federation, with Mr. Hubert Jenkins and Mr. W. P. Nicholas, Solicitor, take all the steps necessary for watching the proceedings."

The shape of the prosecution was that seventeen "informations" for infractions of the Coal Mines Act were laid against the manager and four against the Company. The stipulations in the Act about offences and penalties therefore were very numerous. Thus, though the Act was typical of the positive legislation that had come increasingly into prominence, it was also full of pains and penalties as though the legislators had been aware of how readily industrial laws of this kind were liable to be disobeyed or evaded. The minatory phraseology varies from section to section but there is no question about its frequency.[1]

An Act of Parliament is one thing, its administration another. Legislators do not administrate—except possibly in the case of the eighteenth century Private Enclosure Acts. No doubt local Justices of the Peace are the custodians of the law; but the Latin proverb as old as the law itself sharply raised the question "Quis custodiet ipsos custodes?"—which might be Englished as "Who shall do justice on the Justices?" That same question, in English or in Welsh, was raised amongst the South Wales miners, when the Senghenydd case came before the local Bench of three Justices of the Peace.

Out of the seventeen "informations" against the manager, seven were dropped and out of the remainder that were pressed, the magistrates dismissed several and recorded a conviction only on five. On these five they "gave extraordinarily lenient sentences." So much for the manager and agent. Lord Merthyr of Senghenydd and the other owners were absolved of all offences lodged against them.

The particulars of the five counts on which the manager was convicted may be put briefly.

First, the failure to provide adequate means for reversing the air current, as prescribed by Section 31 of the Act, was met by a fine of £10 or one month's imprisonment. Second, for the failure to carry out Section 62 (Prevention of Coal Dust), the sentence was £5 or 14 days, while the even more serious charge of failure to systematically clear roofs and sides was dismissed. Third, the failure to record the atmospheric conditions (barometer, thermometer and

[1] See Appendix II to this chapter.

hygrometer readings) as required by Section 71: sentence was £5 or 14 days. Fourth and fifth, failure to appoint in writing a surface lamp man, and an underground lamp man (Section 34) for each of these offences the manager was fined £2 or 14 days.

The disaster cost 439 men their lives: it cost the manager £24 in fines.

Contemporary comment was made by Professor Jevons in his book *The British Coal Trade*, where he wrote:

> That is the sum total of the convictions obtained. Failure to provide the means of reversing the air current meant the loss of perhaps 100 lives or thereabouts, which might have been saved had the apparatus been available. If the coal dust had been dealt with, the explosion might have been much less serious. No wonder that the local Labour paper headed its report, "Miners' Lives at 1s. 1¼d. each."

Jevons made the further scathing comment:

> It is interesting to note how advantage was taken of the consideration shown by the Inspector and of the letter of the law, when it seemed to be in favour of the management. As regards means of reversing the air current, this should have been provided by January 1, 1913, but four months later the manager first applied for an extension of time under the Act. After correspondence and a visit by the sub-inspector to the mine, the extension was granted until September 30th. When the explosion occurred fourteen days later (October 14th) no work had been yet commenced for complying with this requirement. As regards measuring the air current, the magistrates decided that as the regulations made only came into force on September 16, 1913, and only required the measurement to be made once a month, the manager had still two days to make the necessary measurement at the time the explosion occurred. It appears to have been overlooked that the Chief Inspector in his report says that though part of the mine resumed work in November, no measurements were, in fact, made until the following January. Why are these laws passed if Parliament does not mean them to be enforced?

This comment was fairly typical of public feeling in South Wales about the results of the trial.[1] Consequently H.M. Divisional Inspector, with the approval of the Secretary of State, lodged an appeal in two selected cases. The first was against the dismissal by the magistrates of the case against the manager for not preventing the accumulation of coal dust. The second was against the Lewis Merthyr Consolidated Colliery Limited in that they had not

---

[1] But the miners beyond the South Wales coalfield shared the feelings of indignation. A minute of the Executive Committee of the Miners' Federation of Great Britain, runs: "*Senghenydd Disaster Verdict.* The result of the police court proceedings in this case was considered and the Committee unanimously passed the following resolution: 'That we express our indignation at the result of this prosecution, and that we take immediate steps to impress upon the Government the necessity for altering the present procedure in these cases; and that the Secretary be instructed to arrange with the Home Secretary to meet the Executive Committee as a deputation from the Federation on the matter'." (*22.vii.1914.*)

provided means for the immediate reversal of the current—for which the magistrates, despite the express wording of the Act, had held the owners to be not responsible.

The first of these appeals was based on the facts of the case, namely that the management, "while clearing the floor of the roads, was doing nothing to remove the dust from the roof and sides": but in the autumn of 1914 this appeal was dismissed. The second appeal, against the owners for having failed in their duty to provide means for reversing the air current,[1] was at first sent back to the Justices by the Appeal Court for a further statement as to the facts. Then in 1915 the appeal was allowed by the Court of the King's Bench and the case was "sent back to the magistrates to convict".

The importance of this case lay in its bearing upon the responsibility of the owners under the Act. The Court decided in the first place that owing to the failure to provide the means in question, the mine was "not managed in conformity with this Act", and that the owners, agent and manager were accordingly each guilty of an offence against the Act under Section 101(2). The Court went on to consider whether the owners had relieved themselves of liability to any penalty as provided for by Section 102. This was the section of the Act containing "escape clauses" under which an owner would not be liable to any penalty "if he proves to the satisfaction of the Court"—that he did not take any part in the management of the mine "in respect of the matters in question" or again "that the offence was committed without his knowledge, consent or connivance". The Court decided against the owners on both points.

The attempt "to drive a coach-and-four" through the Act of 1911 was thus defeated, and safety provisions that had been set at nought by the owners of the Universal Colliery remained thereafter in full legal vigour. It was perhaps fortunate for Sir William Lewis, Bart., Lord Merthyr of Senghenydd, G.C.V.O., K.C.V.O., a Justice of the Peace in the counties of Glamorgan, Monmouth, Brecon, Pembroke, and in the City of Cardiff, that on August 29, 1914, full of years and of honours, he was gathered to his fathers many months before the Senghenydd appeals were determined.

[1] Section 31, Clause 3 as quoted above—on page 344 of this volume.

SAFETY PROPOSALS OF S.W.M.F., FEBRUARY 1914

1. That all trams shall be dust-proof and not filled higher than the top level, so as to admit of a cover.
2. That the workmen shall have the right of the appointment and control of colliery firemen, and that they be prohibited from performing any other duties than attending to the safety of the mine.
3. That it be made compulsory to fill up or stow all gob waste, overhead vacancies, and disused workings places.
4. That the districts be asked to appoint full-time workmen's examiners under section sixteen of the Coal Mines Act.
5. That overhead rollers or sheaves be prohibited.
6. That there shall be a total prohibition of the use of any inflammable or combustible materials in the construction of intake airways.
7. That we press for the general use of electric lamps in mines, provided that a gas testing lamp is available for use in every working place.
8. That a considerable increase be made in the number of His Majesty's Inspectors of Mines, sufficient to enable at least a monthly inspection of all collieries, and that they be required to post up at the pit-head reports upon their examinations of the colliery. These appointments to be made from among the workmen.
9. That no small coal shall be stowed or kept in the mine, but that all coal produced must be sent out.
10. All main roads to be well watered or other effective means used for rendering harmless the coal dust on the roadways, including the roof and sides.
11. That all working places should cease working at least eight hours of every twenty-four.
12. Emergency safety doors to be erected in all main intake airways, as near the working face as is practicable.
13. That the haulage of coal in the return airways shall be totally prohibited.
14. That the workmen shall be given the right to institute prosecutions against the colliery officials for the breach of rules, in the same manner as the right given the officials to prosecute the workmen.
15. That in all cases where practicable, the use of the endless rope system of haulage shall be enforced in place of the main and tail rope system.
16. That it be made compulsory to provide "water zones," i.e. complete portions of roadways saturated with water in all intakes, return and working districts.

Various other safety proposals were sent in from the lodges, which the Council have undertaken to consider. (*3.ii.1914*.)

LEGAL PROCEEDINGS

Examples of Penalties for Offences against the Coal Mines Act 1911

Section 4 (4) runs:

"If any person acts in contravention of any such order [by the Secretary of State] or connives at any such contravention, he shall be guilty of an offence against this Act." Again, Section 6, prescribing certain duties for the owner to notify certain things to the Division Inspector, ends with the words: "and, if he fails to do so, he shall be guilty of an offence under this Act." Section 11 (2) and also Section 83 (2) dealing with Courts of Inquiry set up by the Secretary of State, makes it an offence for anyone who "fails to comply with any summons or requisition of the Court" and makes him liable to a fine "not exceeding one pound for every day during which the offence continues." Again, Section 18 (4) ends with the same sort of warning to the three most responsible persons as did Section 16 (3), namely, that "Every owner, agent, or manager of a mine who fails to comply with this section, or . . ., shall be guilty of an offence against this Act." In the lengthy sections following, namely, 19, 20 and 21, the minatory words recur in each case: until the penalty section (No. 28) at the end of Part 1 of the Act winds it up with the words "imprisonment with or without hard labour for a term not exceeding two years."

Part II with its "Provisions as to Safety" in 45 separate sections ends with a double threat. Not only is he "who contravenes or does not comply with any of the provisions" of this Part of the Act "guilty" as aforesaid, but in the event of any such contravention "by any person whomsoever" then, it is laid down, "the owner, agent and manager of the mine shall each be guilty of an offence against this Act." So it is stated in Section 75: and though a saving clause lays it down that if "he had taken all reasonable means by publishing and to the best of his power enforcing those provisions to prevent that contravention or non-compliance" then he would not be guilty: but the onus of proof would fall upon the accused. So it is clear that there was an exceptionally strong inducement for each one of the responsible trinity to observe Part II, to ensure safety in the mine and to see that all others observed it. The eighth Part of the Act headed "Legal Proceedings" has all-embracing penalty provisions in Section 101 as follows:

"(1) Every person employed in or about a mine, other than an owner, agent, or manager, who is guilty of any act or omission which in the case of an owner, agent, or manager would be an offence against this Act, shall be deemed to be guilty of an offence against this Act.

(2) If a mine is not managed in conformity with this Act, the owner, agent, and manager thereof shall each be deemed to be guilty of an offence against this Act.

(4) Where a person is guilty of any offence against this Act which, in the opinion of the court that tries the case, is one which was likely to endanger the safety of the persons employed in or about the mine, or to cause serious personal injury to any of such persons, or to cause a dangerous

accident, and was committed wilfully by the personal act, personal default, or personal negligence of the person accused, such person shall be liable, if the court is of opinion that a fine will not meet the circumstances of the case, to imprisonment with or without hard labour, for a period not exceeding three months."

CHAPTER THIRTEEN

RETROSPECT AND PROSPECT

By the year 1914 the members of the South Wales Miners' Federation could look back on fifteen years of existence of their organisation. Just as they had been gathered later than other British miners into a single union covering a coalfield, (and the largest of all such within Great Britain), so in their beginnings much had been slow, tentative and bearing the marks of that unorganised and dispersed condition from which the union had arisen. There had been valley associations, varying in number and differing in content and function, from those endeavouring to do the work of a trade union, to others which could not be considered as trade unions at all. Indeed, without lodges and with members associated together only by the compulsory deduction from their wages of a monthly sum to pay for representatives on the joint committee devised by the employers, such a body was more like a company union than a genuine trade union organisation.

Out of this chaotic condition, marked by recurrent outbursts of primitive strike activity, there had grown up a trade union that was to seek to defend the interests and improve the conditions of its members. Thus formed, it had to face the most powerful combination of coal owners that existed in any coalfield in Britain. This employers' combination tolerated the South Wales Miners' Federation rather than accorded it any due meed of recognition, except where it might seem that there was a common interest of all those engaged in the industry, as in the case of the coal tax.

The condition of the workmen was in some ways considerably worse than that of their fellow miners in other coalfields. Their standard of living was often lower, their hours of labour were definitely longer, their housing conditions were only less deplorable than those of the Scots miners, their tale of accidents and disasters was longer, more frequent and with far more casualties.

Not only the colliery owners, associated in their formidable combination, but all the powers that be, seemed at the beginning linked against the miners in their valleys. The magistrates and the police often appeared as hostile forces. Something of the conditions of a subjugated country still bore heavily on the miners of whom at that time, especially in Glamorgan and Carmarthen, a great number spoke Welsh more readily and easily than English.

The career of the Union in its first ten years had been sufficiently peaceful under the leadership of the men from Monmouth who together with Mabon had taken the initiative in building up the union. Their disposition was pacific, and some of them for long enough hankered after the smooth automation of the Sliding Scale Joint Committee which had lasted, by a series of agreements, from 1875 to 1903. They had grown up under it as miners' agents: and they were accustomed to it. Not did the underlying argument for it appear to them in any way implausible: their coal trade, once the needs of the iron masters had been met and house-coal provided, increasingly lived on the export market. Capital was invested in coal, labour was fetched from far and near: but neither of them fixed the price. This fluctuating, ever-shifting series of prices of each different kind of coal, with an average which accountants ascertained quarterly or oftener at the five Bristol Channel ports, was beyond the control of those engaged in its production. Price was settled by what each ton would fetch in the capitalist world market, free and unfettered. They were all at the mercy of the world market and all alike should share in good fortune or ill-fortune, in good times or bad. Thus capital and labour, willy-nilly, could be seen as co-partners in the coal trade: and if this were so, then they should share the results in an agreed proportion. Such was the argument that was first propounded in 1875: and it was only in the terms between partners, the detailed provisions of a sliding scale, that anything could arise to disturb industrial harmony.

In the beginning of the 'nineties it was only the M.F.G.B. supporters who believed that "a living wage," a minimum, should be the collier's claim: and that until this claim was met all else was irrelevant. This agitation, the insistence of the owners upon the changed scale of 1892 and the successive reductions thereafter convinced the miners and some of their leaders that the perpetual truce of the Sliding Scale should be denounced and give way to collective bargaining.

Any attempt by the agents, who in the main made up the Executive Council, to initiate a forward movement, was soon to be subjected to the restraint of the Taff Vale Judgment. The highly lucrative Taff Vale Railway Company had been able in the prevailing atmosphere of South Wales to regard a strike, official or unofficial, of its employees as an affront and a damage to its prestige and profits rather than as a simple dispute: so it sued the union.

On July 22, 1901 when five judges from the House of Lords unanimously rejected the appeal by the railwaymen's union, this decision on the Taff Vale case became the law of the land:

the immunity of trade unions from corporate liability for damages, widely accepted for over a generation, had been swept away in an afternoon. Neither Sir William Lewis who long years before, like a magistrate of Sparta ritually declaring war upon the helots, had set his face like flint against trade unions; nor his fellow owners were the men to ignore this new legal weapon that had fallen into their hands—should the union give them any cause. This the Federation did, and did repeatedly in that same autumn of 1901 by calling a number of "stop-days." The belief was that the rapid decline in coal prices and with it the fall of wages from their zenith of May 1901 (78¾ per cent above the standard of 1879) could be halted by restriction of total output—a belief inculcated, but in another form, by D. A. Thomas, M.P. from 1896 onwards. Accordingly they fell back upon the old device of "stop-days" and were confident that both masters and men would benefit thereby. On this they were undeceived when at the end of November 1901 angry owners took legal action. All but three out of the 74 colliery companies then in the Coal Owners' Association sued the Federation for "wrongfully and maliciously procuring and inducing workmen to break their contracts of service." The result was a foregone conclusion: and the union was nearly bankrupted thereby. In this "stop-day" action they had to pay £57,562 4s. 4d. in damages, being a sum far in excess of the Federation's annual income.

Not only the miners' associations throughout Great Britain but all trade unions were soon pressing the Government for legislation that would reverse the Taff Vale Judgment. But Prime Minister Balfour preferred to set up a Royal Commission and to await its report.[1] Angered by this the Miners' Federation of Great Britain by an Executive Committee resolution made it clear that it "declines to tender evidence" to the Commission whose personnel was "an ex-parte one." (*19.vii.1903.*)

The report of the Royal Commission with the Bill based upon it bore out the miners' apprehensions. By strong pressure before and after the January–February general election of 1906 the Bill was jettisoned, and gave place to the Trade Disputes Act of 1906. For nearly sixty years, this Act was to be the palladium of Trade Unionism, its main protection for activities particularly in strikes or lock-outs. The right of peaceful picketing had been restored: the unions were content. But to British judges this relative immunity in law was to appear for ever after as an offence and "a stumbling block of their iniquity."

When the mounting wave throughout Europe of working class and democratic advance reached Great Britain in 1905 it affected

[1] Royal Commission on Trade Disputes and Trade Combinations. Cd. 2825 (1906).

also the miners of South Wales but less for the moment than in other coalfields. In the latter part of 1904 and throughout the year 1905 there had swept through the valleys a great religious "Revival," called a revival not only for theological reasons, but because it seemed to re-awaken that prodigious movement of Methodism, which from the middle of the eighteenth century till well on in the nineteenth had such a profound and extensive influence in the coalfields of England and Wales. It revived enthusiasm among Baptists (where it had the greatest effect) and among Independents as well as among the numerous smaller sects. It had little effect in the Church of England.

Linked as it was with the temperance movement the Welsh Revival had a marked effect on the miners, both at their work and in the trade unions. For example, the last Rhondda District meeting in the Imperial Hotel at Porth was in April 1905. On May 1st of that year they met in the rooms of the Young Men's Christian Association. At the same time it had the effect that historians have now agreed to be one result of Methodism, that it could damp down the effort of trade unionism and socialism, or, in the case of the former, diverted it into the most pacific channels. Thus it was not until after the wave of 1904–5 had begun to retreat from its crest that the Welsh miners took up the fight for better conditions with an energy that had been lacking in earlier years of the century. The first need was to safeguard their union, sorely stricken in its funds and for four years dwindling in its membership. There then began an effort to deal with non-unionism which in all trades from 1900 to 1907 was, next to wages, the biggest of the seven categories of causes of all disputes as listed by the Board of Trade. The Federation members were in the forefront in 1905 and still more in 1906,[1] and lurid tales are told of the treatment given to recalcitrant colliers.

Meanwhile, and during all the century, unparalleled since the time of Shakespeare the erosion of the standard of living by fall in the value of money was going on.

From 1908 there began a rapid change in the conditions of the South Wales miners and also within the union. Legal judgments that worsened conditions of work confronted them. The pittance that a minority each fortnight or month received as "consideration money" if working in an abnormal place was whittled away. Payment

---

[1] The Report on Strikes and Lockouts for 1905 refers to the growing proportion of "disputes in which the workpeople directly involved declined to work with non-unionists and in these disputes, all of which occurred in the South Wales Coalfield, the workpeople were successful in attaining their object except in one case." Cd. 3065. Next year it is stated: "The figures for 1906 are the highest on record. Of the 50,750 workpeople affected by such disputes in 1906, no less than 45,995 were coalminers in South Wales and Monmouthshire, where a determined effort was made by the members of the South Wales Miners' Federation to compel all non-unionists to join the Federation." Cd. 3711.

for small coal was not given: but the amount of small coal was increasing and the price obtained for it by the colliery owners was on the increase. Nevertheless, it was the further offensive of the owners that stirred up the miners of South Wales in the years after the first decade of the Union's existence. The owners themselves regarded the Eight Hours' Act passed in December 1908 as an offensive against which they must react by altering the Conciliation Board Agreement. At that time in 1909 the Miners' Federation of Great Britain was not equal to giving the support which South Wales expected in the struggles that appeared about to be forced upon them by the South Wales owners.

Thus, backward at the time of its formation in 1898, the South Wales Miners' Federation was still regarded in some respects as backward in 1908. In that year the Labour Party was admitted to the Socialist International as "organised independently of bourgeois parties" though "not expressly accepting the proletarian class struggle": but the South Wales Miners' Federation were not at that time in the Labour Party. It is true that the ballot vote showed that in political consciousness the rank and file of the union were already advancing beyond the stage reached by their fellow miners in the Midlands of England: but their leaders seemed little further advanced than they had been at an earlier stage.

Only from 1909 onwards could a change be seen in retrospect. This change was signalised partly by a struggle inside the union itself between the old and tried Liberal leaders and the younger members many of whom were checkweighers or coming to the fore with a political socialist outlook in lodge meetings, district meetings and coalfield conferences. Some of those were chosen to go to Ruskin College in Oxford where they helped to lead the strike of students against the governors, and in favour of their principal whose lectures did not eschew the doctrines of Darwin and Marx. Many (though not all) of these students as they returned from their brief sojourn in what became the Central Labour College were to prove the torch bearers of a new "socialist enlightenment," one object of which was to transform the South Wales Miners' Federation into a militant "class struggle" organisation.

Soon the strike movement which had been sporadically effective earlier began to be concentrated for a while in mid-Glamorgan. There in a series of valleys and above all in the greatest of the districts, the Rhondda, there was boiling up a ferment of socialist agitation at the same time as the forces of capital were becoming more and more strongly organised and more and more ready to resist any encroachments by the workers. There followed the struggles in the mid-Rhondda of 1910–11, associated forever with the name of Tonypandy.

It was not until 1912 that the reading public became familiar with the word "syndicalism" some 20 months after Tom Mann in his journal *The Industrial Syndicalist*[1] had launched his agitation for militant trade union activity with such slogans as "direct action." Thereafter for a number of years in the newspapers "syndicalism" was often loosely used to denote a general tendency rather than any definite doctrine or theory.

These big industrial conflicts made South Wales appear as the cockpit of the whole British and European struggle of the mine-workers. Every relevant authority, local and national, was brought into play: and in the minds of the colliers there spread a questioning of the basis of that authority: and a growing indignation at the exercise of it. To get the help of their fellow miners, "missionaries" were sent to the other coalfields to explain their plight and in so doing often to stimulate sympathy, support and industrial activity. The proposal to send out some fifty such "missionaries" was sanctioned at a coalfield conference in the year 1911. They went in pairs from the mid-Rhondda to the furthest north-east of England and beyond. Undoubtedly it was this fiery cross that roused the miners' associations and swung the leaders willy-nilly into action[2]. In 1911 and 1912 the South Wales miners, particularly their militant section, saw their ideas triumphant and embodied in the great movement for the Minimum Wage. Here they realised as never before their own strength and weakness as well as the strength of the forces opposed to them or that could be brought into play against them. The result was dramatic. A vote of the South Wales miners showed that they had lost faith in their old leaders whom they replaced with other leaders at the end of 1911 upon the Executive Committee of the Miners' Federation of Great Britain. Another lesson brought home was the need for better trade union organisation. Some changes were made but not enough to satisfy those who realised the need for more far-reaching changes.

In the year 1914 the Executive Committee of the Miners' Federation, empowered by a resolution from South Wales, set about in

[1] In *The Industrial Syndicalist* of February 1911 Ablett and Hay wrote a vindication of the Cambrian strikers' standpoint for a minimum wage. But none of the Cambrian Combine Committee appears to have been an avowed "syndicalist." On the other hand George Harvey, for some years editor of the organ of the (De Leonite) Socialist Labour Party, denounced Tom Mann as a false prophet and no true exponent of the tenets of "industrial unionism."

[2] "Officially, we were 'to seek for additional financial support'. All missionaries had been told unofficially, that 'at their discretion' they must talk to the leading men individually in each lodge and convey that what the Cambrian wanted was 'a national stoppage to enforce a national minimum wage.' Noah Rees and I were in Yorkshire for nearly six weeks, tramping from lodge to lodge. At Featherstone where miners were shot down in 1893 we found a particularly sympathetic lodge official who showed to us a tree in which one of the bullets was still embedded." *W. H. Mainwaring in an interview.* (*17.xi.1966.*)

earnest the task of assembling a larger body of workers for the struggles which they all believed would mature in the near future. This was to bring about the "triple industrial alliance," composed not only of miners but also of railwaymen and transport workers.

At the same time the value that had accrued to the union through the work of those who had been at the Labour College was now felt in every valley, and a decision was taken in 1914 to maintain (jointly with the London district of the National Union of Railwaymen) the Central Labour College in London on a continuing basis.

All this had come from the five years. These were years when the cost of living was rising more rapidly and when unknown to most of those in the valleys the grouping of the European powers in the Triple Alliance confronted by the Triple Entente was driving steadily towards the first world war. It was not realised, except by a minority, that there was already a race between the forces of socialism operating for peace and the forces that were driving toward war.

The prospect of greater struggles opening out within Britain was clear to many of the South Wales miners. The prospect of the slaughter that was to be the actual future and the fate of millions was hidden from their eyes.

GENERAL APPENDICES

SOUTH WALES MINERS' FEDERATION
EXECUTIVE COUNCIL

Table showing District Membership, and Agents, for selected years.

DISTRICT	AGENT	MEMBERSHIP				
		Average for 1906/07/08	1909	1912	1913	1914
ANTHRACITE	D. Morgan J. D. Morgan }	9,918	12,639	14,337	12,460	10,856
ABERDARE	C. B. Stanton	8,490	8,587	5,910	2,514	4,903
AFAN VALLEY	Wm. Jenkins					2,600
BLAINA	J. Manning	3,810	4,390	4,388	4,335	4,284
DOWLAIS	J. Davies	3,448	3,926	4,438	3,696	2,482
EASTERN VALLEYS	J. Winstone	5,467	5,872	5,976	5,691	6,155
EAST GLAMORGAN	H. Jenkins	2,784	4,067	4,006	3,649	3,529
EBBW VALE	W. Vyce	3,231	4,652	4,000	4,000	4,000
GARW	J. Thomas F. Hodges }	2,490	4,403	4,679	4,049	3,747
MAESTEG	V. Hartshorn	4,718	3,134	5,121	4,681	5,435
MERTHYR	J. Williams	3,991	4,769	3,298	4,335	2,257
MONMOUTHSHIRE WESTERN VALLEYS	G. Barker M. Roach }	8,514	10,260	10,013	10,310	10,731
OGMORE AND GILFACH	T. Lucas	3,022	2,711	2,858	1,995	2,077
PONTYPRIDD AND RHONDDA	B. Davies	6,404	8,373	6,975	6,016	3,422
RHONDDA NO. 1	D. Watts Morgan W. Abraham T. Evans }	28,100	31,363	29,985	19,627	18,956
RHYMNEY VALLEY	W. Lewis E. Thomas }	5,355	7,436	7,983	6,780	6,367
TAFF AND CYNON	E. Morrell	7,120	7,242	6,219	4,648	3,376
TREDEGAR VALLEY	A. Onions	5,426	6,872	8,413	8,253	10,051
WESTERN MINERS' ASSOCIATION	J. Williams W. E. Morgan W. Jenkins }	8,697	10,610	8,632	9,000	7,330
SAUNDERSFOOT	J. Williams	276	272	301	331	356

THE EXECUTIVE COUNCIL OF THE SOUTH WALES MINERS' FEDERATION SHOWING SOME OF THE CHANGES IN SELECTED YEARS

PRESIDENT: William Abraham, M.P.
VICE-PRESIDENT: William Brace, M.P.
TREASURER: Alfred Onions, J.P.
GENERAL SECRETARY: Thomas Richards, M.P.
} 1898–1911

PRESIDENT: William Brace, M.P.
VICE-PRESIDENT: James Winstone
TREASURER: Alfred Onions
GENERAL SECRETARY: Thomas Richards, M.P.
} 1912–1914

EXECUTIVE COUNCIL	1900	1901	1903	1907	1908	1909	1911	1912	1913
* David Watts Morgan	X	X	X	X	X	X	X	X	X
† Enoch Morell	X	X	X	X	X	X	X	X	X
* George Barker	X	X				X	X	X	X
* John Williams	X	X	X	X	X	X	X		
George Churchill	X								
Thomas Morell	X								
* Thomas Thomas	X	X							
* David Beynon	X	X	X						
* T. Daronwy Isaac	X	X							
T. James	X		X						
* W. Hopkins	X	X							
* James Winstone	X	X	X	X	X	X			
John Davies	X	X	X	X	X	X			
† David Morgan	X	X		X	X	X	X	X	X
* W. E. Morgan	X	X		X	X	X	X	X	X
* William Vyce	X	X		X	X	X	X	X	
† Thomas Evans	X	X		X	X	X			X

×   × × ×   ×   × ×   × × ×   × × × × ×

× ×   × × ×   ×   × ×   × × × ×   ×

× ×   × × ×   ×   × ×   × × × ×   ×

× × ×   × × ×   × ×   × × × × ×

× × ×   × × ×   × ×   ×   × × × × × ×

× × ×   × × ×   × ×   × × × × × ×

× × ×   × × × × × × ×   ×

× × ×   × ×   ×   × ×

× × × ×

* Ben Davies
** John Thomas
** Evan Thomas
William Williams
* James Manning
** C. B. Stanton
Vernon Hartshorn
John Kemp
†* Thomas George
J. D. Morgan
George Little
* M. Roach
Thomas Davies
† Thomas Lucas
†† W. H. Morgan
† Thomas Harris
William Harris
† Charles Edwards
* Hubert Jenkins
James Baker (Wattstown)
Jabez Jones (Pontnarydd)
* Walter Lewis
† Noah Ablett
Tom Smith
† Noah Rees
* Frank Hodges
** William John
†* W. L. Cook
* Albert Thomas
* William Jenkins

* Miners' Agent
† Checkweigher

INDEX OF NAMES

INDEX OF SUBJECTS